Writing and Selling
Feature Articles

PRENTICE-HALL JOURNALISM SERIES
Kenneth E. Olson, Editor

Writing and Selling Feature Articles

By

HELEN M. PATTERSON

Associate Professor of Journalism
University of Wisconsin

With an introduction by

GRANT MILNOR HYDE

Professor of Journalism
University of Wisconsin

THIRD EDITION

Englewood Cliffs, N.J.

PRENTICE-HALL, INC.

Current printing (last digit):

16 15 14 13 12 11 10 9 8 7

PRINTED IN THE UNITED STATES OF AMERICA
97075-C

Introduction

■▼

It is unusual for a journalism textbook to go into a
third edition. After assisting in launching the First and Second
Editions in 1939 and 1949, I am again gratified to have a small
part in a third version of this book after seven short years. This
new reworking of the subject is evidence of the success that the
book has had, in spite of vigorous competition, both for classroom use and for self-taught students outside the colleges. It is
also evidence that styles and demands in feature articles have
changed sufficiently in seven years to warrant a modernization
of such a textbook. Reactions from soldiers, sailors, and aviators
in uniform who use the book in a course offered by the United
States Armed Forces Institute have shown their strong interest
in mastering this type of writing. In fact, some of the most interesting military students have been older high-ranking officers
who have attained much success in writing and marketing feature
articles in various fields.

This new edition continues the development of the new experiment in "Magazine Article Writing" that was first presented in
the Second Edition. As a pioneer in this field of writing, the
author has continued to teach students how to exploit to the utmost *one field* of article writing in which they have special interest. Most significant in this activity has been the encouragement of writing on scientific subjects for popular publications—
a field that was long neglected in college classrooms. Not only
is this idea of special interest to U.S.A.F.I. students, but the

v

author's campus course—which she launched in 1936—continues to draw an increasing number of students majoring in chemistry, physics, biology, and engineering who wish to learn how to write popular articles on the material with which they have special acquaintance. Interestingly, some of these scientific students later pursue graduate work in the School of Journalism to develop further their writing proficiency.

Although the writing of special feature articles was originally developed about 1909 as a special subject in departments of journalism, the project is being undertaken more and more by teachers of English composition as a specialized writing course of value to all college students. Also it is a field in which increasing numbers of embryo writers are training themselves with the aid of a textbook guide. The popularity of such a course, on a college campus or outside, results from several advantages that may not be obvious at first sight: (1) for any person who has an urge to write, the size and ramifications of the feature article market offer the most immediate possibilities of financial return; (2) for a teacher who seeks a tangible measure of success in his teaching, the feature article is sufficiently within the range of undergraduate accomplishment to bring the goal of publication to students while they are still members of the class; (3) for the young student who is tired of trying "to write out of his head" the course offers a chance to do something worth while with actual facts; and (4) for the student who is taking his first steps toward professional writing, the feature article is much easier to master than the short story—although it may be a preliminary to later success in fiction writing.

The success of this book is, of course, the result of the fact that the author is one of the most experienced and successful teachers of the subject. She has been in charge of the course in the Wisconsin School of Journalism since 1929 and, during those years, has been successful in teaching hundreds of college students to gather facts, carry on interviews, write readable copy, obtain pictures, and sell to newspapers and magazines. Her success is often measured in hundreds, if not thousands, of dollars received by students for articles written while they are members of the class. The secret of her success in this practical writing activity is her emphasis on the study of markets for articles and on the adaptation of articles to particular markets. That secret, together with many other special techniques of teaching that she has developed, has been written into this book so clearly that it will be of assistance either to a student in a university class or to an ambitious writer who is approaching the task alone without the aid of a teacher.

As a colleague of the author, who tried his hand at teaching feature writing and who has watched with interest her achievements in further developing the project, I am delighted to assist in presenting this third version of her very successful book. May the book go on to a Fourth Edition when the time is ripe!

Grant Milnor Hyde

Preface

Many amateurs attempt to write fiction because they feel they will have more freedom and will be happier doing that type of writing. They do not realize that they are competing with hundreds of authors whose names are well known. When they learn of the opportunities for unknown journalists in feature writing, of the freedom in style, of the wealth of subject matter about which they may write, and that they can earn while they learn, they take up the subject—whether in the classroom, writing clubs, or alone at their desks—with an enthusiasm that borders on fervor. They do not find the study of writing to sell a drudgery but a merry adventure. Students like to write features because they do not have to wait until graduation to be compensated for their efforts. Adults turning to it as an avocation find they can get results almost immediately, since they learn to slant and market as they write. Why should amateurs be encouraged to write if they are not taught how to sell what they write?

The book is planned to be helpful to five types of persons: first, the undergraduate majoring in journalism or advertising, who takes the course to meet the requirements of the curriculum and to be prepared to do this type of writing upon graduation; second, the undergraduate who elects the course because he wants to write to sell even though his major is in some other field; third, the graduate student who is preparing himself for a profession or business which offers material that would make acceptable articles or who may be called on, in his chosen work, to write articles; fourth, the adult writing without guidance but who has ambition and leisure and aspires to learn the fundamentals of writing and marketing either for immediate profit or for an avocation after he retires; and fifth, the advanced magazine student, studying Part II to prepare for a career in magazine writing.

Since writing should be fun, the content of the book was planned with but little emphasis before Chapter 11 on the actual writing techniques. An assignment to write will thrill a student rather than bore him if he feels free from the restriction of rules that are necessary in the beginning composition class. After his new-found writing freedom allows him to write as he wishes, he very soon will be aware of his lack of ability and will then seek information from his instructor or from rhetoric and composition books that will aid him in presenting his ideas effectively. Particular emphasis is placed on methods of slanting material in order to aid the free-lance writer in selling his manuscripts. The Publication Analysis at the end of each chapter will aid him in acquiring market knowledge of what editors wish to buy.

The ideas and plans outlined in this book are the result of the author's experience in writing and buying features and in teaching hundreds of students in her classes in the Wisconsin School of Journalism and the United States Armed Forces Institute not only to write but to sell articles, as well as to train for a career in magazine writing. That the methods outlined are practical is proved by the students' sales, which in recent years totaled between $8,000 and $10,000.

This third edition is amplified to include new chapters and a complete revision of Parts I, II, and the Appendix. Included in Part II is the content of the advanced magazine course that has been given at the School of Journalism, University of Wisconsin, since 1936. It probably was one of the first schools, if not *the* first, to offer an advanced magazine writing course. "Training for a Magazine Career," as the proseminary is called, gives the student the opportunity to write in specialized, technological, or science fields of his choice. It offers the science major desiring to write "readable science," or the student in technology eager to interpret that knowledge by means of the written word, the techniques of writing and selling scientific and technological articles to general periodicals. It also gives the journalism student training and practice for a magazine career, either as a contributor or a staff writer.

The Exercises and the Research Reports at the end of each chapter in Part II enable students in an advanced class or proseminary, or working alone in their homes, or studying the course through the United States Armed Forces Institute, to acquire the more professional background necessary in writing articles as a staff worker on a magazine or marketing them as a magazine contributor after they have had a semester or a year course in beginning feature writing, as planned in Part I.

To serve as inspiration to the novice, by showing him what others have accomplished, a few examples of articles, reprinted in whole or in part with permission from the authors as well as from the publications that bought them, are included in the various chapters. But analysis of current periodicals will be more beneficial to a writer.

In using this book, the beginner, whether studying under an instructor or teaching himself, should scan Part I to get a survey of what it contains that will aid him in the production of his first feature. As he writes, he will then know where to turn in the book to find the solutions to his problems as they arise. Teachers long have realized that there is only one way to learn to write, and that is to write and learn the technique afterward. The book is based on that theory.

If the amateur has the opportunity of having his manuscript criticized in small discussion groups, or in the classroom, or by groups of other beginners, or even by a friend, he will be benefited immeasurably by the reader point of view.

A chapter a week should be read thoroughly for the first semester course; a chapter every two weeks for the second semester course. Weekly or daily assignments of the Exercises at the end of the chapter will serve as a teacher-check to inspire a second and thorough reading. Publication Studies at the end of each chapter of Part I may be assigned each week or in alternate weeks. Four articles may be required in the first semester course. Part II includes the Exercises, Research Reports, and three magazine articles for the course in training for a magazine career.

It is not possible to thank, in this brief space, the hundreds of students in university and unseen global classes of the United States Armed Forces Institute who—by proving the author's tenet that beginners not only can write effectively but can sell successfully—have made this book possible.

In presenting this book, the author desires to express her special debt of gratitude for the many helpful suggestions and assistance given by Professor Grant M. Hyde, Professor of Journalism, School of Journalism, University of Wisconsin, who gave generously of his advice during the preparation of the original manuscript and of the two enlarged editions.

The author feels especially indebted to newspaper and magazine publishers and a number of student authors and distinguished writers for their gracious permission to reprint complete copyrighted articles or extracts from them. They are: *The American* and Mrs. Susan Ammann McLane; *The American Home,* Mrs. Dorothy F. Douglas, and Mr. Kenneth B. Stark; *American Milk Review* and Mr. Robert E. Koehler; *American Restaurant* and Mr. Kenneth C. Wagner; *The American Rifleman* and Dr. A. M. Libasci; *Better Homes and Gardens* and Mr. Kenneth G. Johnson; *Capper's Farmer* and Miss Luida E. Sanders; *Charm* and Mrs. Dorothy F. Douglas; *The Children's Bureau and Children* and Mrs. Kitte Turmell; *Coronet,* Mr. E. A. Batchelor, and Mr. John McGiffert; *The Crippled Child* and Miss Marilyn E. Johnson; *Esquire* and Mr. H. E. Wassam; *Field & Stream* and Mr. Edward A. LeHoven; *Florists' Telegraph Delivery News* and Miss Jeanne Arnold; *Ford Farming* and Mr. Ben Logan; *Ford Times* and Mr. Tom McHugh; *Fountain Service and Fast Food* and Mr. Sanford A. Moen; *Fur-Fish-Game Harding's Magazine* and Mr. Don Huibregtse; *Law and Order* and Mr. Earl B. Dutton; *Leatherneck* and MSgt. Fred G. Braitsch, Jr.; *Modern Pho-*

tography and Mr. Tom McHugh; *Motor News* and Mr. Charles
E. Edwards; *Natural History* and Mr. Tom McHugh; *Outdoor
Life* and Mr. Rob F. Sanderson; *Parade* and Mr. John Prindle;
Pic and Mr. William J. Cox; *Popular Mechanics Magazine,* Mr.
John L. Kent, and Mr. Tom McHugh; *Popular Photography* and
Miss Violet Witt; *Presbyterian Life* and Mr. Linn Lewis Brown;
Reader's Digest and Mr. Charles Stevenson; *Restaurant Manage-
ment* and Mr. Bruce Estlund; St. Louis *Globe-Democrat,* Marian
Yocum Newspaper Features, and Mrs. Kitte Turmell; *The Sample
Case* and Mr. James F. Sullivan; the *Saturday Evening Post* and
Mr. Lester Velie; Seattle *Times,* Marian Yocum Newspaper Fea-
tures, and Mrs. Kitte Turmell; the Sioux Falls *Daily Argus-
Leader* and Mrs. Ida B. Alseth; *Sports Afield* and Mr. Lloyd
Soehren; *Successful Farming* and Mrs. Carol K. Johnson; *Today's
Health,* Mr. Howard C. Custer, and Mr. John L. Paustian;
Trains and Mr. William D. Middleton; *U. S. Camera* and Mr.
Tom McHugh; and *Woman's Day* (*The A & P Magazine*) and
Mrs. Dorothy F. Douglas.

H. M. P.

Table of Contents

PART I

1 Feature Writing as a Career or Avocation   3

Slanting Articles to Publications (*Cont.*):

10 Planning and Outlining the Article — 177

Planning and Outlining the Article (*Cont.*):

11   Writing the Article   211

Writing the Article (*Cont.*):

12 Composing the Title   232

13 Revising First Draft of Manuscript   249

PART II

History of Science Writing Aids Writer (*Cont.*):

23 Writing Scientific and Technical Articles 437

42 Magazine Production Is a Huge Industry 475

Magazine Production Is a Huge Industry (*Cont.*):

APPENDIX

Illustrations

██▀█▀█▀▀▀▀▀▀▀▀▀▀▀▀▀▀▀▀▀▀▀▀▀▀▀▀▀▀▀▀▀▀▀▀▀▀▀▀▀██

Part I

WRITING AND SELLING FEATURE ARTICLES

CHAPTER 1

Feature Writing as a Career or Avocation

Demand Is Large for Fact Writing. If you want to make writing your career, or if you want to make it merely an avocation, have no doubts or fears about lack of opportunities to sell your articles. You are living in the golden age of the Sunday newspaper feature section and the magazine. Never have there been so many newspaper feature sections and magazines appealing to such a variety of readers with all kinds of interests. If you have the ability to gather the material and to write the facts into the sort of interesting articles that editors want for their subscribers, you will be successful in getting into print.

Feature Article Developed Rapidly. Some people thought that the much-talked-of inventions to come following World War II would be the death blow to the magazines and the Sunday newspaper magazine sections which had developed in the early nineties and increased in number rapidly during the depression of the early thirties as an institution in American life. War II and the postwar problems were the cause of additional expansion. The economic history of periodical production during the forties, when the United States was at war and later was struggling to make and keep the peace, shows that the feature articles in maga-

zines and newspaper magazine sections were in greater demand by
readers than were short stories and novels.

The sudden growth of weekly and monthly magazines during
the last ten years, which might be termed the "magazine boom"
period, was due to: (1) the popularity of fact articles over fiction;
(2) the wave of increased interest in reading because the postwar
problems touched the life of every citizen and each wanted to be
better informed; or (3) the continuation schools and the adult-
education movement, which awakened in people the desire to be
better informed; or (4) the fact that people realized world problems were their problems and they must study them. At any rate,
they turned to magazines and to newspaper magazine sections as
a means of adding to their information or as an escape from the
problems of keeping the peace, and they found in the periodicals
a substitute satisfaction.

Opportunities for Sales Are Unlimited. No matter what may
have been the cause, today there are approximately 7,733 magazines, with approximately 92,796 issues annually, and 12,885
daily, weekly, and semi-weekly newspapers, with approximately
4,550,594 issues. About 487 of the dailies have magazine sections, with 25,324 issues, in addition to the articles used in the
weekday issues. These publications, totaling more than 20,618,
with approximately 4,643,390 issues annually, each of which uses
from one to twenty or more features, buy from free-lance writers
fact articles that will keep their readers interested in continuing
their subscriptions. Any person who can gather facts intelligently,
write them interestingly, and illustrate them attractively will not
have difficulty in marketing his manuscripts if he will study the
various kinds of publications to see what types of articles editors
want. The free-lance writer has, in fact, more than one and a half
million opportunities annually to write for publications.

Advantages of Features over Fiction. Almost every person
who has any creative instinct thinks that some day he will write.
If everyone really did write, competition would be so keen that
writing as a career, or even as an avocation, would be hopeless.
Fortunately, however, for those who do write, most would-be

writers never overcome their inertia, and thus never become competitors. If one has the urge and the will power to find the time to write (that is, to set aside a definite time each day in which to do his writing; or, if otherwise employed, a certain time each week), he will succeed in getting his ideas upon paper. Then he faces the question of whether to write fiction or fact articles. Perhaps he has just heard of someone in Mississippi, or elsewhere, who has sold for $10,000 a novel to be used as a serial in a leading magazine. He learns also that the author has signed a contract with a publisher to issue it in book form and has signed another contract with a moving picture company for the scenario rights. He probably does not know the new author, but he may actually have met someone who sold a manuscript for $1,000; and of course he knows about the struggling young architect down in the next block who has just had a short story, upon which he had been working for days and days, accepted by one of the "class" magazines for $250. Perhaps he feels he should write fiction, for apparently that is what brings in the big checks.

But before deciding to try fiction writing, one should reflect upon just how many such lucky authors there are. Investigation will show that where one has succeeded, hundreds have had many manuscripts rejected and have never had an acceptance. Where the one has dashed off a best seller or a much-talked-about short story, there are hundreds of persevering people who have written fiction for years without receiving a check. Also, one may be successful with his first novel or story, but may never be able to produce another manuscript that will find its way into type.

In any community, however, there are numerous people who do not devote nearly so much time to their writing as do the fiction writers, but who, because of their interest in persons, places, or things about them, are writing fact articles for Sunday feature sections, trade publications, and general and class magazines. They continually receive checks that well repay them for the energy and time spent in gathering the material and writing the articles. For the average writer, the financial rewards and the personal satisfactions will be greater from feature writing, in the end, than from fiction if he applies what he learns from these pages. His chances of selling his articles are almost unlimited, and the remuneration is more ample for the time and energy expended, since it is easier to sell facts. Reader interest in fact articles has increased manyfold in the last decade. Many successful fiction writers, moreover, started their careers by writing feature articles before attempting short stories or novels.

Writing Affords Personal Satisfaction. It is easy to find suggestions for fact articles. All around us, everywhere, are ideas that can be written into features that will sell. In order to get facts, it is necessary to interview successful people. Successful people are usually happy people; and who is there that does not enjoy coming into contact with happy folk? In the search for facts, one's own knowledge, as well as one's acquaintanceship, is widened. Usually one feature article opens up ideas for several more, whereas in fiction writing, one is so busy with the intricacies of plot and character that he never has time to meet interesting people in real life. His writing keeps him at work alone in his den. His own knowledge is widened only in so far as his story is concerned. To the writer who likes to know successful people, or to learn new or easier ways of doing things, and who has a keen interest in the life about him, no type of writing offers more personal satisfaction than does feature writing. Not only is there the pleasure that comes from sharing the knowledge one gains with others who can profit by it, but the opportunities to sell manuscripts are much greater. If one has the urge to be a missionary as well as to create, but does not wish to devote his entire time to such work, he should turn his talents to writing features. The good he may do by his writing is unlimited. This is shown by the published articles by beginners in a feature writing class, which total between $8,000 and $10,000 annually.

For many persons, the principles of writing feature articles, as discussed in this book, have opened up an entirely new field of work. Some of them have made feature writing their life work; others have developed it into a worth-while avocation; and still others have found, by their success in it, a goal to which they might look forward on that day when they retire from the monotonous routine of their jobs. They may then spend their days writing feature articles and have something interesting with which to occupy their time as well as to add to their incomes. *Even Beginners Sell.* Young people, just average juniors and seniors in a university school of journalism, who never before had written a feature article, have applied these principles of feature writing. As a result, they have written features that perennially brought the class in magazine article writing a total of $8,000 to $10,000 a semester. If college students can, as some of them have, become entirely or partially self-supporting while in school by means of writing features, it seems likely that others, no matter how inexperienced, may be successful, provided they have the necessary qualifications.

Many service people enrolled in the United States Armed Forces Institute global class in feature writing had never before written for print; they never even saw their instructor, yet they sold articles for sums ranging from $5 up to $300. One man's sales totalled more than $2,500 in a specialized field. A young sergeant topped the record by selling his second article for the course to *National Geographic* for $550. If those students, writing alone under all sorts of conditions, thousands of miles away from the help of their instructor, could sell feature articles to newspapers and magazines, others may too, if they will apply the suggestions on the following pages.

Groups of writers in several states have organized writers' associations and are consistently selling their manuscripts. When they are not writing, their members are farmers, housewives, teachers, ministers, and social workers. The members meet about once a month, read their manuscripts to the group, and offer one another constructive criticism. United States Armed Forces groups work together and are equally successful in selling their manuscripts.

A recent survey by a writer's journal reveals that more than 500,000 persons are free-lance writers. About 100,000 are regular contributors, and another 100,000 make an exceedingly good living. The other 300,000 have varying degrees of success.

Of course, one should not plan to be dependent upon an income from free-lancing until he has become established and has acquired some reputation in particular fields or has made successful contacts with enough magazines to be assured at least of a certain degree of success.

Definition of a Feature Article. The special feature article is similar to a news story in that it gives the reader facts in an interesting form and is adapted to rapid reading. But it goes beyond those facts by amplifying them with study, research, and interviews, to instruct, guide, or entertain readers who know about the subject as well as those who do not. They vary in length from a couple hundred words to several thousand.

The news story is written to inform the reader. The feature article not only informs but instructs, guides, or entertains. Where the news story presents the bare facts, the feature article dramatizes and supplements them by giving in detail information that will appeal to the reader's imagination. The reporter writes of what he sees; the feature writer relates not only what he sees but the causes or background of the story. The news story may, of necessity, be hurriedly written. The feature article seldom has to meet a "deadline," and can be written at greater leisure. Thus, it affords the writer greater opportunity to make use of moving narration and vivid description, as well as clear exposition, in order to dramatize his writing. The news story and the magazine article are similar in that they interest the person who knows all about the subject and the one who knows nothing about it. In many respects, feature writing is reporting—at least it amplifies the work of the reporter.

Ability to Write May Be Acquired. Many persons feel the creative urge to write but hesitate to market their manuscripts because they believe that successful writers possess occult powers that they themselves do not have. But writing for publication is not mysterious; it must be reduced almost to a formula if one would write successfully. It is true that there are born writers, but as in almost every other kind of work, one may acquire the knack or mastery through practice and experience. Some have an inherited or natural aptitude for writing, but anyone who can write English correctly can write features if he will cultivate the following qualifications: (1) the ability to be curious and interested in the things about him and the desire to share that interest; (2) the capacity to recognize subjects that will interest readers and that may be developed into features; (3) the confidence and the enthusiasm and the ability to inspire those qualities in his readers; (4) the sympathy and understanding to enable him to see human interest elements in the facts about which he is writing and to make the article appeal to the readers; (5) the qualities of observation, thoroughness, and accurateness, to give the reader as well as the editor confidence in the writer; (6) skill in interviewing, in order to obtain interesting facts; (7) the ability to write clearly, accurately, and with imaginative appeal, to hold the reader's interest to the end of the article; and (8) the realization that feature writing is a business requiring a practical knowledge of the markets and the skill to "slant" articles to appeal to specific publications.

Writer Must Be Sincere and Enthusiastic. Just as the advertising copy writer must be convinced that the product he is describing is the best the customer can buy, so must the feature writer convince or, as the advertising writers say, "sell" himself on his own idea for the feature that he is about to write. Unless it is written with sincerity and enthusiasm, the article will never sell. Even as he plans the article before beginning to write it, he will want to visualize his reader—he will want to have a sincere desire to help, guide, or entertain him. If, as he plans and writes his article, he can picture the reader in his home sitting under the light of the reading lamp with the magazine containing the article in his hand, the writer will be able to write enthusiastically and sincerely.

Curiosity Is Source of Ideas. The person who is interested in people from all walks of life, who is curious, and who is always asking "why" of everything he sees and hears and does, or sees others do—and cannot be content with telling it to one or two friends but must tell it to hundreds, thousands, or millions—will find newspaper feature sections and magazines the most satisfying means of communicating his interests to others.

A young journalist passed a florist shop window that displayed, in miniature, a whirling windmill, a fast flowing brook, and a cool placid pool on whose moss-covered bank little, bright-colored flowers were growing. He stopped along with many morning shoppers, for he, too, was attracted by the movement in the small but realistic scene. He wondered what made the little windmill go, what power kept the water forever flowing in and out of the tiny lake. He was curious. He wanted to know "why." He entered the shop and asked the proprietor the explanation of the mechanism. As he left the store, he met a fraternity brother, a law student, and as they walked back to the campus the young writer told what he had just learned about the window display. At the first opportunity, the lawyer asked if the journalist were going to Evanston for the football game. The novice realized that his audience of one was not interested; but he felt that someone must be interested in that clever device that attracted so much attention to the window.

In answering his own question as to who would be interested, he thought of other florists, and he wondered what they read. Retracing his steps, he asked the florist what he read, and was invited into the manager's office to see copies of several florists' trade journals and business magazines. Some time later the young writer's story of the window display, including snapshots of it (which had been made on "glossy" paper) and a blueprint of the motor and the machinery employed to keep the little windmill and the water moving, appeared in one of the leading floral trade papers. The young man cashed a check for $35, which he felt was a fair reward for his first feature article and for his first assignment in his magazine-writing class. Because his article was written with intense enthusiasm and sincerity and almost absolute correctness, his professor had recorded a grade of "A" for him. Although he occasionally had received a few "A" grades, it was the first time he had ever received a check for a class assignment.

A young woman in the same class passed the window several times and was impressed by the crowd watching the display every time she went by. Each time she passed she noticed that a number of window-shoppers went into the florist shop and made purchases. She wondered how much new business the window display was bringing the owner. A fifteen-minute interview with him gave her the material for her first feature article. A few minutes spent that night taking a flashlight picture of the window display, and her interest in wanting to tell other florists how they could attract more customers through interesting window displays, resulted in an article that was accepted by another florists' trade paper and for which she received a check for $25. Her article was shorter and was not quite so practical, because she did not send a drawing to show how the mechanism worked, as the young man did. Her ability to sense news, store news though it was, and to recognize a subject that would interest readers of a business journal, brought the writer the satisfaction of seeing her article in print and enabled her to earn her first money by means of her journalistic training.

A third student observed another display in the opposite show window of the same shop. It contained an aquarium with tropical fish, which were then coming into vogue. She was interested in the kinds and types of fish bowls and, in talking with the manager, she became interested in them from the point of view of interior decoration and types best suited to the various periods of furnishings. They also talked about the care of the little fish. The young interviewer became so enthusiastic about her idea, or "tip," for her first feature that she wrote it up immediately. Her article was informative and entertaining, but she was not satisfied with it. She went to the library to read all she could find on the subject of small-fish life and rewrote the article entirely. She changed words, sentences, and paragraphs until she had an article that compared favorably with those that appear in many magazines. Before rewriting, she had studied the magazines that appealed to homeowners and housewives and finally selected one whose readers she thought would be interested in her article. She sent it out and in due time received a letter of acceptance. Upon publication of the article, she received a check for $50.

Here were three young students, ages 20, 21, and 22, juniors and seniors in a university school of journalism, who never before had written a feature article, but who sold their first. After the magazines were on the subscribers' desks, two of the writers received "fan mail," or letters inquiring further about the subject matter and expressing interest in the articles.

To Succeed One Must Be a Careful Thinker. Let us see why these three students, and hundreds of others too, were successful in selling their first articles. The answer is easy: in each case the young writers had the eight qualifications for feature writing. Although all three became interested in the same floral shop, each saw a different thing when he looked in the window. Each saw a different angle appealing to a different reader. But they were all interested; they all recognized the news or interest value to other people; they were confident they could write the article to interest others. Through their understanding and sympathy for the problems of florists and home-owners, they made their articles practical enough to appeal to the readers, who were practical people. They were skillful in getting the florist to give them the information, and they were observant and accurate in writing the facts into articles that editors would buy for their readers. They were resourceful in obtaining pictures, blueprints, and drawings to illustrate the articles. They were businesslike in: (1) deciding who would want to know these facts; (2) learning what the shopkeepers and home-owners read; and (3) studying the markets before they began to write their articles.

Perhaps one might conclude that these students had worked on school publications and had had courses in survey of journalism and news reporting and, because of even that small experience, were better prepared to write features that would sell. That was true of one of the three, but the other two had not had journalism experience or previous journalism courses. In the same class, sitting in near-by seats, were other students who had never had a previous course in journalism and had never worked on a student publication. They, too, wrote articles that sold. There was the mother, who had come along to college with her son and daughter, whose interest in an unusual corner drugstore netted a check for $65 from a drug-trade publication. There was the college professor's wife whose children were in school. She had leisure time in which to learn to write of her homemaking experiences. There was the seventy-year-old grandmother who wrote three times as many articles as were required in the course, and she sold them all. There was the minister who later became so successful as a free-lance writer that he abandoned his pulpit for the typewriter. There was the young physician, the lawyer, a priest, a sister, a housewife, the high-school teacher, and a university dean, as well as one hundred and twenty others who were just college juniors and seniors who had enrolled in the course because they wanted to write—and to write to sell.

They wrote about all kinds of subjects for all kinds of publications; they wrote of their own experiences and the experiences of others; they wrote all types of articles because they were interested in everything—and they were so enthusiastic that they just had to share their interest with others. They were successful in selling their manuscripts, not because they were upperclassmen or held degrees of higher learning (for some of them who had not completed a high-school course were enrolled as adult specials), but because they were willing to apply what they learned concerning the technique of writing features. Their success was due, not to their education or their lack of it, but to their interest, enthusiasm, and observation; to their ability to gather and verify facts, use a library, and write simply, clearly, and entertainingly; and to their businesslike procedure in studying newspapers and magazines to find markets and in keeping systematic records concerning their manuscripts (the cost of paper, stamps, envelopes, pictures, drawings, and other expenses, the time spent in gathering and writing the material, the dates on which the articles were mailed out and returned, and the list of publications to which they were sent).

Aptitude for Writing Is Essential. The gift for writing fea-

tures, whether native or acquired, is absolutely essential. But by
no means is it a talent with which one must be born. If, however,
a person thinks he would like to learn to write for print, he should,
first of all, take stock of his native abilities and his likes and dislikes. He should determine, in so far as possible, his capacity for
overcoming his dislikes and the traits of character that would
hinder his success in writing feature articles.

As important as the desire to express himself in writing, and
to share or communicate his knowledge of facts with others, is
his high regard for truth and accuracy. A writer must never be
willing to disseminate false statements or facts, or even to imply
untruths. His inaccuracies will find him out. Then he will lose the
confidence of both the editor to whom he submits his manuscripts
and the reader who detects the false statements. The latter will in
turn lose his faith in the publication to which he has subscribed.

Equally significant is the writer's willingness to search out and
dig for facts and to go to no end of trouble to ascertain the truth
in order to inform the reader correctly. If one finds that he is
bored by searching for facts, and if he is not curious or interested
in the people and things about him, and if he does not wish to
know what others like to read for their information, guidance,
and entertainment, he should hesitate to take up writing either as
an avocation or as a career.

Skill in Interviewing Is Important. If a writer is to gather
facts from authorities, he must develop skill in interviewing, in
order to draw from the expert the information that he desires for
the reader. He must learn to be not only a good listener but an
enthusiastic one. If he does not show interest in the subject upon
which he is interviewing, the person interviewed (or the "interviewee," as the journalists say) will not be enthusiastic or interested either, and the result will be a lifeless article.

If the interviewer does all the talking, or most of it, the interviewee will not have an opportunity to give his expert opinions,
and then the interviewer will have nothing of importance to write
or quote. The good interviewer has been termed a "human sponge,"
or a "blotting paper." He must be able to absorb and assimilate

what he is told and to think through his material clearly, in order to be able to appeal to the reader's interest. The person who is content with foggy thinking will not have readers to whom to appeal, because editors will not buy his manuscripts.

Slanting Manuscripts to Markets. To succeed, a writer must be willing to study the markets. If he cannot sell his manuscripts, he will never attain success. He must be able to adapt his material to conform to the policy and style of the publication that he thinks might be interested in the article. When writing for print, the writer should think, never of the editor, but of the 100,000 or 500,000 subscribers. He should visualize one of those readers—a typical reader of the newspaper feature section or of the magazine to which he is submitting his manuscript—and then he will be better able to write his material for that reader and for the thousands of other similar readers. If he has selected, in his imagination, a typical reader, he will be less likely to go beyond the mental grasp of that reader. Thus, he will avoid writing down to the reader or over his head. Before beginning to write the first draft of the article, the writer must determine the markets to which he will send his article, in order to fit it to the length and style of the publication and to know what pictures or drawings he will need for it. If an article does not have pictures it probably will not sell.

In appealing to the reader's interest, one must write about the things in which the reader will be interested. Yet many young beginners yearn to write their own opinions. A writer will never develop a reader following unless he writes from the point of view of the reader rather than from his own opinions. Very young writers often try to impress their readers with their individual style of writing, which in many cases is merely a poor imitation of some freakish style popular for the moment in some of the magazines that are more interested in fads than they are in facts. Or the embryo writers may refuse to conform their style of writing to that of the publications that they are hoping will buy their articles, because they feel it will ruin their so-called "individual" style. Some beginners have such confidence in their own writing ability that they feel it is a waste of time to organize their material or to write from an outline. There are others who write the first draft enthusiastically but who refuse to edit their copy to correct careless or slovenly writing, bad spelling, and faulty punctuation. Their personal vanity is hurt when they are required to prepare their manuscripts in the professional manner of experienced writers. Many beginners are wordy or fail to use the right words to express their ideas. They express themselves awkwardly because they do not think through the sentences before they start to write them. They have little regard for the rules of punctuation and grammar or for accuracy in spelling. Editors will not have confidence in careless manuscripts and will reject them even though the facts may sound new and interesting. They feel that the authors of such manuscripts may be equally careless in their fact-gathering. Editors have to be careful to avoid making their publications ridiculous in the eyes of their readers and of editors of other publications.

Writers Must Use Businesslike Methods. The successful writer does not wait until he "feels like writing," or until "the spirit moves him," but has a definite time for his writing and lets nothing interfere with his work. Though he thoroughly enjoys writing, he writes for money rather than for "the love of writing." Some sensitive people who are afraid to get a rejection slip say they do not care to write for money because they prefer to write for "the love of writing." There are dreamers who refuse to write practical ideas or to be businesslike in their writing or work. They refuse to keep their files of material and clippings in an orderly manner, and they just cannot be bothered with keeping records concerning the expense and whereabouts of their manuscripts. They think it is artistic to be careless, unsystematic, and slovenly in their thinking and writing, and unbusinesslike in looking after the financial side of their avocation or career.

The enthusiastic beginner who is ambitious to overcome his faults; desirous of adapting the content and style of his article to that of a possible market; willing to work hard, study publications, and analyze possible markets for his manuscripts; always thoughtful of the readers; always thinking of that typical reader as he writes; never satisfied with his manuscript, but always anxious to revise it in any way he can to improve it; careful to prepare his copy in a professional style; and sensible enough to write about things in which people are interested—he will be a success. His own fervor will help him to overcome his faults. If he will be businesslike in keeping his files in order, always to have material on hand, and be systematic in keeping records of profits from his writings, he will soon pass from the stage of the beginner to that of the professional.

Some who start writing features have one or all of the faults enumerated, but, because they have a burning desire to express their thoughts and to write for print, are willing to learn to write in the professional manner. Of course, it is hard work and requires great patience; but in the end they win and their names are seen in the by-lines over leading articles in magazines today, simply because they were determined to write and to write well.

Some Beginners Never Attain Success. Many who would write remain amateurs because they are not willing to adjust their ideas to conform to editorial policies. They fail because they wish to write their own opinions, and, as a rule, beginners do not have opinions of enough value to interest readers. They are not authorities in some specialized field. There are self-satisfied souls who write because they wish to express themselves; they do not want to include opinions of people whose ideas would be new and interesting to readers or whose names would lend weight to the article. These self-centered folk may sell one or two of their opinion articles, but they never progress far in writing for publication. They are not observant, nor are they desirous of learning what readers want to read. Others never climb above the round of the amateur on the writer's ladder because they will not work regularly or systematically; they wish to wait to write until they "feel like writing," until they are "inspired." They are the type who spurn the writing of anything practical that will inform, instruct, or entertain readers.

Others fail because they will not interview people who have new ideas or who are authorities. They do not desire to share credit for anything in the article with anyone. Many will not adjust their ways of writing to conform with the policy of the magazine or will not prepare a manuscript to meet the requirements for publication. They feel their way is superior. They do not want to be informed on the topics of the day because they feel that to do so is not "being literary." As a result of their attitude, their articles are always behind the times, and editors will not buy them. No matter how well written other manuscripts are, those on current subjects are preferred by editors. Or there is the type of would-be writer who cannot bear to send anything out for publication until he has developed a "style." The result is that he writes but little, and therefore never attains the style he is seeking. Some lose their courage at the sight of a rejection slip and become so depressed that they never attempt to send out the manuscript again, or to revise it, or to write another one. They are the cowards of the writing world. Others are too lazy to think: (1) who will read their articles; (2) why they will read them; and (3) how much they will want to read. The consequence is that no one ever reads their articles. They are written so carelessly and contain so little that is informative, instructive, or entertaining that editors will not buy them.

Many remain beginners because they are content to send out manuscripts that are written hastily and superficially; the vocabulary is poor; sentences and paragraphs are not thought through; and the writers are satisfied to write merely what they saw, without telling the reader what was back of what they saw, or what caused what they saw. They are neither enthusiastic nor confident about the subject matter; they write to be writing and do not give any thought to the reader and to his likes and dislikes.

Writer's Attitude Helps or Hinders. The unknown writer has as good an opportunity as the well-known one to have his articles accepted, provided that his manuscript is as well done as the experienced writer's. Editors still depend upon free-lance writers for much of their fact material even though staffs are larger. They are more interested in the content of the article and how it meets their publication needs than they are in the author's name, or by-line, over the article. The amateur's by-line will be welcome to any editor if the writer will adopt the professional way of writing and the attitude of the professional toward his work.

The professional feature writer admits that he writes for money, whether it is to provide his entire income, or, as an avocation, to add to his salary from his regular profession or work. The writer whose by-line is familiar has the spirit of the eager pioneer or adventurer, because he, too, seeks the new, works regularly, and writes systematically. He not only is willing, but desires, to do his work in the professional way. He knows what he is doing, how to do it, and, upon its completion, where to send it for publication.

He succeeds because he gives thought: (1) to the subject about which he is going to write; (2) to the reader and to how much the reader will be interested in the subject; (3) to the publications that people interested in the subject will read; (4) to the sources he will go to for help or ideas; (5) to the person, or persons, he will interview; (6) to the pictures, drawings, and illustrative material that he can use to add to the interest in the article; (7) to the plan of development of the facts, in order that they will have the greatest appeal to the reader; and (8) to writing the article in a way that will make it effective in its appeal to the reader.

Through experience he has learned that writers must be curious, observant, accurate, and well informed. He has found that when he is confident and enthusiastic and has faith in the article, he writes more easily and better. He has acquired the scientific spirit, for he is willing to search for facts until he gets what he wants; then he desires to share them with others through the printed page. By studying the markets assiduously and knowing how to slant his articles to fit the policy of the publication to which he sends them, he avoids rejection slips. He is businesslike in filing the material that he gathers from observation, interviews, experiences of his own and of others, clippings, and notes from his readings. He tries to know a little about everything and to know all he can about several fields of special interest. He does not wait for inspiration to write, but inspires himself by writing regularly, whether or not he feels like doing it.

Often one hears it said that success in writing is just a matter of luck; but success in writing is a matter of hard thinking and careful workmanship. Those who enjoy it are rewarded with the satisfaction that their work has been well done and with the knowledge that the financial remuneration can be as little or as big as they desire, the amount depending upon their determination.

The Amateur Acquires a Journalistic Face. The novice who becomes a success undergoes a metamorphosis before he becomes a professional writer, because a free-lance must develop "a journalistic face." In looking for the new about which to write interestingly, the feature writer develops "a nose for news," as the journalist says; in looking for appeals to the emotions to brighten up the facts, he acquires "an ear for human interest"; in finding fact material that will entertain or inform the reader, he enlarges "his eye for feature stories"; and in learning to slant his material to a market that may buy his article, he strengthens "his jaw of determination" to succeed. In reality, the professional achieves more than a journalistic face, because back of and above his face he must have a mind that is sympathetic, understanding, and desirous of knowledge; and he must have a conscience that will let him write only the truth.

In the eyes of the craft, the amateur becomes a professional writer when he has made his new journalistic features a part of his physiognomy, or his professional face. He gathers his material, writes his facts, and markets his manuscripts in the professional manner. Any beginner who will read and apply the proper techniques can be transformed from an amateur into a professional as soon as he acquires the qualifications that will enable him to write articles that subscribers will want to read, to study markets as diligently as the investor studies the financial pages of his newspaper, and to prepare his manuscript as carefully as does the professional writer.

Learn to Write by Writing. There is only one way to learn to write for publication, and that is *to write.* Creative writing, which is largely self-taught, actually is only a small part of writing. If one could break feature writing up into ten parts, he would find: one part gathering facts; one part interviewing; four parts thinking and planning; three parts knowing how to analyze the editorial policy in order to slant the article and to know where to submit the manuscript; and one part writing—but excellent writing.

The tyro must force himself to write whether he feels like it or not, because creative work of any kind is seldom the result of some spontaneous inner power. The writer can compel or inspire himself by various methods to become so interested in what he is writing that he will forget to go to lunch or will write far into the night without realizing the hour. If a novice will set a time to start his "research," or preparation, for his article, he can call forth the impulse to write by: (1) reading all he can find on the subject; (2) investigating facts; (3) observing things that might apply to the material; and (4) interviewing authorities. By the time he has collected all his notes, material, pictures, or drawings, he will have given his article so much thought and become so enthusiastic about it that one could not keep him from writing. Even before he sits down to his typewriter, he will have formulated a plan or outline of the material he will wish to include. As he was walking down the street, or perhaps he just was dozing off to sleep, or just had turned off his alarm clock, a striking idea may come to him for a clever "lead," or beginning, for his article. Attention-getting captions, or headlines, and leads, or beginnings, usually come to one like a flash after he has given the subject matter of the entire article the necessary thought that spurs the imagination to produce clever ideas with reader appeal.

Some beginners find that to form the habit of writing every day at a regular time not only develops the urge to write, but improves their ability and skill. For others, unusual events often serve as the stimulus that invokes the urge to express themselves on paper; or perhaps a unique experience which the beginner wishes to share with others serves as the incentive to begin his article. A sense of obligation will conjure so-called inspiration for undisciplined writers who must meet a "deadline," even a self-made one, in order to get started; or making a vow to start often aids one in doing so. The hope of compensation, either a financial reward or renown and fame, frequently is sufficient incentive to begin the manuscript. The fervent desire to communicate ideas or experiences with others who may be interested may fire the novice's enthusiasm to the point where he sits down and types off an outline from which he develops his article. Writing will not come by waiting for the impulse or inspiration; it does come by regular and continued practice. Writing for trade magazines enables a beginner to get a good start in fact writing.

Difference Between Amateurs and Professionals. Feature writers are classified into two distinct groups: amateurs and professionals. The amateur works spasmodically and usually takes pride in writing only when he "feels the urge." He glories in the fact that he is not businesslike, he refuses to slant his copy to any particular publication, and he says he spurns the idea of writing for money.

The professional's attitude toward writing is quite the opposite. He writes regularly either to keep in practice, if his writing is an avocation, or, if it is a career, to earn his livelihood. He plans a schedule of articles to be written; he studies and analyzes publications of all kinds to know their editorial and advertising content. Even though he is not writing editorials, fiction, or advertising copy, a careful study of those phases of a magazine may show a writer the kind of readers for whom the editor plans his magazine. A survey of the advertising in a publication will give one an idea of everything he needs to know concerning the readers for whom he hopes to write, because the advertising is written to appeal to them. A fair estimate of the reader's income, buying power, living standards, likes, and interests may be determined from the advertising, as explained in Chapter 9, "Slanting Articles to Publications." The veteran writer takes pride in his sales, which are the result of his careful work. He invests in pictures to help sell the article.

The amateur will remain an amateur until he is able to adjust his attitude toward writing and his writing habits to conform with the standards set up by experienced writers in the craft and demanded by editors. He must: (1) follow the accepted technique in order to do the articles as editors would want them done; (2) be observant in order to develop the nose for news and the eye for features; (3) gather interesting facts that will instruct, inform, or entertain his readers; (4) have ability to use the writer's tools—words, sentences, and paragraphs—correctly and effectively; and (5) never be satisfied with his writing until he feels that it has real merit.

The feature writer is a reporter, who, like the aviator, has a sixth sense. He knows what the general public likes to read and he knows where, when, and how to market his manuscripts. Like the reporter, he must keep on studying, experimenting, and setting himself newer and harder tasks in the writing field. Feature writing is the reporter's normal side line.

Equipment for Writing. Of all the arts, writing requires the least financial outlay. A good typewriter is the first requisite. A supply of a good grade of typewriting paper, carbon paper, and copy paper is necessary; one should always save a carbon of anything he writes for print, in case the manuscript is lost in the mails. Two sizes of manila envelopes, the outside one 13 x 10 inches and a smaller one 12½ x 9½ inches (to fit easily inside the larger one, to be used if it is necessary to return the manuscript), and government postal cards for the editor's acknowledgement of the receipt of the manuscript, are necessary. Bristol board, a smooth lightweight pasteboard, or any other that takes India ink, should be used for drawings and sketches if articles lend themselves to that type of illustration. Every feature writer should, as soon as possible, have a good camera, since informal snapshots are preferred by editors. A professional writer has his office or study equipped with file cases in which he files notes taken from his readings, clippings, bulletins, and other reference material. He will find a small postal scale of great convenience in weighing his manuscripts. His professional library should include a recent, recognized dictionary, a thesaurus, a synonym book, a handbook for writers, a world almanac, and an atlas—all instruments of his craft. Market books listed under "The Free-Lance Writer's Library" in the Appendix will be suggestive of ideas for articles as well as markets, as will the writer's magazines listed there. Access to libraries where newspapers, trade or business papers, magazines, periodicals, and bulletins may be studied is essential if the writer is to achieve craftmanship.

Pretentious equipment is not necessary for the beginner. He may rent a typewriter and a camera. He will find that a pasteboard box large enough to hold manila folders will serve well as a file case, or he may obtain a portable cardboard file from an office supply company. He may buy the necessary supplies (typewriting paper, carbon paper, envelopes of two sizes, post cards, and stamps) as he needs them, in order not to purchase too heavily at a time. Because many people think that they want to write but, when they get at it, find they do not have the aptitude for it, one should be cautious about investing in too much equipment until he is confident that he wants to make writing either his avocation or his career.

Rewards for Writing Features. If a beginner enters the field of feature writing with the determination that he will not be discouraged by rejection slips, disgruntled by the long waiting for either the rejection or the acceptance of his articles, or disappointed by the uncertainty of the financial remuneration, he will find great satisfaction in writing articles—whether he makes it an avocation or a profession.

In considering the benefits and rewards of feature writing as an avocation, the beginner will find mental satisfaction in self-expression and in the communication of his ideas to others. It affords an incentive to improve his writing and to develop a style. It provides opportunities for meeting and interviewing successful people. It also serves as a training school for short-story and fiction writers, in that it stimulates initiative and imagination. Intellectual curiosity and desire for scientific investigation are stimulated in the search for facts, which makes a feature writer a student throughout his life. He is always adding to his knowledge in many fields, because he cannot write features without becoming better informed himself. Since a great variety of material is available to the free-lance, he writes only that which he chooses. The opportunities for his manuscripts to be published are almost unlimited.

The novice should not depend upon feature writing as a means of livelihood, because the markets and the financial remuneration are too uncertain until one has become established in the profession. There have been a few clever and gifted students in almost every journalism school, however, who have abandoned dishwashing as a means of attaining a college degree. They have found free-lancing easier, more pleasant, and more profitable. They have received from $500 to $2,000 annually for their articles. But they had acquired the eight desirable requisites for successful writing of features.

The beginner is paid from one-fourth of a cent to five cents a word or more, the rate depending upon his ability to write effectively and to slant his material to meet the editor's approval. As skill is developed and experience is gained throughout the years in writing and marketing, many adults have added from $1,000 to $10,000 to their incomes in addition to their business or career. Many people find free-lancing a means of attaining little luxuries and pleasures that they could not otherwise have. There was the housewife, for example, who wanted more than anything else to go to Europe. Financially it was impossible; but upon hearing of the success of writers in a beginning class in magazine writing, she enrolled, determined to learn to write and sell articles. She received $5,000 for her articles over a period of about two years. Then, with her husband, she went to Europe on the money earned. She has been writing ever since. The money has enabled her to enjoy other things that she had always wanted.

Invalids and wounded veterans have found a career in writing though unable to leave their beds.

Widens Professional Opportunities. Professional satisfactions include personal influence, public recognition, respect of others, and fame—to at least some degree. Ability to write acceptable articles and to be paid for one's ideas often serves as a cause for promotion or a salary increase in almost any business or profession, as well as increasing the opinions of others as to the value of one's ideas. Doctors, lawyers, ministers, deans, professors, teachers, business people, engineers, housewives, farmers, and others may add to their incomes by sharing their expert knowledge or experiences with readers who are interested.

Fortunately for the journalist, many experts do not have the time nor the inclination to write about their specialities; or they may write too technically for the average reader. Their shortcomings enable the feature writer to interview them and to write the information in a way that will appeal to readers. By submitting features to newspapers and magazines, free-lance writers may make contacts that will bring them offers of positions as correspondents, staff reporters, feature writers, or associate editors. A young woman in a feature class wrote an article concerning the coal and fuel business and sent it to a coal dealers' trade paper. The editors were so well pleased with it they asked her to send in an article a month and made her an associate editor. Numerous other students and free-lance writers have developed similar opportunities through their articles. Feature writing offers many opportunities to enter any of the several fields of creative writing and serves as the door that may lead to the writing of fiction.

Feature Writing as a Career. For the person who has ability and has established a reputation for himself in the journalistic field, writing as a profession has just as much to offer from the financial point of view as has any of the other professions, provided one likes to write and has the determination to succeed. The income of the professional varies with his ability to slant his material for the more remunerative markets and with his capacity to turn out a large number of articles in a year. The income of the proficient writer varies from $5,000 up to $50,000 or more. He is paid from two to ten cents a word, although a number of the big names are paid as high as a dollar a word. Some articles in the *Saturday Evening Post* brought authors $175,000 for their articles.

The road to success as a writer is long and arduous, but no more so than in such professions as law and medicine. To the creative writer, however, it is never laborious nor boresome. His work brings him in contact with successful, happy people, whom he enjoys meeting. Even though one is never certain of his income, if he is businesslike and keeps a score or more of articles in the mail at the same time, and if he is able to turn out from two to three articles a week, he will soon, like the physician and the lawyer, establish definite sources of income from markets upon which he can depend. As some free-lance writers become specialists in a particular field, they give up writing for the other fields. They feel it is better to concentrate on one. They depend entirely upon querying the editors of the field in which they have specialized and in which they are known. Many write only on order. Many class magazines pay from $500 to $1,000, or even more, for an article written upon order by a writer whose by-line will add to the reputation of the publication.

Professional writers who prefer to have a definite and assured income may become associated with publications as assistants, associate editors, or as editors-in-chief when the opportunity arises. Their salaries range from $5,000 up to $50,000 a year or more. Even though one may not have become a renowned writer, there are many openings for experienced writers as editors of trade, business, industrial, technical, fraternal, professional, class, and general publications in addition to opportunities in writing fiction, nonfiction, syndicated features, publicity, and radio and TV continuity, as is pointed out in Part II. Such experience gives one background if he wishes to start his own magazine, as many free-lance writers do when they are interested in the business as well as in the editorial side.

The World Is the Writer's Workshop. Whether one makes writing an avocation or a career, he will succeed only because he likes to write, enjoys meeting people, and has a professional attitude toward his work. To the novice and the professional alike, there is a keen pleasure in writing features, for the whole world may become the writer's workshop. His search for facts to interest readers takes him into all sorts of paths and byways at home or abroad, because wherever one goes or wherever one looks, there are more ideas for feature articles than one can write in a lifetime. In this golden age of the magazine there are more markets than free-lance writers can ever hope to over-supply.

Exercises

1. What are the names of ten magazines that are on sale at your nearest newsstand or corner drugstore or that you find in the library periodical reading room?

2. List those with which you are familiar.

3. Check the names of those listed in Exercise 1 that contain feature articles.

4. List five metropolitan newspapers that have magazine sections and five business or trade papers to which you think you might be able to sell feature articles that you could write.

5. In your two favorite general magazines list the fiction (short and continued stories) and the feature articles that you find in the table of contents. What does this comparison tell you about the reader's interest in each magazine?

6. What is the circulation of your favorite metropolitan newspaper as listed in the N. W. Ayer & Son's *Directory of Newspapers and Periodicals* or in the directory in the International Year Book Number of *Editor and Publisher—The Fourth Estate*?

7. What is the circulation of your favorite general magazine as listed in the last issue of the magazine section of the *Standard Rate and Data Service* or in Ayer's *Directory*?

8. Question yourself concerning the eight qualifications of a feature writer listed in this chapter. Grade yourself on each question as good, fair, or poor. Which qualifications do you need to develop more fully?

9. Go through the advertising in your favorite magazine and make an estimate of the average subscriber's income, living standards, and interests.

10. On the basis of your survey of the advertising in Exercise 9, what kind of subjects for feature articles do you think the subscribers would like to read?

Publication Analysis

Milwaukee *Journal*, Kansas City *Star*, St. Louis *Globe-Democrat* and Indianapolis *Star* (Note syndicated feature sections, *This Week, Parade* and others.)

Do not spend more than three hours in analyzing and typing this report. Use chart form as illustrated in the Appendix.

An analysis of the feature articles in the Milwaukee *Journal*, Kansas City *Star*, St. Louis *Globe-Democrat*, and Indianapolis *Star*. (Glance through the state, local, and national features in one or more issues of the Sunday sections assigned.)

1. Notice length of features. What did you like about them? What did you find less interesting?

2. What did you learn that was suggestive to you in writing your own feature articles?

3. What did you like or dislike about the captions or headings of the feature articles?

4. With what subject matter were the feature articles concerned?

5. What was the average number of pictures used in an article?

6. What kind of readers do you think read these special feature articles?

7. Which article in each paper would you have liked to have written and why?

8. List two tips for feature articles that you could write that were suggested to you by this study. List three markets for each tip or suggested article.

(Report may be in chart form, like the sample given in the Appendix, or it may be typed, double spaced, on one side only. The instructor will assign one form or the other. *Not to be more than 500 words* if you do not use chart form. Fold papers crosswise and out. In upper left-hand corner write your name, course number, name of course, and your instructor's name. In middle of top margin write names of newspapers you are analyzing. In upper right hand corner indicate time spent on analysis and time spent typing as well as total time. It will be interesting to see how your powers of concentration and speed in typing improve.)

CHAPTER 2

Finding Ideas and Material for Features

Recognizing Material for Articles. The inexperienced writer marvels at the variety of subjects for feature articles that the professional finds. But everywhere there is material that even the beginner may write into marketable articles as soon as he develops the ability to recognize possibilities in material about him. In searching for ideas, he develops (1) "his nose for news"; and in finding the facts with which to entertain or inform the reader, he develops (2) "his eye for feature articles." The amateur must train himself to look at every person, every experience, every event, and at everything he sees, hears, tastes, and even smells with a view of seeing what possibilities there are for features in which readers would be interested.

Qualifications for Finding Ideas. A writer, to be successful, must have: (1) an inquiring mind; (2) a keen eye that is all-observing; (3) a nose that senses the new and unique; and (4) an indispensable notebook in which to record the inspirations, or "tips," immediately to prevent them being lost to memory. With this equipment he will never need be concerned about what to write. If he has the curiosity to dig beneath the surface, he will find "gems" for acceptable articles which editors and the reading public are eagerly awaiting.

Sources Are Everywhere. Subjects are never lacking. The alert writer will find within his own world a perpetual supply of ideas for profitable articles. It is not necessary to have specialized training, or extensive travel, or a particular location in order to find ideas, or "tips," for articles. These advantages, of course, will increase the supply and variety of suggestions. Yet if similar ideas cannot be seen and developed into successful features from one's immediate surroundings, the chances are that one will not have the "special feature eye" when he reaches the location of his desire. Everywhere one turns, everything one reads and sees contains possibilities for subjects about which to write. Good material for articles goes to waste every day because no one writes it into features. But in order to train oneself to see features, one must constantly ask "why" of everything he sees, hears, feels, and does. When a writer says that he cannot find anything to write about, he is confessing that he is not alert, or observing, or curious. If he were, he would see material everywhere, along every street, on the train, in the streetcar or bus, in the newspaper, or in daily conversation. Wherever one goes there are more ideas than he possibly can find time to write about, even if his writing day were twenty-four hours.

Even in the most commonplace environment there is unlimited material. One can always find something unusual, unfamiliar, and unexpected. Even the usual and familiar things in one community may be unusual enough in other communities that readers there would enjoy reading about them. Wherever there are people, things are happening. Back of these events there may be interesting ideas, personalities, discoveries, or experiences upon which the alert writer can easily capitalize.

The feature writer in search of ideas is like a first-class reporter who associates with all classes of people in order to learn their points of view, their interests, and their ideas. Through these contacts he picks up ideas for stories of hobbies, avocations, and all sorts of unique and unusual things. He finds ideas in conventions, addresses, sermons, newspapers, radio, television, periodicals, bulletins, advertising, publicity, catalogues, fairs, conversations, exhibits, museums, industries, trades, businesses, professions, educational institutions, holidays, anniversaries, or weather conditions. As the beginner becomes more experienced, he will find that "tips" will "pop" into his mind. With practice it will become second nature to discover subjects that deal with concrete ideas.

Three Classifications of Sources. Because editors consider content more valuable than form, even a writer whose style is clumsy may draw generous checks if he has the faculty for seeing everything through his "feature-article eye." Even though one is not born with this ability, he can soon train himself to see features all about him. The more one writes, the more he will find about which to write. As one readily can see, it is difficult to classify sources as to types, because in many instances an article may seem to have its origin as much in experience as in observation, or even in printed material. But for the sake of examining the sources from which ideas come, we shall classify these sources under three divisions. In so doing, we must keep in mind that the sources overlap, and in some cases it is impossible to classify an idea as definitely coming from one source. Three main sources of ideas and material for special features to be written for newspapers and magazines are: (1) observation; (2) experience; and (3) printed material.

Sources of Ideas Are Unlimited. Observations of one's own, or of others, are rich with ideas and suggestions for acceptable articles. (1) A locality, (2) a prominent person, (3) the new and unusual, (4) conventions, (5) professions, businesses, and trades, (6) farm life and activities, (7) homes and gardens, (8) family problems, (9) welfare of all types, (10) recreations and outdoor life, (11) organizations, and (12) the arts—all, by means of observation, will provide unlimited sources of ideas to the beginner as well as to the professional.

The Locality. Wherever one lives, if he walks down Main Street or through the neighborhood or community or takes a ride in the country, he will have ample opportunities for observation and for developing excellent ideas. To see things happen on the streets, in public places, or at meetings and gatherings will suggest ideas that anyone who enjoys writing will find interesting and lucrative.

Seeing people enjoying their picnic lunches in the park gave a woman writer a good subject for an historical treatment of this custom and its many variations throughout the world. The article was published in the New York *Times* magazine section in July, a picnic month.

A beginner in feature writing stepped into a drugstore to buy some paper for her first article. She was informed that only drugs were carried in this store. She became interested in the owner's business policy and asked so many questions that she found she had a better idea for her first article than the one she had planned originally. She wrote up the druggist and his store and sold her article to the *American Druggist.*

Prominent and Interesting Persons. The great or near great are valuable as a source for articles, because everyone likes to read about them. In almost any community there are persons who would become more famous if the outside world only knew more about them. The alert writer may be the means of bringing deserved recognition to an interesting personality and thus give him and his friends pleasure. The fun of writing and the financial remuneration will be the writer's reward. One can capitalize upon the ambitions of those who may not have attained greatness by encouraging them to talk about the hidden secrets and desires of their lives that may be so written as to inspire readers.

An interview with a Madison Street bridge tender not only told of the crew's work in saving lives in Chicago, but made the readers of the Chicago *Daily News* feel that they knew Paddy Culhane. An account of two young women hiking to Mexico to study social and economic conditions and taking turns in carrying their portable typewriter and camera made a feature in the Brooklyn *Daily Eagle.* Because of his unique ideas concerning city planning and because of his prominence as an expert on urban communities, Gury Greer made an interesting subject for an article in *The American Magazine.*

The New and Unusual. Since human nature is always interested in the unique and the modern or newest, editors are always on the lookout for articles of that type. As the range of subject matter is unlimited, an ever-watchful writer will find this source a lucrative one. It may be a new way of doing something, a new invention, a new idea that has improved old conditions, a new point of view, the unusual things made by man or nature. In fact, anything that is new and unusual will develop into saleable features. Such articles contain many elements of the news story, because they concern the new and, like the news story, must supply the answers to who, what, why, when, where, and how. Although the object about which one is writing may be old to the particular community in which it is found, it may be new and unique to readers in other places, and this fact increases the range of "tips" for this type of article.

Noticing, while on a short motor trip, that numerous small towns in Missouri, Kansas, and Nebraska had adopted city planning and that unsightly buildings were vanishing from the main streets, to be replaced by modernized business sections, an observer made some inquiries at the local chambers of commerce and wrote an article, "Main Street in the Middle West is Going Modern." It was both new and unusual, and was published in the Kansas City *Times*. The great eroding power of rivers and streams and the colossal carving power of glaciers were described graphically as the unusual in *Nature Magazine*.

Conventions. Speakers at meetings of all kinds are usually experts in their fields and are good sources of material. Their talks often are based upon the results of years of research, or upon valuable experience, or upon the presentation of new ideas, any one of which would make interesting articles for magazine readers. From such a source came the following:

Attending a meeting of the American Road Builders Association, a writer gathered information that provided material for an article on building highways with cotton because it was more enduring and the cost less than present road construction materials. The story was printed in the New York *Herald Tribune*.

Professions, Businesses, and Trades. All kinds of professions, businesses, occupations, and trades offer innumerable opportunities for articles for professional, business, and trade magazines, which number 5,817, with 69,804 issues annually. Anyone who is successful in his profession or adept at his business or trade will be glad to tell the feature writer what distinguishes his work from that of others. The story must be based upon the worker's originality, ingenuity, skill, or technique. The writer must get all the information he can and must ascertain how much time, trouble, or expense the professional or occupational worker saves and the pleasure he derives from his tasks, which thus enables the reader to improve his methods, save his time or his money, or add to his pleasures. Pictures, sketches, or drawings, no matter how rough or sketchy, are necessary to show the construction or use if the article concerns the construction of some device that the reader may wish to make. The beginning writer should observe different kinds of professions, businesses, and trades by visiting offices, stores, and shops. The wealth of suggestions he will see will bring in checks. It is easier to sell to this field of publications than almost any other.

An article on a young woman physician whose profound knowledge astounded research men, published in the Milwaukee *Journal,* and one on court judges who show an understanding sympathy, printed in the Chicago *Daily News,* show the ease with which one may find articles concerning professions. Stories on the Christmas-tree business, in the New York *Herald Tribune;* on the turkey-raising industry, in the Kansas City *Star;* on how delivery trucks build sales, in *The Cooperative Merchandiser;* and one on a harnessmaker whose business continued to flourish in spite of changed customs, used as the lead article in the *Spokesman and Harness World*—all indicate what a writer may find in occupations and trades when he is observing and alert.

Farm Life and Farm Activities. Since it has been estimated that 32,500,000 people live on the 6,500,000 farms in this country, farm interests provide a wide range of features that will find a ready market in the 1,068 farm publications with their 12,816 issues annually. The editors of these journals are in the market for all kinds of manuscripts concerning the farm. The marketing of farm products, the cutting of production costs, improving farm sanitation, modernization of farms, crop rotation, erosion control, increased production of dairy products, poultry, livestock, grains, gardens, short cuts in the farm kitchen, canning made easy, decorating the farm home, and planning the farm family's wardrobe —all have reader appeal. Articles on novel sidelines—such as raising bees for profit, growing evergreens to finance the children's education, or conducting a wayside market—are found in magazines because the editors know that they will be read by millions of readers and that they will be a means of helping them physically or financially.

A young woman observed birds eating bugs on grains growing in her father's fields. She interviewed a zoology professor and obtained material for an article, "Birds Aid in Pest Control," which was published in *Capper's Farmer*. It gave the reader information and guidance which, if followed, doubtless saved the readers thousands of dollars and resulted in better crops.

Homes and Gardens. Even if one does not have a home, he hopes to have one some day, and that explains the almost universal reader interest in this subject. It is upon this human desire that 32 well-known home and garden magazines, with 384 issues annually, are founded. Women's magazines and newspapers devote pages and whole sections to these two subjects, which, in many publications, are expanded to include articles concerning not only exteriors and interiors, but interior decoration, home management, household equipment, selection and preparation of foods, textiles, needlecraft, fashions, and science. Material of this type is to be found everywhere, for every home, however humble, may have article suggestions. The writer's own home and garden, or those of others that he observes, may be the source of checks. One writer, who says everything in and around the home is "grist for her mill," has earned more than $10,000 writing for home magazines since she took a course in magazine writing.

A young writer was attracted by an artistic and colorful window display of linens and bedding. She interviewed an expert in interior decoration and buyers in stores and acquired information that would enable anyone to shop more efficiently for a good night's sleep if he read the issue of *American Home* in which the article was printed.

"Highlights in the Colonial Kitchen" was suggested by observing a display of kitchen utensils. It gave the readers of *Better Homes & Gardens* information on how to keep their pots and pans as attractively as did the colonial housewives. Offering guidance and information to the reader, the author of "Going Native with Rock Gardens" in *House Beautiful* gave definite directions in selecting the location and the soil and in choosing the plants for the sunny and shady places among the rocks.

The Family and Its Problems. Not only the social but the physical welfare of the family is a perpetual source of ideas in which a writer will find unlimited opportunities. Many publications are devoted entirely to the subject, and almost all of the 41 home and women's magazines, with their 492 issues annually, use one or more articles concerning the family and its life. Many observing housewives and mothers who have an aptitude for writing and who are alert to their opportunities find that articles on the problems of the family sell as easily as do those written for the home and garden publications. The subject matter may range anywhere from dressing the child for indoors or outdoors or helping the man of the house to overcome his grouchy spells to meeting the problem of the unpopular daughter.

A young mother told a writer of her experiences, with the aid of a psychologist, in helping her small son overcome his fear of dogs. The article, which was sold to *Today's Health* aided many other mothers to teach their children to like rather than to fear their pets. Hints of what a summer vacation at home or away might mean to the various members of the family were given to the readers of *Woman's Home Companion* in the article "Vacation Time."

Recreation, Outdoor Life, and Health. Because modern inventions and labor laws have provided more time for play and apostles of good health have championed the desire for relaxation through play, articles concerning recreation, outdoor life, and health are much in demand by 142 publications, with their 1,704 issues a year, in this field. Since people are much interested in outdoor and indoor sports and games, particularly those beneficial to one's health, a writer will do well to familiarize himself with as many different kinds of sports and recreation as possible and to utilize this information in articles that will sell to outdoor, recreation, sports, and health magazines.

In "Games for Players," in *Woman's Home Companion,* the author emphasized that sports must be fun and not work. "Hit That Ball" tells the young readers of the *Open Road* how they can improve their skill. "Rolling Your Own Home Over Wide America" in the New York *Times* magazine section is equally instructive.

"Let's Make Winter Sports Safer," in *Today's Health,* "Here's a Way to Better Casting," in *Outdoor Life,* and "The New Road to Mexico City," in *Sports Afield,* show the interest in life outdoors, whereas such articles as "The Corrective Value of Swimming," in *Health and Physical Education,* "Sports by Which Hollywood Keeps Its Waist Line Down," in the New York *Herald Tribune,* and "That Waistline Slump," in *Ladies' Home Journal,* indicate that readers are interested in sports as a means to keep or gain health.

Organizations. Commercial clubs, merchants' associations, civic and industrial organizations, church and welfare groups, and study and cultural clubs may be the sources of articles if the writer is observing and alert to what the groups are doing more efficiently or effectively to hold and increase their members' interests and to be of greater service in their communities. There are hundreds of special publications for such organizations that pay well for fact articles. One free-lance writer has earned $20,000 from publications that paid less than a cent a word by writing up church and club affairs and methods of church and club management. The hundreds of editors of church publications clamor for such articles, as do editors of the hundreds of club and association magazines.

The Arts, Statuary, and Carvings. Pictures, to the observant writer, are possible incentives for the production of articles. They may be snapshots in a camera book; illustrations in papers, magazines, books, or advertising copy; ideas from television; or paintings in homes, public buildings, or art museums. A writer may find profitable germ-thoughts in statuary—carvings in soap, wood, and stone—and works of art of all kinds. The picture of a bridge spanning the Royal Gorge in the Colorado Rocky Mountains suggested to a writer an article on great bridges and their engineers in the United States.

A young woman going into the library in search of ideas for her first feature admired a statue so much that she asked a librarian about it. She learned that the sculptor at one time had lived in the city and that her work was outstanding. It happened the librarian had known the sculptor as a child. The novice recognized her first feature "tip," did more interviewing, took pictures of the statue, and was able to get one of the sculptor as a young woman. She wrote up articles that sold to Sunday sections of the Washington *Star,* New York *Herald Tribune,* and the Philadelphia *Record,* because the sculptor's statues were in those cities. She became so interested in the woman's personality that she was able to write a sketch that sold to an art publication. By using her powers of observation, this young woman received four checks for one idea. An interview with a sociology professor and the director of the art department of the University of Oregon related the success of an experiment of a class in sculpture at the Oregon state penitentiary. It was sold to the *Christian Science Monitor.*

Realistic Experiences Are in Demand. Experiences of one's own or of others are a second source for factual material. One can always write better of that which he knows from personal experience or the personal experience of those whom he interviews. Not only are the technique and method of the experiences known to the writer, but also the desires and purposes back of them. A novice will find his own experiences easier than those of others to handle because he is familiar with the facts and can make them appear real and vital to the reader. Beginners, since they are desirous of gathering material far afield, overlook the possibilities of what they, or others near by, have done or are doing that would appeal to readers.

In the early development of the feature articles in the nineties, owing to the rise of popular magazines and of magazine sections of daily newspapers, feature writers assumed the roles of persons whose experiences they wished to relate. The article might tell of the adventures of deep-sea diving; or a professional writer might feign insanity or confess to a crime, in order to be assigned to an institution to tell of the life there; or he might ride in the basket of a balloon to get material to interest his readers. Such articles and methods are out of date. Present-day editors prefer experiences of people who regularly do the things about which they write, or about which they are interviewed, rather than to have a stunt writer relate his impressions, which frequently are inaccurate. Also, readers soon tired of the early type, because the articles were impractical. It is no longer necessary to go far afield or to do stunting to obtain experiences. This is the age of reality, and editors want realistic experiences. One's own (1) university campus, (2) pioneers and old settlers, (3) crafts, mechanics, and hobbies, (4) confessions, (5) travel, and (6) conversations are suggestive of sources for ideas based on experience. That opportunities are unlimited is shown by a few examples of good sources.

University Campus. A gold mine for student writers is the campus. Every day in class rooms and laboratories new knowledge is being imparted, new inventions are being made, and many experiments are conducted, all of which make excellent feature articles. One student writer, whose sales ran into high figures, said he found "editor's checks breezing across the hall, fluttering up the steps of the library, and draping the windows of every college building." Professors, he found, were passing out greenbacks with every daily assignment, and their lectures were as so many gold pieces.

From material in his applied psychology class he wrote an

article with a new angle on the "lie detector" machine, which he sold to a scientific publication; a botany professor's experiments with fruit trees, which resulted in increased production, suggested a story that was sold to a fruit raisers' journal; an interview with a chemistry professor yielded two articles, one on the health value of nuts and the other on the advantages of cane sugar as a sweetening in bakery commodities—both were purchased by bakers' trade papers. New ways to serve tomatoes, appropriate clothes for the school child, planned household finances to cut increased living costs, and temper tantrums overcome at nursery school were articles based on interviews from the department of home economics and sold to women's magazines. Interviews with professors in the College of Agriculture who had done research in corn production, rural zoning, growing soy beans, and erosion control developed into articles that were sold to farm publications. The laboratories in the Medical School were the source of ideas for an article on dogs in medical laboratories that save hundreds of lives; for one on a new cure for athlete's foot; and for an article on a Chinese interne who discovered a relief for colds, which was purchased by a scientific magazine. These were only a few of the articles that this student free-lance wrote during his junior and senior years and from which he cleared more than $2,000 in the two years. Two other students, who had part-time jobs and were carrying a full study program, earned $950 and $785 respectively from the feature articles they wrote during their senior years after they had studied magazine writing in their junior years. All of their articles were based either on their own experiences, or on those of others, and the majority of the ideas were found on the "runs" or "beats" that these young writers developed just as do news reporters.

Pioneers and Old Settlers. Good experience articles may be developed from historical subjects by interviewing old settlers. These old-timers are happy to have the opportunity to recall other days and other events that will add incidents and human interest to the dry facts obtained by the writer in libraries and historical files. New light may be thrown upon present-day problems by the point of view gained from interviewing those who have lived long in a community.

The bare facts of the history of a drugstore that played an important part in the pioneer history of making Kansas a free state, and in the development of the town of Lawrence and the state university, were made interesting to the present generation. The feature writer was not content with the facts gained from her reading in the library, but interviewed one of the old-timers, who related many incidents of those early days when the North and the South were each struggling to control the vote that would determine whether the state was to be slave or free. She gathered so much material that she was able to develop it into three articles: one compared the early days with the present, for the Sunday Kansas City *Star;* another emphasized the part New England played in the history of Kansas, for the *Christian Science Monitor,* and the third showed the influence of a druggist, not only in making state history, but in setting a high standard for the drug business, and suggested how drugstores may still be an important factor in community life. This latter story was accepted by the *American Druggist.* "Wheels Go Round, But—," a feature comparing the pleasures of bicycle riding in the nineties with those of today was based on interviews with old-timers and was printed in the New York *Times* magazine section.

Crafts, Mechanics, and Hobbies. How-to-do or how-to-make articles, better known as utility features, have their sources in experience. It is easy to find markets for them, because many publications are devoted to useful information of this type. Mechanical, handicraft, homecraft, hobby, farm, home, garden, and women's magazines as well as trade publications are only a few that use utility articles of this type. They are much in demand, because readers always are wanting to know how to do things more efficiently or how to make things more effective, more practical, more economical, or more artistic. The sources for these types of articles are found everywhere. The mechanic's or carpenter's workshop, the home, the garden, the farm, the business place, the office, and the laboratory abound with ideas. There is a market for the articles in the many craft, mechanic, and hobby magazines if they are so clearly written that the reader can follow directions accurately. Novices find it easy to gather material for these types as well as to write and to sell the features.

"Scenic Modeling," in the *Model Craftsman,* is the story of one of the most realistic model railroads in the country. "The Story of Bridges," an article on bridge construction engineers in the same issue, shows the diversity of material in the same publication. "Making Modern Dressing Sets," "Jackknife Sculpture," and "Care and Use of Tools" found markets in *Popular Home Craft.* "Tricky Cards for Christmas Made on the Typewriter" was bought by the Pittsburgh *Telegraph.* "Help Your Microscope with Stains and Reagents," in *Popular Science,* and "Color Piano Plays Melody on Rods of Glass," in *Popular Mechanics,* had their sources in university laboratories. "Build This Stinson Glider from Scrapwood," in *Model Airplane News,* came from a young mechanic's experience in his own workshop. "A Collection of Old Wooden Ware," in *Hobbies,* and "Bees in Uncle Sam's Bonnet! National Crazes That Strike Us," in the Detroit *News,* appealed to readers with or without hobbies.

Confessions. A popular form in which personal experiences of the writer or of others may be written effectively is the confession. If the confession is the writer's own experience, it is told in the first person, often anonymously. If it is well written, it is one of the most interesting forms in which to present facts and experiences. When the writer is telling of the personal experiences of another, and if he is able to obtain sufficiently detailed information to make the article plausible, he may use the form of the confession.

Confessions are usually written as though the "confessor" had told his confessions to the writer. The writer in turn tells them to the reader. This form of writing is called "ghosting." It was a device developed by writers some years ago to enable them to write articles of personal experience or confessions of others, as will be discussed in a later chapter. Because the cheaper class of magazines were the first to use confession articles, and since many cheaper magazines are devoted entirely to confession articles, young writers frequently think that they are above writing confessions. The quality magazines—*Atlantic, Harper's, Coronet,* and hundreds of other well-written and well-edited magazines— use numerous articles of this type, although the appeal is different from that in the cheaper, or "pulp," periodicals. Like all current articles they are short. Another type of confession article, which is in part historical, is known as recollections. An example is "Washington Wife," which ran in *Harper's.* Beginners find that if their confessions have reader interest, they, too, can sell their articles as can well-known writers.

A novice wrote of her experience of being left a cripple by infantile paralysis. In a confidential tone she "confessed" to the reader how self-centered and selfish she became before she realized that her friends and her family no longer found her agreeable. She not only overcame her character faults, but by her entrance into sports she overcame her physical handicaps, entered the university, and made all the honor societies. She received a check for $65 for the article, "I Refused to Be a 'Polio' Cripple," which was printed in *Physical Culture.* She was paid an additional $10 for her picture, which the editor requested. Others have sold articles about overcoming bashfulness, transforming the jolly fat girl into a sylph-like prom queen, and the mother and daughter who became pals instead of enemies. These were confession articles because the writers not only wrote of their experiences but confided their thoughts or revealed their secrets to the reader. Every writer has had experiences that he can write in confidential tones and sell as confession articles. Or if he has not had them, his friends have.

Travel. A never-ending source of ideas for experience articles is found in travel. But everyone travels nowadays, and a trip does not have appeal unless it is that of a well-known person, or unless it is into unfrequented parts of the earth, or unless there is something unusual about it. The temptation of the beginning writer, when traveling, is to become too interested personally in the trip itself and to fail to see and investigate the things that would make a manuscript interesting. The writer who can see things "scriptorially"—that is, see things that will make an interesting manuscript for a travel page or travel magazine—will find excellent ideas in short trips as well as in distant travels.

Traveling will open up ideas for other types of articles. A salesman, who has an aptitude for writing and whose work takes him through the Middle West, says that in addition to travel articles he finds material for semi-historical articles, personality stories, and all kinds of informative articles. His work takes him into industrial plants, and he contacts the publicity directors for the necessary photographs and a guide to take him through the plants. He sells articles to industrial trade publications and adds more than $2,000 a year to his income. In addition, he hears intimate stories from the strangers he meets, and from these he develops excellent confession articles that add several more hundred dollars, to bring his total income from his side line to more than $3,000 annually.

A writer does not need to take a long and expensive trip to get material; but the trip should have something unusual about it. The expense, the manner, the plan, or the purpose may be the interesting feature that will make his article marketable. An account of an automobile trip from Chicago to Seattle taken by three college juniors at a cost of $30.40 each brought the young writer a check for $50, because he showed that one can travel economically. He also pointed out the educational value of such a trip to three young men reared in a city. A canoe trip from the source of the Wisconsin River down into the Mississippi was sold to a boy's publication. The article had appeal, not only to youths of that age, but to their parents as well, because it showed how an experience of that kind aids in a young boy's character development.

All types of newspapers and magazines use travel articles. "I Travel to See People," in *Good Housekeeping,* "Two Months in Mexico," in *Woman's Home Companion,* and "Gypsy in a Trailer," in *Harper's,* are excellent travel articles. Each tells of experiences that are different and have an appeal both to the reader who travels and to the one who cannot. Travel articles, like those in the travel magazines, should always have interesting pictures to illustrate them.

Conversations. Discourse with others furnishes ideas for articles. When a friend or visitor takes some of the writer's valuable time, the latter should make this person pay well for the call by entering heartily into the visit and conversation. The alert writer may obtain scores of ideas for future features by talking less and listening more. One should get into the habit of "listening in," not only on the radio and television, but on conversations he hears in the bank, the supermarket, the butcher shop, the bakery, the beauty shop, and the dentist's and doctor's offices. Wherever there is conversation, one will find suggestions for features that will sell at good rates to business and professional journals.

A student journalist stopped in at an auto parts store in Dallas, Texas, and heard a conversation between a salesman and a customer. He wrote up their arguments from three different points of view into stories for three different publications. The three checks more than paid his out-of-state tuition for the second semester at the University. By listening carefully, one not only gains ideas for tips but learns the kinds of things people are interested in. The things that people talk about are the things about which they like to read. From conversations one will garner ideas for personality sketches about prominent people. He will learn about community leaders who will be excellent subjects for general and trade magazines.

Popularizing Facts Makes Interesting Features. To the writer who is willing to look about for some new angle upon which to base, or "slant," his article, printed material of all kinds supplies unlimited suggestions. By finding some person who is an authority and whose name as the person interviewed will add value to the article, one may make dry, uninteresting subjects into excellent features. Or by taking facts and explaining them in such a way as to interest the reader, or popularizing them, one may find a ready market for the new form. Printed material includes: (1) newspapers; (2) periodicals; (3) books; (4) pamphlets; (5) trade and scientific publications; (6) advertising of all types—display, classified, direct-mail, circulars, catalogues, store announcements, and outdoor advertising; (7) questionnaires and surveys; and (8) contents of libraries.

Current Newspapers. A necessary part of a writer's equipment is the current newspaper. It abounds in suggestions for acceptable articles. Every free-lance writer should read several good newspapers every day, because in addition to getting ideas for his own writing, he learns the trends of reader interest and is able to foresee what subjects are likely to be future features. To be a thorough newspaper reader will enable the free-lance writer to watch the trend of current news and to detect undercurrents of interest before it is too late. The writer must be able to anticipate the public's interest before the public is aware of that interest. Many free-lance writers read regularly such staunch newspapers as the New York *Times,* New York *Herald Tribune, Christian Science Monitor,* Kansas City *Star,* Milwaukee *Journal,* Portland *Oregonian,* Atlanta *Constitution,* and many others. From those papers they regularly get many ideas for articles. Valuable information can be garnered, which can be clipped and put into one's files. Any part of the paper from the front-page news to the death notices and the "want ads" will yield material that will offer a diversity of topics. The writer must let the material he reads, or collects, filter through his own mind, in order to absorb it and make it his own.

Newspapers in one's own city, town, or village offer "tips" that the writer easily develops into marketable material by visiting the place mentioned, interviewing the persons concerned, and gathering additional material. With practice, one soon learns to recognize in the local newspapers ideas that will develop into lively and interesting articles. Every paper, metropolitan or rural, prints events of the day that are rich in possibilities. If an article has a news angle that is timely, it stands twice as much chance of being accepted as one that does not have—and this explains why many journalists are prolific and successful magazine writers. If one is a thorough student of current and public affairs, has an inquiring mind, and even an average amount of imagination, he will do well to specialize in writing features based on the day's news. There is an added pleasure in writing features from this source, in that one feels he is not only up with the news but a step ahead of it. A successful free-lance writer found that it paid to subscribe by mail for a newspaper from each of the twelve largest cities in his state. The many articles suggested brought checks to him of varying sizes, paid for the subscriptions and the expense of preparing the pictures and manuscripts, gave him a liberal income, and afforded him pleasure and satisfaction in his writing.

Old Newspaper Files. A valuable supply of ideas that are not limited to historical or reminiscent stories may be found in old newspaper files. Past incidents often suggest a new point of view on some current problem of civic or public interest. Comparison articles may concern prices, fashions, customs, etiquette, entertainment, recreation, anniversaries, and anything else in which there would be an appeal to the reader. Such articles find a ready market in the Sunday magazine sections of newspapers. A novice who had access to an excellent library of newspaper files specialized in writing articles of this type, which he sold to newspapers throughout the country. His problem of finding illustrations was solved by photographing articles in the museum that fitted in with those of the periods about which he was writing. The income from his Sunday features enabled him to give up his job as assistant janitor that had formerly paid for his meals and room while he was in college.

Periodicals. Factual articles, fiction, poems, and advertising in periodicals will start the mind of the free-lance thinking in terms of definite "tips." Even an incident in a short story may suggest an idea to start him making investigations that will uncover worthwhile material. One magazine article may suggest another. The fact that something has been written up in one magazine is no reason to think that the subject cannot be handled again for an entirely different publication with a different appeal. Investigation in the library and interviews with authorities in the field will suggest new material and enable the author to write from a new angle. A dozen people might write upon the same subject, but their articles would not be alike. No two people approach the subject from the same angle, and one cannot write even a short article without putting some of his personality into the manuscript.

Trade publications devoted to specialized fields, which appeal to only one class of readers, are a source of article ideas for periodicals that have a general circulation. A beginner, while waiting in a science professor's office for an interview with him, looked at some magazines. Among them was a copy of one of the learned scientific journals. In glancing through it, he saw an article telling of the results of research on potato chips, which showed that the health value of potato chips was greatly over-rated by the advertisers. The young writer read the article carefully, did considerable reading on the subject in the library, interviewed a home economics professor and obtained some recipes using potato chips, and sold the article to a women's magazine. A few days later he interviewed a professor in the business school on advertising and then rewrote his material into an article to appeal to grocers. He suggested ideas for advertising potato chips in the store and pointed out that, although the potato chip wasn't a complete food any more than other foods, it was still potato, and contained nutritious food elements. The second article sold to a grocer's magazine. He received for the two articles two checks, which totaled $55.

Almost every trade and profession has several magazines that carry news and feature articles concerned with one kind of business activity. In addition, there are many magazines devoted to specialized fields, such as music, art, the dance, nature, and archaeology. A writer need never be without ideas or markets to which to sell them. The advertising in these publications is also suggestive of articles to the writer.

Books. The title, as well as the content, of a book may stimulate the writer to new ideas. A novel may give some sidelight on human nature that would make a saleable article. Nonfiction often is suggestive of ideas that will grow into checks for features. Even poetry has been known to be the source of articles. Frequently the title of a book will suggest an article.

Pamphlets. Scientific and government bulletins, reports, documents, printed proceedings, and monographs giving results of research and investigations done by experts, bureaus, commissions, or committees may be had for a small charge. They are worth their weight in gold to the free-lance because of their wealth and variety of ideas. Generally they are written in so technical a style that few people ever read them. The journalist may profitably popularize the material for the general public. The expert who made the scientific discovery then becomes known outside of the technical field and may even become famous through the information that the writer sells to general publications. Some time ago, a scientist working in his laboratory "bottled" sunshine in a way that practically meant the revolutionizing of the manufacture and production of many of the foods of the world. Up to that time his name was scarcely known outside of the world of science. Today Dr. Harry Steenbock's name is a household word because feature writers popularized his material and readers of general magazines were informed of his scientific discoveries. A writer was inspired by a government bulletin to do an article on removal of stains. She sold it to a women's magazine, and through it helped thousands of readers to reduce their cleaning bills and to keep their clothes attractive. She received a generous check for doing a good deed for her fellow women.

Bulletins issued by federal, state, or local governments, or by universities, are concerned with new and better methods of doing all kinds of things. They are written by experts in federal and state laboratories, universities, agricultural colleges, and home economics departments. When popularized, the material develops into articles that are easy to sell, because they are concerned with the new in the field of science and research. State commissions issue reports that are fruitful sources for timely articles on industries, insurance, health, sanitation, welfare, relief, railroads, commerce, conservation, and other subjects with which government is concerned. Official documents are seldom read by the general public, yet from them may be gleaned suggestions for the writer who will present the information in a bright, interesting manner to attract the reader. Teachers' bulletins are good sources, for the material there can be expanded and presented to appeal to parents' and women's publications.

Advertising Copy. Display, classified, direct-mail, radio, television, outdoor advertising, circulars, catalogues, and store announcements are rich in subject-finding material. An attractive display advertisement of linoleum suggested an article on the selection and care of linoleum. This article in turn suggested another one on various uses of linoleum in the home. The first was sold to a woman's magazine and the second to a farm publication. A classified advertisement in a metropolitan newspaper concerning guinea fowls for sale was investigated: the result was another pair of articles. One was on raising guinea fowls for market and was purchased by a farm magazine; the other was about the preparation and serving of guinea fowls and sold to a restaurant trade paper.

A circular advertising jelly made from wild fruits and berries growing on Wisconsin hillsides turned into a success story. It told of a woman who gathered the fruit and berries, canned the juice, and, when the orders came in, made the jelly, which she put in attractive containers and shipped in neat cartons to any part of the United States. The first story, emphasizing the local state angle, sold to the Milwaukee *Journal.* The second one sold to *Capper's Farmer* and played up the angle of how this farm woman operated a thriving business in her home. Even catalogues suggest all kinds of articles, if one only takes time to turn through them. An article sold to *American Home* magazine on the care of blankets had its origin in a mail-order catalogue. Many articles on flowers for garden magazines were suggested to the authors by seed catalogues.

The Survey and Questionnaire. Another source of articles, although not used so frequently because it is a rather involved and expensive method of getting information, is factual material gathered by means of the survey and questionnaire. Public and private businesses and professional people usually will consent to fill in a questionnaire if it is so planned that it does not take much of their time. A student journalist was interested in a newspaper item concerning the amount of milk consumed by the students on her campus. By getting out a questionnaire and interviewing managers of dairies and the director of the student clinic, she gathered information for an article, "College Students' Drinking," that sold to *Hoard's Dairyman.* Another student, who was attending college on the income from a life-insurance policy taken out for that purpose, wondered how many other students were similarly supported. After carefully thinking out the questions, she ran off several hundred mimeographed copies of a questionnaire. With the permission of her professors, she circulated the questionnaires in her classes, tabulated the results, and wrote an article which she sold to *The Insurance Salesman.*

Libraries. Next to the daily newspaper, the library is the feature writer's biggest help. Not only must he know how to use books, but he must have an intimate acquaintance with reference books, biographical dictionaries, gazetteers, encyclopedias, and periodical readers' guides, as well as books, magazines, learned journals, house organs, and trade papers.

Anniversaries, historical events, holidays, seasonal events—all give rise to many timely articles, material for which can be found in the library. By looking over tables or lists giving significant events, a writer may always anticipate the special days sufficiently far in advance to have his material collected. Prolific writers usually start collecting material for articles for special days a year in advance.

Filed away in university libraries are hundreds of master's theses and lengthy reports of graduate research. These, boiled down and rewritten with a popular, practical slant, would make articles of the type editors clamor for, because they contain information and guidance to interest the readers.

In addition to developing the library habit, one should make friends with the librarians. A few minutes of conversation with them may open up numerous ideas for marketable articles. Then, too, a cordial friendly librarian can save hours of time for a busy writer who cultivates her acquaintance.

Keeping an Advance Book. The feature writer should keep an advance book, as does a city editor of a newspaper. When he learns of events, coming conventions, people returning from unique trips, and other news happenings that could be developed into features, he can jot down the notation. For as little as ten cents one can buy a diary with a space for each day of the year, which serves the purpose very well. A larger book, of course, has the advantage of more space under each date. By looking forward three to six weeks or more for the newspaper magazine sections, and six months or more for the magazines—because editors plan their publications long in advance—a feature writer can select subjects and gather material that will be timely and seasonable. Free-lance writers who support themselves entirely by their writing keep their advance books systematically, in order never to be without ideas about which to write. If one has his advance book full of "tips," he may start collecting material from various sources long in advance of the time he wants to start his article. Then, when he is ready to begin writing, he has his material at hand.

One Feature Often Leads to Another. As one can readily see, finding subjects is the easiest part of writing magazine articles, after one develops a nose for news and an eye for features. Even the amateur learns to see articles all about him, and he wonders why he ever thought it would be difficult to find things about which to write. In addition to seeking material for all sorts of features, the beginner learns how interesting it is to meet the successful people with whom his search for material brings him in contact. Their enthusiasm and happiness is contagious. He also finds that when he searches for material for one article, he is likely to uncover ideas for another. And that, in turn, uncovers other ideas for other features.

Self Test for Determining Salability of a Feature "Tip." If the amateur will consider the sales possibility and the reader interest in the idea, or "tip," which he thinks he will use for his feature article as carefully as do experienced writers, he will be less apt to receive rejections. Before deciding upon the idea for a feature article, the tyro should ask himself the following questions:

1. Will such an article be interesting to readers six months or a year from now? Or six weeks from now? If the former, then it should be slanted to a monthly magazine; if the latter, then it should be slanted to a Sunday newspaper magazine section. If the answer to either question is no, then select another "tip."

2. Why will the article be interesting six or twelve months or six weeks from now?

3. What kind of readers will be interested in reading such an article?

4. What will they want to read about the subject? Why?

5. What periodicals do such readers read?

6. What kinds of illustrations do the editors of those periodicals use? Photographs—size and number used in average article?
Drawings—size, type, and number used in average article?
Charts—kinds and number used?
Graphs—kinds and number used?
Maps—kinds and number used?

7. What is the average word-length of the fact articles in those periodicals? (Count number of letters and spaces in one line. Divide by 7, the average word length. Then multiply the number of words to a line by the number of lines to a column inch. Multiply that figure by the number of column inches in the article.)

8. What style of writing do the editors seem to prefer?

9. Note peculiarities of style. What kinds of sentences? Length? In what person are the fact articles written? How are articles constructed? Is vocabulary simple? Are figures of speech used? Does narration, description, exposition predominate?

10. Study the advertising in these periodicals to determine the class of readers and their interests, education, and financial status. Are there advertisements for private airplanes, yachts, or expensive cars? For servants' uniforms and vacuum cleaners or for carpet sweepers and brooms? (The quality of goods advertised in magazines tells the writer much about the private lives and interests of their readers because the advertising agencies placing advertising copy in periodicals know who the readers are.)

11. Is factual material for the article available in the community, or does it necessitate a long and expensive journey to obtain facts and illustrations?

12. Are there well-known "interviewees" or authorities available whose names or whose quotations will aid in selling the article?

13. Will it be possible to gather the facts, write them into an article, and obtain illustrations before the date the article is due?

14. Would it be better to defer this tip until I can give it more thought and time? (If the answer is yes, select another idea and test it.)

15. List five ideas for tips from your "advance book."

Examples of Students' First Sales. To show students how other beginners wrote and sold, the following examples were selected from a newspaper, a trade paper, and a business magazine. The ideas came from observations and walks down Main Street. The sales of the three articles totalled $110.00 for the three beginners. Each article had from three to five pictures because current periodicals, almost without exception, do not buy articles that are not illustrated. The grocer cannot sell his wares if he does not have groceries on his shelves; the writer cannot sell if he does not have pictures for his articles.

(1)
Memorial Rites Held Each
Year Since 1891 At Grave
Of Unknown Boy Near Elrod*

By Ida B. Alseth

Perhaps, with the exception of the Tomb of the Unknown Soldier at Arlington cemetery, no grave of an unknown person has received the care of that of the little Italian boy buried one and three quarter miles west of Elrod, S.D., on the railroad right-of-way.

Though well off the highway, a number of people gather there each Memorial Day, despite the early hour, to watch the little passenger No. 107 come to a stop and to witness the decorating of the grave.

The crew gathers at the grave. After a moment's silence a prayer is said and the wreaths are laid on the grave. The crew solemnly returns to the train and little 107 continues on its way.

"Little Fellow"

It all started back in 1889 when "Big Bill" Chambers was a brakeman on the train hauling ballast for the repair work on that section of the Chicago and North Western railroad. The boy's parents were cooks for the gravel gang that placed the ballast. He was about 12

* Reprinted by permission of The Sioux Falls, S.D. *Daily Argus-Leader* and Ida B. Alseth.

at the time. No one remembers the name of the parents or of the boy. He was small for his age and they called him "Little Fellow."

Two years later, 1891, he died of smallpox. "Big Bill" and his crew buried him on the right-of-way—the only grave so located in the United States except one in New Mexico.

For a period of 40 years "Big Bill" Chambers—then conductor —never missed placing flowers on that grave on Memorial Day or near that day—the train does not run on Sunday. Then on April 8, 1931, he, too, went to meet his Maker.

For some time after his death his sister, Miss Lydia Chambers of Watertown, furnished flowers for the train crew to place on the grave. Later the work was taken over by Mr. and Mrs. Vince Ford, Redfield, daughter and son-in-law of Mr. Chambers. Mr. Ford was a conductor on that run and for many years placed the flowers. He is now retired.

CEREMONY CONTINUES

This year will be no exception, for, according to E. J. Carland, freight passenger agent, Winona, Minn., arrangements are being made so that Train 107, the morning of May 30, will make a stop at the grave of "Little Fellow" near Elrod and the usual ceremony will be conducted by the railway employes.

Thus has been kept alive the unique friendship between "Big Hearted Bill" Chambers and the "Little Fellow."

(2)
Promote Easter Sales
with Black Light*

BY JEANNE ARNOLD
UNIVERSITY OF WISCONSIN

If you are looking for something original and different in display techniques that will boost your Easter sales, why not consider black light? According to experts its application is simple yet most effective as a traffic stopper, attracting window shoppers and flower buyers alike.

Black light is a comparatively new, yet commercially available, and already widely applied light source, rich in near-ultraviolet light normally invisible to the eye. When turned on surfaces or materials

* Reprinted by permission of *Florists' Telegraph Delivery News* and Jeanne Arnold.

treated with fluorescent paints the colors burst forth in a brilliant neon glow.

Today there are black light installations on outdoor signs everywhere. Effectiveness of black light has earned it a permanent and important place among display advertising techniques. In recent months its applications have spread rapidly into window and interior displays with results equally outstanding.

Because of the mystical, almost magical color effect of black light on fluorescent materials, many believe it is difficult to work with. But, it is said, it requires no special talent to use this fast growing display medium.

MATERIALS AND EQUIPMENT

The fluorescent paints are as versatile and easy to use as ordinary colors. The black light fixtures are compact, long lasting, and are available in sizes ranging from nine to forty-eight inches long. Lamp ratings range from six to eighty watts. The units are safe to use, do not burn hot, and the cost of replacing their special tubes is not much more than the cost of regular fluorescent tubes.

> Color recommendations suggested by Samuel F. Chase for the sample Easter window display sketch:
> Use a fluorescent (F) White White on the lilies and the cross. Outline the width of the cross in regular bulletin black. Use F Green for the greens in your sketch. If you wish, you can add the F Red Red for the ribbon on the flower pots. For the background, a stained Gothic window screen, use a regular non-fluorescent white, and outline it with regular non-fluorescent black. Under black light this will make your stained glass window appear an orchid color.

The light units are the biggest cost of the display. Prices range from about $9 to $47. But, after they are bought they can be used again many times for other displays throughout the year, featuring occasions like Halloween, Thanksgiving, Christmas, St. Valentine's day, Fourth of July, Mothers' day, Fathers' day, New Year's day, Labor day, and St. Patrick's day.

COLORS

Ordinary colors tend to appear black under the light, but a pure white will appear as a soft bluish-purple, because it reflects some of the small amounts of visible light that get by the special cobalt glass filter.

Fluorescent paint under ordinary light has a color value comparable to regular colors, but under the ultraviolet black light, these colors glow brilliantly due to fluorescent pigments in the paint.

The fluorescent paints are available in twelve brushing oil and brushing water colors and twenty-three silk screen colors. These include the "invisible" paints which have a neutral or near-white color in daylight, but show blazing color under black light.

APPLYING BLACK LIGHT

If a flashing, changing color effect is desired in the display, use a flashing white light to "overcome" the steadily burning black light. Black light cannot be flickered. When the white lights are off, the fluorescent or invisible colors will immediately come to life in full glowing colors.

For greater emphasis of black light letters, outline them with a dark, non-fluorescent background for contrast. A flat white undercoat is necessary for non-white and porous surfaces before coating with fluorescent paints.

Samuel Chase, Lawter Chemicals, Inc., who has guided many black light beginners, outlines seven steps on how to make a black light window display. They are:

1. Select a window that is not surrounded by too much competing white light; the darker the surrounding area, the more effective the bulletin. This does not mean that fluorescent displays must be located on side streets or in poorly lighted areas, but it is important to consider the effect of very brightly lighted locations.

The points to check for lighting are:

1. Incident light falling on the display can be checked by the following methods:

    (a) Readability without illumination.

    (b) Measurements with a light meter (reading should be taken at the middle of the painting surface.)

    GOOD—Very dark—Under one foot candle

    FAIR—Medium dark—1-3 foot candles

    BAD—Too bright—Over 3 foot candles

2. Bright lights in the line of sight from 200 feet or closer.

3. Bright lights in the area of vision around the board. If the location is bad on point 1, or on 2 and 3, it should not be considered for black light. If the location is bad on point 2 or 3, but rates good under 1, it can be made into a good location with special treatment. If this is the case, perhaps the display should be ar-

ranged in the form of a shadow box or stage to shield the fluorescent areas from outside light.

2. Check the fluorescent colors available and select those to be used. Plan to use contrasting and dark non-fluorescent colors to set them off.

3. If possible, try to get an experimental kit that contains the six basic water or oil colors; each costs a dollar a jar. An experimental 6-watt black light unit can also be bought with the kit. These samples will enable you to make sketches or miniatures of the proposed display. You will save time and money by knowing exactly what to do and what the display will look like when finished.

4. Determine the kind and texture of materials to be treated with fluorescent colors and select the proper oil, lacquer, or water base paints.

5. Check the height and width of the display and use the chart on "How to Position Black Lights" to select the size and number of lights needed.

6. Check the chart to arrange fixtures for maximum effectiveness. It shows a simple rule for positioning black lights in front of your display. Measure the height of the display. If, for example, the fluorescent area to be covered is 6 feet high, then place the lights to reach maximum effectiveness in activating the display.

7. Add a flashing white light if you want the changing color effect.

If these seven steps are carefully followed, poor color combinations or ineffective lighting can easily be avoided. Properly applied, black light can stimulate active interest in your window displays and, more important, in the things you sell.

(3)
Why Her Customers Come Back*

By Kenneth C. Wagner

"If it doesn't taste so good that you want to eat it yourself—even if you have just eaten a big meal—it isn't good enough to serve the customers."

This rule, which she insists her cooks abide by, and a second which she herself follows: "Give the customers as much as you can afford to give them," have enabled Mrs. Gerda Grant, of Madison, Wisconsin,

* Reprinted by permission of *American Restaurant* and Kenneth C. Wagner.

to build up a flourishing business. She has had to double the floor space of her original establishment, and in addition has taken over two other restaurants in other sections of the city. Originally employing only five persons, she now has 30 people on her weekly payroll.

When she took over the Uptown Grill on Madison's historic State Street in 1939, it was a financially precarious, ordinary looking restaurant; now it does an ever-growing volume of business, and has a personality all its own. When business is slack at many other places the Grill is crowded—and with good reason. Superb food at amazingly low prices, a delightfully quiet and relaxing atmosphere, and a beautifully decorated room keep customers coming back time after time.

No newcomer to the business when she undertook the revitalization of the Grill, Mrs. Grant had had eighteen years of experience as manager of the popular Woolworth Cafe in Madison before going into business for herself. By 1942 her rigidly adhered to rules had built up such a volume of trade that she felt the need of expanding, and took advantage of an opportunity to rent the adjacent store space to secure additional room. It was in adding this floor space that she had an opportunity to create a room with a distinctive atmosphere, and to make use of her natural flair for decorating which has made the new Grill an artist's—and her customers'—delight.

To attract customers she decided to create an unusual window display, and has succeeded in doing so. For example, one eye-catching display consisted of beautifully hand-painted rosemaling plates, some of which were imported, others procured from importers in Chicago. This display alone was enough to make the Grill stand out as unusual from among the many restaurants which crowd that area.

Not content to stop there, however, Mrs. Grant created an interior just as striking, and just as unusual. Avoiding the chrome and gleaming metal surfaces now seen so often, she preferred to select a color scheme which would provide a homey, relaxing atmosphere, and at the same time be light enough to make the room look clean and bright. After having the walls painted a dusty rose to give the room warmth, she had a Norwegian artist, who paints rosemaling plates similar to those used in the window display, paint similar abstract designs of her own creation on the two side walls, using rose and light green on a cream background. This design provides the basic color scheme, as well as the inspiration for the remaining decorations, which are as unusual as the basic motif which they follow.

Additional hand-painted plates with beautiful floral designs adorn the walls at intervals on either side of the central designs and over the door, while a maple cupboard near the rear of the room displays more of Mrs. Grant's collection of unusual china. A bright basket of flowers, flanked by two colorful pottery vases, sets off a second cupboard which stands against one wall.

A final touch of color is provided by a row of green "mother-in-law's tongue," the tips of which border the railing of the small mezzanine floor at the rear which serves Mrs. Grant as an office. Two rows of cream colored booths line the walls, and a row of maple tables covered with different colored table cloths makes additional seating possible. White candles and crisp, white paper doilies for each place provide inexpensive, attractive table decorations. Everything in the room was carefully selected to harmonize with the basic color scheme —even the menus, which are enclosed in deep rose leather covers.

Her preference for homelike decorations was influenced by practical reasons as well as her personal artistic taste, for in a university city of 96,000 she caters to students and the average middle class customer. She explains her simple but strikingly effective redecorating by saying that she could have put in expensive, leather-upholstered booths, heavy rugs and ultra-modern furnishings, "but then I would have had to raise prices and make it 'exclusive,' and I didn't want to do that. I think of the students—especially the veterans—and the average man who has to eat out, and I give them as much as I possibly can for their money."

The meals for which the Grill is noted are in themselves more than enough to promote a thriving business. A typical Sunday dinner consists of shrimp cocktail (artistically presented in a small dish within a larger, long-stemmed dish filled with crushed ice), fruit cocktail similarly presented, chicken noodle soup or tomato juice, as an appetizer; a generous serving of tender turkey with dressing, and French or American fried, oven-browned or mashed potatoes; a fresh or frozen-fresh vegetable; fruit gelatin or tomato salad, attractively served with lettuce, delicious hot rolls and butter; a side dish of crisp carrot sticks and celery, with fresh radishes or onions; and a choice of beverage and dessert.

All the pastries are baked at the Grill (formerly by Mrs. Grant herself, now by one of her experienced chefs), and are famous for their "home-made" taste, which so many establishments try unsuccessfully to attain. She credits this to the fact that she insists on using plenty of shortening or butter and other key ingredients which determine the quality of the food. "God gave the customer a palate just as He did you and me," she tells her cooks, "and he uses it just as we do."

GRILL'S PRICES ARE REASONABLE

The price asked for the Grill's delicious dinners is another important factor in Mrs. Grant's success. Although Madison is rated as one of two cities in the United States having the highest living costs, the turkey dinner is priced at only $1.15; week-day meals, by comparison, are as low priced. Beef tenderloin or two good-sized pork chops are listed on the menu for 75 cents, with the same choice of potatoes, fresh vegetable, bread and butter, and choice of drink. A typical 45 cent luncheon consists of meatloaf, potatoes, vegetable, salad, and bread and butter—all in generous portions, and with the real "home-cooked" taste which makes all the Grill's food outstanding.

Patrons of the new Grill are also impressed by the unusually courteous and competent waitresses. The reason for their efficiency is quite simple, according to Mrs. Grant. She tells them this: "You're not working for me—you're working for yourself. When that little machine over there stops ringing (indicating the cash register), you are out of a job. So it's up to you to be at your best." And, she adds with a twinkle, they get amazingly large tips.

The quiet and relaxing atmosphere which always prevails is another feature to which customers invariably react favorably. The usual rush and hurry just isn't there. The waitresses serve quietly and quickly, but never give the impression that they are trying to hurry anyone through his meal—which adds appreciably to the average patron's enjoyment of the food.

The lack of noise can be attributed to the fact that all the dishwashing is done on the second floor; the cooking and baking are done in the basement. There is a definite reason for the latter—again to carry out Mrs. Grant's motto of giving her customers nothing but the best. "Cooks are inclined to be horrified at the discard of unused butter," she claims, "or else want to save apparently untouched dishes of vegetables or pieces of meat for the soup kettle. And customers know that. I figure that the food was paid for once, and that is enough. And my customers always know that their food is absolutely fresh."

A rather amazing fact about the Grill's outstanding success is that not one bit of advertising has been done to secure customers, except for a "courtesy" ad which is run every year in the University of Wisconsin daily newspaper, "The Cardinal." Her customers do all her advertising for Mrs. Grant, and do it so well by word of mouth that her only concern is in being able to accommodate everyone with a minimum of delay. In appreciation of her policies, many veterans and other students from the University patronize the Grill regularly whenever they have occasion to eat away from the campus. They are joined by many families in and near the city who consider it a treat to eat in such delightful surroundings the food prepared by Mrs. Grant's expert cooks.

Not dependent on any unique, money-saving buying scheme, the Grill's prices are both the result and cause of the tremendous volume of business done by Mrs. Grant.

Despite the fact that it is three blocks from the main shopping center and the heaviest pedestrian traffic, the number of steady customers who prefer to walk extra blocks to enjoy the Grill's delicious food continues to increase steadily. The volume of business maintained is even more astounding when you know that there are 117 restaurants listed in the Madison telephone directory, seven within a block of the Grill—and nine more are within three blocks, on the same street!

After eight years of increasing success since it was revitalized, the Uptown Grill promises to become ever more popular as the result of Mrs. Grant's determination to give her customers nothing but the best—and as much of that as possible.

Exercises

1. Walk down Main Street and come back with six ideas for feature articles for metropolitan Sunday newspapers or for magazines. Type out and hand in at class.

2. Walk across the campus and find six suggestions that will make features suitable for Sunday newspaper magazine sections or for general magazines. Type out and hand in at class.

3. After attending one class in each of the courses in which you are enrolled, type out one "tip" for a feature article that you got out of each of the lectures, which you could develop into a newspaper or magazine feature.

4. In reading your afternoon or morning newspaper, find three ideas from local news stories for which you could gather the material and which you could write into features that would be acceptable in metropolitan newspapers or magazines.

5. Recall recent conversations that you have had to find one idea for a suggestion that could be written up for a marketable article.

6. From a convention, a speech, a sermon, radio, or television program, find one idea that you could expand into a feature to sell.

7. From bulletins, advertisements, publicity, or catalogues, find two ideas for features.

8. Find a "tip" for an article from some industry, trade, business, or profession that you could sell to a trade or business magazine.

9. Suggest a "tip" from your own experience, or the experiences of others, that you could write.

10. From the eleven sources for ideas for features listed in this chapter, jot down one "tip" from each that you think would sell.

11. Every day during the coming week write down the ideas that have come to you from observation, experience, or printed material that you think would make good future "tips" for articles. At the end of the week transfer the good ones to your permanent "tip" notebook, "assignment book," or card file, and plan to write them when you can gather the material.

Publication Analysis

New York *Times,* New York *Herald Tribune, Christian Science Monitor,* and Philadelphia *Inquirer*

*Do not spend more than three hours on this report.
Use chart form as shown in Appendix.*

Look at Sunday feature and magazine sections in the four newspapers.

A. 1. What can you say of the general policy of these papers toward features?

2. How do local, state, regional, national, and international features compare in space in these newspapers?

3. What do you think would be your chances of selling to these papers?

B. (Put emphasis of report on this section.) In chart form classify the features as to: (1) types; (2) variety of subject matter; (3) use of cuts; (4) average length of features; (5) type of readers to whom features appeal; (6) ones that you might have written.

C. Analyze briefly four features articles—one each in the *Times,* the *Herald Tribune,* the *Christian Science Monitor,* and the Philadelphia *Inquirer*—preferably something you might have written and of the type that you are now writing for your first feature article.

D. At the end of the report—and in every report hereafter—list two tips for feature articles that you might write that were suggested to you from this study or some other source. List three possible markets for each tip.

CHAPTER 3

The Interview Article

No Definite Distinctions of Types. The number of classifications of feature articles is as great as the number of feature writers, for almost every writer has his own plan of grouping the various types. In any classification one arranges, considerable overlapping is likely to occur, because almost any article has elements of one or more types. In the majority of newspaper and magazine offices the editors classify them into the following types: (1) the interview; (2) the utility article; (3) personal experience story; (4) the confession article; (5) the personality sketch; and (6) the narrative. Thus, a writer will do well to adopt the journalistic names for the different types. Nevertheless, he must bear in mind that any article may contain elements of one or more of the types enumerated in addition to the predominating one.

Popularity of the Interview. The success of an interview article depends upon the interest in the interview, which is in proportion to the "interviewee's" prominence, or to the interest in the topic, or both. It is true that editors are more willing to buy interviews with well-known persons, because readers recognize them; but they are equally interested in unknown persons whose opinions and ideas are new and unique. The interview article offers the writer a good device for giving information. Because the material for many features is obtained by interviewing, a writer may present it more effectively by developing it as an interview article. People are questioned for the information they can impart, for their opinions, and for their ideas concerning particular subjects, which may make up the major part, if not the whole, of the article.

As a means of obtaining material, the interview also is used for the other kinds of articles listed, as discussed in later chapters. However, when editors speak of the interview article, they refer to one that is more concerned with one phase of a person's opinions or ideas. Usually that person must be a recognized authority on the subject about which he is interviewed, or he must be so well known that his prominence gives weight to his opinions or ideas even though he may not be an expert in the field in which he is being interviewed.

The interview article may be defined as one concerned with one or more phases of the opinions or ideas of a recognized authority, or authorities, on the subject, or of the opinions of a person, or persons, so well known that his or their prominence gives value to the ideas expressed.

Personality and confession stories are similar to the interview in that they contain opinions and ideas, but they are presented from a different point of view. In the confession article the writer confesses or confides his ideas, or "sins," whereas in the personality sketch not only the person's opinions but his personality and character are revealed by relating the interesting experiences in his life.

Technique of Interviewing. In looking about for ideas for interview articles, the writer is attracted to persons because they are experts or because they are distinguished in some particular field. After selecting the person to be interviewed, the writer should make an appointment, either by telephone or letter, for an interview at the time and place designated by the interviewee. One problem is to know whether it is better to meet the interviewee in his office or at his home. Some persons think better away from their desks, whereas others think better in the atmosphere of their work. When the interviewer makes the appointment, either by telephone or letter, he may solve this problem by asking whether he should go to the person's office or home.

As a rule, it is a poor policy to interview a person without giving him several days or more to think about the subject. One will get much more interesting material if the interviewee has had time to do some thinking. The interviewer should give his name and explain briefly that he is a free-lance writer who wants an interview for an article to be published because the person to whom he is speaking, or writing, is considered an outstanding authority in whose ideas magazine readers will be interested. He should indicate the amount of time that he thinks he will need for the interview; then he must be careful at the conference not to outstay his time, unless the person being interviewed assures him that he may have more or shows by his attitude that he is willing to talk longer.

The interviewer should learn all he can about the subject upon which he wishes to base his interview by: (1) looking, in the library, at the Periodical Readers' Guide and reading all the material he can find listed pertaining to the subject, in order to be as well informed as possible and to ask intelligent questions; (2) looking in all available sources, such as *Who's Who,* or the *Who's Who* of the special field in which the interviewee might be listed, for the facts about the person's life; and (3) talking with friends and acquaintances of the interviewee to learn about his hobbies, his pet theories, his likes and dislikes, in order to plan the interview carefully. If the writer acquires this knowledge before he meets the interviewee, he not only will save time, but will be able to start the discussion from the angle he desires and to control the interview. By being well prepared, he will gain the person's confidence and respect, because he knows what he wants and because he is accurately informed.

Interviewing the Interviewee. A series of questions, perhaps as many as twenty-five, should be planned and memorized by the writer in advance of meeting the person to be interviewed, in order to acquire the exact information he desires. The questions should be cleverly phrased, to arouse the interviewee's interest. In planning the questions, the writer constantly must keep his readers in mind and think of the questions that they would ask the interviewee if they had the opportunity to talk with him. For this reason the writer should pretty well determine, even before he has had his interview, to which markets he will submit his manuscript. Thus he will have some idea who his readers will be and in what phases of the subject they will be interested. Nothing is more irritating to a person whose time is valuable and who has granted a twenty-minute interview than to have a feature writer take an hour of his time because he knows nothing of the subject and did not have his questions planned in advance. Nothing labels a person as a beginner more quickly than the lack of adequate preparation and the failure to carry on the interview in a businesslike manner, thus saving time for the interviewee as well as for himself.

One should be on time, or a few minutes ahead of time, for his appointment. He should be attractively and appropriately dressed, as is any successful professional writer. It is only in the movies and fiction that journalists go about their business hatless and slovenly dressed, or dash past secretaries without presenting their cards or names, instead of waiting to be asked into the interviewee's office. It is only the young writer portrayed on the silver screen who achieves success by entering his interviewee's office chewing gum or smoking and who sits slumped in his chair, hat, if any, on the back of his head, while he takes a few notes on any scraps of paper he has at hand. The successful writer is extremely careful to see that his personal appearance is attractive and that his manner is gracious and considerate toward office boys and secretaries as well as toward the interviewee. As much care and thought should be given to these matters by a writer as by a person who is going to apply for a position. Like the employer, the interviewee forms his impressions of the writer as he enters the room. If that impression is favorable, the writer will be more likely to get better material for his article, and perhaps the way will be opened to more features.

Writers find that business cards with their name, the words "Free-Lance Writer," and their address and telephone number, to be presented to the interviewee upon entering his presence, serve to bridge over any awkward pauses following the self-introduction. The card may later aid the interviewee in getting in touch with the writer in case he wishes to correct some statement or wishes to add to the material he has already given. Even young journalism students find the cards useful. If they do not have engraved or printed cards, they can type the necessary information on blank cards, and these serve the purpose until more professional-looking ones are necessary.

Fig. 1. Free-lance Writer's Business Card.

A well-trained memory is preferable to a notebook or folded pages of copy paper, unless the feature writer knows that the interviewee wishes to be quoted verbatim or that he is accustomed to being interviewed. Some people feel there is less danger of misquotation if the interviewer takes notes in their presence. A person less experienced in being interviewed will feel ill at ease and self-conscious of his speech and expression if he sees a writer taking notes. Such note-taking may result in an atmosphere of formality that will prevent his giving all of his interesting information. The writer must remember that the interviewee may be frightened, because many people hold writers, even beginners, in great reverence, if not in awe. Or he may be nervous for fear the writer, whom he recognizes as an amateur, will misquote him and make him appear ridiculous in print. The free-lance should conduct the interview in as cordial and informal a manner as possible, and thereby put the interviewee at his ease. The interviewee can be tested to see whether he will be more comfortable when notes are taken, or when they are not. A good device is to get him talking and then ask, "May I write that down?" The writer can see the interviewee's reaction to such writing down of quotations, and then he will know whether or not to take notes during the remainder of the interview.

Like a psychologist, the interviewer, to be successful, has to know how to judge people and how to draw them out to say the things that will make a good article. If one feels that he is not clever in drawing people out to say things that he wants them to say, he should practice on his friends, classmates, and anyone with whom he comes in contact. To interview successfully, knowledge of human nature will help one more than anything else. One must be alert, enthusiastic, and interested in the person he is interviewing as well as the subject. By his own interest he will elicit greater interest and better material from the interviewee.

A young writer may find that he is inclined to let the interviewee lead him astray from the topic, not because he wants to, but because it is human nature to ramble in conversation. The interviewer may be kept off the subject for several hours by a too talkative interviewee, whereas he could have obtained his material in twenty minutes. The interviewer must put a value on his own time just as do people in such professions as medicine, dentistry, and law. Even though one is only a beginner and evaluates his time at only a dollar an hour, he cannot afford to spend two hours in an interviewee's office to obtain material that could be his in a tenth or a sixth of that time.

Although it is the interviewer's place to keep the conversation moving by means of questions, to draw out the interviewee, and to keep the discussion in the direction that he wishes it, he must remember that his chief business is that of a listener. When he sees that he has taken as much of the interviewee's time as he had asked for, he should suggest that perhaps he should leave. If the person is willing, of course, the interviewer should stay until he has all the desired information; but if the interviewee is busy, then the writer should ask if he may have another appointment to complete the interview.

If the material is of a technical nature, the free-lance should ask the interviewee to be kind enough to read the copy of the interview for approval before it is submitted for publication, in order to avoid any inaccuracies. Experienced writers find it to their advantage to have an interviewee's approval of a completed article, even if it is not technical. It is easier to deal with objections before rather than after publication. When the final draft has been approved by the interviewee, indicate this in the note to the editor on the cover sheet (as explained in a later chapter) by saying: "This article has been approved by Mr. Blank." When the editor knows that the interviewee has seen and approved the manuscript, he will feel more secure in printing the article, especially if the writer is a stranger to the magazine.

A considerate writer will remember, when he leaves, to thank the expert, or authority, for his valuable information and for the time that was so graciously given. The information the interviewee has given the writer may be the result of a lifetime of study and research. The time that was given by the interviewee for the conference may be worth ten or more dollars an hour to the expert. If the interviewer has taken fifteen minutes of his time, he should consider that the expert has given him $2.50. For such generous gifts, the writer should express his appreciation, and, if the article is published, should supply the interviewee with a copy of the periodical containing it.

Preparation for Writing the Interview. Immediately, or as soon after the interview as possible, the writer should fill in the exact words and phrases and complete his notes, whether or not he took notes during the interview. If he has done a good job of interviewing, the interviewee's words will be ringing in his ears. Now, with the quotations in hand, he may wait to write the article until he has: (1) thought through his material carefully; (2) investigated possible markets thoroughly; (3) decided how to "slant" the article to give it the greatest possible reader interest; (4) selected the style and form in which he can write it most effectively; (5) planned the type and number of photographs or snapshots; and (6) arranged for other illustrative material, such as drawings, maps, and charts.

A well-written feature is the result of careful thinking and planning before one begins to write. For this reason, it is essential that the interviewer transcribe his notes completely, in order that he may take time to think and plan his interview into the type of article that will market easily and profitably. He should manage to relate his interview aloud to someone. In the telling of it he will remember points that he forgot to include in his notes, and new ideas of development may occur to him as he talks about it.

The interview article may (1) consist almost entirely of direct quotation, with a limited amount of explanatory material concerning the person interviewed; or it may (2) be made up partly of direct and partly of indirect quotation, combined with necessary explanations; for greater variety it is advisable (3) to alternate direct with indirect quotation; and (4) a description of the person and his surroundings, generally by way of introduction, gives the reader a distinct impression of the individual under characteristic conditions.

Although a good beginning is important in any article, it is even more so in the interview article. Unless one puts a great deal of thought into organizing his material, the beginning, or "lead," is the hardest part to write. But if he has thought through the plan carefully, he will be able to introduce the person interviewed to the reader in the lead paragraph or paragraphs by giving a vivid description of him, his appearance, and mannerisms, his surroundings, or his background. Thus he will give a distinct impression of the individual and make the reader feel he really knows the person as well as what he says and thinks. Or the writer may feature in the lead something unusual, or a striking statement, followed by a paragraph of description of the interviewee, just as a news reporter includes the "W's" in his speech story.

No matter which type of lead is used, early in the article, probably in the second or third paragraph, an explanation should be given the reader as to why the interviewee was interviewed, and a brief sketch of him should be included. In the paragraphs following the feature and the identification of the interviewee, the writer may continue with the direct and indirect quotations, description, narration, and exposition, in any order that will add to the effectiveness of the article, just as though he had not interrupted himself to give the interviewee's background or the reason for the article.

The artistic writer keeps himself in the background entirely, remembering that his readers are interested in the interviewee rather than the interviewer. He avoids writing so that his questions stand out. He knows his readers are interested in the answers rather than the questions. He refrains from mentioning that there was an interview, for that is obvious to the reader.

In many ways the interview article has an advantage over the other types, in that readers are attracted to it because they like to feel they know prominent or successful people. If they cannot know them personally, they like to read about them, and that is why editors buy interview articles to supply the subscriber demand. Verbatim quotations give life to the article and make the reader feel that he is conversing with the person interviewed. Descriptions of him or of his surroundings make the reader feel that he has seen the speaker, and the statements of an authority have greater weight than do those who are not well known or experienced in a particular field.

The symposium interview is developed in the same way as the interview, except that it is based upon interviews with several authorities whose opinions on the same subject may or may not agree. The writer may compare or contrast the opinions, according to the "slant" he decides to give the article. This type generally is more dependent upon the prominenc of the persons interviewed than upon their opinions.

Rewards Are Many. Beginners often are surprised at the willingness of prominent people to be interviewed and at their generosity with their time. They do not realize that even the well-known are not averse to becoming better known; and in most professions, businesses, and trades, people interviewed are benefited by favorable publicity. For that reason they are not only agreeable to being interviewed but are extremely grateful to the writer for making them, their views, or their work, better known to the public. Although the interviewer is asking valuable information and time from the interviewee, the latter will be more than compensated by the favorable publicity when the article appears in print.

Sometimes, however, the reverse is true. One may have to exercise his ingenuity in approaching the interviewee. Not all experts and celebrities are easily seen, and many of them become interview-weary. One writer tried to see Fritz Kreisler but was not admitted. However, she did not give up. During the last encore number at a concert she slipped back stage, and as Mr. Kreisler was entering his dressing room, she said, "I'm interested in one thing about your violin."

The great musician beamed down upon her and, although he would not talk about himself, he would talk about his violin, for he loved it. Before he realized it, he was being interviewed; but he did not object, because the writer had given him an opportunity to talk about what he wanted to talk about.

An ingenious interviewer will have little difficulty in approaching the celebrity whom he wishes to interview, if he hits upon his main interest—which, of course, requires a knowledge of the interviewee's likes and dislikes.

Rewards to the writer who interviews are numerous. In getting one article, frequently he gets material for others. While he is interviewing to earn, he also learns, and thereby adds to his own knowledge. From these contacts he acquires new acquaintances and friends, many of whom may prove valuable in years to come. From a financial point of view, the free-lance finds that well-written interview articles are always in great demand. Every Sunday newspaper and almost every magazine, as well as scientific and business publications, are in the market for this type of article.

As a writer, one does a great deal of interviewing, not for interview articles alone, but for most of the other kinds. For that reason, much of the discussion of the technique of gathering and writing the interview article applies to developing other types of features.

Examples of the Interview Article. An analysis of the articles that follow will show how the writers gathered their material by research and interview, and how they arranged the quotations to present them effectively. A few magazines follow a fad of "hiding" the interview element by not using any quotations, others will not use interview articles unless they have direct quotations. The first interview, published in *Fountain Service and Fast Food,* was the author's first article. The second article, also the author's first, sold to *The Sample Case* and shows how one type of article contains the elements of several. The third article had its source in a senior investigating scholarships for graduate study. Because he slanted his manuscript to *Pic* magazine, which at the time did not use direct quotations, he wrote the interview material without direct quotations. In reality it is an interview but it appears to be a utility article. The writer received a check for $150.00 and later was awarded one of the scholarships for which he had applied. The sales of the three authors totalled $250.00.

(1)
Planning Scientifically Is Jayaness Formula for Keeping Out of the Red*

BY SANFORD A. MOEN

Are mounting costs giving your fountain the "inflation blues?" If they are, then you can understand the plight of two ex-GI's in Stoughton, Wis. who went into business two years ago. They nearly included bankruptcy as their silent partner because they had no experience. They borrowed the necessary capital and bought a business whose inventory had sunk to zero.

Among other worries was the inflationary spiral which added $2000 more to the original buying price. The fountain lacked adequate glasses, silverware, and stools. Its patronage had gone in the

* Reprinted by permission of *Fountain Service and Fast Food* and Sanford A. Moen.

same direction as the inventory—down. Only optimism and a barrel of promises kept this business from heading down foreclosure road during those first few months.

Today if you enter the Jayaness Soda Grill in Stoughton you will find little evidence that it once faced collapse. New equipment has been installed, inventory has increased 600 per cent and customers instead of bill collectors come through the doors.

And all this change took place because the two young partners learned one important thing—how to plan scientifically.

Only when things became so desperate that a few weeks could determine the success of their business did the management adopt a new approach. It was then that Douglas Stokstad and Curtis Larson started analyzing the reasons for their continual losses.

"Where was the profit going?"

This was the first question they faced and the answer was given by Mr. Stokstad, an easy going young man of 25.

"We made a quick survey and then itemized the cost of everything in the store, including the sundaes and malteds," he said. "We discovered that our profit on these items was being lost due to improper measurements. We figured the actual cost of our items and learned that our profit margin could be greatly increased if we set up a system of uniformity.

"We instructed our dispensers in fountain item preparation and the first week we noticed that we had less waste. A few weeks later we discovered that our profit on these fountain items was steadily increasing."

After having found how effective reducing waste on these items was, Mr. Stokstad and his partner started along another line. They reasoned that if waste was occurring in handling fountain items perhaps profit was also being lost because of old methods of management.

As Mr. Stokstad related the story of the early days in business, he glanced over at his new dishwasher.

"That cost of $400 seemed at that time like the straw that would break our business back but before we invested we investigated. We figured the cost in laundry and soap bills, plus the time spent washing dishes. There were other things that couldn't be figured in, such as the number of customers we lost through lack of dishes during rush periods. All these things added up to the purchase of that machine."

He grinned when asked the results.

"We have cut our laundry bill by one-third, our soap bill by 90 per cent and above all we paid for the dishwasher in less than a year from these savings."

"The dishwasher was only the beginning," he continued, "but it was the start that enabled us to see more clearly how proper equipment could save us time and labor and help us make that all important profit.

"After we had the dish problem taken care of we turned our attentions toward a sandwich-grill. This was another detail which wasn't included in the purchase price. It involved a more complicated estimate because we had no way of knowing what our savings, if any, would be. Countless times, customers would ask for hamburgers and other hot sandwiches only to hear us say 'I'm sorry but we don't have any.'

"This continued until we realized that each request that was refused was a potential order lost and above all a dissatisfied customer.

"Though we were hard pressed for cash we managed to spend $150 for a grill without our creditors knowing it. Our sales as a result of this expenditure were so great that five months later we owned the grill. No longer did our hamburgers have a mortgage on them!"

Mr. Stokstad's enthusiasm mounted as he related how thorough investigation of all their equipment and methods showed a chance for improvement and eventually a profit.

"One of our big headaches was furnishing our fountain drinks with clean chipped ice. We had been buying chipped ice but invariably it was dirty and this resulted in full glasses remaining on the counter after the customer had gone. We invested in an ice chipper and the savings paid for the gadget in three weeks."

* * *

Another important change were the methods of paying. Until the owners studied the situation it had been satisfactory to let the customers pay their bills as they left the soda grill. He set up a plan.

"We were astonished," said Mr. Stokstad, "when our ice cream representative informed us of a dealer in Illinois who kept a check of all his accounts that were actually paid. He noted the number of stubs given to his customers and the number that had been returned to him with the proper amount of the bill.

"Much to his surprise he learned that 19 per cent of his sales were going unpaid. We consider our customers the best that ever patronized a fountain. But operating on a small profit margin it is necessary to take every precaution to protect our investment. Now we employ a system with no losses.

"We have also learned through the different trade magazines and fountain salesmen what types of fountain items to promote for greater profit. For instance, on our cola drinks we made a profit of 65 per cent. This certainly makes it advantageous to encourage the sale of this item.

"However, it hasn't all been smooth sailing. We were forced out of our first location and it became necessary for us to buy the building in which we now operate. If this had happened early in our business life we would have been stymied. But our profits and patronage have increased enough.

"We never would have remained in business had we continued to plod along in the old way. We examined every phase of our business to determine how we could start advancing toward profit instead of retreating toward debt," he concluded.

(2)
Small Business Enters the Classroom*

New Program in Distributive Education Improves Selling Techniques.

BY JAMES F. SULLIVAN

It was another Horatio Alger story and the hero was an ambitious young fellow who wasn't afraid to get out and work, as far as people in Milwaukee, Wisconsin, are concerned. To Joe Anderson, it was more than that. A training program called Distributive Education prepared him for the climb to one of the best men's clothing businesses in the city.

Joe Anderson discarded his fire-fighting tools and left the Civilian Conservation Corps in 1937 to go to work for the largest clothing retailer in Milwaukee. He liked the clothing business and decided to make it his future. He heard of a new program being taught evenings at the local vocational school.

He joined thousands of adults throughout the United States who returned to the classroom each evening to learn sound business techniques by participating in the federal program authorized by an act of Congress known as the George-Dean law. Essentially, the act provides for further development of vocational education in agriculture, home

* Reprinted by permission of *The Sample Case*, official publication, United Commercial Travelers, and James F. Sullivan.

economics, trades, and industries. It includes an annual appropriation of $1,200,000 for training in the distributive occupational subjects which will improve business techniques. Federal funds are matched dollar for dollar by local boards of education.

Higgler or huckster—jobber or retailer, all look upon selling today as a holiday task with the buying public ogling for their favor while bidding for scanty wares that dribble back to the consumer market after the prolonged wartime drought.

Joe Anderson, and businessmen everywhere, recognize, however, that the public is developing a growing consciousness of the approach of the period when the wheels of peacetime production will gush forth with long-awaited items. They notice an increased inclination to clasp a wary hand on the pocketbook and hold out for the day when they will be able to express their own preference at the downtown store.

Every corner merchant knows that when new stock piles up on his shelves, it is his cue that all the subtle techniques of better salesmanship will assume new importance. His chances for success will be no better than his efforts to satisfy his customers.

Distributive education has been introduced to curb the high mortality rate of the small retail business in the United States. The course teaches the merchant to substitute successfully applied methods for the trial and error system so commonly applied in the retail field.

Federal subsidies for training are provided, according to the bill, to "give those businesses engaged in the distributive field an opportunity to render better, more economical and more efficient services. The social and economic benefits that will accrue from an adequate program in distributive education will be shared by the consumer, the retailer, and the manufacturer."

Joe Anderson was eligible to participate in the program because he was interested in operating a business making goods and services available to the consumer. He was seeking to learn methods of reducing the hazards of a small business, both by acquiring knowledge of operation problems, and by applied sales techniques that have resulted in increased efficiency. While working for the clothing store he was in a position to immediately apply his schooling to improve his salesmanship, and he also brought new ideas into the classroom.

Distributive education, as now applied in each of the 48 states, is the product of an experiment attempted by the Wisconsin Board of Vocational and Adult Education in 1932. It evolved out of the ideas of Wisconsin business leaders seeking to reduce the number of business failures in the state. One of the pioneers that helped guide the program through the infant stage is Roy Fairbrother, supervisor of distributive education for Wisconsin.

Mr. Fairbrother takes almost an evangelical attitude toward the program. When it was introduced on the crest of the 1932 economic depression, he threw his 5 foot, eight inch frame and his winning personality behind a salesmanship program of his own. He traveled Wisconsin from end to end selling local school boards on the possibilities of this new type of education.

The fact that distributive education courses are now functioning in 40 state vocational schools, and is operating throughout the nation as well, is ample evidence of the success of his selling techniques. But Mr. Fairbrother would rather judge the value of the program in the increased enjoyment brought to thousands of former students in their daily work, in increased earning power for both the store owner and his employees, and in greater stability brought to the distributive industry.

Mr. Fairbrother describes what the program can do in his simple, direct manner:

"The average purchaser knows little about color, lines and designs when he stops in to buy a new tie or a suit of clothes. He never realizes that a proper fit includes such things as wearing colors that blend well with the skin, hair and eye coloring, or with his height and girth. He depends upon the salesman's advice for a proper fit.

"When the man walks out of the store with a new suit, he expects compliments from friends. The friend, trying to decide 'whether the clothes look nice,' is of little help in telling just why the clothes don't look right. The fitting of clothes of appropriate textile and style is an exacting science. The clerk is usually blamed when the clothes don't draw compliments and the store will likely lose a customer.

"A well trained clerk who knows how to fit clothes properly is going to give better service. This means greater earning power to the employer and the employee. It gives both of them a greater enjoyment of their jobs, results in greater application, and ultimately it means a lower turnover in the store's personnel."

Joe Anderson went over to his vocational school after completing his day of work and took a full course in salesmanship and management. His courses included a study of textiles, store arithmetic, elementary principles of retailing, fashion trends, specialty selling, applied display, art principles, nontextiles, fashion merchandising, English for salespersons, business behavior, consumer relationships, and merchandising information. He completed a full course in the college of better selling.

Distributive education includes more than retail sale of clothing. The program is designed for all workers employed in commercial exchanges making consumer goods and services available to others. A retail grocery store manager, for example, is a typical distributor, since he assembles from wholesalers, jobbers and producers a wide variety of goods which he sells to his customers. He directs the managerial activities, the salespersons who do the selling, and the deliverymen who transport the purchases.

*   *   *

The program is sponsored nationally by the United States Department of Education, under the Secretary of the Interior. Supervision is provided on a state level by each state department of Vocational and Adult Education. All contacts with individual schools are through the state supervisor's office. The duties of the state supervisor include the promotion, inspection and supervision of instruction. It is also his responsibility to see that adequately trained instructors are available to meet the demands of the local schools.

While direct financial support of the local programs by local businessmen is prohibited by law, they are encouraged to recommend the courses of training most appropriate to local conditions. Because larger business establishments can provide their own training staffs, the program has been designed to appeal to the smaller concerns.

High standard is required of teachers participating in the program. A bachelor's degree from a recognized university is required, preferably in marketing. In addition, specialized training in teaching business courses, and at least three years' experience in the distributive field is required.

Mr. Fairbrother sounds a note of warning to American businessmen:

"Approximately 80 per cent of all small businesses in the United States turn over every ten years, and half of our new merchants lose out in their first year. With thousands of new concerns entering the field for the first time since the war ended with only a willingness to work hard as a qualification, it is more important than ever that we realize the value of distributive education.

"When our present general prosperity slackens, it is the distributor that isn't applying scientific methods that will be forced to retrench first. An investment of time now in learning improved methods is the best investment that can be made in your future security.

"Your failure to succeed is a blow to your community, to the producers and to your employees. The economic welfare of the nation is dependent in a very real sense on your success in business."

Thus, American business is brought back to the classroom.

(3)
Scholarships
Go Begging*

*You Don't Have To Be a Phi Bete To Get One
of the Thousands of Grants for Study
Offered Each Year.*

By WILLIAM J. COX

Take stock of yourself—and the scholarship field—and you may be studying at Oxford next winter. Even if you were not the class' bright boy, a surprising amount of financial backing to further your education is available. But you must investigate—and apply early.

Every year around 70,000 scholarships worth from $12,000,000 to $15,000,000 are awarded by American colleges. Many go unused simply because too many people think they cannot qualify, that scholarships are for Phi Betes and valedictorians only.

Financial backing for scholarships comes from three sources: (1) joint arrangement between Federal agencies and colleges; (2) city and state grants; (3) individual colleges. The third bracket is the toughest to crack if you haven't a straight A record. For some of the others you need merely to be a resident of a certain state.

Basis for the award of scholarships is as diverse as are the schools offering them. Thirty-five states provide scholarships to orphans of World War I. Some schools have Gold Star scholarships, in honor of World War II dead. Others offer concessions in their fixed charges for tuition, room, and board for the benefit of sons and daughters of naval personnel. A complete list of these concessions and scholarships can be obtained by writing the Bureau of Naval Personnel, Navy Department, Washington, D.C., and asking for the booklet entitled, "Schools and Colleges Granting Concessions to Sons and Daughters of Officer and Enlisted Personnel of the U.S. Navy."

Almost every state provides aid of some sort to resident students seeking higher education. This aid usually consists of reductions in tuition and various other charges as well as ample scholarship funds. Because of the vast number of veterans taking advantage of the GI

* Reprinted by permission of *Pic,* Street and Smith, and William J. Cox.

Bill of Rights, the number of grants open to non-veterans has greatly increased. You can get information about state scholarships either by writing your state's department of education or your state Board of Regents. Over 1,700 municipal scholarships are awarded each year, so write your city's board of education, too.

Rhodes scholarships to Oxford, granted for a minimum of two years, are offered to college or university students in their junior year. Students must be unmarried and between the ages of 19 and 25 on October 1 of the year in which they are elected. The Rhodes trustees have also authorized a limited number of War Service scholarships. Applicants for these scholarships must have completed at least one year of war service, have attained sophomore standing, and have been between the ages of 19 and 25 at any time since October 1, 1940. Married as well as single students are eligible. Information about them can be obtained from almost any college or university.

La-Verne Noyes scholarships, which vary from $35 to $50 per student per semester, are awarded in 49 colleges and universities in the U.S. They provide for the payment of tuition, in part or in full, of deserving students needing this assistance. The applicant must either have served in the Army or Navy in World War I, or be a descendant of one who did. Eligible students should make application to the university or college they wish to attend. For a copy of a circular on this, send a stamped, self-addressed envelope to Estate of La-Verne Noyes, 2500 Roosevelt Road, Chicago, Ill.

The Fulbright Act provides for the use of certain foreign currencies and credits, acquired through the sale of surplus property abroad, to be used for education.

*   *   *

Programs [Fulbright] have been set up in the United Kingdom, Australia, New Zealand, Finland, Netherlands, Denmark, Belgium, France, Czechoslovakia, Austria, Hungary, Poland, Italy, Greece, Turkey, Egypt, Iran, China, Netherlands East Indies, Philippines, Siam, and Burma. Financial assistance granted to students includes the payment of transportation, tuition, maintenance, and incidental expenses, which means that the extent of each grant will vary in accordance with needs of the student. Candidates are selected from all parts of the country. Write to the Department of State, attention of the Division of International Exchange of Persons, Washington 25, D.C., to be placed on the mailing list of available detailed information.

Information in periodicals about scholarships is listed in the "Readers' Guide to Periodical Literature," available in most libraries. You can get complete lists of scholarships available in the school in which you are interested by writing to its registrar. A good overall picture is offered in a helpful, 25-cent volume entitled, "Scholarships and Fellowships," published by the Office of Education, Department of the Interior, Washington, D.C.

Here are scholarship leads for special fields, and addresses you can follow up:

Humanistic sciences—American Council of Learned Societies, 1219 16th St., N.W., Washington, D.C. Medicine—Association of American Medical Colleges, 5 So. Wabash Ave., Chicago, Ill. Biological sciences, medical sciences, physics, chemistry, mathematics, technology—National Research Council, 2101 Constitution Ave., N.W., Washington 25, D.C.

Chemistry and related sciences—Lalor Foundation, Lancaster Pike and Old Baltimore Rd., Wilmington, Del. Economic, political, and social sciences—Brookings Institution, 722 Jackson Pl., N.W., Washington 6, D.C. Forestry—Charles Lathrop Pack Forest Education Board, 1214 16th St., N.W., Washington, D.C.

Government—National Institute of Public Affairs, Investment Bldg., Washington, D.C. Social Work—Social Science Research Council, 230 Park Ave., New York 17, N.Y. Library Science—American Library Association, 50 E. Huron St., Chicago, Ill.

Here is the general procedure in obtaining a scholarship after looking over the field: write the college or university you wish to attend. State the specific scholarship in which you are interested. Most schools then require the student to submit a statement of approximately 500 words in which the applicant gives a brief sketch of his life, stating his present and future plans, together with the extent of his financial need. Letters of recommendation from several people are usually required, and must be sent directly to the school. Applications are generally required to be submitted by April for students expecting to start the fall term but now is a good time to get a line on available scholarships.

The duration of most scholarships is for two semesters, though there are some that last but one semester, and others that extend for the entire four years.

Exercises

1. Select the last issue of your favorite Sunday newspaper and go through the magazine section, listing the articles that are interview articles as defined in this chapter.

2. In chart form: (1) list the captions; (2) indicate the source from which the writer probably got the article; (3) list the type of person who you think will be interested in reading the article; (4) estimate the number

of words (roughly estimating there are almost 50 words to the typical newspaper column inch); (5) list the number of pictures or drawings for each article.

3. In the sixth column of the chart indicate which persons were interviewed because they were recognized authorities and indicate those who were interviewed because they are prominent.

4. Selecting one of the articles, list six of the questions that the feature writer probably asked the interviewee.

5. Selecting a recent issue of your favorite monthly magazine, go through the feature articles, selecting the interviews, and make a chart for them as you did in Exercise 2, except that in estimating the number of words to the magazine column inch, you will have to count the average words in a magazine line and multiply by the number of lines. (To get the average word length of a line count the number of letters, or units, or characters, as they are spoken of journalistically, and divide by the number of letters in the average word, which is seven.) Complete the chart as you did in Exercise 2.

6. Compare the two charts and write a topic of not more than 200 words on "The Difference in the Treatment of Features in Newspapers and Magazines."

7. Select one of the interview articles in the magazine and see if you can detect the questions that the interviewer asked the interviewee. List as many as you can find.

8. List five persons in your community that you might interview and indicate whether you would interview them to give readers information or to tell their opinions or ideas to the readers.

9. Give two sources from which you could get information concerning each of the five persons you listed in Exercise 8.

10. List five questions that you would ask one of the persons you selected to interview. Check them to see whether they are worded to bring forth the replies that you want and that you would be able to use for direct quotations, or whether the interviewee could simply answer "yes" or "no."

11. To what five markets would you send each of the five interview articles as suggested in Exercise 8 if you actually were to write them?

12. Interview a classmate as to what he thinks the prospects are for a winning football team, but do not take any notes during the interview. Then try to reproduce on paper the exact words that the interviewee used. Check with the interviewee or others present to see if you quoted all he said, and correctly.

13. Write a beginning, or "lead," for the interview you obtained in Exercise 12.

14. Where would you obtain material for the second or third paragraph

of the article or that concerned with the explanation of why the interviewee was interviewed and a brief sketch about him?

15. List one idea and three persons that you could use for a symposium interview.

Publication Analysis

Detroit *News,* Atlanta *Journal,* Chicago *Tribune,* Los Angeles *Times,* Minneapolis *Tribune,* or Seattle *Times*

Do not spend more than 3 hours on this report.
Use chart form as shown in Appendix.

NOTE: Read the following questions carefully, then turn through several issues of the papers to get a general idea of the publications as a whole before writing your report. Then discuss the following:

1. (a) What are the opportunities for a free-lance writer, such as yourself, to sell features to the above papers?
   (b) Prove your answer.
2. (a) List the titles of the feature articles in each paper, and from only the titles and lead paragraphs classify the articles as to type, as listed in the beginning of this chapter, and indicate to what class they appeal.
   (b) What is the general tendency or nature as to type of the feature articles in each paper?
3. (a) How many interview articles did you find?
   (b) Why was each interviewee interviewed?
   (c) List the subjects that the interviewees were interviewed upon.
   (d) Which interview article did you consider the best and why?
4. (a) What sections did you find in the one paper that you did not find in the others?
   (b) What would be the prospects of your selling articles for these special sections?
5. What are the interesting things about the articles (one from each paper), in reference to the *way they are written,* that you might have or would like to have written?
6. List two feature tips that you might write, including source, authorities, and markets that were suggested to you by this study.

CHAPTER 4

The Utility Article

Aim Is to Help Reader. Because it is a trait of all human beings to want to be (1) wiser, (2) healthier, (3) wealthier, and (4) happier, magazine readers are always interested in articles that will benefit them mentally, physically, emotionally, and financially. If a writer succeeds in showing people how to be more efficient, more useful, or more practical, or how to increase their wealth, editors will buy anything he writes, provided it is well written. It is upon these four factors that all magazines are founded. If free-lances write to help and guide their readers, they will find it easy to sell.

In order to help the reader, the writer must think of the subscriber constantly. With his nose for the new and his eye for special features, he must observe things that will be useful, beneficial, or remunerative to the reader. Parts of publications, and even entire magazines, are printed on the theory that everyone wants to know how to advance, how to get more pleasure out of living, how to live more easily, cheaply, or comfortably. The utility article is one that aims to help the reader in some way, by giving him definite directions and advice for doing or making something in a better way to satisfy human needs, wants, or desires. There is great interest in these how-to-do-it articles.

The similarity between the utility article, the personal experience story, the confession, and the narrative is marked. They all are written to aid the reader. They may be distinguished by remembering that the utility article guides the reader by giving him definite directions. The personal experience story may benefit the reader, but it is based on experiences of the writer or experiences of others whom he interviews. The confession article helps the reader ethically, religiously, or morally, but it does so only through confiding one's sins or shortcomings. The narrative, which is written in the first or third person, may help the reader as well as entertain him, although it is written with many of the techniques used in the writing of the short story.

Sources of Subjects. Ideas for utility articles may be found anywhere and include all sorts of subjects. Anything from a recipe giving simple directions for making a salad or a cake to an account of producing new building materials or saving hundreds of dollars in business operations will develop into marketable manuscripts. The people who made the salads or devised means by which they improve their businesses will be only too glad to tell a feature writer how they did it. It is a human characteristic to like to appear favorably in print. By observation or by conversation with people in homes, industries, trades, businesses, and professions, a writer, in a few minutes, may uncover material for telling the reader how to do something or for giving him practical guidance. The technique of arranging for the interview and planning the article is the same as for the interview article.

Before deciding to write, the free-lance should ask himself: (1) whether the idea for the utility article he wishes to write is new; (2) if not, how can it be written to be of value to a certain class of readers; (3) whether it will interest a large number of readers, or, in other words, is it the type of article that could sell to any one of many publications; and (4) is the idea of the utility practical for the reader from the standpoint of the expense involved and the results that may be expected?

The illustrations for utility articles often include drawings or charts as well as photographs. If the various steps of a process described can be shown by drawings, even very simple ones, they will aid much in making the directions clearer for the reader.

Planning and Writing. Because the purpose is to give practical guidance, the plan of writing the utility article varies considerably from that of the interview article. Any type of beginning may be used, but the writer must select one that will attract and appeal to the reader and make him curious to read on. In the shorter utility articles, dialogue makes an effective beginning. Unless it is handled well, however, it is a poor device. To dramatize the opening by putting people and their problems into the article sometimes makes the effect more realistic for the reader. If it is written in the first person, the article has the advantage of making the reader feel that the writer actually made or did the thing about which he is writing. However, with the frequent use of the personal pronoun, the reader is likely to get the impression that the author is conceited and is "preaching." The writer can modify this tone by frequently warning the reader not to make the mistakes that he did. To give confidence and encouragement to the reader, the author may point out that although he was an amateur and did make mistakes, he finally succeeded. The simplest and most direct method is to write the article in the second person imperative; it is then easier to give the directions clearly. But one must guard against making the tone dictatorial. Recipe articles, mechanical guidance articles, and other short concise pieces of similar nature, in which the reader will prop the magazine up on his work table or bench and follow directions exactly and quickly, often are written in the second person. The third person is used in writing utility articles only when the material is unusually dramatic and entertaining and is written more in a narrative style. The questions that the readers would be likely to ask, if they were present when the method, process, contrivance, or device was explained, must be kept in mind by the writer, since it is his duty to anticipate the questions and answer them before the reader thinks of them.

In giving directions for practical guidance in utility articles, one must remember that the reader is unfamiliar with the process. Great care must be taken to explain and describe every detail and step clearly and simply. Include approximate costs and suggest ways to reduce costs. The person who made the contrivance or the expert who draws from a rich store of knowledge is inclined to forget that the reader has not had the same experience and information. As a rule, he does not write so simply and understandingly as the feature writer, who has not had the experience nor the knowledge but who does have the ability to express clearly what he sees or hears. If a single direction is omitted, it may be impossible for the reader to follow the procedure successfully. A writer should not insult the intelligence of the reader by telling him things he already knows, but he may assume tactfully that as he "may know," or, that as he "remembers," or that he "may have forgotten." Perhaps the greatest problem in the writing of utility articles to give practical guidance is the avoidance of being "preachy" in tone. In giving instructions to others, one easily appears to be, in print, superior and overbearing. Young writers, because they have been preached at all their lives by their parents and teachers, are quite inclined to talk down to their readers in an imperative tone.

Throughout the body of the article, the writer must avoid choking the reader with facts. Everyone agrees that encyclopedias are excellent books because they are full of facts; but they are used only for reference. One may keep his article from sounding like an encyclopedia by getting people and action into it. An article on how to play golf could be full of facts and still be most uninteresting. But if awkward John Smith is taken out on the course by the professional for his lessons, and the reader learns along with John and profits by John's mistakes, he will be interested, whether or not he plays golf. A real person always adds to the interest of any article. After the article is finished, one must go over it, unit by unit, or paragraph by paragraph, to see that all the needed information is there, that every step of the process is clear to the reader, and that it is written concisely, since wordiness detracts from the clearness of the meaning.

Results Are Easy Sales. For his interest and efforts in giving the reader practical guidance and telling him how to do something, the writer of utility articles is rewarded by the ease with which he can find material and sell his manuscripts. Of course, he must study carefully the magazines that use this type of article, in order to "slant" it correctly. If he has the missionary urge to do good and help his fellowmen, but his temperament or circumstances prevent adoption of a religious career, he can find a sense of satisfaction by writing utility articles that will help other people by the hundreds and thousands to find life more enjoyable. Hence, editors are constantly in the market for all kinds of utility articles if the ideas are expressed clearly, accurately, and concisely. If rejected by one type of periodical, articles may be reslanted to other markets.

Periodicals Buy Manuscripts for Service Bulletins. An additional market for utility manuscripts is that of the service-to-the-reader utility leaflet or bulletin which some magazines list for sale for a few cents. A writer should keep a list of periodicals which provide such reader services and should obtain a few such leaflets in order to analyze their style. Such magazines as *Ladies' Home Journal, Woman's Home Companion, McCall's Magazine, Good Housekeeping,* and many others, frequently purchase utility manuscripts for their service booklets.

The utility leaflet or bulletin, like the utility article in the magazine, must be written in a clear, definite, practical style, with illustrations to aid in explaining each step to the reader. Emphasis in the utility leaflet or bulletin is placed on the cost or the saving of effort or money to the purchaser of the bulletin who desires that information.

Examples of the Utility Article. The first of the following utility features was published in *Capper's Farmer.* It tells how-to-do it by interviewing an authority on the teaching of reading and makes the article realistic by getting children into the article. The second article developed from a newspaper item which attracted the author's interest sold to *Successful Farming.* It shows the techniques of combining several types of articles. The third article, which sold to *Popular Photography,* shows a reader how he too may have a photomobile. All of these articles were the first features the authors had written. They sold the first time they were mailed out because the writers applied what they learned in Chapter 9. Each article had several pictures. The three sales totaled $170.00.

(1)

Reading Is Fun*

BY LUIDA E. SANDERS

Reading can be fun! Fortunately, many children discover this delightful truth for themselves at home or at school. But suppose your youngster, like too many others, doesn't like to read and is having difficulty with school work. Let's see what can be done about it.

* * *

"The starting point for parents who want to help their children," says Dr. Lois G. Nemec, Assistant Professor of Education at the University of Wisconsin, "is to do a lot of reading themselves."

When the rest of the family read and there are books around the house, a large part of the problem is solved. A child simply accepts the fact that reading is the natural thing to do.

There are a number of special things that can be done, using as a base the child's main interest. After discovering what that is, the parents need to develop a sincere interest in the subject themselves. How can anyone show the proper enthusiasm for doll houses or for cowboys if he knows little about them? It doesn't hurt a bit to do a little research on the side after the young fry have gone to bed. There can be long and delightful conversations about what is in an action-packed rodeo picture, for example. You can ask, "What is this called? Can you guess what happened before this? What will happen next?"

Mrs. Nemec then suggests, "Using this interest as a base, you can find some very easy books, so that vocabulary won't get in the way. That is a place where a conference with the teacher is helpful. She can tell you about the child's readiness to read and suggest books that are right for him."

* * *

"At every step of the helping process there should be sincere praise and encouragement," Mrs. Nemec declares. "Never, never compare him to some other child to his detriment."

She points out that each child is his own best measure. He develops his skill in reading in the same order that other children do, but at his own rate. If he can read books of second-grade level, that is the

---

* Reprinted by permission of *Capper's Farmer* and Luida E. Sanders.

place for him to be reading whether he is 7 or 10 years or older. He will go on from there. He should never be told that he doesn't read as well as big brother did when he was that age. And don't forget to invite him to tell the story to the family. This gives him a purpose for reading.

(2)
Clubwomen Start
a Country Library*

BY CAROL K. JOHNSON

Mrs. Ruth Dietz, reading to the youngsters in the photograph on the opposite page, had an idea. Mrs. Lola MacLean hit on the same one. They told their clubwomen friends about it, then things began to happen.

It all goes back to three years ago when the last echoes of "No more classes, no more books" died away in the 75-year-old country school, just outside of Madison, Wisconsin. The school population had dwindled in the area and the remaining children were sent to nearby city schools. It looked as if old Hillcrest School would share the fate of thousands of one-room schools thruout the country— complete abandonment.

Weeds began to grow abundantly around Hillcrest. Dust collected on the neglected books and desks. Except for an occasional home-maker's meeting, the school was idle.

But it was at one of these homemaker's meetings that the idea of the community library began. This particular meeting of the Home-makers Club emphasized the value of reading, and the need for readily available books. Almost simultaneously, Mrs. Dietz and Mrs. Mac-Lean hit upon the idea of using the school for a library.

Mrs. Dietz pointed out that, "Rural residents can use the Madison city library upon payment of a fee, but the distance most Hillcrest residents live from the library has kept them from using it to any extent."

Mrs. MacLean, who had taught at Hillcrest School, knew the school's library books had been left behind when the building was vacated. There were 500 books that could serve as the beginning for a children's section of the new library.

The response to a community library was immediate and enthusi-astic. Mrs. MacLean volunteered to be librarian and to lead a story

* Reprinted by permission of *Successful Farming* and Carol K. Johnson.

hour for children. Mrs. Dietz offered to help with the organization. The Homemakers Club as a group agreed to sponsor the library. The project was under way.

Five high-school girls made library cards for the children's books that were available. Homemakers, armed with dust mops and pails, invaded the then-quiet classroom. When Mrs. Dietz completed arrangements for obtaining 175 additional books, children's and adults', from the traveling library, everything was in readiness for opening day.

Families from the surrounding area and representatives from two local newspapers responded to invitations of the homemakers to celebrate opening day.

Since that opening day, Wednesday afternoon finds the once-deserted school full of life again. The library is open from 2 to 4 p.m., with a story hour at 2:30.

"We have averaged 10 children per story hour over a period of several months," said Mrs. MacLean. "This, of course, does not include the mothers or older brothers and sisters who come to bring the children. Most of the youngsters, who range in age from 2½ to 9 years, come from homes within a radius of two miles. However, several families come from as far as five miles."

As librarian, Mrs. MacLean believes that the children should learn library discipline. "During story hour and while they choose their books, we encourage them to be as quiet as possible," she said. "We also try to make them aware of the responsibilities of caring for books and of returning them on the date due. A one-cent fine for every day the library is open, is charged for overdue books."

One mother who had never visited the library exclaimed, "I don't know what you told them at the library, but whatever it was, it certainly worked. My children were completely destructive with their own books. In fact, at first I was afraid to have them bring books home. Much to my surprise, they haven't done a bit of damage to any of the borrowed books."

For the parents who bring their children to the story hour, there are magazines and books to read. Of the magazines, Mrs. Dietz said, "Since we have no funds available, some of us have been contributing our own magazines to the collection. We hope to encourage more people to read them and to get them for their own homes."

Most of the adult books available are from the state traveling library, which almost every state has. This service sends out 175 books which may be kept for three months and then exchanged for others. The only charge for these books is the postage, one way.

Several other sources of books have sprung up. When the local newspapers publicized the opening day of the library, readers called to offer books and sets of magazines to Hillcrest. Homemakers told their friends, and many of them have been giving books from time to time. Several donations, to be spent on children's books, came from the men in the neighborhood. Whole families are interested and enthusiastic about the Hillcrest project because it includes something for every group.

A total of more than 700 books is now available. Many more are waiting to be catalogued and prepared for use.

The leaders of this project have many plans for the future. One of their greatest needs is more shelf space. Already, one of the men in the community has volunteered to build shelves as soon as plans are complete.

Evening reading and study periods for adults are among the future plans of the library. "We hope to encourage adults to do more reading. We also hope that the library will bring them together and help them to become better acquainted," said Mrs. Dietz. Mrs. MacLean expressed the hope of organizing the reference books into a reference section for high-school students in the community.

In conclusion, Mrs. Dietz said, "We are pleased with the results of our project and hope that we can inspire other groups to do the same type of thing. If there is no country school available, perhaps some other abandoned building could be made into a community center."

So dust no longer gathers on the books and chairs in the little Hillcrest school. Because of a community-minded Homemakers Club, the old school is now a well-managed library and social center, where boys and girls answer roll call with, "I'm always here!"

(3)
In a Merry
Photomobile*

*Milk Wagon Becomes Darkroom As Two
Ex-GIs Enter Night Club
Photography.*

By VIOLET WITT

The pretty girl with the press camera and the speedlight stops in front of your ringside table, smiles, and says "Like to have your

* Reprinted by permission of *Popular Photography* and Violet Witt.

pictures taken?" And although you have three cameras, do your own processing, and have had prints exhibited in international salons, you probably will grin at your date and mug self-consciously as the flash goes off.

But you may be just a little surprised when, about twenty minutes and two drinks later, the camera girl returns with your pictures—and they turn out to be sharp, snappy enlargements, thoroughly dried and mounted in attractive folders. About then you will begin to wonder how speed and quality can be combined so effectively.

If all of this has happened in Madison, Wisconsin, the chances are that the secret of the whole process is the "Photomobile." Property and invention of two ex-GI's, Monte Couch and Art De Jong, the Photomobile is a darkroom on wheels which shuttles between three different night spots. Formerly a conventional milk wagon, it has now been converted into a most unconventional unit for very rapid developing and printing, and the result is the speedy service that most night clubbers now take for granted.

* * *

Couch and De Jong started literally from scratch, but within a year and a half, their venture, known as "Freelance Photographers," has proved itself a successful young business. The photomobile and its equipment represent $4,700 in assets, which includes two Speed Graphics and a 4 x 5 view camera, with accompanying electronic flash units. The latter were purchased because of the shortage of flashbulbs at the time.

* * *

Today they have more orders than they can handle and expansion is becoming a necessity. They are enthusiastic about the Photomobile and believe that it has a place in all types of freelance assignments. With it, a photographer can produce the goods immediately, thereby saving both the buyer and himself a great deal of time and anxiety. Certainly their own experience with it has proved its value in at least one line.

De Jong and Couch now have a thriving business, but it took a lot of persistence, and the ride wasn't always jolly. But today, as the blue truck with the painted camera on its side goes jogging down the street, you'll know that someone's picture is having a merry—and a fast—ride in the one and only Photomobile.

Exercises

1. In any newspaper of your choice, list all the utility articles. In the first column of a chart indicate whether the article was written to aid the reader in becoming more efficient, more useful, more practical, more wealthy, more healthy, wiser, or happier.

2. In the second column indicate the source of the material for each article listed.

3. In a third column indicate those articles that do not meet the four-pointed test that the free-lance should give himself before deciding to write.

4. In a fourth column indicate what kind of illustrative matter was used with each article.

5. Suggest one tip, gained by observation, for a utility article for your near-by metropolitan newspaper.

6. Suggest one tip, gained from conversation, for a utility article for any newspaper magazine feature section. Indicate to which newspaper you would send it.

7. In any magazine of your choice, list the utility articles. In the first column of a chart indicate the type of lead that was used for each article.

8. In the second column of the chart indicate in which person the article was written.

9. In the third column of the chart indicate the type of illustrative matter used for each article.

10. From your two charts write a paragraph of not more than 200 words. Point out the kinds of utility articles that the two publications use.

11. Suggest two tips for utility articles for magazines, and also suggest three possible markets for each one.

12. Suggest illustrations for each of the articles suggested.

Publication Analysis

General Magazines

Compare, by using the chart form illustrated in the Appendix, any four general magazines. There are many magazines of this type and they may be obtained at newsstands, from magazine dealers listed in the Appendix under "Aids for Writers," or in library periodical reading rooms. Suggested ones are *American Magazine, Collier's, Coronet, Cosmopolitan, Life, Look, National Geographic, Pageant, Reader's Digest, Red Book, Saturday Evening Post,* or others of your choice.

Do not spend more than three hours on this report.

I. Identification: Names, publishers, editors, where published, price.

II. Make-up: Including typography, size, style, etc. What do you like about the magazines? What do you not like about them?

III. Advertising: To whom does the advertising appeal? Is it different in any way from that in the other magazines studied? From the advertising, what type of material would you expect to find in the magazines? List at least one tip suggested to you by some advertisement in *each* magazine.

IV. General Policy:
1. From the table of contents, estimate roughly the amount of different material used.
2. What do you think are your chances of selling to these publications?
3. What do you like about the magazines?
4. If you were editor, what would you change in the magazines?

V. Features:
1. What feature articles could you have written for each of the publications?
2. Which types of features seem to predominate?
3. Write a comment concerning the photographs or other illustrative devices used in the publications.
4. Analyze one feature article in each magazine in any way you wish, but do it from the point of view of what you can learn about writing your own articles.
5. How many utility articles did you find in each magazine?

VI. Slogan: Make a slogan for each magazine.

VII. Two Tips: Source, authority, and three possible markets suggested by this study. (Six tips in all, including tips suggested by advertisements.)

CHAPTER 5

The Personal Experience Story

▪▪▪

Interest Depends upon Uniqueness. The interest in a personal experience story depends chiefly upon the extraordinary and unique events with which the account is concerned. People view television, listen to radio, go to movie houses and entertainment palaces, and buy millions of magazines and books because they wish to escape from the commonplace things in their own lives. To satisfy this demand for "literature of escape," editors are in the market for accounts of unusual events and novel happenings. The personal experience article is one concerned with unusual experiences of either the writer or of other people, and is written to entertain, help, or inform the reader.

This type of article, perhaps more than the others, may contain elements of the interview, the utility article, and the personality sketch. Occasionally the personal experience story will contain much that, in part, might be classified as a confession article, except that it must concern the unusual or extraordinary rather than the typical. It is similar to the narrative but differs in that it deals entirely with experiences that are personal and unusual.

Ideas Exist Everywhere. Amateurs as well as professionals may write this type of article. Everyone has taken trips, has had adventures in his diversions or at work, or has done something different or something out of the ordinary that will make interesting features. Of this type were articles entitled, "I've Been Around," or "Duck Hunting in Japan," or "Thrice Married." Everywhere there is material for this type of article, which makes its possibilities for the free-lance as great as those of the interview.

The article may be the writer's own experience, written under his name, or a pseudonym, or anonymously. If the experience is not his own, the feature writer, whom we will call John Jones, may: (1) write it in the third person; (2) "ghost" it, by writing it in the first person as if he were the one who had had the experience, but with the permission of the interviewee, signing the latter's name to it; or (3) write the "by-line" as that of the person who had had the experience, followed by the phrase "as told to John Jones." With the advent of "ghost writing," feature writers realized that, although they were paid well for the "ghosted" manuscripts, the glory of authorship went to the person for whom they were writing. Consequently, someone devised the phrase "as told to," in order to enable the writer to put his name in the by-line, or more accurately, the second by-line underneath the by-line of the person who has had the experiences.

Many public officials, artists, specialists, and scientists use the services of ghost writers. They may not be able to write their own articles or, if they are, they may not have the time to spend in what to them is "the tedious business of composition."

More magazines now have research departments and supply their contributors with research workers who collaborate in obtaining the factual material from research sources. In such cases the writer and the research workers are on a salary basis and their articles are not given a by-line but are published as the work of the magazine staff.

Style Must Be Convincing. Whatever device is used, the writer must present his material realistically and convincingly. The more personal and intimate the tone of the article, the greater the interest.

Descriptions of persons, places, and objects, conversation by means of dialogue, and vivid narrative, all help to make the article more realistic and personal to the reader. Illustrations, such as photographs, drawings, and charts, add immeasurably, as they do in other types of articles, to the reader's interest.

Added Compensation Is Meeting Interesting People. Whereas the newspaper readers and magazine subscribers enjoy reading lively and well-written personal experience articles, the feature writer enjoys gathering the material and writing it. He is brought into contact with interesting people who have done something out of the ordinary, such as "Making $50,000 a Year in the Turkey Business," or "Taking a Dixie Detour." As when writing the utility article, the feature writer is rewarded for his efforts in writing the personal experience story by finding material everywhere and in knowing that there are innumerable markets for this type of feature. A writer will more readily find a market if he analyzes the newspapers and magazines (as is suggested in a later chapter), in order to make his manuscripts and illustrative material conform to the policies and style of the publications to which he submits his articles.

Examples of the Personal Experience Article. The first of the following personal experiences, written in the third person, appeared in *Restaurant Management,* accompanied by several pictures of the restaurant's interior taken by a fellow student who was an experienced press photographer. The author learned that the owner had been written up in the trade paper when he owned a restaurant in another part of the city. He used the idea in a former student feature writer's conclusion as his lead. In a short time the author received a check for $60.00. The second article sold to *Parade,* a syndicated newspaper magazine section. It is an example of a picture story as well as a personal experience since the writer illustrated the vacation with 15 pictures which he had taken. The author wrote of his experiences in the third person. Probably because beginning writers are reticent about writing their experiences in the first person, the third article, too, was based on the writer's own experience in a hospital. It sold for $50.00 to *Today's Health* not only for the patient viewpoint but for the subtle humor which the student injected into his experiences. It was illustrated by several clever sketches since he did not have any pictures to illustrate the points emphasized.

(1)
How Rural Italy Inspired
a New Decorative Theme*

*Using Imported Art To Establish
Authentic Restaurant
Atmosphere.*

BY BRUCE ESTLUND

"However, his imagination is not bounded by his current receipts and profits. He has plans for expansion which will offer even more atmosphere."

These words concluded the article, *An Italian Restaurant Rich in Native Atmosphere,* in the February, 1950, issue of RESTAURANT MANAGEMENT. But the story, describing Mathew Lombardino's Italian Village in Madison, Wis., might well have been tagged: "To be continued," because Mr. Lombardino couldn't satisfy his imagination with only one success.

Mr. Lombardino began by turning over the management of the Italian Village to his nephew. Then, with his wife, he left on a trip to his native Italy—a place he had not seen since his arrival in this Country 32 years ago.

While sightseeing through the length of the sunny, boot-shaped peninsula, Mr. Lombardino began his preparations for a new restaurant he planned to open on his return.

*   *   *

Judged by the type of clientele the place has been attracting since its opening about a year ago, Mr. Lombardino's decorations have proved appropriate. The Garden has become a favorite rendezvous for University of Wisconsin students. But collegians aren't the only ones who have become regular customers. The combination of bright, lively colors, fine art and ornamental iron work has attracted many different groups.

The leisurely atmosphere has lulled many a customer into lingering over dessert and coffee. The proprietor is proud of his art objects and

* Reprinted by permission of *Restaurant Management* and Bruce Estlund.

takes great pains in their display. "Put yourself in the customer's place," he says, "and you'll have a regular and happy business." His creed as a restaurateur is as simple as that, and his two successful ventures testify to its soundness.

"Years ago, when I first came to America, I worked in many kitchens," Mr. Lombardino reminisces. "Over 30 years ago I swore that if I ever owned a restaurant I'd never serve anything to anyone that I wouldn't enjoy completely myself."

And now, with two beautiful and successful restaurants of his own, is Mathew Lombardino finally content? "No sir! I want to have the most beautiful restaurant in the Midwest—no, in the entire Country!"

Considering his past achievements, this appears to be no idle remark. To be on the safe side it might be wise to conclude this part of the Mathew Lombardino story with the words: "To be continued."

(2)

The North
Woods*

*There's a Lake for Every Taste in Wisconsin.
Here's One Family's Choice
for Fish and Fun.*

BY JOHN PRINDLE

Across Northern Wisconsin (and adjoining Michigan, Minnesota and Ontario), thousands of pine-bordered lakes stretch in an almost endless galaxy. To the John Prindle family of Madison, Wis., this vast playground posed a problem: how to single out one lakeside family vacation spot?

When they made their choice, it was a little like stabbing a pin in a map blindfolded. But after a week at Lac Court Oreilles, near Hayward, in Wisconsin's Indian Head country, they were convinced they had made the best possible choice for family vacationing. They marked it down mentally as a place for next year—and probably the year after.

Originally, the attraction was fishing. Hayward is muskellunge country; the world's record muskie (69 pounds, 11 ounces) was caught in nearby Lake Chippewa, dethroning two previous record fish taken from Lac Court Oreilles. But the Prindles found that the

---

* Reprinted by permission of *Parade* (syndicated newspaper magazine) and John Prindle.

lake also had appeal for all the family—John and Ruth Prindle as well as Jimmie, 5, and Johnnie, 3.

*   *   *

Some 13 miles from Moccasin Lodge, the Prindles visited the Court Oreilles Chippewa Indian Reservation. The kids hobnobbed with little Indian children in full costume, while their parents discussed the ceremonial dances which are held twice a week in Hayward during the summer months.

Many of the Indians hire out as fishing guides (fee: $11 a day) to take guests to the best muskie spots. The world's biggest muskie remains to be caught (the Wisconsin Conservation Commission says Lac Court Oreilles has some weighing over 80 pounds); for fishermen shooting at records, a guide is absolutely necessary.

*   *   *

Wherever you choose in the North Woods—and however you choose to get there—you'll find the rugged charm of the great outdoors. And, the Prindles can guarantee you, if you choose Lac Court Oreilles, you'll also find that something extra that makes for ideal family vacationing.

(3)
Are Patients Human?*

BY JOHN L. PAUSTIAN

Have you ever felt that your membership in the human race was in jeopardy? This question may seem trifling and ridiculous to many, but to anyone who has ever been a hospital patient, its significance is readily apparent. In fact, he might even answer in the affirmative. On behalf of the Society of Present and Former Hospital Patients, I should like to start a movement to convince the world that patients definitely are human beings.

One of the great mysteries of our modern society is why an otherwise normal human being becomes something akin to a zoological specimen upon hospital admittance. The patient is physically sub-par, it is true; but more often than not the medical staff, in its attitude toward him, seems to assume he is mentally incompetent, too.

* Reprinted by permission of *Today's Health* and John L. Paustian.

Consider for a moment what happens to the unsuspecting soul who leaves the normality of the outside world to enter a strange new existence behind the medical iron curtain. First, he is shorn of his civilian individuality and becomes a nonentity in drab hospital attire, and a number in the files. Next, the innermost secrets of his life are extracted from him in a manner that would cause a Gallup pollster to blush.

As our friend's hectic orientation continues, he is hoisted into a stilted bed. Before he can acclimate himself to the dizzying altitude a thermometer is stuck in his mouth, an urgent hand is wrapped around his wrist and a set of busy fingers beats out a tattoo on his chest. At this point he may already have come to the realization that hospital peace and quiet is an overworked myth.

*　*　*

Our hospital guest soon learns that medics aren't the only ones who forget that patients are human. At times the public forgets. We all know the type who is afraid even to go near a hospital for a visit, no matter how close a friend is involved. Then there's the visitor who enters the hospital, but unsteadily approaches the bedside as if he were confronting some unearthly creature in human form. He seems to forget that this patient displayed average interests and tendencies just a few days or weeks ago. Just because he is temporarily horizontal, it does not mean he has forgotten about everyday human activities.

The reclining host, if he could choose, would center the conversation about familiar things—late news, gossip, sports or movies. It's wise to keep the patter in a light vein, but he doesn't expect you to amuse him with a steady stream of snappy repartee. Even Bob Hope requires gag writers. Don't avoid all reference to his condition. After all, it is of immediate importance to him, and if you don't mention it or inquire about his progress at all, he may get a mistaken idea of your concern. But don't overdo it and display morbid fascination; you should bring in part of the cheerful outside world with you.

A prize exhibit is the type of visitor who is just running over with a complete list of everyone who has ever had the same ailment. To make the statistics complete, this cheery soul usually includes the number who have died of it.

Let's get going on this "Be Kind to Patients" movement. Possibly recuperation would be aided if this simple maxim were remembered by one and all: patients are human, too!

Exercises

1. Select a magazine section of a newspaper and list the personal experience stories in chart form. In the first column indicate the elements of the other types of articles that you find.

2. In a second column indicate whether the experience is that of the writer or of others.

3. In a third column indicate the purpose the author had in writing the feature.

4. Indicate whether the article was written under the author's name, a pseudonym, anonymously, ghosted, or as told to, and indicate the reason that the writer adopted the method he did.

5. In a brief paragraph discuss the devices the writers used to make the articles personal and realistic.

6. Select two general magazines and list the personal experience stories in each in chart form. In the first column list the sources of the information from which the writers obtained the material.

7. In the second column, in less than four words, indicate what is distinctive about each article that influenced the editor to buy it.

8. In the third column list the number of pictures, drawings, or charts for each article.

9. In the fourth column indicate whether the experience is that of the writers or of others.

10. In a paragraph of not more than 200 words enumerate the points that you learned to make the personal experience stories you write more realistic and personal in order that editors will buy.

11. List a tip for each of the following types: personal experience of your own; personal experience of others; and a ghosted or "told to" story. Indicate three markets for each.

Publication Analysis

Business, Farm, Trade, Professional and Association Periodicals

Compare, by using chart form as illustrated in the Appendix, one magazine of each of the above types. There are thousands of them and they may be obtained at newsstands, from magazine dealers as listed under "Writer's Aids" in the Appendix, in library periodical reading rooms; or they may be borrowed from subscribers. Some suggested ones in the business field: *Department Store Economist, Forbes' Magazine, Hardware Age, Motor;* in the farm field: *Capper's Farmer, Farm Journal, Farm and Ranch, Farm Quarterly, Ford Farming, Milk Review, Successful Farming;* in the trade field: *Aero Digest, American Baker, American Druggist, American Restaurant, Floral Telegraph Delivery, Fountain and Fast Food;* in the professional field: the *American Doctor, American Rifleman,*

Association Periodicals, *Oral Hygiene,* the *American Scholar, Law and Order, National Geographic, The Sample Case,* or others of your choice.

Do not spend more than three hours on this report.

I. Identification: Name, publisher, editor, where published, price of each magazine.
II. Make-up:
1. What do you like about each magazine?
2. What do you dislike about each magazine?
III. Advertising:
1. What is the difference in the appeal in the advertising of the magazines?
2. From the advertising what kind of a reader do you visualize for each publication?
3. One tip from the advertising of each magazine (four tips in all).
IV. General Policy:
1. If you were editor, would you change any one of these magazines in any way?
2. Give reason for above answer.
3. What types of articles could you submit to each magazine?
V. Feature Articles:
1. What types of articles do you find in each publication and to whom do they appeal?
2. Analyze a personal experience article in each magazine and list five suggestions for improving the writing of your own feature articles.
3. Did you find any "as told to" by-lines?
VI. Four Tips: One from each type of magazine; source, authority for the articles suggested, and three possible markets for each one that were suggested by the study of these magazines.

CHAPTER 6

The Confession Article

Popular Because of Tone. The confession article is popular because readers like: (1) unvarnished tales related in a confidential style, in which the writer confesses or reveals his "sins," shortcomings, or frustrations; or (2) exposés of conditions in classes of society with which the reader is unfamiliar. It may aid the reader by showing how personal faults and problems, which may be similar to his own, have been overcome either by the writer or the person about whom he is writing. An article of this type is "How I Improved My Disposition." Or it may present to the reader an intimate revelation that will give him an insight into some phases of life with which he is not familiar. His attention may be attracted in order to interest him in helping to remedy conditions or in aiding the solution of problems revealed. Such an article was "The Life of a Summer Hotel Waitress."

The confession article is a feature in which the writer reveals in a confidential tone: (1) personal and intimate experiences of his own, or those of someone else, which he would not care to give in a signed article; or (2) the "inside story" of conditions or problems normally unknown to the average reader. It may entertain, reform, or inform the reader. It may be written seriously or humorously.

Although the confession is similar to the personal experience article, it is different in that the things related, revealed, or con-

108

fessed should be typical rather than exceptional or unusual. A writer may relate his own confessions, or he may obtain interesting revelations of others. They may concern emotional problems, personal conflict, human greed or desire, fears or hopes. Existing conditions may be criticized constructively and entertainingly by the device of the confession article. The reader's concern in problems about which he previously knew little or nothing may be aroused. The tone, however, must always be confidential—as though the writer were whispering in the reader's ear.

Experiences Must Be Typical. The experiences described must be typical of those of other human beings. Facts and figures may be incorporated to prove that the incidents are not unusual. The more nearly the writer can make the problems correspond to those of the reader, the greater will be the appeal.

Illustrative material for this type of article is more difficult to plan. Frequently the person, or persons, concerned in the confession article does not wish his picture included. Sometimes the confession is of such a nature that charts or graphs add to the clarity and simplicity. In confessions written anonymously, photographs cannot be used because they might reveal the identity of the confessor. Pen and ink sketches often make good illustrations.

Plan and Style of Writing May Vary. The personal or psychological confession may be written to show the author's fall from a happy, prosperous existence to one of continuous calamity. It may present forceful examples to the reader, to warn him to avoid similar failures. Or, if the article is of the opposite type, which is so popular, the author will show how errors of judgment or faults of character were overcome and how in the end he triumphed over all. The reader is thus told how he, too, may do the same. Such articles were "I Cured Myself of the Blues," "The Dentist Made a New Man Out of Me," and "The Confessions of an Undergraduate."

By writing anonymously, or under an assumed name, a confessor may write more freely and intimately, since a large part of the success of the article depends upon the confidential tone in which the revelations are related to the reader. To write anonymously, however, is no excuse for poor workmanship. Simplicity and directness characterize the style of the confession article. The more straightforward the manner in which it is written, the more effective it will be. If the writer is "ghosting" the confessions of another, he must try to put himself in that person's place and reveal his thoughts and experiences as clearly as though they were his own. Even though this type of article may be written anonymously, readers are keenly interested. On the printed page it takes the place of the confidential neighborhood gossip that people like to hear, even though they are reluctant to admit their interest. The happy ending is greatly in favor. No matter how realistic the confession is, the writer should always show that there was a reformation or that experience taught its lesson. If one writes with faith in his own story, he may present many good sermons that will leave the right impression without appearing didactic. If the author wishes his confession to appear without his name, he may so indicate in the note to the editor on the cover sheet. This is explained in Chapter 14, "Preparation of the Manuscript."

Writer Rewarded by Self-Analysis. In addition to the financial reward and satisfaction of seeing one's confessions (or those of others) in print, there is the added advantage that the writer may benefit from the self-analysis, or analysis of others, that he makes in revealing his problems or existing conditions to the reader. In helping the reader, the writer may help himself.

When considering the markets, the writer must ask himself who buys magazines containing confession articles. He will find that housemaids and policemen, housewives and business men and women, priests and gamblers, spinsters and bachelors, youths and maidens, laborers and professional men, the young and the old— everyone—are readers of these tales. They all want to read about something that might have happened to them. Markets are abundant and of great variety. Many pulp magazines consist largely of confession or "true story" articles, and almost every general and class publication includes at least one confession article in each issue. The successful writer of confessions studies all the magazines that print such articles. Their policies concerning the kind of confessions they print differ widely, and he must know the differences in order to "slant" his articles accordingly.

Examples of the Confession Article. Personal and psychological confessions as well as those of the exposé type are popular with mass and class readers. The first two of the following articles were selected from *Coronet.* They each concern problems that are similar to ones the readers experience. Why did *Coronet* buy them? After reading them you will agree that each writer treated the subject cleverly, skillfully, and in a style that attracts and holds the attention of the reader, although his problem may be a "fresh-air fiend," or a poker or bridge addict. The third article, selected from *Children,* has elements of the narrative and the utility article as well as of the confession article. It is written in a serious and informative tone but covers the problem tactfully and understandingly.

(1)
I Married a Vegetarian*

*Curiosity and Sympathy Are Served Up
in Equal Portions When People
Learn That . . .*

BY JOHN McGIFFERT

What happened to me could happen to you. You meet a charming girl—beautiful, intelligent, humorous, understanding. You commit yourself; she appears to care; you set the date. Then you discover the shocking truth: she is a confirmed vegetarian! You, of course, are a confirmed meat-eater.

What's to be done? Should you try to convert her? Impossible. Should she try to convert you? Unwise. Should you call the whole thing off? Unthinkable.

So all I did was marry her. It has been two years now, and we are still on better than adequate terms.

My wife is a non-meat-eater, and I'll thank you to let it go at that and not ask why. I refuse to plunge into the various complexities that a conviction like hers can stem from—complexities that may

---

* Reprinted by permission of *Coronet* (copyright by Esquire Inc.) and John McGiffert.

be hygienic, metaphysical, mystical, emotional or moral. Refusal to eat flesh, fish or fowl is, I believe, a legitimate human attitude; but it is not one of my attitudes. Hence our first two years of marriage have called for more than the usual adjustments.

Once we decided to get married, we made a provisional nutritional contract for a two-year period (the contract has now expired and is up for renewal). "It makes me unhappy to have meat (etc.) in the house," my wife said, "so unless it makes you too unhappy, we will have no meat (etc.) at home. Since you eat lunch out except on weekends, eat whatever you want for lunch. And when we eat together at a restaurant, you can also eat what you want—I think."

This seemed to me a fair arrangement depending slightly, of course, on what our home meals turned out to be. Fortunately, a spiritless plate of unadorned vegetables did not prove to be her idea of a fine meal. She had only the mildest reservations about eggs, on which I dote. She was partial to flavorsome sauces. Her salads were vital with garlic, cheese, avocado, nuts and even raisins. In addition, her entrees were actually stimulating.

My wife, I learned, was a sensitive disher-up of delicacies; of spaghetti and macaronis in all their bewildering varieties, and of rarer forms like lasagna, manicotti and especially gnocchi—all with garlic sauce; of artichokes baked with garlic; of mushrooms stuffed with bread crumbs, cheese and garlic; of eggplant in countless combinations, tinged with garlic; and of a sensational lentil soup in which the ingredients cannot be isolated.

True, I occasionally stopped off at the corner delicatessen on my way home and bolted a guilty salami on rye. Once or twice, I pretended to go for a walk in the evening and actually dropped in at the tavern for a quick steak. But these were only the early aberrations.

My day-to-day eating became casual. I ate flesh, fish or fowl for lunch five days a week, and feasted on my wife's exotic cookery in the evenings. I even came to appreciate her favorite dictum: "To cook meat (etc.) is nothing. You stick a hunk of something under a broiler or into an oven. To cook without meat (etc.) calls for imagination and manual labor."

*   *   *

I am happy to say that my wife has never urged me to eat at a restaurant of the strictly vegetarian or "health" variety. Just last week, in fact, she said to me: "You know that 'Verve and Vitality' place downtown? I ate there today. It's nothing but a vegetarian clip joint!"

All in all, I see no reason for not putting our provisional nutritional contract on a permanent basis. I propose to draw up the necessary papers—as soon as I have devised an amendment to cover the one serious dilemma that remains: the midnight snack. It still seems to me that a carton of creamed cottage cheese is mighty cheerless fare for the wee small hours.

(2)
I Was Cured of TV*

*The Story of a Confirmed Addict
and His Long, Hard Fight
Back to Life.*

By E. A. BATCHELOR

When in the course of human events, an individual has recovered from a malady previously believed to be incurable, a respect for the good of mankind requires that he declare the causes of his recovery.

If that is reminiscent of the first paragraph in the Declaration of Independence, the resemblance is purely intentional. Specifically, I have been saved from a fate worse than death—hopeless addiction to television. I have rejoined the human race from which I was snatched by Channels 2 to 7 a matter of approximately five years ago.

Today, I can either take television or leave it. But instead of the intolerance that frequently characterizes the reformed, my resurrection has left me with a heart filled with sympathy and compassion for those many people who still are in bondage. To them I relate my story.

First of all, let me warn my readers that there is no quick and easy way to shake off TV addiction. It is a long and a hard process, fraught with disappointments. Your gains will come slowly: one day of backsliding may wipe out all the progress made in a week. But it can be done, and whatever the price, you will find it worth paying.

Next, I began to read the headlines on the front page. From them I learned that a lot of things were going on in the world to which television was giving scant attention. From headlines I progressed to rather a thorough reading of the papers, even to the extent of taking time for this activity while all channels of the TV set were offering competition. Then, it was only a matter of a few weeks before I found myself thumbing through magazines I had once subscribed to.

* Reprinted by permission of *Coronet* (copyright by Esquire, Inc.) and E. A. Batchelor.

At first, I merely looked at the pictures, but in due time I progressed to reading some of the articles. In fact, I developed such an avid interest in some of the material that I blushed guiltily when I passed the television set.

Full emancipation came at Christmastime when some people who didn't know about my abasement sent me books. Most of these had exciting jackets and in due time, I opened one just for curiosity. It was a fortunate step, because before I knew it, I had begun to read the text and continued to do so from cover to cover.

But still I didn't feel that my cure had been complete, for these Christmas books were of the type known as "light reading." At last came the happy day when I tackled a ponderous volume that had neither pictures nor entertainment *per se*. I picked it up as a test of my resolution to be free, expecting to read it or bust. It was a grim chore but I made it, without skimming, and I retained a fair idea of the book's contents.

Then I knew that I had been saved. Then I determined, by way of showing my gratitude for my escape, to tell others about it so that they, too, might try to reestablish themselves as human beings. This article is the result. You, too, can be saved—if you are willing to heed my story, and to tackle the problem with the same energy and will power that I have displayed.

(3)
How We Told
Our Adopted Children*

By Kitte Turmell

We have had the good fortune—my husband and I—to adopt two children, each in infancy, 3 years apart. We have been able to tell our son and daughter—successfully we think—without strain or self-consciousness—that we adopted them. Our son, the first adopted, very soon heard the word "adopted" in improvised lullabies; when he was 2 he was proud to translate its meaning as "you picked me out"; at 3 he joyfully went with us to the nursery on the day when we were at last to take home his newly acquired sister.

How did we know what to say and when to say it? By asking advice of the social agency that found our son for us, as many other parents of adopted children have done. Ours was the Children's Home

---

* Reprinted by permission of *The Children's Bureau and Children* and Kitte Turmell.

Society of California, a State-licensed private organization. A staff member of the agency suggested something like this:

The story of adoption should start as soon as possible. A baby can be helped to feel that "being adopted" is something that makes him loved, even before he is old enough to learn that being adopted is being "chosen." The story of his adoption should unfold as his understanding unfolds. When the story unfolds gradually, and is pleasantly told, he will think of it as natural and pleasing. He will look at it just as the parents do who have gone through the experience of choosing a child who is to be theirs for life.

The story starts with the way you say "adopted." If the word is used often, affectionately, easily, with an endearing phrase or a song or a nursery rhyme, and emphasized with a hug or kiss, it will carry warm overtones. It should never be heard first as a playmate's taunt or an adult's whisper.

As soon as a toddler asks, "What's 'dopted, mommy?" he is ready for an explanation of "chosen" or "picked out." This can be made personal, as a compliment to the child's desirability, with the phrase, "We chose—or picked—or wanted—you."

The age at which a child is old enough to be told more about it varies with different children, the worker told us; it is usually between 3 and 4, and certainly before school age. Whenever he does ask, or is ready to be encouraged to ask, tell him simply as much of the story as he can then follow. If you repeat it, and amplify it a little as his interest grows with his capacity to understand, he can enjoy this true story as much as he does a favorite fairy tale.

"To be our very own for always"

But say it your own way, the social worker's advice continued, using as much as you like of this suggested version: For a long time we wanted a baby just like you. We were lonely; our house seemed empty. Then someone who knew where there were some babies who wanted mommies and daddies helped us find you. You were bright and lovable and beautiful, just as you are now. You were the baby we wanted, so we brought you to your new home to be our very own for always.

*   *   *

Be logical and truthful in whatever you say. Do not parry a specific question with a vague answer.

If there are any could-be-disturbing factors that need to be told bring them out early, and gradually; when a child grows up knowing the essential facts they will become as much a part of him as his build or his voice.

Give as vivid a word picture as you can about his natural parents. Often curiosity is easily satisfied with a pleasing description. Tell what the child seems to relish, but do not build up such a fascinating picture that the child will feel robbed when he compares, in his imagination, his natural parents with his adoptive parents. He should not be given the feeling that he has been deprived of a more interesting life or a more colorful heritage than you, his parents, can offer him.

Do not let your child feel isolated by his adoption. Talk with him about other adopted people he knows about or that he can be introduced to in normal social contacts. If his national background is different from yours to a marked degree, see to it that he is helped to like and respect "his own kind." He may learn about his background at school, or through his reading, or through other association with the culture of his forebears. Perhaps he will find out more about it through travel.

Satisfy the craving of every adopted child to be told that he bears some resemblance to his adoptive parents, or to some other relative whom he would like to resemble. Often environment develops similarities that you can point out by identifying "his mother's ready smile" or "his dad's dependability" as a characteristic shared by parent and child.

School the child against any future embarrassment from prying questions by explaining that he may tell as much or as little as he chooses about his adoption story. Help him to realize that he can be proud to tell anyone that he and his parents are more than satisfied with every detail of his history.

Long ago my husband and I learned that we also could ward off impertinent questions (and you'll be surprised to know how many strangers are bold enough to ask whether the adopted child's first parents were married). We say that we want the child to be the first to tell his story to outsiders, in order that he may tell as much or as little as he chooses, without feeling, uncomfortably, that others might know more than he does about his personal history.

Perhaps the keystone of the arch through which the child enters into knowledge of his history is this principle, as stated by the children's agency:

"You must guard against projecting any emotions that might disturb the child about his adoption story. He will be influenced by your attitude; aware of any tension or uneasiness. If you are afraid that the child will not accept his true story, then you, his new parents, need to reexamine your hearts, rebuild your feelings of security, refresh your mind on all the favorable factors that convinced you before the adoption that this was the very child for you. Until you have quieted any qualms of your own you are not emotionally ready to start the continued story we are here considering. If you do learn to tell the story well, your reward will be your child's acceptance of his adoption and of you."

Exercises

1. Turn through the magazine feature section of some newspaper and list the confession articles in chart form.

2. In the first column indicate whether the article reveals the writer's "sins" or is an exposé of conditions of life.

3. In the second column indicate the purpose the author had in writing the article.

4. Indicate in the third column the methods by which the writers gave a confidential tone to the articles.

5. In the fourth column list the number and types of illustrations used.

6. In the fifth column indicate whether the writers wrote anonymously or under their own by-lines.

7. Turn through three general magazines with which you are familiar and list in chart form the confession articles.

8. Indicate in the first column whether the confession is a revelation or an exposé and if it is written seriously or humorously.

9. List the purpose of each article in the second column.

10. List the methods by which the writers give a confidential tone in the third column.

11. In the fourth column indicate the devices by which the writers kept the articles from being didactic in tone.

12. In the fifth column indicate the probable readers of the articles as listed in this chapter.

13. Indicate in the sixth column the number and types of illustrations used with the magazine confessions.

14. Write not more than a 200-word discussion of the differences in content and method of confession articles in magazine newspaper sections and in general magazines.

15. Suggest a tip for a newspaper confession and one for a magazine and include a market for each.

Publication Analysis

Women's Magazines and Men's Magazines

Compare, by using chart form as illustrated in the Appendix, two magazines of each of the above types. There are a large number of first- and second-class magazines for each sex and they may be obtained at newsstands, from magazine dealers listed under "Aids for Writers" in the Appendix, or in library periodical reading rooms. Some suggested women's magazines: *Good Housekeeping, Ladies' Home Journal, McCall's Magazine, Woman's Day, Woman's Home Companion;* men's magazines: *Argosy, Esquire, Male, Men, Sir, Stag, Swank, True, Gentleman;* both sexes: *Life, Lifetime Living,* or others of your choice.

Do not spend more than three hours on this report.

I. Identification: Name, publisher, editor, where published, price.

II. Make-up:
  1. What do you like and dislike about the make-up of each magazine?
  2. Point out briefly how they differ in make-up and indicate which you think has the best make-up.

III. Advertising:
  1. What appeals do you find in the advertising copy?
  2. Give a tip for a feature article suggested by the advertising in each publication.

IV. Appeals:
  1. To what class of reader do the features in each magazine appeal?
  2. Discuss briefly the kinds and variety of appeals in the feature articles in each publication.

V. Feature Articles:
  1. Classify the confession articles as to type.
  2. List three points concerning the style of confession articles in each magazine that will help you in writing confessions.
  3. What did you learn concerning the other types of features in reference to type, length, quality, and illustrations?
  4. How many of the articles are written by well-known or "big" names?

VI. Two Tips: Source, authority, and three possible markets for each tip suggested by the study of these magazines.

CHAPTER 7

The Personality Sketch

Deals with Achievements. Readers like to know the innermost details of personality and character of prominent and successful people, and even of some who are not in the limelight. The personality sketch, success article, profile, biography, or vignette (as it is termed in some offices), is therefore in great demand by editors of newspaper magazine sections, syndicates, trade and business publications, general and class magazines as well as for TV scripts.

The purpose of such an article is to portray the intimate details of the character and personality of someone who has done something important or shown great character in his or her every day living. They are written so vividly that the reader will feel he has not only met the subject of the sketch face to face, but knows him personally. This type of article has a strong reader appeal. Everyone desires to attain success, and he hopes that in reading about the eminent or near-eminent he will find the key to their success and be able to benefit thereby. Perhaps the interest in this type of feature is due to the fact that the reader is interested, first of all, in himself and is constantly seeking guidance in the solution of his own problems and adjustments. He reads of the struggles of others and how they avoided failure in the hope that he can find a way to overcome his own hardships and handicaps.

Personality, success sketches, or profiles are features dealing with the achievements of men and women, prominent or otherwise, and how they surmounted obstacles to acquire character, fame, or fortune. They serve to inspire, to instruct, and to guide the reader in seeking solutions to his problems or adjustments to life about him.

Although this type of article has elements in common with those previously discussed, it differs from them in many ways. It gives interesting information about the interviewee's life rather than just his opinions, as the interview does. It may be like the utility article in that it aims to help the reader, but its major concern is to inspire the reader to improve his personality or character. It differs from the personal experience article in that the experiences, as a rule, are not unusual. It is similar to the confession article in so far as it reveals intimate experiences, but they are not so personal that the subject of the sketch wishes to keep his identity concealed. On the contrary, he probably is glad to share them with others who may be inspired and helped in overcoming difficulties, for the aim of the personality sketch is to give inspiration, instruction, or guidance.

Gathering Material Depends on Skill. In gathering material for the personality sketch, a beginner will attain success more quickly by interviewing and writing up little-known people who have attained some degree of success. Skill in interviewing and in drawing out information concerning character and personality of lesser celebrities should be acquired before interviewing those better known. That is why newspaper training and trade paper writing are invaluable to one who aspires to become a writer of interview and personality sketches. It teaches him how to see sources of material, to interview skillfully, and to write quickly and accurately.

The novice's first sketch may be about an old gentleman who lost his job because of his age but who turned coppersmith and attained some financial success. It may concern the clever puppet show by which a young physician has become somewhat well known. Beginners will find that it is better to leave the great statesmen, theatrical, television, radio, and screen stars, and others already renowned, until they have improved their techniques for gathering material and writing it. It is not that the already well-known and prominent people are harder to interview, but the writer will obtain better sketches after he has developed more skill in drawing out the interviewee to relate incidents that have not appeared in previous articles. Everywhere the writer looks he will see opportunities for success-angle personality sketches about people who overcame obstacles and achieved success, and whose experiences will serve as inspiration to readers.

As in writing all features, the markets should be fairly well determined before the article is too definitely planned or the interview obtained. The policies of publications should be studied: (1) to determine whether the aim of the article is to afford food for thought; (2) to inspire to action; (3) to give guidance; (4) to estimate the length of the publication's manuscripts; and (5) to see kinds and number of photographs or drawings the publication would be likely to use. Then, when the writer meets his interviewee, he will know what illustrative material he wants. He can arrange for the pictures and thus save time for the celebrity and for himself. He should secure informal snapshots rather than professional portraits; if possible, he also should obtain pictures of the person as a child or youth, for they will add to the reader interest of the article.

Sources of Material. Material may be obtained: (1) by conversations with people who know intimately the subject of the sketch; (2) from an interview with the person to be described, supplemented by talks with others who can contribute information; (3) from printed sources, reference books (such as *Who's Who* and the *Who's Who* in the person's specialized field; and (4) from friends and associates of the subject of the sketch. It is easier for the beginner to write a straight personality sketch if he selects a subject whom he knows. Until he has had considerable practice, he should not attempt to write of those whom he does not know, or whom he knows but slightly. But he may, without any experience, attempt a personality sketch with a success angle, for trade or business publications and, like thousands of beginning free-lance writers before him, receive an acceptance almost immediately.

After some experience, however, a writer will be able in a single interview to get impressions from which to write a satisfactory sketch, because he will have learned to observe carefully, to judge people quickly and accurately, and to know how to find additional material to weave in with his own impressions. Some publications combine the personality sketch with the interview by printing the sketch followed by the interview.

If one wishes to specialize in this type of writing, he will find additional prospects for his sketches by scanning memberships of clubs and organizations, particularly business and service clubs. Usually the secretaries are pleased to furnish suggestions about members who overcame obstacles and who are doing unusual and successful things. Newspaper stories, pictures, radio, and television will serve as tips for articles for syndicates, trade and business publications, general or class magazines.

The writer must bear in mind that personality stories do not always deal with people who, because of fame or riches, are prominent in the day's news or the world's work. Many excellent stories are to be found in the personalities of those who have overcome physical handicaps and struggled to success. These stories are worthy of the time and attention of any writer. They have a wider human interest appeal than do the stories of the eminent and wealthy. On every college campus there are available achievement stories of talented young people who are educating themselves by their own efforts. Publications are always in the market for this type of success story because of the inspiration and help it will give their readers. Even newspaper files, previously published articles, and books are sources of ideas and material for personality sketches.

Persistence must be one of the qualifications of the writer of personality sketches. He will meet many people who (1) are indifferent to being written up; (2) will not see the story in their own achievements; (3) will refuse to be interviewed from a sense of false modesty; or (4) will be afraid their rivals will profit if they reveal the methods by which they attained success. Occasionally a writer will meet someone who simply cannot talk in an interview, but who, upon the request of the writer, is willing to write out a few notes and facts about his business or invention or whatever has been the foundation of his success. From these notes, a skillful, observant interviewer will be able to write a marketable personality sketch.

Writing the Sketch. The easiest part of the personality sketch is the writing, if the writer has gathered all the material available and given careful thought to the selection of facts, data, and details. As he plans his outline, he must keep in mind the policy of the magazine at which he is "slanting." To sell success stories, the writer must learn to distinguish between the types suitable for the newspaper feature section, syndicates, trade and business publications, general and class magazines. For the newspaper, syndicate, and magazine, the human interest angle should be emphasized, but for the trade and business publication the characteristics that made the person successful in his business or profession should be stressed.

Personality sketches should contain the following: (1) biographical data; (2) description of the person, the details of the setting, surroundings, and general atmosphere; (3) quotations from the interviewee, in which he gives his principles for attaining success and the advice or guidance to others; (4) a general account of success in the words of the interviewee, or friends, or of the writer; and (5) the person's philosophy of life.

To portray the subject of the sketch to the reader, the method of describing characters in fiction may well be adopted to avoid using general descriptive terms, but by: (1) actually describing the subject's personal appearance, demeanor, facial expressions, and dress; (2) telling of characteristic mannerisms and actions; (3) using direct quotations in a characteristic manner; (4) giving opinions of others about him; and (5) showing how his friends, associates, and employees react to him. Any combination of methods should be used that will enable the writer to make his readers feel they have met the person face to face, heard him speak, seen him act, and know his thoughts or opinions sufficiently to understand his past life and see how he attained success.

The reader may be enabled to visualize the subject through a short opening paragraph of vivid sentences that (1) dramatize the hero before he attained success or renown; (2) describe the person as he is now, after he has become known; (3) answer the question of what is the secret of his success; (4) quote the motto or principle by which the subject has lived and to which he attributes his success; or (5) give the chronological beginning, if that is of sufficient interest. No matter how the story is written, it must be handled sympathetically and understandingly. If the article concerns one who has overcome physical handicaps, it must be free from any suggestion of pity or it will thwart the very purpose for which it was written.

Personality sketches, more than any other kind of article, demand that the writer have a definite purpose, as well as market, in mind before beginning to write. If the article is about a person in some unique work, then its aim would be to inform. If it is about a character in a field of work that others could enter, it would instruct. If it is about someone in hazardous employment or work that requires unusual fortitude, or one who is victorious over illness or triumphs over old age, then it would inspire.

Aids in Humanizing Writer's Style. Many beginning writers overlook the advantage, both financial and inspirational, of writing personality or success stories. The field is wide and offers excellent material and well-paying markets. Such copy is eagerly sought by all kinds of publications and syndicates. Nothing brings the writer closer to humanity nor develops his understanding and sympathy (prime requisites of the writer) than does the writing of personality stories; and nothing can be more inspiring to him than to relate the achievements of men and women with the knowledge that others, too, will be inspired.

Examples of Success and Personality Sketches. Ideas for sketches come from many sources. The first one, which sold to *American Milk Review* was developed by a student writer by background reading, interviewing, and writing it in a descriptive, factual style that should inspire any reader. The second article selected from *Esquire* shows how one's interest may be developed into an article if one slants judiciously and writes enthusiastically as did the serviceman author who was on foreign soil when he wrote of his favorite historical character. Yet some people say you can't sell articles about historical people or events. The third article, selected from a serviceman's magazine, *Leatherneck*, also was written by a student taking the United States Armed Forces Institute feature writing course. It was selected because of its thorough coverage, its interesting style of writing, and to show how even a busy soldier can look about him and find article ideas that sell. The sales of these three articles totaled $300.00. Beginners can write successfully if they *will* to do so.

(1)
Portrait
of a
Dairyman*

By Robert E. Koehler

Dotting the rolling, grassy farmlands of Wisconsin are herds which produce almost one-sixth of the nation's entire milk supply and earn for the Badger state the title of "America's Dairyland." But Wisconsin dairymen have never been content with mere quantity alone; they likewise produce some of the finest milk on the market.

One of the state's top boosters of quality milk products is John C. Schuman, president and general manager of Dairy Distributors, Inc. Co-operative, whose new $500,000 pasteurizing plant in Milwaukee is a dream of cleanliness.

The story of the co-operative is also the story of a man who through the years has fought for and promoted sanitation in milk production, both as a dairy plant executive and as a legislator. Serving as a state senator for eight years in the 1920's, Mr. Schuman was instrumental in developing Wisconsin's quality milk program and laws regulating the operation of co-operatives.

*   *   *

Operating 45 routes in Milwaukee and 16 out of the Watertown area, Dairy Distributors produce a complete line of dairy products.

* Reprinted by permission of *American Milk Review* and Robert E. Koehler.

But the organization's real success is found in almost unbelievable sanitation, a word that has been part of Mr. Schuman's active vocabulary ever since he entered the dairy industry.

President of the Dairy Research association, a statewide co-operative group, he is also a director of the Midland Co-operative Dairy association. It is because of men like John C. Schuman that Wisconsin has earned its great prestige in the dairy world.

(2)

Indomitable
Old Hickory*

Rough Andy Jackson, 7th President,
Gambled with a Pistol
for His Lady.

By H. E. Wassam

By the beginning of the nineteenth century, most Americans had given up settling their differences with dueling pistols. The honor involved had come to seem hardly worth the obvious risk. But there were still plenty of hot-blooded young men who found an outlet for their energies and imagination in pistols at dawn.

Inevitably, the bone of contention that brought two young blades to the field of honor was politics or a woman, and it was the memory of a careless remark about a lady that led to one of the famous encounters in American history, involving a future United States President and the best pistol shot in Tennessee.

Normally, a duel was simply a slightly modified form of murder. The romance was largely a fabrication of fiction writers.

This one was different.

The cause was the good name of a beautiful lady with a not-unblemished past. Before the matter was finished, a story of courage, iron will, hate, love and death had unfolded that sounded as if it had come from the pen of a Dumas.

It happened well over a century ago, in 1806, in a secluded place in southern Kentucky, just after sunrise. If the result had been only slightly different, Andrew Jackson would never have seen the inside of the White House.

The story begins with love. Old Hickory was smitten with a pretty

* Reprinted by permission of *Esquire* and H. E. Wassam.

lady named Rachel Robards. Sometime after they were married they discovered that Rachel had not been legally divorced from her previous husband. This could scarcely fail to cause talk, and so Jackson, never a temperate man, swore he would kill any man who besmirched the name of his beloved Rachel.

* * *

It was just a question of whom he would hear about first. The gentleman turned out to be a dashing young Nashville socialite named Charles Dickinson, reported to have spoken lightly of Old Hickory's lady.

* * *

There was a dull clack as Jackson's pistol stopped at half-cock. Deliberately he drew the hammer back again, aimed and fired.

Dickinson staggered and dropped to the ground with a ball through his stomach. He died that night, after fourteen hours of agonizing pain, without having learned how close he had come to killing Old Hickory. His shot had broken two of Jackson's ribs close to the heart; the loose fit of Jackson's coat and the thin body had fooled him.

Andrew Jackson never fully recovered from his wound. But he had avenged the honor of his lady. And he lived to become President. When people said he had been lucky, Andy always admitted it. "But," he would say, "I would have hit Dickinson if he had shot me through the brain."

(3)
Lady Recruiter*

*A Pleasant Smile and Sparkling Eyes Convince
Skeptic Gals That Life in the Corps
Is for Them.*

STORY AND PHOTOS
By MSgt. Fred G. Braitsch, Jr.

Frances is a pretty girl with flashing brown eyes. Her neatly starched uniform and "Welcome to the Corps" smile give her that Marine Recruiting Poster look.

And that's her job—recruiting girls like herself for the lady Marines.

* Reprinted by permission of *Leatherneck* and Fred G. Braitsch, Jr.

Sergeant Frances M. Capps was sworn into the Corps two and a half years ago; now she's back in her own native North Carolina answering the southern belles' questions about the Women Marines.

She was fresh out of Recruiters' School at Parris Island and full of enthusiasm when she reported to Major W. E. Brandon, Officer-in-Charge of Marine Corps recruiting for her home state. "I like coming back to North Carolina," she told her new boss. "I know the people here and from my own experience, I know how North Carolina parents feel about their sons and daughters entering the service."

Major Brandon smiled at the eager young girl sitting across from him. "It's not going to be easy Sergeant Capps," he told her frankly, "there'll be times when you'll wish that you'd never become a recruiter. The travel will be tiring and the task trying, but I believe you can do the job."

Frances has found that recruiting women is far from an easy task. Most women applicants must be completely sold on the Women Marines before they'll enlist. Good employment, skeptical parents, and unsympathetic boy friends are the woman recruiter's biggest obstacles. But Frances is a good talker; her pleasant smile and sparkling brown eyes have convinced many a skeptical gal that life in the Corps is for her.

Along with interviewing applicants and talking to their parents, the public relations and information aspect has equal importance with recruiting. Frances drops into newspaper offices to place news articles on the Women Marines; she visits radio stations to tell audiences what the women of the Marine Corps are doing. Then, there are speeches to be made at high schools and women's clubs.

Talking to newspaper reporters and radio announcers is a chore Frances likes. "They seem to be such nice friendly people," she says. "Somehow, I feel they know just how big a job I have and are trying to help me."

*   *   *

Her busy schedule is rough on her social life. Right now, she's still getting acquainted with North Carolina from a woman recruiter's standpoint and is extra busy. When her schedule is worked out she'll be able to devote more time to dates and parties.

Frances is proud of her place in the Marine Corps, and happy as a woman recruiter. She likes her North Carolina beat and is anxious to do a good job and sell the Women Marines to the public.

All over the nation, women recruiters like Frances are scouring towns, cities and even the hills for eligible young women who'll make good Women Marines. Just any girl won't do. Before a gal can even be considered for the Marine Corps she must have a high physical, educational and moral standard. If she's not a high school graduate, the girl must pass an equivalency test. These high standards make the job difficult for women recruiters but they know that someday they may serve side by side with the women they enlist.

The quest for America's best women for the nation's finest service is often trying, tiring and exasperating but the job is in capable hands.

Exercises

1. How many personality sketches did you find in the magazine section of your favorite newspaper?

2. Of that number, how many were concerned with unknown or comparatively unknown persons?

3. In chart form, list each personality sketch in your favorite newspaper and indicate what appeal was made to the reader in each one.

4. By adding a second column to the chart in Exercise 3, list the purpose of each sketch.

5. In a third column, list the number of pictures, charts, maps, or other illustrative material used with each article.

6. List five ideas for personality sketches for Sunday features that you could write about persons in your community, and tell briefly why you think each would make a good feature article.

7. List one idea for a story about some person who has overcome a physical handicap and list three possible markets for it.

8. In chart form, list each personality sketch in your favorite magazine and indicate the appeal to reader interest made in each.

9. In a second column to the chart in Exercise 8, indicate which one of the five methods of portraying the subject of the sketch to the reader was used for each personality sketch.

10. In a third column to the chart indicate the purpose of each article.

11. List three ideas for personality sketches that you could write about persons in your community. Indicate which you would submit to magazines or trade or business publications to inform, instruct, or inspire the reader. Tell briefly why you think each would make a good feature article.

12. List a series of six personality sketches that you might write for a syndicate and indicate to which syndicate you would submit the series.

13. List four possible success stories for trade or business publications and tell why the persons would make good subjects for articles.

14. Indicate a possible market for each of the above success stories.

Publication Analysis

Young Women's Magazines and Young Men's Magazines

Compare, by using chart form as illustrated in the Appendix, two magazines of each of the above types. There are an increasing number of magazines for young women and young men. They may be obtained at newsstands, from magazine dealers listed under "Aids for Writers" in the Appendix, or in library periodical reading rooms. Some suggested young women's magazines: *Bride-to-be, Charm, Glamour, Business Girl, Mademoiselle;* young men's magazines: *Future Magazine, Man to Man, Pic, True;* both sexes: *Living for Young Home Makers, Red Book,* or others of your choice.

Do not spend more than two and a half hours on this report.

   I. Identification for each magazine: Name, publishers, editors, where published, price.

  II. Make-up: What to you, as a future magazine editor, are the interesting things about the make-up of the four magazines? Give reasons for your answers.

III. Advertising:
1. From the point of view of what you know about advertising, do you think the copy in each publication will appeal to the reader?
2. What did you like about the advertising in each publication? Give reason.
3. What did you *not* like about the advertising in each publication? Give reason.
4. What tips were suggested to you by the advertising?

IV. General policy:
1. To what types of readers do the four publications which you analyzed appeal?
2. Why should you as a free-lance writer know these magazines?
3. What features might you have written?
4. Anything of special interest in either publication?

  V. Features: Read a personality sketch or a success story in each magazine and list suggestions for each feature read that will enable you to write better personality sketches or success features.

 VI. Slogans: Write a slogan for each magazine.

VII. Four Tips: Source, authority, and three possible markets suggested by this study.

CHAPTER 8

The Narrative Article

▄▀

Uses Devices of Short Story. Readers like rapid action, thrilling adventure, and vivid description along with facts. The narrative article, like the well-written short story, is extremely popular with magazine readers in America. Its purpose is not only to instruct or guide the reader but to entertain him by the same devices that the short-story writer uses, except that the feature writer never uses fictitious nor exaggerated details.

A narrative article is defined as one used to present facts by using devices of the short story—conversation, rapid action, vivid description, thrilling adventure, and sustaining suspense—to heighten the effect and to entertain as well as to inform the reader.

Although similar to the interview, the personal experience, and the confession article, in that they all contain narrative, the "narrative article" is more effective if written in the third person, whereas the others may not be. It may be somewhat like the utility article by aiming to help the reader with definite directions or advice, but it is written in a narrative-descriptive style to appeal to the reader's imagination. Its purpose is to entertain as well as to inform. It differs from the personality sketch in so far as it is not concerned with achievement from the personal point of view; nor is its purpose to inspire; rather, it is to *tell*.

The writer will find it advantageous to present material in narrative form, if it can be so treated. It is easier, in many ways, to interest the reader and to hold his interest by presenting facts along with action and adventure. Suggestions for gathering material for the other types of articles may be applied in planning the narrative. Adventure, travel, historical, and biographical data, as well as material presenting processes and the results of scientific research, can be presented effectively by the devices used in fiction writing.

Narrative Affords Variety in Form. In writing the article, one must remember that narrative affords variety and action and that description must be vivid enough to make the reader hear, smell, taste, feel, or see as the writer desires. The writer must, however, guard against overdoing the description in his attempt to produce dynamic impressions. The clever writer may frequently find opportunity to inject humor into his narratives, but the beginner, unless he is particularly gifted, should avoid making too great use of it. If humor is overdone, the article may be ridiculous instead of funny. Later, when one has attained skill and ease in his writing, he should attempt writing humorous narratives or adding a humorous tone to narrative articles whenever his material lends itself to such treatment. Editors pay well for articles with a humorous slant, and they find it difficult to obtain clever ones.

Using First Person or Third Person in Narrative Writing. Whether to use first person or third person in narrative writing depends upon the story the writer wishes to tell and the effect he is trying to achieve. The writer must determine whose story he desires to tell in order to choose the viewpoint from which the reader will see what happens. He must consider which person used to tell the narrative will seem the most natural.

First person may make the article sound "preachy" in tone, and the personal pronoun may become monotonous to the reader. But, if the article is written with skill, the first person is effective because of its naturalness and directness.

The inexperienced writer usually uses the third person with greater skill than the first. Then, too, the use of the third person can produce all of the effects of the use of the first, but without making the writer sound "preachy," or egotistical, or without giving a monotonous tone to the narrative. Fact writing probably uses the third person more than the first, with the exception of the confession article. The latter, to be effective, is generally written in the first person. In a recent study of ten issues of twenty magazines, it was found that only one narrative article out of five was written in the first person. Most of those were travel articles. The historical and biographical articles were told in the third person.

Large Demand Due to Popularity. By developing his ability to write narrative articles, a writer will acquire variety in style and type. He will be rewarded by facility in marketing his manuscripts, and he will be rewarded well financially. Editors constantly need well-written narratives, since the popularity of feature articles written in fiction style has increased so rapidly.

Examples of Narrative Articles. Clever writers can take simple incidents to interest readers as shown in the two following articles both of which were generously illustrated with pictures. The first article taken from *The Crippled Child* gives an interesting article a fiction-type of lead to catch the reader's interest. Then the author skillfully narrated the story of the Mitchell Motor Chair. The second article contains elements of several types but it does *tell*, so it was classified as a narrative. It grew out of the student's interest in juvenile delinquency and how a university town was solving its local problems. He too, used a fiction descriptive lead —or it might have been fact—to "take the reader by the hand" as it were, to show him the Community Center. He injected facts into his narrative so skillfully and submitted six excellent pictures to show the Center in action that the *American Home* sent him the following letter:

Mr. Kenneth B. Stark
c/o School of Journalism,
University of Wisconsin
Madison, Wisconsin

Dear Mr. Stark:

It makes me happy indeed to tell you that we are accepting your manuscript "Citizenship, Inc." for publication.

A Check for $150.00 in full payment of this material has been ordered and should reach you shortly.

Sincerely Yours,

Virginia Herrod
Feature Editor.
The American Home

VH:bl

Later the editor requested a short sketch of the author and his picture which was included in the first part of the magazine where the editor "introduces" the top writers for each issue.

(1)

**He Made His
Magic Carpet***

BY MARILYN E. JOHNSON

To the man in the United States Patent Office, the sheaf of papers in front of him was one more routine job. He took off his glasses, wiped them carefully, and moved his chair nearer the well-littered desk. Putting on his glasses, he read "Patent application, Mitchell Motor Chair." Even to an old hand at bright ideas, this design looked like something new.

But the detailed drawings, photos and yards of descriptive adjectives fell far short of telling the whole story of the motor chair, and how 25-year-old Kenny Ginsterblum happened to have his invention in line for those coveted abbreviations, "Reg., U.S. Pat. Off."

Back in 1924, when immunization wasn't quite as universal as it is today, Kenny, a blond two-year-old, was stricken with diphtheria. Doctors and the boy's determination pulled him past the crisis, but he mended slowly. Months later, when allowances for his illness had been made and made again his parents realized that his legs had been affected, and he would never be able to walk.

*   *   *

When the test came this time, Kenny made sure everything was perfect. His balloon tires had been tested, the motor ran like a top. The best part of the mechanism, for him, was the "airplane control," which enabled him to operate speeds and make turns at the slightest touch of the steering wheel.

* Reprinted by permission of *The Crippled Child* and Marilyn E. Johnson.

He pressed the starter, and after a long second, the solid hum of the motor reassured him. Another second, and it was running as he had so often dreamed it would! He motored hesitantly down the sidewalk, then a little faster as he neared the end of the block. Turning, he drove confidently back. All his years of work had been for this, and it was worth it!

* * *

Setting November 3 as the deadline for the new Mitchell Motor Chair to roll off the "assembly line," they worked day and night. Kenny, as owner, had a myriad of jobs, and as he supervised and directed each step of the work, and assembled the hard-to-get supplies, he could see his machine taking shape.

At midnight on November 2, after grueling hours of hard work, Carl put down the paint gun with a grin—their chair was completed. Kenny's shoulders relaxed with a feeling of accomplishment, a thankfulness for the friends that had made it all possible. And that day, Attorney Joseph Casey filed the patent on his motor chair in Washington, D.C.

If you happen to be in Osage, Iowa, on a weekend this summer, you'll probably notice a slight, fair boy, driving slowly down a tree shaded lane, or motoring on a downtown sidewalk. You may see him cheering enthusiastically at a baseball game, or he might be seeing his first circus. You'll recognize him because he'll be riding in a streamlined chair, and by the way the townspeople greet him as he passes. But don't expect to run into him during the week, because Kenny, as President of the Mitchell Motor Chair Company, is one of Osage's newest businessmen—and proudest citizens!

(2)
Citizenship, Inc.*

In Madison, Wis., the Community Center Is Neither Makeshift Nor Substitute; It Is Citizenship and Democracy in Action.

BY KENNETH B. STARK

On the crowded dance floor, the jitterbugs twirled and swung as the hard-working orchestra gave its all in a colorful rendition of "Shoo-

* Reprinted by permission of *The American Home* and Kenneth B. Stark.

Fly Pie." Soft lights cast wavering shadows on the dancers' eager young faces. In an adjoining room, teen-agers thronged about small tables, drinking, talking, or just looking on. The snack bar was another bedlam, and a juke box in the corner competed valiantly with the toiling band. Couples strolled in and out of the dance hall, oblivious to everything but the fact that here was a chance to have fun. In an upper room, shaded bulbs lighted up green surfaces of pool tables and outlined the players in vague relief. At near-by card tables, games held others intent. The click of the balls and low-spoken comments punctuated the steady hum wafted from the floor below. . . .

That scene might have been a night at some unsavory club or roadhouse—but it wasn't. Here, everything, though jubilant and enthusiastic, was orderly. No pall of cigarette smoke deadened the air. The bottles from which the youngsters drank bore the trademark of a world famous soft drink manufacturer. Behind the snack bar, two motherly ladies worked feverishly handing out sandwiches, pop, coffee, and ice cream at nonprofit, mere cost-of-operation prices. At the entrance, a young man checked the admission cards of all arrivals, each card bearing a picture and brief description of its owner. Another young man alternated between the groups at the downstairs tables and those in the card room, answering questions, offering suggestions, helping in various ways. And all through the dense crowd moved a quiet, inconspicuous man, nodding a cheery greeting here, pausing for a brief, friendly word there. Thus we meet Mr. Robert ("Bob") Hurd, director of the Madison (Wisconsin) Community Center, and his assistants employing their own unique methods for showing the young people of that city a good time. Methods which, however, could be used just as effectively in any community where citizens and civic and business organizations are willing to work earnestly together to combat juvenile delinquency, develop civic spirit and neighborhood unity, and in many other ways raise the living and recreation standards of the entire family and all the people.

Madison's Community Center opened on February 1, 1946, as a result of that community's realization of the need for a place where Madisonians of all ages and walks of life might gather for recreation and citizen-building activities. During its first year, an average of 18,000 people per month have used its facilities. What it has taught them about good citizenship, fellowship, and the profitable use of leisure time, no one can say. What it has prevented is suggested by the high praise given its work by the city's juvenile probation officer. The budget for the Center amounts to 11.3 cents per capita of Madison's population, certainly an insignificant price to pay for the welfare of the community and its citizens. It is a challenge to other urban areas of the country, for there is no question and no secret about the manner in which it is achieving success.

*   *   *

A "Code of Good Sportsmanship" motto hangs over the door of the game room, where devotees of pool, table tennis, chess, checkers, cribbage, dominoes, etc., exercise their skill. The only restriction in sight is a sign above a pool table: "Please do not try Masse Shots,"— the result of a would-be Willie Hoppe's attempt that didn't come off. YAC dances are usually held Wednesday evenings; Thursdays the OAKS take over, and Fridays and Saturdays are for the Loft Club dances. Sunday afternoons, the hall is used for roller skating by all ages; Loft members skate by themselves Monday afternoons, and the older folks are given Monday evenings. Skates bought with budgeted funds are loaned in exchange for the skater's membership card. A high spot in the Loft Club activities is a monthly radio program broadcast over a local station in co-operation with the Madison Youth Council. But perhaps the most American (and heart-warming) activity of all is the Center's Tuesday evenings for crippled children, when those whom life has treated harshly are given the run of the place. Parents bring favors and help with decorations, but the youngsters have their own officers to plan and carry through the programs. Magicians rate high at the meetings, and barbershop quartets are frequently a major part of the entertainments.

Exercises

1. How many narrative articles did you find in the magazine section of your favorite newspaper?

2. By referring back to your previous exercises, tabulate the number of each kind of article found to show which type seems to be most favored by the feature editor.

3. In chart form, list the narrative articles, and in the first column indicate in what way each feature is similar to the short story.

4. In a second column in the chart indicate the purpose of each article.

5. In a third column indicate from what sources the writers obtained their material.

6. In a fourth column enumerate the appeal to the reader's senses which the writers have used.

7. After summing up your findings by means of the chart, write a paragraph of not more than 200 words pointing out why your favorite newspaper is, or is not, a good market for narrative articles.

8. How many narrative articles did you find in your favorite magazine?

9. In chart form list the names of the articles, and indicate: (1) the elements in the article that are similar to the short story; (2) the purpose of the article; (3) the sources of the material; (4) appeal to the reader's senses; and (5) the person in which the narrative is told.

10. After totalling up your findings, write a paragraph of not more than 200 words pointing out why your favorite magazine is, or is not, a market for narrative articles.

11. List two ideas for narrative articles for a newspaper section and two ideas for narratives for a magazine, and indicate a market for each "tip."

12. List one "tip" for a narrative that could be treated humorously and indicate a market to which you might send it.

Publication Analysis

Psychology and Inspirational Magazines

Compare, by using chart form as illustrated in the Appendix, two magazines of each of the above types. There are a number of these periodicals and they may be obtained at newsstands, from magazine dealers listed in the Appendix under "Aids for Writers," or in library periodical reading rooms. Some suggested psychology magazines: *Modern Psychologist, Popular Psychology Guide, Psychology Digest;* inspirational magazines: *Human Nature, Your Life, Your Personality, Woman's Life,* or others of your choice.

Do not spend more than two and a half hours on this report.

I. Identification for each magazine: Name, publishers, editors, where published, price.

II. Make-up: What to you, as a future magazine editor, are the most interesting make-up devices used in each publication? Give reasons for your answers.

III. Advertising:
 1. To what class is the appeal made in the advertising of each magazine?
 2. What novel ideas in advertising make-up did you find in each publication?
 3. From which one of the four magazines you analyzed do advertisers get the best returns?
 4. Suggest one "tip" for a feature article suggested by the advertising in each magazine.

IV. General Policy:
 1. Make a comparative summary of the four magazines which you analyzed as to content and appeal.

2. Make a brief comment on the fiction as to type, titles, appeal, writers, and the amount of space devoted to it.
3. What did you learn of each publication's policy by reading its editorials?

V. Features:
1. Make a comparative summary of the features, as to style, subject matter, content, length, and writers (whether they are, or are not, well known).
2. Make a comparative comment on the illustrative matter (pictures, charts, graphs, maps) used in each magazine.
3. Read a narrative article in each publication and list two suggestions for each feature read that will enable you to write interesting narratives.

VI. Slogans: Write a slogan for each magazine.

VII. Four Tips: Source, authority, and three possible markets for each suggested by this publication analysis.

CHAPTER 9

Slanting Articles to Publications

Magazine Growth Makes Slanting Necessary. Although feature writers are fortunate to be writing in this period—which might well be known as the "boom" age of the magazine, at least as far as numbers are concerned—they have to have a keener knowledge of markets today than did their predecessors. Never in the history of journalism have there been so many publications as there now are. Writers must ever be alert to the constant change in periodicals. Seldom a week passes that a new magazine does not appear on the newsstands; or another disappears because it has failed financially; or two combine and change the editorial policy and appeal to reader interest in an attempt to meet tremendous competition.

Until the last three or four decades, few publications existed, and they all had similar conservative policies. Today there are 12,398 daily newspapers, of which 487 have Sunday editions, according to N. W. Ayer and Son's Directory.* It lists 8,220 periodicals. The magazines publish 98,640 issues annually, each carrying from one to twenty feature articles. Each magazine makes a different appeal to its readers. Each offers to the writer an

* Ayer, N. W., and Son, *Directory of Newspapers and Periodicals,* 1955.

opportunity to market his manuscripts if he will study its issues and learn its needs.

Slanting Defined. When beginners in feature writing classes sell their articles, it is because they study the markets assiduously. They avoid rejection slips and returned manuscripts by being ever alert to opportunities to sell. One often thinks of salesmen as people who travel with samples. Feature writers, too, are salesmen. Their sample kits, or manuscripts, are not exhibited personally, as are the traveling salesman's. The articles are sent direct to the middleman, or editor, the writer thinks most likely to be interested in buying for resale, as a merchant, to his customer-consumers, who are the readers of the magazine. There is a place in some publication at some time for every well-planned and well-written feature. It is the writer's job to be extremely businesslike and to see that his manuscript is at the right place at the right time.

A slanted article is one written to the editorial requirements of a particular publication. The writer's problem is to find the particular policy for each publication before he even outlines his article. Some writers, who like to think of themselves as "literary artists," object to deciding beforehand where they will send their manuscripts. But they never become known as authors, since their works seldom are printed. The practical, businesslike person determines his markets before he writes. He sells if he writes, or "slants," to suit a certain publication or type of publication. The formula of any publication may be found by analyzing not only the articles but the entire contents of several of the most recent issues, and by studying the style of other contributors in recent issues.

Problems in Slanting. Writers with something worth writing do not have to go begging for a market if they apply the same intelligence and study to the salesmanship of the article as they did to the technique of gathering and writing the material. Markets are as numerous as feature writers. But the majority of beginners are not competitors. They refuse to study periodicals; and their copy, sent out hit or miss, is rejected. Novices will find slanting an insurance against rejections instead of a baffling problem. Of two writers, otherwise equally experienced and versatile, the one who is practical and prepares in advance to aim at definite markets will get acceptances instead of rejections.

Qualifications for Slanting. A businesslike attitude toward the selling of his copy is the author's first requisite in slanting an article. He must be familiar with all kinds of publications and observe closely the type of article and the subject matter most favored by the editor of each. After a writer selects his subject, he should have the ability to visualize his readers or market and seek a publication that goes to such subscribers.

It is important that the writer be a close newspaper reader and a keen observer, in order to see the trends of current news and to determine the undercurrents of thought before it is too late to gather, write, and submit material while interest is high. Magazines change their purposes to keep up with the times. If a writer is determined to know the markets, his determination will make the business of publication analysis interesting.

Finding Specific Buyers. Ambitious beginners hope to have their articles appear in the "slick paper," or class, magazines. If their articles are accurately gathered, carefully planned, skillfully written, and wisely slanted, the writers need only stamps and envelopes. Although the big magazines receive from 2,000 to 3,000 articles a week, they do look at every manuscript. One can assume that every successful magazine is satisfying its readers, at least to some degree. The surest way to determine the interests of its readers is to study carefully the contents of the entire publication to which one is submitting a manuscript, and then to plan and outline the material to fit it. It is a waste of postage, effort, and time to send articles out to the first market that comes to mind. The manuscript is sure to be returned so promptly that the writer will marvel at the speed of the mails.

An unskilled writer is inclined to offer his manuscript indiscriminately and frequently. This practice tends to prejudice the editor against future contributions and, in addition, wastes the writer's time and postage. Nothing labels one as an amateur more quickly than sending his manuscript to the wrong type of publication, as did the junior journalist who sent an article on student health to the *Christian Science Monitor*. After being carefully slanted and rewritten, the article later sold to *Today's Health*. But if an editor receives a feature showing that the writer senses the reader-appeal of his magazine, even though the particular article is not acceptable for some reason, he will often suggest in a personal note that he would be pleased to see more of the writer's work. If beginners would only be willing to study the magazines thoroughly before attempting to write articles, and then "tailor" their articles to fit the periodical selected, they would have little difficulty in marketing.

Though there may be obvious defects in a manuscript, if it has some merit and is well pointed to a specific publication, it may be salable. Finding buyers for one's manuscript may be likened to finding a position. It takes a lot of searching, and sometimes a bit of luck, but in the long run most worthy people do find work if they apply where their services can be used. A manuscript, like any merchandise, is marketable when the right buyer is found. Editor-buyers can be found easily if the salesman-writer will display only the wares that will appeal to the middleman-editor because he knows his customer-readers will be interested.

Feature Article Is a Commodity to Be Sold. Not many beginners sell, because only a few are willing to learn: (1) market requirements; (2) editors' methods of handling manuscripts; (3) ways of impressing the editor favorably; (4) price scales for features; (5) the great number of possible markets for their articles; or (6) what the interests of the readers are. The result is that a small number of nationally known magazines receive almost the entire output of the multitude of novices.

It is not surprising that relatively few writers attain success; proportionately, only a few are willing to recognize their manuscripts as a commodity that must be designed for definite markets. Manufacturers of furniture do not let their product remain in their warehouses; they see that it is sold. Many writers, however, feel that when they have struck the last period on their manuscripts, their work as writers is done. They refuse to be salesmen. They are too lazy or too indifferent to study the magazines in detail in order to manufacture a commodity that the middleman-editor and his public will want. Such an analysis would increase their chances to sell at least 500 per cent.

Usually they complete their final drafts and mail them out to the first market that strikes their fancies. They shoot in the dark, trusting to luck instead of devoting (1) considerable time to the study of thousands of opportunities and (2) serious thought to marketing their articles.

Two Ways of Marketing. From the commercial point of view, there are two ways in which creative writers may approach their work. First, they may write what they feel like writing, in whatever way they wish to write it, and then, if they feel like it, see what they can do about selling. One beginner, in spite of being advised to study markets, wrote what he "felt like" writing. He thought his "self-expression" was nearer to "real art." He did not sell the article. Meanwhile, his classmates, who had analyzed the markets before outlining and writing, received checks. He changed his plan of work, and since then has sold many articles. He admits now that it is much more fun to have readers and checks than to write as he "feels." He found that writing to a plan was much more enjoyable and successful than writing in a haphazard manner. Those writers who yearn to "express themselves" generally send out what they do write to the best-paying of the class publications. They do not realize that thousands of other beginners are sending to the same markets because they, too, do not know or will not learn of the existence of thousands of other publications where there is but little competition. They receive rejections and become greatly discouraged. There are exceptions, of course. Occasionally someone does sell the first time he sends out his article, without giving the marketing any thought.

The second way is for the beginners to learn everything they can about the needs of all the current newspapers, syndicates, trade, and business publications, and magazines. After they have learned of the existing demands of the markets, they attempt to supply them by: (1) selecting subjects that they hope will be suitable; (2) writing articles in a style similar to that of articles already published, in order to fill the needs of the editors in the way that they seem to want them filled; and (3) obtaining photographs and other illustrations of the type the editors seem to want. They succeed where the would-be "artistic" novices fail.

Adapting Professional's Technique Is Helpful. These beginners who attain success do so by adopting the devices of the professionals already writing for the publication to which they are slanting. Concrete incidents and instances, people, direct quotations, and interviews with authorities whose names may interest the reader are devices that most editors like. Each may have his own notions about what his readers like, but frequently they change their ideas. A semi-professional who, over a period of time, had sold a number of articles to a well-known magazine, neglected to continue his study of the publication. He had an article returned with a personal note suggesting that if he would take out the expert's name and quotations, rewrite the manuscript to conform to the new policy, and return it, the magazine would accept it. In making a study of the publication, he found to his surprise that the editor, several months previously, had discontinued the use of interview articles.

Learning Editor's Desires and Needs. To insure acceptance, a manuscript must fit a particular magazine, as previously pointed out. In reality, it must appeal to the editor who buys what he believes his subscribers want. As the middleman, he buys from the producers what he thinks he can sell to his customers. Unless his customer-readers are satisfied, they will shop elsewhere for their reading matter.

Editors buy those articles in which the reader can visualize himself, or herself. Human beings are interested, first of all, in themselves. People go to movies, read current magazines and best sellers, listen to radio, and view television to escape from their prosaic lives and live for a brief time in a world of their own, in which they see themselves as the hero, or the heroine, of the film, article, or story. Why do people look at the advertising in publications? Psychologists say it is not that they are interested entirely in the commodity, but that the readers like to see themselves— consciously or unconsciously—in the illustrations and in the copy. The women like to think they look like the radiant girl in the swimming suit advertisement; the men see themselves as the handsome young chap in the collar advertisement. It is only human nature for readers to identify themselves in everything. If writers base their work on that principal of psychology, they are more successful in interesting editors.

Another principle upon which editors base their selections is appeal to subscribers. Most magazine readers are from the great middle class. They have grade-school and high-school educations. They read little else than their newspapers and the magazines. They look at them for their entertainment and their information. They go to the movies, play bridge, and tune in on their radios and television sets. They are buying their homes or they have borrowed money in order to build homes. They drive "popular-priced" cars. They like romance, adventure, and the things close to their own lives. They want to be healthier, wealthier, wiser, and happier. They are the average American families.

This is the kind of reading audience the average editor has to consider. With them in mind, he attacks his daily pile of manuscripts, always with the hope that he will discover a new writer whose work will lend distinction to his publication, or at least will compare favorably with the work of his staff writers or those who write articles "on order" from the editor. But no matter how well written the manuscripts are, he cannot accept any of them unless they are what the readers want. Readers are interested in accounts of what someone has done more efficiently, more satisfactorily, or more profitably than they have.

Amateurs and semi-professionals long have had a wrong conception of editors because of the rejection slips they receive. They do not stop to think that had they sent in well-written articles containing something new to inform, guide, or entertain the reader, and written for the editor's particular subscribers, he would have been only too happy to have sent a check instead of a rejection slip. All editors are constantly on the lookout for new contributors. After analyzing a publication and before even outlining his article, a writer should imagine himself in that editor's place in order better to keep the readers in mind as he works. Just as the editor, were he writing the article, would (1) make himself master of the subject before beginning to write, or (2) interview an authority whose expert opinions would add to the reader's faith in the content of the feature, so must the beginner, if he would satisfy the editor's wants and needs. Editors are easy to please if the writer will apply himself to learning what they want. Beginners should remember that duck hunters do not load their guns, shut their eyes, and shoot into a duckless sky when they wish to bag game. But the feature writer who does not "slant" is doing just that.

Factors Determining Editorial Selection. Every magazine's success depends upon the ability of its editor to visualize his readers—their incomes, their expenses, their problems, their likes and dislikes, their entertainment, their ambitions, and their aspirations—in order to publish the kind of periodical that will please them. A great editor producing a home magazine to appeal to the middle class saw in his mind a typical community of 1,500 inhabitants, somewhere in the Mississippi valley. He selected everything that went into that publication—editorials, articles, fiction, and poems—with a view to satisfying an average American family— a father, mother, and three children, aged 14, 9, and 6. For two other magazines that he published, he employed editors who as accurately visualized their readers. The subscribers in one case were country gentlemen; in the other, business people. The owner of these three magazines became one of the outstanding editors and millionaires of his time. He attributed his success to his capacity for visualizing his readers. If an editor can attain great success on that principle, so may feature writers if they will visualize their readers when planning and writing their articles.

Distinguishing Factors as Markets. To determine where to sell an article, a writer must decide whom the article will interest and where will he find a ready market. Both factors are dependent upon the subject matter. However, if this subject matter would interest the newspaper reader as well as the magazine reader, or would interest only the former, the writer will find it is easier and quicker, perhaps, to sell to the newspaper's local magazine sections. Their editors buy from three to six weeks in advance, while the magazine editors buy from four to six months before publication. Although Sunday newspaper sections are not so numerous now as magazines, many papers run daily features on their editorial pages in addition to those in the large Sunday, or Saturday night, feature sections or syndicated sections which many papers buy. Newspapers are broader in reader appeal as well as more varied in style of writing and the type of features they use, and the author's name does not need to be well known, as it must be with some of the class magazines. But whichever type of publication one writes for, he must know its readers' interests.

If one is slanting for a newspaper, he should learn to know the people who read that newspaper; he must talk to the elevator boy, the judge, the waiter, the minister, the janitor, the teacher, the laborer, the banker, and all the other kinds of readers. Newspaper reporting experience affords excellent background for anyone who desires to write features. The reporter is writing regularly, whether or not he "feels" like it; he writes under the constant criticism of the city editor; and he is continually coming in contact with all kinds of people. If one cannot work on a newspaper, he should write every day and he should attempt to know as many kinds of people as he can.

Diversity in Publication Appeals and Policies. It is the purpose of every publication, magazine or newspaper, to have a definite appeal to a particular reader; it is the writer's task to learn the appeals of the publication. The magazine differs from the newspaper in that its appeal must be national, while the newspaper's is local or sectional. Newspaper readers living in the same community or in the same section of the country have similar interests, but national magazines cannot appeal to people throughout the country in a single issue. To satisfy the demand of a widely varied appeal, editors developed the class magazine, to attract readers of certain types throughout the nation. Timeliness is more important in the newspaper, because its very name signifies giving the news. If an article has a news angle, is has twice the chance of being accepted for the Sunday section.

The newspaper and the magazine are business enterprises, as is pointed out in Chapter 24. As they must sell their products and retain their reputations, they buy only those manuscripts that help them to carry out their business policies of dependability and reliability. The newspaper and the magazine are constantly changing, but the latter is a greater follower of fads and fashions than the former, and it is easier for the beginner to slant to the newspaper than to the magazine.

Knowledge of Circulation Aids Slanting. Since publications are business ventures, they are dependent upon circulation. In this phase, more than in any other, lies the greatest difference between newspapers and magazines. Most popular magazines have nationwide circulation to people of many classes. Some agricultural and trade journals are published for a distinctly sectional circulation because climatic conditions or geographical locations present different problems and give rise to different interests in different sections of the country. Others are published for subscribers interested in the same profession, business, or industry who live in all parts of North America, and a few magazines publish editions for other countries.

It is essential, in selling, that the writer know, as does the advertising agency buying space in publications, just what the circulation is and who the subscribers are. By knowing the variances, the writer will be able to slant his articles accurately.

High Standards of Writing Are Required. Some beginners believe that it is easier to write for the newspapers than for the magazines, and that the former will buy poorly written and carelessly constructed articles. They are mistaken. Newspaper feature editors have an abundance of material from which to choose, and competition is keener today than it ever has been before. Therefore, writers must turn out good manuscripts for the newspapers as well as for the magazines. In writing for the former, the free-lance has to compete with other free-lance writers, regular staff members, and syndicate writers, many of whom are well known in the world of letters. No writing is ever too good to appear in the Sunday sections. The articles of the best writers appear in both types of publications.

Slanting to the Newspapers. The newspaper is an excellent field for the beginner if he slants his article to it. In every city there are daily newspapers publishing feature articles. Even in the smaller city there is at least one daily, and it, like the metropolitan paper, will use articles on local subjects that are right at the beginner's door. Since only local writers, as a rule, submit manuscripts to the smaller papers, the novice does not have as much competition in free-lancing. In addition to giving the news of the locality, a newspaper also prints the important news of the world. So, too, does it publish, in addition to its local features, articles of a broader scope, and herein lies the beginner's opportunity. His financial remuneration will be smaller, but he will gain in experience and will learn how to write for print. Small city dailies have offered apprenticeships to hundreds of writers who later moved on to larger opportunities.

Because of their broad appeal, metropolitan newspapers offer a ready market for articles, or "feature stories" as newspaper workers term them. Some newspapers, such as the Kansas City *Star* and the Milwaukee *Journal,* even publish articles daily on the editorial page, as well as elsewhere in the paper. Four hundred and eighty-seven newspapers have Saturday or Sunday magazine sections containing features similar to those found in general magazines. Newspapers obtain the articles they publish from: (1) members of the newspaper staff—reporters, correspondents, special writers, or editors—who are employed for the purpose or who, on some papers, are paid for the features they write in addition to their routine work; (2) syndicates, which are companies that buy articles from writers and sell them to a number of newspaper feature editors in different cities for release on the same dates; and (3) from free-lance writers, either amateurs or professionals, who submit their stories to the feature editor. Staff workers on smaller papers frequently submit articles to the larger ones, as do news correspondents, if the paper upon which they are employed does not desire them. Through their feature writing, they develop a sideline that adds to their regular income and affords them the opportunity of seeing their by-lines in papers other than those upon which they are employed.

Analyzing Newspapers to Detect Differences. Each newspaper should be studied to learn the differences in reader appeal. Some papers, such as the New York *World-Telegram,* may stress local color and atmosphere; the Chicago *Daily News* may emphasize human interest; the New York *Times* may require scholarliness and timeliness; the *Christian Science Monitor* may demand accuracy; the New York *Herald Tribune* may use features of national and international importance; and the great majority, such as the Kansas City *Star,* the Milwaukee *Journal,* and the Indianapolis *News,* publish anything of general interest if it is unusually well written. Newspapers, like persons, may appear to be alike; yet upon analysis one finds that they have as varied personalities and as many dissimilarities as do individuals. The character of the readers of a newspaper determines the character of its features, just as readers influence the presentation of the news.

It is not a waste of time to study publications. If tailors or dressmakers made up suits or dresses in styles and sizes different from those their customers could wear—because they "felt like expressing themselves in that way"—or if they made the garments several inches too long or too short—because they did not take the measurements accurately—their customers would refuse to accept them. The editor feels just that way when unsolicited manuscripts are not cut accurately to fit the pattern of his publication.

Kinds of Features Wanted by Newspapers. Current topics, because timeliness is the keynote of the newspaper, furnish the basis of the majority of daily feature stories. They may contain elaborated details of past news or they may anticipate coming events.

To satisfy the reader's curiosity concerning the details of the concise announcements of news events, by interviews and research a writer may elaborate them into features. These features may be concerned with accounts of scientific discoveries or inventions; sketches of personalities and successful persons; reports of industrial, social, economic, or political conditions; narratives of seasonal occasions, such as holidays, vacations, opening and closing of schools, and the fishing and hunting seasons; synopses of local, state, national, and international affairs; or reviews of historical events that may be timely because of some news angle or because of some approaching anniversary. The daily news columns are provocative sources of "tips" for features, either for Sunday sections or for magazines.

To entertain subscribers by giving them reading matter with which to occupy their leisure, or to serve as "literature of escape" from their workaday worlds, newspapers often print articles on subjects of little or no value, simply because they are written in an amusing and entertaining style. Sensational newspapers devote considerable space to topics that lend themselves to melodramatic treatment in features. The sensational paper is about the only market for highly dramatized features, with the exception of a few periodicals. Most periodicals generally do not attempt to attract readers by that means.

Sunday Magazine Features. The magazine sections of the Sunday newspapers, and the syndicated Sunday sections, like the daily editions, contain features concerning (1) rare, unusual, novel, romantic, tragic, and adventurous things in life everywhere; (2) outstanding achievements in the arts and sciences; and (3) authoritative opinions on current and historical issues and events. The articles in the sections devoted to features are similar in subject matter to those used daily. They are much longer than those used in the weekday issues, and frequently they are as long as those in general magazines. The Sunday magazine sections use more pictures and other illustrations than the daily does; often these equal in number those in the magazines.

By noting the subjects of the articles, the types most used, the point of view from which they are written, the form, the style, the length, and the appeal to the reader, a writer will soon discover what the feature-section editors desire. The newspaper and periodical studies at the end of each chapter in this book indicate the points to keep in mind in studying publications in order to slant material to the newspapers.

Syndicated Features. Newspaper syndicates buy series of articles from free-lance writers, but they seldom buy the work of a novice. They obtain most of their material from writers of already recognized prominence, because professionals are better judges of reader interest, have "big" names, and have the ability to produce a series of articles. Occasionally a beginner will be able to sell a series to a syndicate, but as a rule he is wasting his time and stamps to attempt it before he has become an authority, or at least recognized as an outstanding and reliable writer.

Slanting to the Magazines. Most beginners are familiar with the magazines of big circulations, the majority of which use articles only by well-known names. But they are not acquainted with the thousands of lesser-known periodicals that have achieved such success in their fields that advertising agencies consider them excellent media for their clients. Each has an appeal to a certain class of reader, and each has its special field. Each is like a store on Main Street: it has something definite to "sell" to its readers.

The personality of a magazine is the result of its editorial policy or program, developed over a period of years. It portrays the purpose behind the magazine, its motives, and something of the personality of the staff and writers. A magazine's identity is measured and its worth evaluated by the extent to which it serves its readers by understanding their problems and seeking and finding practical solutions. Every editorial staff attempts to develop in its publication a personality that its readers will like and of which the staff may be proud. If free-lance writers would learn something of the personalities of publications before outlining their articles, they could help editorial staffs to be of greater service to the subscribers, as well as insure the sale of their own manuscripts.

Slanting Requires Thorough Study. In learning the personalities of magazines, one should try to know all the publications that cover the same field and what distinguishes one from another.

Writer's market books and periodical directories are valuable aids to the writer. If an article does not sell to the first periodical to which it is submitted, it may then be sent out again, with but minor changes, to one with a similar personality. As a writer becomes more experienced in the art of slanting, he will develop a sixth sense, or instinct, for discovering publications to suit the things about which he desires to write.

A novice should analyze several publications each week, in order to acquire a knowledge of the markets. Because of the great number of publications and the constant change in their policies, a writer probably will never know all of them thoroughly; but he should know every publication in each of the fields for which he is writing. If possible, three or more issues of a newspaper or magazine should be studied in order to see what the editor avoids and in what he specializes.

Magazines Vary in Appeal. Unlike newspapers, which interest persons of all classes, each magazine has its own particular group of readers. Since appeals are not in the same proportion to all persons, the class magazines were developed. Some appeal to a limited class group with similar ideas, while others interest a number of classes. Still others are directed toward the business man, the housewife, the home-owner, or the farm family. For every group, no matter how it is classified, there is a magazine skillfully edited to consider the reader's problems, interests, and pleasures.

Classification of Magazines. Magazines are divided into two classes, the "slicks" and the "pulps," according to the quality of paper upon which they are printed. The former are printed on "slick paper," or high grade stock. Their contents include all types of writing—fiction, features, poems—in which the editor thinks his readers will be interested. The "pulps," or action magazines, as they are sometimes termed, are usually all fiction and are printed on pulp, a rough heavy paper. Since they seldom use fact articles, the feature writer is not usually concerned with them.

The "slick" periodicals consist of class, general, business, religious, and farm magazines. Standard Rate and Data Service lists a total of about 7,000 publications, with about 200,000 issues annually. Each is a possible market for unsolicited manuscripts. The class and general magazines number about 800, with about 15,000 issues a year. Each prints from one to fifteen or twenty feature articles, covering a wide range of subjects, in every issue. Business papers—trade journals and house organs—are listed as numbering 4,749, and publish 56,988 issues a year. Some of the journals consist entirely of features; others carry one or more in each issue. They make up a class of periodicals that, for the most part, pays a lower rate than the class and general publications, but their editors buy more articles, not only because there are more of them, but also because they receive relatively few unsolicited manuscripts. The majority of free-lance writers are not aware of their existence. They are edited to appeal to people in the professions, businesses, industries, and trades. They are concerned largely with aiding the subscribers to overcome their problems, inspiring them to greater effort in attaining success in their work, and pointing out occasions to widen their services or to increase their opportunities.

House organs are published by commercial organizations and business houses to appeal to limited groups. Their purpose differs from that of the trade or business journal in that they aim to serve as a means of establishing feelings of good fellowship and friendly relations among the subscribers, their staffs, or their customers. Railroad companies, shipping lines and commercial concerns of all types issue such publications. Many of them have circulations that compare favorably with the trade papers. They afford markets for novices, because the editors do not have many manuscripts submitted to them and because writers are not aware of them. Many of them feature hobbies, amusements, sports, success stories, and guidance articles of all types. They offer advice or suggestions on everything of interest to their readers, who are members of the organization, employees, or customers of the firm issuing the organ.

Religious periodicals listed in the Standard Rate and Data Service directory number 683, totaling 8,196 issues annually. Their editors, like those of the business papers, do not have as many manuscripts submitted to them; and so they, too, are in the market for articles. The majority of the religious journals contain shorter features than do the general and business magazines, and as a rule they do not require as many illustrations. Although their rates are lower than those of other types of magazines, writers find them profitable. Sales are quicker and, if the articles are aptly slanted, sales are easier.

Agricultural and farm publications are listed as numbering 1,068, with a total of 12,816 issues annually. This group, along with the business papers, offers the novice an excellent market for all types of practical articles of interest to the rural reader. Successful farm men and women, county agents, extension division leaders, and professors and research workers in agricultural colleges are excellent sources for articles for farm publications. They have knowledge and experience that will enable the beginner, by means of the interview, to write articles helpful to farm dwellers with problems.

When the beginner realizes the great variety of markets in all classes of magazines, he can look about him—no matter whether he lives in the heart of a great city or on a remote farm—and find numerous subjects that may be used by the five classes of "slick" paper magazines.

Manuscripts Are Submitted by the Thousands. The beginner need not be discouraged when he learns that magazines like the *Saturday Evening Post* receive more than 10,000 manuscripts a month, that *Good Housekeeping* gets more than 2,500 and, that *Harper's* receives 2,000. The larger publications buy very few unsolicited manuscripts. Most of their articles are written "on assignment" or by special contract with well-known writers. But when the beginner recalls that there are 20,618 newspapers and magazines that publish from one to twenty articles in each of the 4,643,390 issues, and that a great majority of these periodicals receive only a few unsolicited manuscripts, he will realize that opportunities are about him everywhere if he will slant his articles.

Surveying the Contents of a Publication. Editors have said that 95 per cent of the failures to sell are due to the writers' lack of market knowledge. Many novices write an article and then consider where they can sell it. It behooves the writer to make thoughtful surveys of all classes of publications. The wider his market knowledge the greater will be his sales. As soon as one decides definitely on an idea for an article, he should select three or more markets to which he believes he could slant the material to fit the publications' policies. Strange as this method may seem to a beginner—determining the possible markets before doing the "research," or background reading, interviewing the interviewee, outlining the material, or starting the actual writing—it is the secret to success.

The survey of the publication should include a thorough analysis of the (1) reading matter, (2) photographs, kodachromes, and illustrations, (3) advertisements, and (4) circulation.

Analyzing the Reading Matter. Sending articles to magazines to have them rejected is not only costly in time and postage, but the delay in finding markets may make the articles out of date, since newspaper feature editors plan their sections from three to six weeks, and magazine editors from four to six months, in advance. The professional as well as the beginner must study the markets constantly. Publications change policies by varying the appeal, the purpose, or the content. As soon as one becomes a free-lance writer, he becomes a perpetual student of publications if he wants to see his articles in print.

In examining the content and policy of a publication to which one is planning to submit a manuscript, one should: (1) study the table of contents, to see whether the by-lines are "big" names, the names of well-known writers, or names entirely unknown, in order to get an idea of the editor's attitude toward accepting manuscripts from beginners; (2) note the number of pages of features as compared with fiction, to perceive why the subscriber buys the magazine; and (3) scan the editorials, to ascertain the editor's point of view on topics that he discusses in addressing the reader, which may be a key to the policy of the publication.

The feature articles should be examined carefully to note: (1) the subject matter; (2) the types of articles that are used, particularly those that predominate and those that are used sparingly or not at all, in order to submit only the kinds that the editor uses; (3) the writers' general approach and point of view, in order to learn the editor's point of view; (4) the appeal and the kinds of persons to whom it is made; (5) whether the article contains the opinions of the writer or whether he interviewed an expert whose name or experience gave an authoritative tone; (6) the interest-arousing qualities of the paragraph beginnings; (7) the literary style, including figures of speech, and the vocabulary, to see if the publication has any preferred or standardized presentation; (8) the average length of the sentences, paragraphs, and the articles, in order to have a measuring stick for one's own manuscripts; and (9) the style and length of the captions, or headlines, in order to "pattern" one's own after them, because if the editor uses sprightly and short ones, so should the writer.

Consideration should be given to the fiction, poetry, and special departments. The fiction and poetry indicate the editor's appeal to the subscribers' interests in reading for entertainment and relaxation, particularly if the former predominates. The special departments reveal the practical interests of the reader and the publication's policy of helping and guiding him. In addition, one may find possibilities and opportunities of submitting manuscripts to the departments.

Planning Pictures to Fit the Publication's Policy. Never have pictures been so important as they are today. Because "a picture is worth ten thousand words," as Confucius said, beginners and professionals alike must give considerable thought to the illustration of their articles. One student wrote an article around some unusual pictures he had and sold the article and the pictures to a national magazine for $550. Writers must learn to think in terms of pictures. As a nation, we have become picture-minded. By means of pictures, editors hope to create an even greater demand for their publications. If the editor "sells" his publication to his readers on the appeal of pictures, the writer, in turn, must "sell" the editor his manuscript on the same basis.

Snapshots are preferred to the formally posed photographs

taken in a photographer's studio, although some editors use both as well as kodachromes, or color transparencies, as explained in Chapter 15. One, however, must know which kind the editor prefers before he arranges for the illustration of his manuscript. Other kinds of illustrations, such as drawings, charts, graphs, and maps, should be noted, because some newspapers and magazines have the policy of using them, although others would reject them.

Advertising Analysis Is Clue to Reader Interest. A feature writer must develop the habit of investigating the advertising to gain an insight into the reader's income and interests and to know the manuscript markets better. Advertising agencies spend thousands of dollars annually to learn all they can about the readers of each magazine that they use as a medium for their clients' copy. By means of surveying the subscriber, they know the source and range of his income, his buying power, his living standard, his education, his class standing, his recreational interests, and his likes and dislikes. They know where the magazine's readers live and how they live. They know the number of readers who buy the publications by subscription and the number who buy it on the newsstands. They know whether they are professional, business, industrial, or agricultural people. The agencies know how much the readers spend on necessities and how much on luxuries. They know whether they are single or married; the size of their families; and whether they own their homes or rent them. They know whether they go to church or to the golf course on Sunday.

On the basis of these tabulations, made from questionnaires and surveys, the agencies place their clients' advertisements. Because the advertising agency must know where it can get the best returns, it must know everything it possibly can about the readers to whom the appeal is made in the advertising copy. Thus, one sees that the advertising is a safe guide for the writer if he would know all about the readers. A knowledge of a publication's advertising will enable a writer better to interest the reader in his article. Agencies do not buy space at anywhere from $50 to $30,000 or more a page without knowing who will read and be influenced by the advertising copy. For his purposes, the writer does not have to spend thousands of dollars, nor even a single dollar, to learn about the readers, if he will use the agencies' knowledge. He can profit by their studies simply by familiarizing himself with the advertising.

By noticing whether or not the magazine carries advertising for servants' uniforms, vacuum cleaners, carpet sweepers, or brooms, the writer will learn a great deal about the reader. Or it may be the kinds of floor coverings, kinds of refrigeration, kinds of automobiles, or prices and brands of wearing apparel advertised that may serve as a guide to knowing the subscribers. For example, if a brand of shoes is advertised for $2.95 or for $35.00, the writer will know a great deal about the reader's income, spending power, and interests. Immediately in his mind he will picture an average person in whichever group the appeal is made. With this definite picture of the reader in mind, the writer will be able to slant his article to appeal to the reader better.

The percentages of reading matter and advertising copy should be compared to indicate something of the probable income of the publication. A comparison with other magazines that are similar in appeal also should be made, in order to determine which publication is regarded by the advertising agencies as having the greatest reader interest.

Because the income from advertising and from subscriptions is so closely related, one may profit in slanting by knowing the circulation figures of a publication. This may be obtained by looking in one of the publication yearbooks or directories listed under the "Free-Lance Writers' Library" in the Appendix. The appeal of the advertising and the subscription price are clues to the kind of reader a publication has. Careful and thoughtful analysis of advertising and circulation will repay the writer manyfold, because it will lessen his opportunities to receive rejections.

Examining the Advertising Tie-up. In modern publication production, the business and advertising departments influence the editorial department either consciously or unconsciously. Successful periodicals must have an editorial policy that harmonizes with the salesmanship aims of the agencies that place the national advertising. The readers of the magazine also read the advertisements, and this means that the two policies must necessarily consider the same reader. If the magazine is to obtain subscribers and the advertising copy is to sell the goods displayed in the advertising, the two divisions must cooperate with each other.

A recent study of seven of the largest women's monthly magazines, made by the author over a six-months' period, revealed a decided "tie-up" of the editorial copy, or reading matter, with the advertising copy of each of the periodicals analyzed. For example, an article on cosmetics either described the container or pictured it so distinctly that the brand name showed or that the reader-consumer could recognize the brand by the shape of the jar or carton. In some instances the advertised brands were mentioned in the article. The survey disclosed a range of from 36 definite advertising "tie-ups" in the *Ladies' Home Journal* to 147 in the *Woman's Home Companion*. The remaining five women's magazines over the same period averaged 85 "tie-ups" for each publication. In sixteen outstanding monthly farm publications for the same six months, the advertising "tie-ups" varied from 2 to 66 in two magazines. The other fourteen magazines averaged 28 apiece. The percentage for the two classes of magazines was practically the same, because the farm publications, on the whole, are much smaller in size and have a lower number of advertising accounts. Because of the nature of the appeal in both reading matter and advertising copy, it is easier to plan advertising "tie-ups" in these types of magazines. But even a scanning of other publications will show that almost every magazine makes use of the opportunity when it is offered. Even if the "tie-up" is not obvious, the article may begin where the advertising leaves off, because the policy of magazines is to help both the reader and the advertiser as much as possible.

From analyses that writers make, they will find that they should give heed to opportunities to write articles for farm and women's magazines that lend themselves to possible "tie-ups" with advertising copy. A young writer observed that a farm magazine did not carry advertising copy of washing machines or other laundry equipment. She interviewed an authority on household management and several housewives, and then wrote an article on "Short Cuts to an Easy Washday." In the note to the editor she called his attention to the opportunity to solicit laundry equipment advertising. The editor bought the short article for $25. The advertising staff contacted manufacturers of washing machines, automatic dryers, mangles, and soap (or the agencies placing their advertising copy), and increased the magazine's advertising lineage and revenue. Another writer, basing her material on an uncopyrighted government bulletin for authority, used the same approach in her note to the editor and sold an article on "Canned Meat That Keeps" for $30 to a women's magazine editor. The article was used to contact national advertisers of pressure cookers and resulted in added advertising lineage for that publication.

Antagonizing advertisers in manuscripts should be avoided. Editors will not purchase articles that will offend their financial supporters. A novice wrote an article on "Making Your Own Face Creams," in which he pointed out the money that women could save by not buying commercial products. He insisted on sending it to a well-known women's magazine that carries a great amount of "copy" advertising high-priced cosmetics. He could have saved his time and postage on the manuscript had he given thought to the attitude of the publication's advertisers toward such an article. Eventually he sold the article to a periodical that did not carry cosmetic advertising. In writing for the "slick" magazines that take advantage of advertising "tie-ups," one writes to the advertisers as well as to the readers, while the fiction writer slanting to the "pulps" writes only to the readers, because that class of publications depends on support from subscriptions and newsstand sales rather than from advertising.

Developing a Selling Technique. A card file, even a small one that costs only a dime, will be convenient for recording for future reference the market information one acquires from his publication studies. Since magazines are changing constantly, one must keep up to date and add the changes to the cards as he notes them.

By analyzing the articles that have been accepted and by slanting material to the editor's needs, beginners and semi-professionals will soon have prospective feature writers examining *their* articles as they appear in print, to see how they attained their acceptances.

From this five-pointed plan, the prospective writer realizes that success is not due to being a good writer entirely. He must also be a good judge of markets. Like the aviator, he must have a sixth sense; but instead of a sense of balance, the writer has the sense of slant that enables him to plan and write his manuscripts to appeal to a definite editor of a definite publication.

Beginners Should Aim at Small Markets. Novices frequently are torn between the urge to submit their manuscripts to the better-known class publications, in order to satisfy their hope for renown, and the desire to submit to the less familiar ones and receive acceptances instead of rejections. This problem can be solved in their minds before it is formulated if they stop to realize that the bigger and better known the magazine is, the greater and keener the competition. Most amateurs are astonished when they learn of the number of publications for which they could write. Because they are lazy or indifferent, they continue submitting manuscripts to a few well-known magazines—with the result that the articles are returned in an astonishingly short time.

Amateurs often feel that they are handicapped if they do not live in one or the other of the three great publishing centers, New York, Chicago, or San Francisco. The experience, however, of many professionals proves the fallacy of their desire. The advice that successful writers and editors give to the beginner is to stay in the community that he knows and where he can find marketable material to interest readers. Since the great majority of subscribers do not live in the publishing centers, the editors, in order to interest their readers, desire manuscripts concerning things close to the readers' lives—another point that the writer must keep in mind as he writes.

The Use of Manuscript Market Guides. Guides to the manuscript markets are available for writers who wish to learn more about opportunities for selling. Their greatest value lies in acquainting the writer with the fact that such markets exist. If possible, he should examine copies of the publications suggested in the market books before writing the article. If none are available, he should write for sample copies. The market books are suggestive in supplying ideas for "tips." Upon learning that there is such a market, one may think of subjects that he quickly may turn into salable features. A young man turned through a market book and noticed a trade journal for barbers. He wrote up the experiences of a student who became a barber in order to earn his way through college. He received $25 for the manuscript. Another saw listed a magazine for shoe-repair men, and that reminded her that the manager of the shoe-repair shop where she had just had her shoes mended would make a good subject for a success article. She sent in the story and received $25. Used with intelligence and ingenuity, the market lists may be of real value in suggesting not only markets but ideas for articles. A number of the market books are listed in the Appendix.

In writing for a sample copy of a publication in order to slant to it more accurately, always enclose at least 3 three-cent stamps, or a dime. The writer should not ask the editor to pay the postage.

Querying the Editor. A beginner does not need to be concerned about querying an editor in order to get approval before writing an article. Editors do not buy manuscripts unseen, except from professionals with whose work they are familiar. In that case, there are times when the professional might save his time, energy, or expense by querying the editor. As a rule, however, the best plan is to write the article and submit it. The editor might accept it because of the way it is written, the clever style, or its unique point of view, which, of course, he would not discern in a note of query.

The Use of Literary Agents. The feature writer wastes his time in depending upon literary agents to market his manuscripts. (1) They are interested only in selling articles for professionals who write regularly and whose manuscripts demand high prices. (2) One may have more difficulty in persuading an agent to accept him as a client than he would have in marketing his material himself. (3) If the article is timely, it may get out of date while it is on the agent's desk waiting until he has the time or inclination to try to place it. Even writer's magazines discourage beginners' queries as the following shows.

Sir:

I have just completed my first manuscript and am seeking to obtain an agent to represent me. It has been recommended that I work through a writers' magazine, and in accordance I have chosen yours because of its evident superiority in this field.

This is the first time that I have ever written, and I have no connections with publishing firms and no knowledge of literary agents. I would appreciate it if your magazine could either contact such an agent or recommend where a connection might be made.

> Mary Jones
> *Chicago, Ill.*

We advise beginning writers not to seek an agent. Most reputable agents will not accept beginning writers as clients, unless it is an unusual case. It is far better for the new writer to submit directly to the editors. Rest assured that the manuscript will be read—no editor can afford to overlook a manuscript. Editor.

By having the services of an agent, the writer is less likely to keep up his analyses of magazines. As a consequence, he is not as familiar with reader interests and is not as adept in slanting his material as he would be if he marketed his own articles. Then, too, he has to pay a fee to the agent.

If a writer finds it necessary to employ an agent after he has become well known, he should make careful investigation as to the agent's reliability before contacting him. One should avoid making any agreement with an agent who makes extravagant claims and promises and who requires a fee in advance. The writer who receives offers from unknown agents should resist the alluring contract. Reliable agents who have the confidence and respect of the big magazines do not have to solicit clients. If an article has merit, any editor to whom it is submitted will recognize it without the influence of an agent. In fiction writing, however, a reliable agent may save even the beginner hundreds of rejections. Marketing unsolicited stories or serials presents a more difficult problem to the author than does selling features.

One Sale Leads to Another. Just as experience is most valuable in applying for a position, so is success in selling. The acceptance of a manuscript gives the beginner confidence because he has learned to study the markets with an eye for slanting his material. With success in selling just one article he loses his fear of a rejection slip. Because the editor is generally more willing to trust a writer whom he has tried once and found competent, it is a good plan to try to follow up one sale with another. Personal contacts with an editor, or taking him out to dinner, mean nothing unless one can prove to him one's unfaltering dependability as a writer.

Contacts Resulting from Sales. If a writer sells regularly to a publication, particularly to those in the trade field, he may be offered an associate editorship or a position as a staff writer. If the publication is a monthly one, it is not difficult for the writer to produce the required articles in addition to his regular work. If an editors finds a free-lance writer dependable, he may ask him to do articles on assignment, or on order. If a writer wants a position on the staff of a particular publication, he may attract the attention of the editor by submitting unsolicited manuscripts. Strong friendships often spring up between editors and contributors who submit manuscripts regularly over a period of time.

Basis of Payment. Financial compensation varies with publications, because they pay upon the basis of their incomes. The income of most periodicals is dependent entirely upon the circulation and the advertising, with the latter contributing the largest percentage. The *Saturday Evening Post,* for example, which at the end of the first six months of one year carried more than 1,500,000 lines of advertising at $16,800 for a black-and-white advertising page and $50,090 for a center spread in color, surpassed all records of any other weekly magazine during the same period. Its net paid circulation at that time totaled 4,597,987 copies. The magazine broke its own record by buying 1,100 unsolicited manuscripts from the 100,000 submitted by free-lance writers. It now leans heavily on contributions from free-lance authors, as about 75 per cent of the editorial content for the same year was purchased from "outside" contributors. From this sketch of the magazine one may see at a glance that such a magazine should be able to pay generously when it does accept an unsolicited article.

Naturally a less-popular periodical with a smaller income from advertising and subscriptions could not pay as much for a free-lance article as the well-known magazine does. On the other hand, the smaller magazine, in comparison, does not receive many manuscripts from free-lance writers, and, because it cannot pay professional writers big sums, it depends more on the unsolicited manuscripts of the beginners and semi-professionals than on those written by well-known writers. Until his name becomes well known, the beginner will fare better if he slants to the smaller markets.

Another well-known woman's magazine carried the largest dollar volume of advertising of any single issue of any magazine up to that date. The 264-page issue carried $2,146,746.20 worth of advertising of 334 advertisers, which was read by 4,500,000 buyers—the largest all-woman audience up to that date.

It is a tradition in free-lancing that no matter how much time, energy, and expense the writer may have put on his manuscript, he does not set a price on his work but accepts what the editor offers. If he feels the price is not sufficient, he may refuse it; and when the manuscript is returned to him, he may submit it elsewhere. As a rule, the wise beginner accepts what he is offered, because he cannot set a price until he has become established in free-lancing. Professional writers, whose by-lines are known, may benefit by shopping about for a better price. One writer, who had been having his manuscripts accepted for years, was offered $75 for one that he felt was worth more. He refused the offer and later sold the article to a larger publication for $300. Such instances, however, are the exception even for the professional.

In writing for the newspapers, one may expect anywhere from $2.50 to $25 per column; from the magazines one may expect anywhere from $25 up to $3,000 or more, the price depending upon the publication's ability to pay, the importance of the article, and the name of the writer.

Slanting Has Its Rewards. A good writer likes to think of himself as a literary artist, but he must also consider himself a practical business person. He must be a good salesman. And like the salesmen in other lines of business, he must know where to sell his wares. A writer's ability to slant his manuscripts, or the lack of it, either lifts him into the rank of the professional or dooms him to failure. The first law of free-lancing is that the manuscript must be slanted to fit the publication to which it is submitted. Slanting not only enables the writer to sell, but also provides him with ideas for more articles.

An ambitious, enthusiastic student, in spite of her instructor's advice, did not wait to study the markets in order to slant her material. She wrote the article, and, like a blind hunter, shot hit or miss at the magazines. The result was that the article always came back. By the end of the course, she had sold all the other articles she had written because she slanted them carefully. After analyzing a publication that she was confident would take the material if it were slanted for it, she rewrote the first article. A couple of weeks later she sought out her instructor to report a check for $65, which completely converted her to the doctrine that "it pays to slant."

When a writer has an article in print, he should always obtain a copy of that issue, not only to serve as a source of gratification but to be kept in his files for future reference. He may wish to present it in applying for a staff position on a publication; or, if his articles are along a certain line, he may want to publish them later in book form. Whether or not he ever makes use of his file of published articles, it will be a satisfaction to see his printed articles increase as he becomes more adept in slanting and has greater success in selling.

Examples of One Article Slanted to Different Markets. Almost every article, though it has sold to one publication, may be entirely re-slanted, re-organized, re-outlined, and re-written for another or even several other markets if the writer analyzes markets carefully and slants accurately to them. In that way a writer may receive several checks from several different publications without having to find several more ideas, or several more interviewees, or spending additional hours on research, as he would if he were writing on new subjects.

A graduate student sold the same idea to four different publications, but each article was re-written to the readers of each of the four publications, whose circulations did not overlap. Because of limited space the articles are used here in part only. The first was accepted by the *American Home,* the second by *Woman's Day,* the third by *Charm,* and the fourth by *Woman's Day,* for a later issue, because the author had given it a different slant than she had in the other article purchased by *Woman's Day.* The writer not only added to her own prestige in her profession but also endorsed checks totalling more than $300.

(1)

**More Basil
and Thyme***

BY DOROTHY F. DOUGLAS

Probably no housewife in the Middle West is so skilled in the raising and using of herbs as Mrs. Flora Rich Toole of Baraboo, Wisconsin. She grew up with herbs in her back yard, and she learned the art of using them from her mother, who acquired it from Mrs. Toole's grandmother back in Vermont. At Garry-Nee-Dule, which in Irish means "Garden of the Tooles," one needs only to follow his nose to a magic land of special smells. In the garden the delicate odor of sweet marjoram entwines with that of lemon-scented balm. In the drying room the aroma of sweet basil blends with that of chives. An enticing fusion of herb smells fills the air in the grinding room. Delightful odors pervade everywhere—in the packing room and herb kitchen.

"Any housewife can bring a little of the romance of herbs into her daily cooking," suggests Mrs. Toole. "Once she tries chives in omelet and sweet marjoram on a pork roast, there is no telling the compli-

* Reprinted by permission of *The American Home* and Dorothy F. Douglas.

ments that will pour forth. Cheaper cuts of beef enhanced with savory, thyme, and rosemary can have the flavor of expensive steak. Tomato cocktail has a piquant taste when seasoned with thyme, savory, tarragon, or basil . . . and all mothers should try sweet marjoram with spinach."

The ancients were noted for their use of herbs in cooking. Europeans, Orientals, and Egyptians have always used more herbs than Americans, but today American women are becoming more herb minded. Herbs are magic. Mrs. Toole suggests that a new user of herbs buy small, assorted quantities. Her experiments will help her discover her family's favorite tastes. Use a level teaspoonful for six portions—green herbs require more.

In her own kitchen, Mrs. Toole is an experimenter just as she is in her garden. She likes, for instance, ham seasoned with brown sugar, savory, marjoram, basil and thyme, or twice-baked potatoes enhanced with chervil, thyme, chives and sage, besides thick cream, butter, salt, and pepper added after potatoes are whipped. Her favorite salad is green pea and English walnut salad mixed with French dressing, and sprinkled with mint.

*   *   *

[Several paragraphs followed, explaining the use of herbs, and four recipes were given.]

(2)
Herb Jellies*

*Stir a Little Imagination into the
Jelly Kettle. You'll Be Proud
of the Tasty Results.*

By Dorothy F. Douglas

Roast beef served with purple thyme-and-grape jelly, or veal with green mint-and-apple jelly, can become the high spot of any meal. Chicken looks like Thanksgiving fare alongside a bright-yellow jelly of sage and cider. Even sausage can be a main dinner dish accompanied by savory-and-grapefruit jelly. Herb jellies are ideal, too, with cream cheese for crackers and open-face sandwiches.

Fresh herbs and juices are best for making herb jellies; but good results can be had with bottled juices and dried herbs or oil of herbs. Vegetable dyes make the jellies colorful as autumn leaves—green for mint, yellow for savory and sage, and red for basil. Any combination with grape won't need coloring.

* * *

[Directions for making herb jellies, and four recipes were included.]

(3)
Herbal Vinegars*

By Dorothy F. Douglas

Although there are over sixty varieties of vinegars, most American cooks are acquainted with only one—plain, ordinary, cider vinegar. Yet other varieties—such as the herbal—are easily accessible at most large department stores or at herb shops. An exotic choice is offered for your spice cupboard: tarragon, mint, burnet, marjoram, garlic, elder, or the mixed herbal vinegar.

Herbal vinegars have a genius for retaining the essential flavor of herbs fresh from the garden. In mid-winter, they taste of summer warmth and fragrance. Used on dull vegetables or meats, herbal vinegars bring out elusive, tangy flavors. They are as much a part of fine cooking as spices and sugar.

Tarragon is probably better known than any other of the herbal vinegars. It may be used for marinating chicken before baking, or to give a sharp, spicy taste to broiled fish. Any green salad (especially string-bean salad) with French dressing made with tarragon vinegar is extremely tangy and delightful.

Mint vinegar may be used in a variety of foods. Two or three table-spoons on a lamb roast will give it a delicate fragrance when done. String beans or green peas—fresh or canned—cooked the last five minutes in ½ teaspoon mint vinegar and ½ teaspoon sugar, taste fresher and sweeter. Cole slaw and fruit salad need a few drops of mint vinegar to sharpen their flavor.

* * *

When making mixed herbal vinegar, be careful not to overpower a weak herb with a strong one. Basil, chives, and mint are especially strong. Chervil, marjoram, and tarragon are delicate and weak. Equal parts of thyme, basil, chives, and lovage make a tasteful blend, as does one part of basil to two parts each of burnet and borage.

A word of warning: Use herb vinegars sparingly. They are meant to bring out the natural and delicate flavor in foods.

* Reprinted by permission of *Charm* and Dorothy F. Douglas.

(4)

Plain Foods
with Herbs*

*An Interview with Carson Gulley, Lecturer on Food Planning
and Food Preparation, and Head Chef of Van Hise
Dining Hall at the University of Wisconsin.*

BY DOROTHY F. DOUGLAS

"Men don't like fancy foods as well as they do tasty baked beans, cole-slaw, and goulash," says Carson Gulley, popular lecturer on food planning and preparation, and head chef of a men's dining hall at the University of Wisconsin. "From a man's point of view it is better to cook plain foods with an original touch than to stun him with new creations."

Mr. Gulley came to this heart-warming conclusion after having supervised the preparation of 10,000,000 student meals during the last twenty years at Van Hise dining hall on the University of Wisconsin campus. Year after year Mr. Gulley satisfies his student guests by using herbs and spices sparingly to bring out the hidden flavors in plain foods. From his collection of 127 different herbs, spices, salts and vinegars gathered from all over the world, Mr. Gulley has experimented with almost everything in everything, and he speaks from experience when he warns, "Herb cookery is a dangerous thing."

"If the housewife uses too many herbs or uses them indiscriminately, their elusiveness is lost, and a badly flavored dish is the result," the chef explains. "Every cook should remember that herbs are not to smother the flavor of foods, but to delicately lift out the real flavor. If an herb doesn't do that, no cook should use it," continues Mr. Gulley. "That's why I call herbs dangerous. I don't recommend them for all foods."

Exercises

1. From observation of your favorite newsstand or from talking with its owner, estimate how many new magazines have come out during the past year.

2. How many have ceased publication in that same period?

3. What magazines with which you are familiar have changed their policy during the last year? What change or changes were made?

4. Have any of the big magazines changed ownership during the last year? If so, what ones?

* Reprinted by permission of *Woman's Day, The A & P Magazine,* and Dorothy F. Douglas.

5. List all the publications with which you are really familiar and list their appeals to the reader as you recall them from having read the publications for some time.

6. Select four from the list and enumerate the feature articles and short stories.

7. In recalling the appeal of the advertising copy, do you believe the editors have planned the publication for the lower, middle, or upper intellectual class?

8. What item in the current news suggests to you an idea for a feature that might be hung on a "news peg" for one of the magazines that you already know?

9. Select a feature story in the magazine section of your Sunday newspaper and one in your favorite magazine and list all the differences that you can find.

10. After looking up the circulation in one of the directories listed in the Appendix of the four magazines on your list in Exercise 6, jot down the ideas you have about what kind of appeals you should incorporate into articles if you were writing for them.

11. Make a chart for the material in your favorite metropolitan newspaper by listing the feature articles in the feature section in one column. In the second column indicate the probable sources from which the editor obtained each.

12. Add to your chart the information concerning: (1) the classification of the articles; (2) the points of view from which they are written; (3) the form; (4) the style; (5) the length; and (6) the kind of reader to whom they would appeal, to judge from the advertising appeal; e.g., vacuum cleaner or carpet sweeper advertising, etc.

13. In a sentence, tell what kind of feature articles you think the Sunday newspaper magazine editor wants for his readers.

14. For what departments, other than the feature section, do you think you could write features that the department editor would buy?

15. How many of the features listed in Exercise 11 concerned current, timely topics?

16. Indicate in your chart for Exercise 11 the features that are local, state, national, and international in appeal.

17. From your chart in Exercise 11, what did you find was the length of the shortest feature? of the longest? When you slant an article to this newspaper, how long should it be?

18. Add to the chart in Exercise 11 the number of pictures that each feature had. What does this tell you in reference to the policy concerning pictures?

19. Write a definition of the editorial policy of a newspaper and a

magazine toward feature articles and point out how one varies from the other.

20. What is the subscription price by the year and by the single issue of your favorite general magazine? From this, can you tell whether it is a magazine to which people take yearly subscriptions, or do they depend upon getting it at the newsstand?

21. How many advertisements does it carry?

22. Using as the basis the goods advertised, to what income level do you think the magazine appeals? What kind of subject matter would a free-lance writer send the publication?

23. List the names of one magazine of each of the five types of "slicks."

24. List four ideas, or "tips," for features that you could write for each publication you listed in Exercise 23.

25. Work out a chart for your favorite magazine as you did in Exercise 11 for the newspaper. Include the information suggested in this chapter on Analyzing the Reading Matter. Include the three points concerning the content and policy of the publication.

26. In analyzing each of the feature articles, list the nine points suggested in this chapter on Analyzing the Reading Matter.

27. In analyzing the fiction, list the two points suggested in this chapter on Analyzing the Reading Matter.

28. Are formal or informal photographs used to illustrate the features, and how many pictures of each type does each article have?

29. Does the publication use any other type of illustration besides photographs? If so, list them on your chart.

30. Analyze the magazine advertising to see whether it appeals to the readers in the home equipped with a broom, a carpet sweeper, a vacuum cleaner, or with servants in uniforms? Or take any other commodity advertised as a basis for your judgment in studying the appeal of the advertising copy.

31. What percentage (by page) of the publication is devoted to advertising? How do you think the advertising agencies regard it as a media for their clients?

32. Look in one of the periodical directories (N. W. Ayer & Son's *Directory of Newspapers and Periodicals,* the International Year Book Number of *Editor and Publisher,* or the magazine section of Standard Rate and Data Service) and find the circulation of your favorite magazine.

33. Scan the articles again to see in how many there are any evident "tie-ups" with the commodities advertised. What were they?

34. From a brief survey of the market books to which you have access (see list in Appendix), indicate the individual purpose of each book in addition to that of listing the markets.

35. Suggest a "tip" for an article that came to you while you were examining the market books.

Publication Analysis

Teen-Age Magazines and Family Periodicals

Compare, by using chart form as illustrated in the Appendix, two magazines of each of the above types. There are a number of these types of publications. They are available at newsstands, from magazine dealers listed in the Appendix under "Aids for Writers," or in library periodical reading rooms. Some suggested teen-age periodicals: *American Farm Youth, Boy's Life,* "Junior Bazaar" section in *Harper's Bazaar, American Girl, Compact, Seventeen;* family magazines: *American Family, Home Life, Household, Parents' Magazine, Town Journal,* or others of your choice.

Do not spend more than two and a half hours on preparation of this report.

I. Identification: Name of magazine, name of editor, where published, price. Do single sales or yearly subscriptions attract the purchaser?

II. Make-up: What do you like or not like about the size and make-up of these magazines? If you were the editor, what changes would you make in them?

III. Advertising: To what classes and types of purchasers does the advertising appeal (broom, carpet-sweeper, or vacuum-cleaner class)? Did you notice any advertising that appealed to a particular class? Judging from the advertising, what types of features do you think these magazines would buy?

IV. General Policy:
1. Do these magazines have editorials? What is the content and appeal of editorials?
2. What percentage (rough estimate) is devoted to fiction in each, and to whom does it appeal?
3. What is the circulation of each magazine? (See one of the directories.)
4. What are the chances for selling, to judge from the names of the writers?

V. Feature Articles:
1. What type of feature articles and what subjects did you find in these magazines?
2. What devices were used to make the feature articles attractive to the reader?
3. List the things that you liked about one feature.
4. List the things that you did not like about it.

5. List the things that you learned about "how to write features" or to "slant" to these magazines.
6. Did you find any announcement of "clubs" or contests? What is the purpose of a contest? Do you have any "tips" you could write to submit?

VI. Slogan: Make a slogan for these magazines.
VII. Four Tips: Source, authority, and three possible markets suggested by this study.

CHAPTER 10

Planning and Outlining the Article

The Purpose of a Plan. Planning the feature article has been likened by some writers to architecture. The architect cannot build without a plan; neither can the writer "build," or write, without one. Others have compared the work of the artist with that of the writer. Like the artist, the writer must get all the details, in order to enable the reader to see the article and understand it as the writer wishes. The writer uses words rather than a brush, but the purposes and the results are the same. Still others have compared writing to public speaking. The writer, like the speaker, must catch the attention of the reader. But the writer has to hold his reader-audience after he gets his attention. If he does not, the reader will go on to the next column or page, while the speaker's audience will not often be so rude as to walk out of the meeting. The work of the writer is more similar, in that respect, to that of the person who speaks via television or radio. If the person before the microphone does not hold his audience's attention, his audience will turn the dial to another station. Neither the broadcaster nor the writer can expect to hold attention if he attempts to work without a plan.

The writer of a feature article is much like the pioneer who crossed the frontier and blazed a trail in order to start a new life in a new place under new conditions. Although the pioneer had definite ideas of the kind of place to which he hoped he was going to establish a home and occupation or business, he had to adjust those plans to meet the actual physical conditions of the new land, the living standards of his fellow settlers, and the opportunities or the hardships as he found them. The true pioneer always knew what he wanted to do and why he wanted to do it, and he never became discouraged. No matter how much writing one may have done, each article offers new frontiers, like the pioneer's trail into a new and unknown land. The writer, like the pioneer, must have a purpose, a definite goal, and he must plan his trail, or outline, just as carefully and as enthusiastically.

Writers Write to Help the Reader. The newspaper feature section or magazine that helps the readers is the most successful. As previously pointed out, in order to help the reader, one must think of him constantly—that is, not of readers in a mass, but of a particular reader. If one would write successfully, he should think in terms of a person whom he knows. But he must remember that instead of talking to one person he is talking to hundreds, or even millions, of people who are like the one person or the several persons he knows.

Writer Writes to Please Readers. The writer who receives checks for his manuscripts, rather than rejections, never writes to please himself, but always to please the readers of a particular publication to which he wishes to sell his manuscript. He does not outline the material nor write the article until he has given those readers a great deal of thought as to: (1) who will be interested; (2) why he will be interested; (3) how much he will be interested; and (4) which periodicals does he read. Not until the writer has answered these four questions can he successfully plan his article.

In order to please his readers, the writer must visualize them. Only the businesslike writer is able to do this. One cannot visualize readers unless he knows who the readers are. By careful analysis of the advertising in the publication to which one is slanting, one may visualize the subscribers accurately. Not until then can the writer plan and write the article interestingly and sincerely.

Timeliness Is Important. Because the contents of magazines must be timely when they are published and on the newsstands, writers must plan their articles long in advance. For magazines, a writer should plan his material six months in advance, because many editors plan the contents of their magazines that far ahead. They work on several issues at a time—reading proof on one, making the layout for another, and planning the content of still another issue six months in advance. If the article is returned the first time it is mailed, there is then still time to send it to one or two other publications. In submitting to newspaper feature editors, the writer should plan his material six, or at least three, weeks in advance, if possible. Even newspaper feature editors must plan their make-up, art layouts, and engravings some time ahead. Writers as well as editors must be almost clairvoyant to know what will be news-worthy months in advance.

Catching the Attention of the Reader. In the planning of the article, much thought must be given to the devices of obtaining the reader's attention. The feature writer, like the advertising writer, must (1) catch the reader's attention, (2) arouse his interest, and (3) hold his interest throughout the article, by making the body of it so interesting that the reader cannot lay down his newspaper or magazine until he has finished reading the article.

When one visualizes hundreds or millions of readers intensely interested in an article, the amateur may think that it will be difficult to catch and hold reader interest for his own work. In reality, however, it is very simple if the writer gives a great deal of thought to planning. Before beginning to write, he should have a definite idea of: (1) the title, or caption, or heading; (2) the lead, or beginning of the article; and (3) the plan of development of the body of the article; (4) the conclusion; and (5) the illustrative material, including photographs, snapshots, drawings, maps, charts and graphs. In the planning of the outline, one frequently may determine the caption last, or he may plan the illustrations before he outlines his material. The order of planning is not important, but the five elements of the tentative outline, or plan, are essential to success.

Determining the Aim of the Article. There may be so many interesting phases of an article that the writer may attempt to include all of them, with the result that the article will be aimless and uninteresting because it does not make a definite impression on the reader's mind. An amateur interviewed an authority in home economics concerning vitamins in foods. Before completing his material, he had talked to several experts and, when he came to outline the article, found that his notes included not only the nutritive value of foods, but the canning, storage, and preparation. He felt that all these phases were important, and he included them, forgetting that the magazine to which he was slanting the article was concerned with the health value only. After class criticism of his article, he eliminated all material except that which pertained to the health value for the health magazine. From the remainder of his notes he wrote an article on canning and storage of vegetables for a farm publication. A third one, on food preparation, he slanted to a home magazine. In due time he received three checks, which made him feel well repaid for the thought and time he had given to re-planning the three aims for three articles instead of crowding them all into one manuscript without a definite aim.

The writer, whether amateur or professional, before planning his outline should always ask himself, "Whom am I trying to help or please and how am I going to do so?" In other words, one must determine the aim or purpose of the article before selecting from his notes the material that he wishes to include. After having selected the aim, the writer must never fail to stick to that aim or angle of the subject that pertains to it.

Articles Have Three Aims. In turning through magazines and newspapers, one finds that each article has one of three purposes. It aims to (1) inform, (2) give practical help, or (3) entertain the reader. A clever writer frequently can treat the same subject and the same material to accomplish two or more of the aims. If his purpose is to give facts to inform or add to the reader's scope of information and knowledge, he will present them in a manner that will impress and stimulate the reader's mind. If he desires to help or guide the reader in his practical pursuits, work, or recreation, he may include all the details that will enable anyone to use the suggestions in a practical way. But if one step of the process is omitted, the reader's efforts will result in failure. If the article's aim is to entertain, the writer will select a style and the aspects of the topic that will provide amusement, diversion, or recreation for the reader. An amateur found that in gathering material for an article on trout fishing he had accumulated notes that would inform, instruct, and entertain the reader. His good judgment told him that he could not catch and hold the reader-attention if he tried to accomplish all three aims in one article. He sent the informative one to a general outdoor magazine, where it was purchased after the writer had revised it to meet the editor's suggestions. A helpful lesson in trout fishing under the caption "Beginners Can Catch 'Em Too" was sold on its second trip in the mail. The third, "Trout and Mosquitoes Are a Lot of Fun," was purchased by an adventure magazine to amuse its subscribers. Had the writer tried to incorporate the three aims in one article he would have failed to interest any one reader for any length of time.

Informative Articles. Every free-lance writer has unlimited opportunities to write articles containing interesting and significant information. Nearly everyone who desires to be better informed depends on features in newspapers and magazines for latest news and opinions concerning current affairs, as well as biography and history with which the current events may be concerned. The average reader, after graduation from high school or grade school, turns to newspapers and magazines for his further education. Only a small proportion of the people living in the United States go on to college. In planning the informative type of article, the writer must select only those facts that are worth remembering or that will stimulate the reader to think about the subject. By keeping the purpose firmly in mind, the writer will be able to select the material intelligently and to determine the point of view from which he should write the article in order to attract and hold the reader's interest.

Practical Guidance Features. Articles giving the reader practical help, suggestions, or guidance have increased not only in number during the past decade, but whole magazines are now devoted to such features. People want to get more pleasure out of living, to advance, to be more successful, or to do for themselves what others have done successfully. The simplest guidance articles are found in the recipe features in women's magazines.

Utility articles may be written as simple how-to-do articles in which definite directions are given. Or they may be written so that the utilitarian purpose is not obvious to the readers, because the detail of carrying out the process is presented so interestingly that the readers are not bored with all the information necessary to accomplish a similar enterprise. They will be interested because the narration and description appeal to their imagination.

In writing articles of this type, the author must consider carefully the class of readers whom he hopes will be reading the article, and must give thought to their ability to carry out directions. A device that will often serve to hold the reader's interest is that used by the writer who confides to the reader that he has made mistakes. Such a device can be used only in a personal experience article written in the first person. If the third person is used, the writer may relate how the interviewee made some mistakes because he tried some short cut or did not follow directions accurately. If the reader feels that the writer or the interviewee was not perfect the first time he undertook to do or to make the thing described, the reader will have not only more interest but more confidence in attempting the undertaking. This device also softens the egotistical or "preachy" tone that is so easily given to guidance articles.

Leads must be particularly attractive in this type of article. The writer has to make the article appeal to the reader by means of a clever beginning. Dialogue makes an effective beginning if it is handled well; or direct address is a good beginning by which to attract the reader's eye.

Entertaining Articles. The supply of entertaining articles has never exceeded the demand. Not every free-lance writer seems to have the ability to write features containing humor, pathos, adventure, or romance in a style that will hold the reader's interest to the end. But to the writer who can see the comedy and tragedy or the adventure and romance in life about him, the opportunities are unlimited for writing entertaining features. Because the reader's desire for this type of feature article is never satisfied, he turns to fiction, drama, radio, television, and the moving pictures.

To prepare such articles is not difficult if the writer has a sense of humor, a sympathetic point of view, an understanding of human nature, and can express himself clearly by means of an apt vocabulary. The larger part of the success of an article aimed to entertain depends upon the way in which the writer stimulates the reader to see what he wants him to see. This is done by avoiding general terms and using specific words. Every verb should be scrutinized to see that it is a colorful, suggestive word. Use of figures of speech, if original and clever, adds much to the style of this type of article.

Articles aiming to entertain are the most difficult to write before the writer has acquired considerable experience, unless he is particularly gifted or has practiced writing this type of article in his spare moments. Just because editors have difficulty in supplying the demand for good entertainment articles, a writer—amateur or professional—need not think that it is useless for him to attempt such features. On the contrary, he should practice writing them—even short pointed paragraphs—until he finds he has developed a skill to write in an entertaining style.

Young beginners frequently have the mistaken notion that in order to write in an entertaining style they must stoop beneath the best journalistic standards and write articles that, if printed, would have a pernicious influence. No matter what the editor's personal standard of ethics may be, he will not buy articles that will result in adverse criticism of his publication and in cancellation of subscriptions. To sell entertaining features, one must always write in a constructive vein and never stoop to gratifying a reader's taste for the morbid.

Formulating the Purpose. In order to write marketable features, the writer must obviously have a definite purpose—not only when he gathers his material, but when he outlines and writes his article. To avoid drifting away from the purpose as he outlines or writes, the free-lance will do well always to write down in one sentence at the top of the first page of his outline a statement of the aim and purpose of the article. When the writer cannot decide which of his notes do or do not pertain to the article's purpose, a glance at the statement at the top of the outline may aid him in sticking to his aim and subject. With the purpose clearly defined, it is easier to devote the proper amount of space to each division of the outline, and thus avoid too much detail in some parts of the article and too little in others. If the purpose is not clear as the writer plans his outline, the finished article may lack coherence and unity, which lack may necessitate the rewriting of the article.

A definite objective in outlining and writing each article will result in sales; without it the writer will have rejections rather than acceptances to show for his efforts at the typewriter.

Planning the Reader Appeal. The millions of people who read fact articles in newspapers and magazines differ in their interests because of differences in race, temperament, environment, education, society, occupations, professions, recreation, health, and wealth. There are, consequently, thousands of publications to appeal to those particular interests. In planning the appeal to make in an article to catch and hold the reader-interest, the writer must realize that keen competition faces him.

Appeals Are Based on Psychology. No matter what appeals the writer uses, he must base them on common sense and the principles of psychology. In every article he must assume that he is addressing people who are uninformed and uninterested and who need their attention not only pricked, but stabbed, to catch and hold their interest. A writer does not need to be sensational, but he must know how he can get and keep the reader's attention. The various psychological devices by which this may be done are: (1)

an emphatic caption and lead, to catch the reader's attention; (2) emphatic paragraph leads throughout the article, so that as the reader's eye wanders down the column he will retain his interest and will read on to the end; (3) association, by means of reference to people, places, or things with which the reader is familiar; (4) recall of things the reader has experienced at some previous time; and (5) using the point of view of the reader, in order to aid him in seeing himself in the article.

In addition to knowing the devices by which one may appeal to the reader, one must know: (1) how widespread the reader-interest in the subject is; (2) just how much it will appeal to the reader of the publication for which the article is being slanted; and (3) what phases of the appeal will have the greatest interest for the greatest number of readers. These things one cannot determine without knowing and liking people, or without knowing the likes and dislikes of the publication's readers. The things that a reader likes to see, hear, and do are the things that in his reading will give him pleasure and satisfaction.

Every human being wants to be healthy, wealthy, wise, and happy to at least some degree. In appealing to readers, remember that magazines are based upon this principle. If the writer succeeds in showing the reader the way to health, wealth, wisdom, and happiness, the editors will buy what he writes.

Select Appeals with Wide Interest. Eight out of ten articles that come to an editor's desk cannot be used because the interest does not have an appeal to his particular readers. If the writer observes closely, he will find some appeal in every experience. "What I Think of My Boss," which appeared in *Harper's Magazine,* had an appeal to each boss. When he read the article, he immediately wondered what his workers thought of him. It had equal appeal to every employee, because as he read the feature he compared his superior with that of the writer's. The article had wide appeal. It caught the attention of every employer and every employee. Consequently, the article had practically 100 per cent interest for that particular magazine's readers. After the writer had selected her subject, she visualized her audience and sought a publication whose readers she knew would be receptive to the topic.

When a writer is tempted to give but little attention to the development of the article's appeals, he should imagine that he, along with 100,000 others, is at a football game where he is called upon to make a speech between halves. He sees the packed stadium, the press box with its alert reporters from the metropolitan newspapers and press associations, and the amplifiers to carry his voice to all parts of the huge structure. In the seats are people from all walks of life with all kinds of interests. What subject will the speaker select? If he knows how to appeal to his audience, he will not attempt to discuss the Einstein theory—for two reasons, perhaps. He will choose a simple subject with a wide appeal, the one thing in which every one of the 100,000 would be interested —football. Editors of magazines and newspaper feature sections must find articles that will appeal to even larger crowds, since some of them have ten million subscribers.

Subjects That Have Reader Appeal. If a writer studies the features in newspapers and magazines, he finds a wide variety of subjects to attract readers. They have been selected by editors because they will appeal to the readers. For convenience, the subjects may be divided into the following classes, but, as in any grouping one might arrange, there is bound to be considerable overlapping: (1) current topics; (2) the unusual and extraordinary; (3) mysteries and catastrophes; (4) romance and sex; (5) adventure and exploits; (6) competitive contests; (7) child, teen-age, and adult life; (8) animal life; (9) recreations and hobbies; (10) the familiar and well known; (11) business, professional, and home interests; (12) social welfare; and (13) success and happiness.

Current Topics. Human beings are instinctively curious about what goes on around them. Therefore, timeliness of subjects is an important factor in writing features. Readers like to be the first to know the news, to get the latest and most recent facts, and to know the details of most recent developments. It is easier to sell features that are current, and a writer will profit by finding a timely angle in any subject about which he is writing. Current topics have such a wide appeal that entire magazines are devoted to articles that depend on the appeal of timeliness to interest the reader.

The Unusual and the Extraordinary. The alert writer finds articles everywhere in which he can make use of the appeal of the unusual, unique, extraordinary, or novel. Readers are ever curious about the things that are not commonplace and familiar in their own lives. The biggest, the smallest, the greatest, or the first of anything—all have appeals. For this reason, the extraordinary and novel in the physical, industrial, commercial, and social life about us provide subjects to interest subscribers.

Mysteries and Catastrophes. People are fascinated by anything they cannot understand or by events producing subversion of the usual order of things. Fiction abounds with these appeals. They are the basis for the ever-popular mystery story in which readers from all walks of life find relaxation. The journalist will find in life all about him events that will furnish subject matter sufficiently mysterious or startling to appeal to this type of reader, who is curious or superstitious about the unnatural and the calamitous.

Romance and Sex. Of the elemental instincts, that of love is one of the strongest, according to psychologists. The romance in the life about him is more interesting to the reader than that in fiction. It has been said, "All the world loves a lover." If that is true, all the world loves a romantic feature. Never before has there been so much space devoted to the discussion of sex, but to sell, the articles must be based upon expert authority and avoid an appeal to the morbid.

Adventure and Exploits. New and hazardous enterprises and heroic acts have a wider reader appeal. There are few subscribers who do not enjoy escaping from their monotonous lives for even a few minutes by reading daring tales concerning their fellow men. Many fiction writers capitalize on this method of appeal, and the feature writer could do well to pattern after the novelist. The thrilling tales of the aviator, the radio operator, the explorer, the seaman, the engineer, or the pioneer in any field offer an opportunity to catch and hold the reader's interest.

Competitive Contests. Any struggle for superiority, victory, or defense—whether friendly or hostile—has a strong appeal. Human beings have an inborn love, or competitive instinct, for a good fight, whether it is a battle between prize fighters or contestants in a recreation room, or at the bridge table. Everywhere the writer will find material for an article based upon man's inward impulse to fight to win. Business, politics, sports, strikes, revolutions, conquering the air, the atom, the water, and communication are but a few of the topics that people read because they give a zest to their humdrum existences.

Child, Teen-Age, and Adult Life. Living beings, whether children, youths, or adults, attract the reader. All types of articles concerning child, youth, and adult life are of interest. Love for children and for life is instinctive to all mankind. A child, even the most unattractive urchin, is given sympathy and admiration. Every person recalls his own childhood and sees in the youngster before him the image of his former self. Articles on the education and welfare of children are in great demand, because of parent interest in them.

The appeal of association is the basis for reader interest concerning adult life. In each article concerning a person or persons, the reader finds interest, because he, too, is a human being. It is instinctive to want to know more about that with which we may be familiar to at least some degree.

Animal Life. Features about animals have a perennial charm for readers. They are attracted by the animals' traits—those similar to as well as those dissimilar to human beings. Love for pets is almost as universal as love for children. Interest in animals of all kinds is the reason that the zoos are crowded by young and old, and that many Sunday editors regularly assign a "zoo story" for their sections. In addition to attention given to animals in captivity, there is keen interest in wild-animal life as evidenced by people crowding movies to see "true to wild life" pictures. Fishing, hunting, and trapping have an appeal to many as a sport, while to others it affords an occupation. The care and breeding of all types of domesticated animals on the farm supplies subject matter, not only for articles, but for entire publications that are in the market for free-lance articles.

Recreation and Hobbies. Diversions, amusements, and pastime pursuits pertaining to all sorts of interests are always popular with readers. The instinct to play is one that even adults never lose entirely. The writer will find an easy market for articles with the recreation appeal, since editors buy them to intersperse between the more serious types, to use in special departments in both newspapers and magazines, and to use in magazines which contain only recreation features or hobby articles.

The Familiar and the Well Known. It has been said that the most thoroughly read publication is one's home-town newspaper. If the statement is true, it is because the news concerns people and places familiar to the subscriber. Alert news editors always try to find a "local end" to add to the appeal to news accounts that happen elsewhere. Just because a person, place, or object is well known in one community is no reason for it not to be known in another. All the critizens in a county may have known for years about the druggist who has been in business in the same building for fifty years. They may know something of his policies, which have made his business a success for half a century. But druggists all over the country do not know about him unless a free-lance submits an article about him to a trade publication for druggists.

Well-known persons, places, and objects that readers have never seen may be as familiar to them as those that they see daily. Royalty, statesmen, cities, parks, planes, boats, and trains are well known to many readers, because editors are constantly in the market for such articles that have wide reader-interest. Some of the people best informed about faraway places have never set foot on plane, boat, train, or foreign shore, but they are avid readers of travel articles and of the travel magazines.

Business, Professional, and Home Interests. Whether one's business, professional, or financial interests are in the business district or in the home, there are articles and publications to appeal to all. There was a time when magazines designed to appeal to the business or professional reader contained articles to interest only men, but since women have entered many fields hitherto monopolized by men, many publications have widened their appeals to include business and professional women. Special writers for the business and professional magazines are eager students of all matters pertaining to their readers, such as labor disputes, tariffs, taxes, price fixing, consumer relationships, co-operatives, and legislation concerning the fields for which they write.

Homemaking is still the chief business of the majority of urban as well as rural women readers, whether they "live alone and like it," or live with their own families. A sufficient number of men, however, have turned to keeping their own homes or apartments, and magazines and newspapers, ever alert for new subscribers and an opportunity to serve, have installed departments to guide and help the men homekeepers, just as a half a century ago they developed departments and publications for the housewife. If writers have not had personal experience with the various phases of homemaking, there are unlimited opportunities to interview those who have had. Reader-interest surveys have shown that articles pertaining to the home and welfare of the family in the women's magazines are still in greatest demand. In addition, women's interests outside the home are being appealed to by features pertaining to civic, political, and cultural life. Women's magazines are in the market for any article that will catch and hold, not only the women readers, but men, too.

Social Welfare. Sympathy for and extensive interest in others are instinctive with practically all mankind and, because of this widespread "human interest," the demand for articles concerning all types of social, educational, and religious welfare is never filled. The subject matter may concern aid for those in distress, better hygiene, improved health and living standards, self-improvement along educational and religious lines, increased recreation, and legislation for better working conditions.

Success and Happiness. Each human being is born with the protective instinct that makes him interested in himself first, above all others. Consequently, articles concerning success, prosperity, and happiness are in such great demand by the public that whole magazines are devoted to this appeal. The reader hopes to attain happiness by means of his success or prosperity, and he is interested in reading how to make or save more money, how to do his work more easily and more efficiently, how to improve his physical well-being or his mental capacities, and how to find more pleasure. Because he wants to be wealthy, healthy, wise, and happy, he subscribes to publications that will give him the information he desires.

Using Appeals Effectively. To make the articles interesting, the writer must make it possible for the reader to see himself in everything he reads. It is because an individual wants to see himself that he and millions of others view television or go to the movies. He wants to hear himself—and so he and millions of others turn on their radios. He wants to read about situations in which, in his imagination, he is the center of interest—therefore he and millions of others buy publications containing articles in which they can see themselves, or how they think they would look, speak, or act under the same circumstances as those of the heroes.

The same instinct that compels people to look into mirrors compels them to wish to see themselves in everything they see, hear, and do. It is that same instinct that compels magazine subscribers to turn through the advertising. The men like to think that if they only had that brand of collar, they would look like that handsome young chap. The women like to think that if they had that swimming suit they could look like the bathing beauty pictured there.

To make the reader see himself in every article is not difficult if the writer gives vigorous thought to the appeals he can use most effectively with the subject matter. In many articles it is possible to use several of the appeals, either simultaneously or successively. A student writer, relating the discovery of a simple preventive for pellagra and its cause, for instance, combined nine of the appeals enumerated. If a number of appeals can be combined at the beginning of the article, it will have interest for a greater number of readers. This is the key to success for the writer who plans his article thoughtfully.

Outline Is Essential Part of Plan. Since a writer is an artist in much the same sense as an architect is, he must, to accomplish his goal, work much as the master builder does. While the latter uses building material, the writer uses facts, thoughts, and words. Like the artist, if the writer is to make his finished product a work of art, he, too, must first make sketches and draw plans of what he desires to accomplish. He should make two outlines: first a tentative one, later a final one. If the final one is well planned before the actual work of writing is begun, the article will have a style that will add greatly to its value. The manner in which the article is written determines to a marked degree the price the writer will receive. The better the style, other things being equal, the greater the value each word in the manuscript will have. Therefore, it is good business to make the article in every way just as nearly perfect as is possible, by giving careful thought to its construction.

The more carefully one thinks out the outline, the more quickly he can write the article and the more easily he can sell it. A good outline saves time, produces more money, and enables the writer to turn out more, rather than less, work in the course of a year. The time the beginner or the professional spends on outlines will be time well spent. As a matter of fact, the person who begins writing articles without first making outlines is taking a great risk. Unless he is a genius, the articles he writes without plans will be badly written and will create a poor impression upon editors. This, in turn, will make it more difficult to sell future articles. A well-written feature often leads to an opportunity to become a regular contributor.

The well-planned outline compels the writer to keep in mind the purpose of the article and aids in avoiding digressions and overlapping of material. It helps to evaluate the space to be given to the various divisions, and it calls attention to omissions of necessary information. It reduces time and energy spent in revision.

Three Rings of Interest. In predetermining the construction of an article, a successful writer will pre-establish the three rings of interest. The point of the reader's presumable interest in the article is represented by the center ring. It is determined by the editorial policy and the advertising appeal. The reader's actual interest in the subject matter is embodied in the ring on the right.

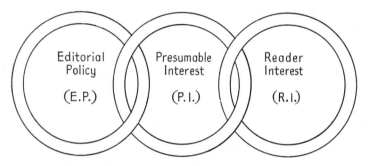

Fig. 2. Three Rings of Interest.

The editorial policy, which is in reality the editor's interest, is shown by the ring on the left. The writer's problem is to link the three rings together briefly and effectively by giving consideration in the outline to the three elements in such a way that the editorial policy, or the editor's interest, the reader's presumable interest, and the actual interest will not only be attracted but held to the very end.

Features Are Built on Pyramid-like Structures. In reporting courses, journalism students are frequently taught to outline and write their news story to the "inverted pyramid," as the story form required of Associated Press correspondents is termed in the classroom. Some writers construct their feature articles like a pyramid, but they do not invert it as does the correspondent writing his news story. They use an upright pyramid, large at its base, and its apex at the top.

The apex, or the first section, represents the point of presumable interest between the reader and the editorial policy, with its one or more appeals. Since this point of contact between the reader and the periodical is often slight, the writer must plan in his outline some sort of a lead that will immediately get the reader's attention. It should contain a startling, or at least an astonishing, idea that is sharp and brief, and that will attract attention. One authority compares the writer to a skater who breaks through the ice. The latter gets immediate attention by crying out "Help!" The thoughtful writer will get his reader's attention by crying out, although he does not need to resort to sensational devices. Just as

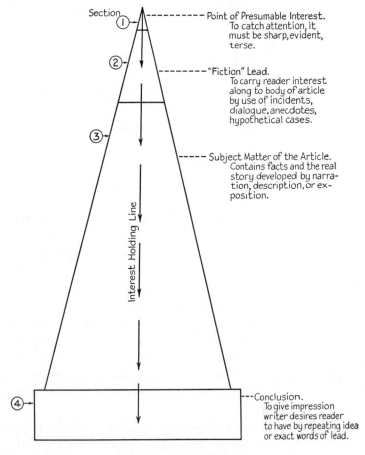

Fig. 3. Pyramid Construction.

the skater did not give a detailed account of how he happened to be skating where the ice was thin before he cried for help, neither should the writer begin his article with detailed explanations. He, too, must get immediate attention.

A writer used such a device when he began an informative article on insurance with: "You who begin this sentence may not live to read its close. There is a chance, one in three or four billions, that you will die in a second, by the tick of the watch." That writer found an immediate point of presumable interest, or contact, whether or not the reader was interested in insurance as an investment. Death has an appeal, although not an attractive one, since it is mysterious and familiar.

Even after the point of presumable interest (P.I.) is established in the first section of the pyramid, the writer must plan to carry it into the second, or third, or possibly the fourth and fifth paragraphs in order to establish in an interesting way the purpose of the article, which is really the publication's editorial policy (E.P.), and to hold the reader's interest (R.I.). This "fiction lead," or "second lead," or "light opening," as the device is spoken of in editorial offices, is represented by the second section. It may approximate the beginning of a short story in an effort to appeal to the imagination, or it may be concerned with relating an incident, or an anecdote, or with dialogue—imaginary or real. The writer of the insurance article carried his reader's interest along and appealed to his imagination by pointing out that the very chair in which he sat reading might collapse, or that he might have an automobile collision, his plane might crash, or his heart might suddenly cease to function.

The third section of the pyramid, following the "fiction lead," is the real subject matter of the article. It contains facts, opinions, and figures to inform, guide, or entertain the reader. It is presented by means of narration, description, or exposition. The real story in the insurance article told why insurance companies are willing to seem "to bet" on the span of life of their policyholders, because they gamble on a sure thing: the average death rate.

The fourth section of the pyramid is the base upon which the story rests, or the conclusion of the feature. It contains the impression that the writer desires the reader to have when he has finished the article.

Whether the presumable interest lead, or the "fiction lead," or both, are used, the writer must plan in his outline a conclusion

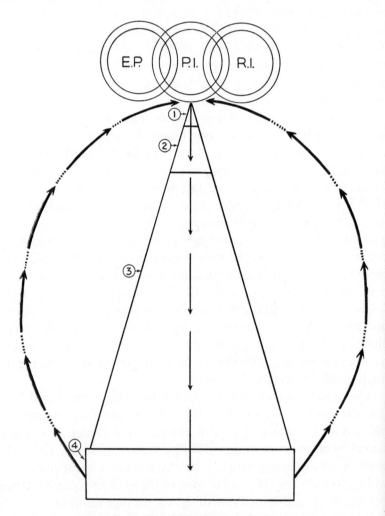

Fig. 4. Entire Plan of Construction of a Feature.

that will be forceful, yet artistic. This conclusion is easily accomplished by repeating either the exact words or the main idea of the lead paragraph in the concluding paragraph, in order to clinch the idea of the entire article in the reader's mind. In the diagram this point is illustrated by drawing an extended semicircle around the pyramid in such a way that its middle touches the apex of the pyramid and the ends touch the base. This device indicates that the writer will take the reader by the hand, as it were, back to the beginning, or apex, in order to leave the reader with the impression he planned when he wrote out the purpose of the article before starting his tentative outline.

General Outline Is Similar to Advertising Copy Writer's. Courses in advertising teach students that there are definite steps the copy writer must take if he would write forceful copy. The same principles may well be applied to the feature article. They are:

1. *Catch the eye.*
   Use a short picture-making title that will make the reader begin to read the article.
2. *Hold the attention.*
   Make statements in the first sentence and the first paragraph that will grip the reader sufficiently to cause him to read on.
3. *Arouse interest.*
   Follow the first paragraph with statements of an interesting nature and with which the reader will agree, or at least that will continue to hold his interest.
4. *Gain confidence.*
   Continue holding reader interest in the body of the article by making comparisons, drawing analogies, or using hypothetical examples; or in other ways show that the ideas set forth are informative, helpful, or entertaining, and that they add to the reader's knowledge, wealth and health.
5. *Convince the reader.*
   Conclude the article by showing the reader in a subtle or suggestive way how much the ideas set forth will inform, guide, or entertain him if he acts upon them or adopts them.
6. *Test the outline.*
   Test the plan of the article to see that the reader will be left with the impression that you, as the writer, wish him to have.

Factors Determining Points in Outline. The architect keeps in mind the width, length, and location of the lot, the roll of the land, the relation of the lot to others in the block, and the structure and color of the neighboring houses. So must the feature writer give thought to the publication and its readers when he outlines the article.

Before the outline is started, the length of the article must be determined for the publication to which one is slanting. Editors frequently return articles that do not fit their publication's length. A young man wrote an article of the length and in the style used by his church magazine, for which he received a check for $85.00 for the article and $12.00 for the pictures. In the row ahead of him in his class sat another student who received his manuscript back from the same publication on the same day. A personal letter said that because the article was "mid-length," the editor was forced to return it. It added that if the author would write a 300-word digest, the editor could still use it in one of the departments. The second young man, as well as the entire class, profited by his mistake.

To write out in a brief sentence the statement of the purpose of the article before making even the tentative outline will save time and energy. It will prevent the writer's getting off the subject by eliminating those portions that will not contribute to the reader's grasp of the content or to the purpose of the article.

The amount and the nature of the subject matter selected from the notes, and the order of their presentation, must be planned before one can determine even roughly the main points, parts, or divisions of the outline. Again, the writer must work like the architect, who has to determine the size of the house that can be built on the lot before he can plan the number of rooms. Just as the master builder sketches the floor plans, so must the writer think through his material and sketch out the points or blocks of material in order to find the best arrangement and relationship of paragraphs. Thought must be given to the outline as a whole, to see that the parts are all in relation to one another. Care and thought given to this phase of the outline will result in the best possible arrangement of material, because there will be simplicity of effect and harmony throughout the article.

Details Must Be Planned before Outlining. The successful writer has every detail worked out both in his mind and on paper, in a tentative outline, before he even starts to make his permanent outline. Changes are difficult to make after the article is written, if it has been carefully thought out, because things will not be in a right proportion. Before starting the final outline, the writer will have transcribed everything—notes from the interviewee, notes from his research, ideas from books, bulletins, or publications, ideas gained from talking with others. Some journalists put their notes on cards, as do the historians, but the majority of professional writers prefer sheets of typewriter paper; they transcribe their notes on the machine, and paper is easier to handle. Another advantage of the latter method is ease of cutting the paragraphs into separate blocks, or of pasting or pinning the various parts together to make a unified whole. Such a plan will prevent an article from being a mere juggling of ideas.

Organizing the Material for the Outline. After all material has been transcribed to typewriter paper, the writer spreads the sheets—much as if they were parts of a puzzle—out on a long table or series of tables, and arranges the material in order of the outline. Such a process gives him the opportunity to view the material as a whole and to make the necessary shifting of pages or paragraphs to give the article emphasis, coherence, unity, and interest. It also enables him to see what space he should give to the various points, and this aids him in planning the lead and the conclusion of the article.

By checking the material with the outline—or checking the outline with the material, as the case may be—the writer cuts, rearranges, pastes, or pins the transcribed notes into whatever order he desires. By this process of double checking, the outline is modified or revised where necessary or where greater effectiveness will result. However good one's outline may be, he should never let himself be dominated by the first arrangement. As he organizes his notes, a better arrangement of parts may suggest itself.

The writer checks and rechecks the material with the outline, or vice versa, and satisfies himself that: (1) the plan is as effective as he can make it; (2) the purpose of the article has been adhered to throughout; (3) all possible appeals have been used to catch and hold the interest; (4) the parts of the outline fit together naturally and readily; (5) the reader will get the impression the writer wishes him to have; and (6) a close relation exists between the article and the magazine for which it is being slanted. He may then determine the style of treatment to which the various divisions of the outline lend themselves.

The writer may find it profitable to save time by writing in the margins of the outline whether to use dramatic incidents, anecdotes, typical instances, hypothetical cases, description, narration, or exposition to keep the reader interested to the end. He then determines the style in which he will write the article and sits down to his typewriter, ready to start the actual writing. By this time the writer has become so enthusiastic about the subject that, unless he writes very poorly, he cannot help writing an interesting article.

Sales Are Results of Planning and Outlining. For the amateurs who are willing to give vigorous thought to planning and organizing material, success will come as it did to the young man who made the tentative plan as follows:

Tentative Outline for Article: *Students' Have Own Church*

I. *Purpose*
  1. To inform readers of church paper how a young congregation organizes, runs, and governs its own church.
II. *Source*
  1. Background reading of printed material in library and material given by minister.
  2. Interviews student members of church.
  3. Experiences of student members.
  4. Interviews with the Rev. John R. Collins, minister; the Rev. Robert J. Villwock, assistant, and Prof. A. C. Garnett, University philosophy department.
III. *Plan of organization*
  1. How church originated.
  2. How supported.
  3. How directed.

4. Church Governing groups.
   a. Ministerial staff
   b. Study groups
   c. Choir Council
5. Planning of programs.
   a. Social calendar
   b. Study groups
   c. Religious reverse of lend-lease minister
6. History of "Pres House."
   a. The part of the Synod in the plan.
7. Student governed churches at other Universities.

IV. *Results*
   1. Value of church to students, church, community.

V. *Conclusion*
   1. Show that youth is successful in church administration.

VI. *Possible Markets*
   1. *Presbyterian Life*
   2. *Christian Advocate*
   3. *Christian Herald*

VII. *Requirements of Possible Markets* (If typed on separate sheet of paper, this market analysis may be used later with the final outline.)

Periodicals:	Presbyterian Life	Christian Advocate	Christian Herald
Headline Style?	2 decks, 3 1 (lines) 2nd dk. 2 1.	not unusual	Variety of heads
Article Length in Wds.?	800-2,000	1,000—2,500	2,000—2,500
Illus., kinds, No., size?	b & w., 7-12 8x10 glossies	Buys photos	none
Peculiarities of Style?	writes out Rev. friendly, infor.	none	wants quality
Art. in Reader's Guide to Periodical Literature?	Found none about youth and churches	Found none	Found none
Pay rate in Market bk.?	2¢ a usable wd.	1½¢ up	varies with quality
When pays?	Pays before or on publication	on acceptance	pays on acceptance
Circulation (See S.R.&D.)?	758, 142	253, 470	377,713
Authors—known or unknown?	both	both	well-known
Any other information?	Any phase of Protest. Faith	Reports in 2 weeks	

Why I Slanted to *Presbyterian Life*
1. Uses many pictures which I can obtain from minister.
2. Style is nearer what I can write.
3. Market book says interested in youth.
4. Length nearer what I can write for first article.
5. Biggest circulation of three should enable it to pay well.

After the young writer had interviewed the interviewees, gathered, evaluated, and organized his material, he made his final outline as follows:

Final outline: *The Church That Students Call Their Own*

(Outline to be made after interview.)

I. *Purpose*
1. To inform church members how young people can be church leaders and show how one youthful congregation has organized and governs its own church.

II. *Rings of Interest*
1. P.I.: Show how churches could develop youthful leaders.
2. R.I.: Present plan and work of youthful congregation.
3. E.P.: Only religious publications that are interested in developing youthful leaders.

III. *Plan of Development*
1. Presumable interest: Appeal to church subscribers who are desirous of encouraging youthful members to be church leaders.
2. Use fact rather than fiction lead because the fact here is "stranger than fiction."
3. Body of article—emphasize it is students' own church.
Cooperation results in confidence and leadership.
Organization: 12 elders, choir council.
Planned programs to meet demand and need.
Social activities.
Study groups.
Choir of 90 voices.
Two services to accommodate all.
Points of view that attract young people to church.
Students develop leadership.
Church and club lounge open every day.
Ministers are counselors and advisors.
"Lend-lease" minister.
History of "Pres House," one of first all student churches.
Started in 1921 as overflow from downtown church.
Synod (governing body) created Student Center foundation.

Built beautiful chapel.
Student governed churches at other universities.
Repeat lead: Students have own church.
IV. *Interviewees:* The Rev. Collins, The Rev. Villwock, Prof. Garnett, and student leaders.
V. Market:
Presbyterian Life
(Attach sheet from market analyses (see No. VII) from Tentative outline.)

Example of Outlined Article. After the final outline was completed, the amateur spent considerable thought on developing the various parts of the outline in an interesting way to appeal to as many readers as possible. The completed article follows:

The Church
That Students
Call Their Own*

*Students Are Elders, Deacons, and Trustees
at Wisconsin's "Pres House."*

By Linn Lewis Brown

The students at the University of Wisconsin in Madison have a church they can really call their own. It is an all-student church that is so in every meaning of the word.

The young people there organize, run, and govern the University Presbyterian Church. Students are elders, deacons, and trustees. They conduct services and social programs. They are the church.

"Pres House," as the students nickname their church, is kept moving and growing by the forty-six key students who are church officers. Their time and skill focuses the activities of a parish which numbers almost 1,000 collegians.

The Wisconsin student body is the sole source of its membership, which requires the minister, the Reverend John R. Collins, to preach two services every Sunday. Mr. Collins, whom the students know simply as "Jack," has been at Pres House for five years, but is still amazed at the vitality of the students. "At the pace we go," he says, "if it wasn't for the hard work, loyalty, and wisdom of the student officers, we'd have left the road at the first turn."

* Reprinted by permission of *Presbyterian Life* and Linn Lewis Brown.

The students not only belong to the church, but, they feel, the church belongs to them. If they want a new program or activity, that's all that's necessary—they organize it. And they've rolled up their sleeves more than once to deserve this freedom. They raise $7,000 a year from pledges and donations (about one fifth of the total budget —the rest comes from the Board of Christian Education, Wisconsin churches, alumni, and other sources).

The collegians do their own landscaping, and have even dug out the entire front of the church foundation to waterproof the basement and install a new drainage system. They keep their membership growing by personally calling on every Presbyterian student who comes to the university, and they hold on to that membership by creating a program that functions seven days a week. In order to direct their activities, they elect their own officers.

The twelve elders direct the spiritual life of the church. These students prepare for the Sunday services, conduct evening vespers, plan midweek services and forums, and, each in turn, read from the Scriptures during the Sunday services. It's their job to keep the worship and sacramental life of the church paramount. However, they don't neglect other phases of student interest. Years ago a weekly "Skeptic's Hour" to discuss all the aspects of the "why" of religion was started by the elders. During the past year they realized that the church might help students in their studies, so under the guidance of Associate Minister Robert J. Villwock, they set up their own unique educational program.

They organized weekly study groups to work in parallel with courses offered on the university campus. The first experiment was with a philosophy of religion course taught by Professor A. C. Garnett. The students met for evening discussions that followed Professor Garnett's lectures—with Mr. Villwock helping them on the religious significance of the phase they were studying. Due partly to the enthusiasm of Professor Garnett and the encouragement of Bob Villwock, the experiment was an overwhelming success and the program was expanded to encompass a history and a Biblical English course. Mr. Villwock expects the program eventually to be broadened to take in a basic anthropology course so as to compare different ideas on man's beginning. "The young people's experiences in this church," the ministers hope, "will help them integrate Christianity with a college education."

The social calendar is handled by the twelve student deacons. They arrange a coffee hour between the Sunday services, and scores of other recreational projects. It's their job to keep the social side of Pres

House's life active and attractive. The trustees handle the business administration of the organization. These ten students keep complete records of Pres House's activities, and handle the budget, stewardship, and relations with the Synod of Wisconsin.

"Even though the students control the normal boards of the church," Mr. Collins explains, "they were not satisfied with this and organized another—their own Choirs' Council." The twelve members of this group complete the church officers and have the responsibility of organizing two separate choirs, one for each Sunday service. The participation in the music program is unusually high, with the combined choir numbering ninety students. Each year Miriam Bellville, choirmaster, assembles 110 students to sing an Easter oratorio, which is recorded for sale.

It's the students, then, who actually make the wheels turn. "No hierarchy would work at Pres House," Mr. Collins told us. "We all try to cooperate to get what we want done. We let the students do it, and they get it done."

It's confidence and leadership like that that give Pres House the cohesion it has. And it's the young, alert personality behind that leadership that keeps students ardent about their church. Mr. Collins's sermons are slanted carefully at the university congregation. Each is always a serious, intimate talk realizing the presence and privilege of doubt and hesitation on the part of some. It's a point of view like this that draws students to the University Church who never dreamed they would be spending Sunday mornings out of bed. He gives the students a firmer conviction in their beliefs, and allows others to inspect unashamedly the realities of their own doubts. His calm logic makes his congregation think.

But sermons aren't all the students take away from Pres House. Mr. Collins believes that the students' participation in the church gives them a "full experience of leadership." "Work such as this helps them to grow as persons," he says. "They come out of Pres House with an appreciation of what kind of life they want to lead—and that gives them the sense of security they need."

The church and lounge are both open every day, and the students come and study or just have a talk with Jack Collins. Working with young people and watching his church click seem to give him a great satisfaction. "Administering a church like this is a wonderful and challenging ministry," he confides. "The ministers and staff here have to be preachers, plumbers, and counselors, be wise as professors, and still at all times be genuine friends to the students." Mr. Collins sees himself as a "resource worker" whose main job is one of counseling and advising students. Whenever a student has any kind of problem, he is encouraged to stop in and talk it over with Jack and Bob. They have handled problems ranging from dating troubles to potential suicides, but whatever the trouble, "I will never force an opinion on anyone," Mr. Collins states; "I'd rather make a mistake."

A church as progressive as Pres House has a natural affinity for being first in line when something new happens. The students in Madison took another first place this year when they welcomed the young Reverend Jacques Beaumont of the French Reformed church in Paris to their church for a year's stay at Pres House. In a new sort of religious reverse-lend-lease program Mr. Beaumont is the first European minister to students to be brought to the United States by the Board of Foreign Missions of the Presbyterian Church U.S.A. Mr. Beaumont slipped right into the smoothly running mechanism at the University Church and made a quick hit with the student congregation.

Pres House was one of the first all-student churches when it got its start in 1921. It was to be a sort of an experiment to catch the overflow from Madison's Christ Church. About two hundred young people moved to the center for their activities, but the group became increasingly popular and the building increasingly inadequate. The students wanted to hold their own services near the heart of campus life, but the building wasn't large enough to do this easily. So in 1931 the Synod created a new corporation known as the Presbyterian Student Center Foundation, and collected enough funds to build the present chapel. The experiment had become a reality, and as its attraction grew, it helped curb the mutterings about a "Godless campus."

Today, Pres House shares the idea of student-governed churches at state universities with the Illinois and Purdue student congregations. It can be done, Mr. Collins believes, in many more churches that skirt university campuses. One look at Pres House will tell you how it can be done.

Writer Receives Check. The article, which was the author's first feature, was written in an unusually attractive style and to the length that his first market was using at the time. Three weeks later the student writer received a check for $97.00.

The Value of the Outline. The amateur who has never bothered to make an outline for any writing may be tempted to start his first feature without making a tentative and, later, final one. Professional writers who have attained national success say that they cannot urge too strongly the use of the outline, whether one is a beginner or a writer of experience. It is true that the writer who makes free-lancing his career and who sells perhaps hundreds of articles during a year may not make as detailed an outline as he did during his earlier writing years, but no matter how many decades one may have written, he will outline his material, consciously or unconsciously.

Although the careful planning and outlining of every article does take time, in the end it: (1) saves a great deal of time and energy; (2) enables one to write in an attractive, interesting style, because his mind is free from planning and arranging; (3) permits him to write rapidly, and at the same time effectively; (4) results in but little revision, except perhaps the improvement of vocabulary and the correction of minor errors and the final retyping of the manuscript to give it a professional appearance; (5) aids in making an almost 100 per cent aim in slanting; (6) brings a check to the writer instead of a rejection; and (7) increases the writer's earning power, because publications pay more for well-written articles.

The majority of writers admit freely that writing is difficult because it requires thinking, and for most persons thinking is difficult. A beginner must not have the notion that he can sit down to the typewriter and dash off an article. Even most professional writers cannot do that. But it is true that if one has given thought and care to planning and outlining his material, he will be so inspired that he will find great fun and satisfaction in the actual writing, even though it is hard work. With practice, the beginner will acquire spontaneity and alacrity. These qualities—which will make the writer feel that he is inspired—will come with a suddenness, as did the ability to play the piano or to learn to use the typewriter. Then even the embryo will write with confidence and skill.

Just as the advertising copy writer cannot write effective copy with strong sales appeal unless he firmly believes in the product about which he is writing—or, as advertising writers say, unless he is "sold" on it himself—neither can the feature writer write an article effectively without enthusiasm for the subject. But one cannot give careful thought, make a tentative outline, and then make a final one without becoming enthusiastic about the subject matter. By the time he has completed his final outline, one could not keep the beginner from writing his article.

Exercises

1. In your favorite newspaper select three features. Jot down in chart form the captions. Indicate in the first column what purpose each author had in writing the article.

2. Select three articles in your favorite magazine. In another chart form indicate the purpose each of those authors had in writing the features.

3. In the second column of your newspaper chart indicate who the probable readers are.

4. In the second column of your magazine chart make the same indication as in Exericse 3.

5. In the third column of the newspaper chart indicate why they will be interested in the article.

6. In the third column of the magazine chart indicate why those readers will be interested in each of the three features.

7. In the fourth column of the newspaper chart, indicate, by a rough estimate of the number of words, just how much the reader will be interested according to each editor's judgment in selecting the length of the article.

8. For the magazine chart indicate in the fourth column, by making a rough estimate of the word length, just how much the readers will be interested.

9. Enumerate in the fifth column of the newspaper chart the devices that each writer used in catching and holding the newspaper reader's attention.

10. In the fifth column of the magazine chart list the attention devices for each article.

11. In the sixth column list the aims of the three newspaper articles.

12. List the aims of the magazine features in the sixth column of the magazine chart.

13. Select one of the newspaper features and list in the seventh column any psychological principles that you find.

14. Select one of the magazine articles and in the seventh column list psychological principles that you find.

15. After classifying the reader-appeals for each newspaper feature, list them in the eighth column.

16. In the eighth column of the magazine chart, list the reader-appeals for each of the three articles.

17. Underneath the chart for each type of publication write down the word "Outline," and the title of the feature you select to outline. Beneath that write a short, concise statement of the purpose of the article. Then outline each of the two articles as you think the writers must have done before they wrote the articles.

18. For each article outlined, draw a construction pyramid similar to Fig. 4 in this chapter. Apply its four sections or parts to each of the features you outlined. Does the treatment of material permit you to put an extended semicircle around the pyramid, or did the writer fail to bring the reader back to the beginning of the article?

19. Test the article outlined and "pyramided" to see if the writer failed to apply the principles listed under the general feature outline.

20. List any suggestions for the improvement of the outline, or, in other words, the rearrangemnt of the article as it is written.

Publication Analysis

Home, Shelter, and Garden Periodicals

Compare, by using chart form as illustrated in the Appendix, four magazines of the above types. There are not many of these types of publications, but they may be obtained at newsstands, from magazine dealers listed in the Appendix under "Aids to Writers," or in library periodical reading rooms. Some suggested home and garden magazines: *American Home, Better Homes & Gardens, Flower Grower, House & Garden, Household,* the *Home Desirable,* the *Home Garden, Popular Gardening, Town and Country,* or others of your choice.

Do not spend more than two hours on this report.

  I. Identification: Name, publisher, editor, where published, price.

 II. Make-up:
1. What do you like about the make-up of the magazines?
2. What do you dislike about them?
3. What changes would you make if you were the editors?

III. Advertising:
1. If you were placing advertising, what appeals would your copy have to have?
2. After glancing through the advertising, do you think that the advertiser gets returns from his copy?
3. Give reason for your conclusion.
4. A tip suggested by the advertising in each magazine.
5. If you were advertising manager, what changes would you make?

IV. Feature Articles:
   1. What types of articles do you find and to whom does each one appeal?
   2. Analyze any article that you wish and in any way that you wish, but also include the pyramid form of analysis.
   3. What do you think are your chances of selling to these magazines?
 V. Illustrations:
   1. Kinds and number of pictures used?
   2. How many articles were illustrated by use of blueprints?
   3. What use was made of drawings?
   4. Were maps, graphs, or charts used? How?
VI. Four Tips: Source, authority for the article suggested, and three possible markets for each one that was suggested by the study of these magazines.

CHAPTER 11

Writing the Article

Plan of Writing. When the amateur starts his first article, he thinks he must first write the caption, or heading. He is surprised to find that the title is generally written after the completion of the first draft—sometimes not until after the final copy has been revised. The idea for the caption frequently comes to the writer like a flash if he has given much thought to the planning and outlining. The best advice to the tyro is not to be concerned about the caption at the beginning of his writing. He may not write it until just before he mails the article to a market. For this reason, the discussion of writing the title is left until Chapter 12.

Some authorities advocate writing the body of the article and then going back to the first part and writing the beginning. If the writer, however, has followed carefully the plan suggested in the previous chapter, and has constructed his article on the pyramid form, he will have the idea for the lead transcribed into his notes, or at least have it definitely in his mind. The beginning is an integral part of the article. It must be written so that the reader is never conscious of where the lead ends and the body of the article begins. Both time and energy are saved if the writer composes the lead first.

The novice who has given thought to his article does not wait until he starts writing to ask himself, "How shall I start?" He not only asked but answered that question when he developed the

plan. At that time he selected the most interesting fact or anecdote to be used as the point of presumable interest.

The Function of the Lead. The beginning of the article, like
the advertisement, should: (1) catch the eye and lure or guide
the reader on into the article; (2) give the reader an idea of the
content of the feature and the movement and spirit of the article;
and (3) provide the point of presumable reader interest.

The Importance of the Lead. The beginning is the critical
point. The article is dependent upon it to obtain and hold readers.
The first few paragraphs are the determining factor in whether
the reader will read on or turn the page over to the next article.
One realizes the importance of the lead if he stops to consider the
competition an article has with the many others, even in a single
publication. Just as the "cub" reporter learns that the lead of a
news story is similar to the merchant's show window, in which the
most attractive merchandise is displayed, so may the feature
writer compare his lead to the show window of the ultra-exclusive
shop that displays but one suit or one dress. By its very interest,
individuality, or style it will attract the attention of hurried pedes-
trians, who stop to "window shop." The feature lead attracts
attention, although it, like the exclusive shop on Fifth Avenue or
Michigan Boulevard, has hundreds of others with which to compete.

Ease of Writing Lead. The article writer has a greater freedom
in drawing on his imagination and his originality than the news
reporter does. Thus, the writing of the lead is not so difficult as
one may think. After all, it is just an introductory paragraph that
is appropriate to the content and that will appeal to the reader.

If one has thought out the plan and outline carefully, he will be
so enthusiastic that he will write with a spontaneity that will cause
him to type hard and fast. If, as he types, he pictures in his imagination not only the reader but the printed article in the publication, with its art layout of photographs, drawings, or charts, he
will write with inspiration.

It is always difficult to begin any project with which one is not
familiar. Starting the feature is not an exception. But if the novice

will take time to examine a number of leads in any publications at hand, or those at the library, he will find he has stimulated his own enthusiasm until he can hardly wait to get to his typewriter to begin his lead. Of course, he will save time and will attain success more quickly if he will analyze carefully the leads in six or more issues of the publication to which he is slanting. Even the professional writers study leads constantly to find out how other writers challenge and hold readers' attention. The more one thinks about and analyzes beginnings, the easier it will be to write them.

Constructing the Lead. Upon the basis of the three rings of interest and the pyramid construction, one realizes that although the lead is a unit by itself (serving to catch the reader interest and to link it to the policy of the publication), in reality, it consists of two parts. The first serves as the point of contact between the reader's presumable interest and the article in such a way that he will follow on down the interest-holding line to the conclusion. The presumable interest lead is the most vital part of the article, since it strikes the keynote of interest and holds it—or should.

The second part of the lead, the "fiction" lead, carries the reader interest along to the body of the article. It may consist of one paragraph of one sentence, or a long paragraph of several sentences, or of several paragraphs, as diagrammed in Fig. 3. Whatever type is used as the lead—summary, striking statement, narration, description, quotation, question, or direct address—it should be a complete unit in itself and give the reader a unified impression.

The point of presumable interest must be sharp, evident, and terse, and yet be a structural part of the article, else it will fail in its purpose. Its connection with the "fiction" lead and the body of the article must be logical as well as enticing. The transitions must be accomplished so skillfully that the reader is not conscious that the point of presumable interest and the "fiction" lead are separate units. Above all, both must be brief, not longer than 5 to 10 per cent of the whole article.

Faults to Be Avoided. In writing the lead, eight faults to be avoided are: (1) packing the lead with too many details that will prevent the reader from getting the unified impression the writer desires him to have; (2) neglecting to make the lead a significant part of the article by uniting it with the body of the article; (3) developing the details of the beginning to a length out of proportion to the body of the article; (4) failing to make a skillful transition from the lead to the body of the article; (5) exaggerating incidents; (6) making the dialogue stiff and unnatural; (7) using pointless or inapplicable anecdotes; and (8) resorting to dissociated and irrelevant hypothetical cases.

Classification of Types of Leads. The entire article is dependent upon an effective lead. Much thought, therefore, should be given to the type as well as to the way it is written.

Each writer has his own classification, but for convenience the types used in the majority of publication offices are: (1) summary; (2) striking statement; (3) narrative; (4) descriptive; (5) quotation; (6) question; and (7) direct address.

The novice will find many suggestive examples in his weekly or biweekly Publication Analysis and in his continual study of current periodicals. Styles in features, particularly in leads and captions, change as rapidly as fashions in wearing apparel. It behooves the writer, amateur or professional, to keep posted on feature fashions.

Summary Lead. Material for a beginning often lends itself to a bird's-eye view, or summary, treatment. As the news reporter groups the important facts in the first paragraph for the hurried reader, so may the feature writer. The average news reader has become accustomed to finding the happening, the persons or things concerned, the cause, the result, the place, and the time all assembled in the first paragraph in answer to the questions, What? Who? Why? How? Where? and When? This type of lead will attract reader interest if the most striking element is "played up" in the first sentence, or the first part of it. If the writer is in doubt as to which of the types of leads enumerated to use, he will do well to select the summary to emphasize the most salient facts.

Striking Statement. An unusual idea, or one that is expressed in an unusual way, commands attention. Because of its brevity and its force, it may be similar to the reporter's "snapper" lead, which is aimed to make the reader jump—at least, mentally. Its purpose is to lead the reader on by arousing his interest or curiosity. It is used with other types as much as it is used by itself.

In turning through feature sections and magazines one finds many articles where the striking statement concerns numerical figures or things of enormous size, or pertains to startling discoveries. If the size of the revelation is of such magnitude that the reader will not comprehend it, the writer should interpret it in terms that may be readily understood.

Subject matter that is unique, predicts the unusual, is paradoxical, or is novel may be made all the more effective if this type of lead is used. Forceful figures of speech, startling, exact, and crisp words, or gripping phrases may be employed to attract the reader's attention, but the writer must resist the temptation to exaggerate or to make false statements.

Narrative Lead. A fiction-like tone may be given to the lead by beginning with narrative. This lead is popular because Americans are great fiction readers. Practically all devices common to the narrative fiction story may be incorporated in this type. It is best suited to personal experience, adventure, and narrative articles. Incidents, anecdotes, conversation, and definite examples may be used. They may be developed by means of dialogue as well as by active narration.

Descriptive Lead. Dealing with images rather than ideas, and appealing to the senses, the descriptive lead may be used artistically for those articles where the aim is to stir the reader's emotion. It must be suggestive rather than detailed, because the former is easier to grasp. Words that have an emotional connotation or an association for the reader, or that are picture making, are essential for this type of lead. If the description is forceful and vivid, the reader is impelled to read on.

Quotation Beginning. Although quotation leads are out of style because of overuse, they are still effective when they have pointed or unusual application to the article. If the quoted portion is one with which the reader is familiar, however slightly, it will serve as an attention-arresting device. Not only actual quotations, but any unique form—such as an advertisement, a menu, a sign, a budget, or a bit of prose—will appeal to the reader. Even though the source of material is unlimited, particularly if one resorts to the quotation books as sources, a quotation lead should never be used unless it has a close association with the subject matter and body of the article.

The various typographical forms in which quoted material may be arranged adds to the attention value. If the writer desires a verse printed in smaller type, he may indicate on his manuscript by setting the quoted lines single space. Quoted slogans and phrases may be set as separate paragraphs. Advertisements may be set off in "boxes," made by placing around the quoted portion a box-like structure. Reproductions of telegrams, menus, price lists, invitations, or clippings are used, as in fiction, to attract the reader.

Question Lead. Although the question beginning has waned in popularity, as has the quotation, there are times when it is the most advantageous. If the writer desires to arouse the reader's curiosity, the form is occasionally excellent. The lead may consist of a single question, or a series of them. Or each of the questions of the series may be used separately in a series of paragraphs if the writer's purpose is to give greater emphasis to each question. This type is often combined with direct address.

Direct Address Beginning. Used occasionally and appropriately, the direct address makes a strong reader appeal. The reader feels that the writer is speaking to him personally rather than to the thousands or millions of other subscribers. Utility articles are often built on this type of lead, but the writer must be constantly on his guard to keep the article from having a dictatorial, or "preachy," tone. He must remember that the reader has been preached at all his life—at home, at school, and at church, and by his associates and friends—and he certainly does not want to be preached at in his reading. The use of the second person makes the reader feel that he has been "buttonholed," and he resents that, unless it is done unobtrusively. Since the imperative verb is the most forceful form of direct address, it is effective; but one must use it tactfully and with caution in the lead.

It is true that the use of "you," or "yours," or "Mr. Reader," or "Mrs. Citizen," and other similar forms aids in personally appealing to the reader, but one must avoid overuse of the device; it soon becomes monotonous. Indirect address may be employed, although, of course, it does not have such strong appeal.

Methods of Using the Types. From studying features in current publications, it is apparent that many of the most effective leads are not used singly, but that two or more types are combined. Because the types overlap, no hard and fast rule can be laid down for their use. The only rule that is applicable in selection of the type of lead is to choose one, or combinations, that will be appropriate and that will attract the attention and hold it to the end.

The two methods in the use of the type of the leads are: the deductive, in which the writer begins with the general and goes to the particular or the specific (although this is the oldest method, it is less interesting); and the inductive, which opens with the particular and concrete and then takes the reader to the general. The second has the greater attention-getting value.

Writing the Body of the Article. After the lead is completed, the main part of the article almost writes itself, if the novice has made his final outline thoughtfully. The feature is in his mind, and all that remains to be done is to write it.

The possible markets have been selected, the reader interest in the subject has been deduced, the amount of material has been ascertained, and the approximate length has been adjudged. The style has been determined, either consciously or unconsciously, as a number of articles in the same field have been analyzed, in order to slant accurately. The beginner knows just how he plans to develop the units that he blocked out on the construction pyramid, because he indicated on the outline which are to be narration, description, and exposition, and where dialogue, anecdotes, and incidents are to be used. The transition from the lead to the article itself will follow smoothly, as will the changes from one paragraph to another. Thus, the reader's curiosity is carried down the interest-holding line enthusiastically to the end.

With a wealth of material on a promising subject, a well-organized outline, and the creative zeal of the artist, the beginner is ready to put the units together to make an interesting article that he hopes will appeal to an editor's eye and checkbook.

Determining Factors. With the problems of how to begin and where to begin solved when the outline was made, the writer must consider in what person he will write the main part of the article. It is a common fault of most novices to write their features in either the first or second person, whether or not it is a confession, personal experience, or a utility article. The personal pronoun becomes extremely monotonous and should be avoided unless the feature cannot be written effectively in any other person. As a rule, a writer will be much more successful if he keeps himself out of the article, except in the types noted. The second person becomes wearisome to the reader unless the writer softens the "preachy" tone by relating his own mistakes, as pointed out previously, to show the reader that he, too, is not perfect, or that results may not be successful if one attempts short cuts. When in doubt, the amateur or professional will do well to write in the third person. Then the reader will not be so conscious of the writer. This style is not as emphatic as writing in the first or second person, but the clever writer will find other devices to hold the reader's attention without running the risk of seeming to "talk down" or to "preach" to him.

In writing the story, the beginner must keep in mind: (1) the reader and his interests; and (2) the interest-holding line, which is the most direct approach from the point of presumable interest to the conclusion. By keeping the reader in mind, the writer will constantly think, "What will the reader want to know about this?" He will be less inclined to miss or bury important facts. Neither should he lose sight of the reader's interest in himself. The psychological devices of recall and association will bring the reader into the article and keep him on the interest line. One should put himself in the reader's place as he writes, to see how he will react to the article. If he, as the possible reader, finds breaks in the interest line, he will do well to incorporate a few of the appropriate appeals listed in the preceding chapter. If the writer would meet the reader upon a common ground, he must bear in mind the latter's limitations. These he will have learned by an analysis of the advertising in the periodical to which he is slanting.

Qualities Characterizing Writing. The first characteristic of a good article is the ease with which it may be read. This is dependent upon simplicity of style and repetition of thought—in different ways, of course—to stress the points. Spontaneity and enthusiasm result from sincerity of purpose. The content should be presented so that the reader may discover ideas for himself, or think that he has. A beginner is inclined either to underestimate or to overestimate the reader's knowledge and ability. Facts with which the reader may, or may not, be familiar should be presented tactfully by such phrases as "one recalls," or "one remembers." One should resist the temptation to moralize, to preach, or to advise: readers resent it. But if it is done by means of adequate reference to authority, it will give weight and credence as well as aid in taking away the dictatorial tone. Facts must be presented, but there is no reason why they cannot be presented interestingly. By inference and by appeal to the reader's imagination, the writer can make dull facts sparkle.

Even though the novice has made a well-planned outline, he constantly will be confronted with decisions. He must have several times the amount of material he will need. From this he must select with precision. Too much detail destroys clarity and emphasis: a lack of it prevents adequate treatment that will result in loss of interest.

Length of Feature Articles. The fact that feature sections and magazines are not static in their policies makes them interesting to the subscribers but makes a problem for the free-lance writer. Just when he has discovered by analysis that a publication uses articles of from 2,000 to 3,000 words, he may find in the current issue on the newsstands that it has changed its style of make-up and is now using 800 to 1,500 word articles, or perhaps it is not using anything less than 5,000 words. Why the professional, as well as the amateur, must study the individual periodicals is obvious.

The beginner should not attempt long articles. The structural problems will be more complicated and more difficult, and he will be inclined to become discouraged with resultant loss of interest. He will find that articles of from 750 to 2,000 words offer good practice and that the demand is large for short to medium-length articles. Thus, selling will be easier.

Structural Units Must Have Variety. The study of articles in the Publication Analysis at the end of each chapter shows how articles are built out of blocks, or units, such as (1) incidents, (2) examples, (3) hypothetical cases, (4) statistics, and (5) processes.

Incidents and Anecdotes. The use of incidents, anecdotes, and episodes helps to entertain, to make the reading more interesting, to illustrate points, and to drive home facts in the development of personal experience, narrative, and confession articles. In studying the articles in current publications, one finds that most features contain one or more of the devices. They offer opportunities to make use of description and dialogue that gives variety to the subject matter and the form.

Specific Examples. Concrete cases give a realistic tone and appeal to the reader's imagination. At the same time, they enable him to comprehend the facts that the writer is presenting. For instance, one might be writing an article on taxation, which would consist of factual material. The reader, at first glance, might think he was not interested, because it looked as though it would be dull reading. But if the writer takes his tax receipts, or those of his friends, and shows how the citizen's tax dollar is distributed, and how he is benefited by the services his tax dollar helps to finance, the reader will be interested immediately. He will realize that the facts touch his own life. The writer must remember always that the reader is interested in himself first of all.

Humorous matter may be incorporated into articles by use of

examples of that type. Such material will make a dull article entertaining. An alert writer will find such aspects in most subjects, but they should be used only when relevant.

Hypothetical Cases. Suppositional incidents may be resorted to when the writer does not have an appropriate concrete example with which to illustrate his point. They must be typical and plausible, or they will fail to add to the reader's interest. One should avoid the overuse of this type of unit. It may result in monotony and a feeling of lack of confidence. Such cases may be introduced by such phrases as, "Suppose, for instance, that," or "If, for example."

Statistical Material. Any systematic computation of facts is generally avoided by young writers. They do not realize that there are various ways in which such material may be presented interestingly for the reader to grasp the information readily. "To find ways of making units of statistics appeal to the reader is like playing a game with oneself," a young writer exclaimed after he had overcome his dread of using sheets of figures that his interviewee had given him.

The first principle in using statistical units is to translate the figures into terms that the reader can comprehend. This may be done by reducing large figures to smaller ones with which the reader is familiar, in order that he will understand them at a glance. A student wrote a story explaining how railroads know at every minute where each one of their thousands of freight cars are. He impressed the reader with the huge number of cars on the tracks of railroads in the United States by explaining that if they were in one long train they would extend around the circumference of the earth three times. Realizing that the comparison would not mean much to the average reader, he explained the terms in how many rows of cars there would be if placed side by side extending from New York to San Francisco. Since he was writing it for a state newspaper feature section, he broke the figures down even further by showing how many rows of freight cars there would be side by side if they were placed on tracks between Chicago and Minneapolis.

Scientific Processes. The average individual avoids scientific and technical information just as he does statistics, unless the writer makes the terms sufficiently simple for the reader to understand them. Narration and description are the best methods of presentation for technical and scientific procedure. Utility articles based on processes and techniques may be given variety by presenting the material through interviews, dialogue, quotations, charts, or tabular form.

Methods of Presenting Units. The articles at the end of the previous chapters and in current publications illustrate how units may be presented to the reader in such a manner that they will be varied yet forceful. The methods of presentation of the five units may be done by means of: (1) narration, (2) description, (3) exposition, and (4) occasionally, by argumentation, or the elements of it.

To give variety to the forms of discourse the writer may employ: (1) dialogue, (2) interview, (3) quotations, direct and indirect, and (4) tabular forms, graphs, or charts for statistics and recipes. By frequent checking with the notations made on the outline opposite the various units, and their methods of treatment, the writer will avoid unconscious repetition and will attain variety in presentation of material.

Paragraph Is Flexible. Although form is second in importance to content in fact writing, yet knowledge of its technicalities enables one to progress more rapidly out of the amateur class. The paragraph is pliant and affords the writer the opportunity to employ individuality in its development. In many respects each one is a distinct unit and offers a separate problem of composition, but, of course, each must have unity and coherence. In planning one paragraph, consideration must be given to the manner in which it may be linked to the one following. Although it is developed as a unit, it cannot stand as one by itself, because the outline was designed upon the theory that each paragraph is dependent, more or less, on the preceding one.

Paragraph Development. The connective idea between paragraphs should be in the first sentence of each to make a smooth transition. These word-links give variety throughout the article. A few methods by which they may be used, selected at random, are as follows: hypothetical instances; illustrations; questions; analogies; descriptions; figures of speech; reasons; causes; effects; and phrases such as, "to continue," "to put it another way," and the like. Natural ability, observation, and practice skill will enable the tyro to include in each paragraph word-links appropriate to the content and the style of the subdivision.

After the selection of suitable word-links, the writer states the paragraph topic, and then gives attention to the expansion and amplification of the paragraph subject. He presents the facts he wishes to use by means of anecdotes, figures of speech, and examples. These are followed by the paragraph conclusion, which emphasizes the idea of the paragraph, either by giving a new angle, or by repetition for emphasis.

Like the feature article, every paragraph consists of a beginning, the paragraph itself, and an ending; or, as rhetoricians say, the connective link, the developed topic, and the conclusion.

Factors Determining Paragraph Length. Just as the advertising copy writer plans sufficient white space for the display of his advertisement, so does the feature writer when he makes the outline, with its numerous paragraphs. Short pithy paragraphs make for variety and for easy, rapid reading. They break the solid appearance of the column, and the prominent display of the paragraph topic aids in catching and holding the reader's interest.

Paragraph length is determined by the magazine to which one is slanting rather than by the nature of the subject, although that is secondary in importance. Emphasis may be based on brevity, as illustrated by the lead paragraph in a press association story, "The President is dead." The average paragraph for feature sections or for magazines with mid-length lines is from two to five sentences. One successful writer said he never had less than two paragraphs on a typed page, double spaced; but he found that usually three or four paragraphs were better and were more attractive to the eye. If he were writing for a newspaper section, with its shorter line, he made his paragraphs even shorter. The magazine with a wider line can use longer paragraphs, since the width makes the paragraph appear shorter and easier to read.

Sentence Structure Must Be Evident. Sentences—particularly paragraph lead sentences—are important. They serve to get the reader's attention as his eye glances down the page and to convey ideas to a more or less hurried reader. The first requisite of a good sentence, whether it is the lead or not, is that its grammatical structure should be obvious. If the reader cannot see at a glance the relation of the parts, he cannot read rapidly. Then he will lose interest.

Sentence lengths vary in features for the same reasons that paragraph lengths do. Short ones contain fifteen words or less; long ones have thirty words or more. Because the meaning is easily grasped, short, simple sentences are more emphatic than longer ones and they serve better as transitions between paragraphs. Variety in sentence length is necessary to prevent monotony.

Importance of Words. As the beginner trains himself for his career or avocation, he should develop skill in selecting the right word while he writes. He should not leave the task entirely until revision of the article, as some novices are inclined to do; because they dislike to think, they defer it as long as possible. One should choose words that: (1) are familiar to the reader for whom he is writing; (2) are concrete, to stir the imagination and to paint vivid, modern word pictures; and (3) are likely to have associated ideas and feelings that will enable the reader to recall literature that he has read or experiences that he has had. An up-to-date dictionary and a thesaurus are the writer's best friends.

To write effectively, the writer will check his manuscript to see if all unimportant words or details have been deleted and that the writing moves fast because of active adjectives and verbs. He also should check for clarity, concreteness, and conciseness.

Arrangement of Material. Fortunately for people with a creative instinct, the actual arrangement of material is flexible. There are very few rules for the development, other than to arrange the content of the article logically, in order that it will be interesting. Beginners as well as professional writers enjoy freedom in their writing. An article should be written in any way that will be effective and that will keep the reader on the interest-holding line (Fig. 3) to the end.

Because of the many varied arrangements, owing to the initiative and originality of writers, it would be difficult to plan an elaborate classification. There are four methods, which, in general, apply to most plans. They are: (1) the logical order, which consists of a systematic arrangement of the related ideas and events in which the relating of one thing suggests another; (2) chronological order, which, as the name indicates, follows the time elements in which the events happened, so that the article is developed as the events occurred; (3) general news story order, in which the most important points are placed at the beginning, with the less important material following; and (4) the "snapper" news story order, in which the point of presumable interest is a brief paragraph, consisting of an anecdote or a hypothetical case, that fairly reaches out and grabs the reader's eye. The main part of the article following the "snapper" lead may be developed in logical or chronological order. The order of development in most well-written articles may include elements of one or more of the several methods listed.

Formula for Writing. The conventional method for writing features is not a very set form. The writer writes what he has to write; he writes it interestingly, and with a purpose. He employs the writer's artifice wherever it is needed, and thus pleasantly surprises the reader just when he was about to become bored. He sustains the interest throughout by withholding some of the best units until the end.

Many professional writers take a week, or a month or even more, to prepare an article of 5,000 or more words. They know that editors wish literary workmanship in the features they buy. Therefore, they regard the writing of the article as of first importance.

From the preceding paragraphs the amateur has learned how to avoid tiring the reader's mind by giving him too many weighty facts at a time, or too-ponderous paragraphs of narration, description, or exposition. He knows how to incorporate the various units in order to relieve dullness and to give variety and crispness to the style. He understands the technique of making his style vigorous by means of colorful description, lively narrative, and lucid exposition. He knows that his vocabulary must be vivid and exact and his figures of speech appropriate and effective to aid in making the article appeal to the reader.

He has learned the formula, if there is one, for writing features. He is ready to start the first copy of the article.

Putting the Units Together. In the writing of the first draft, the novice checks the various parts of his pyramid-like outline as he writes, in order to ascertain that he has all the units and their elements in their proper relationship. He aims at clearness in every sentence, although he does not devote too much attention to the English mechanics until revision (which will be discussed in Chapter 13).

As the beginner writes, he should imagine that he is speaking his article to a friend. His diction will then be fresh and vital. He will find that it is not difficult to dramatize the facts by means of the varied units, since all he has to do is to put them together. He will give attention to making the paragraph transitions smooth. But his main purpose at this stage of writing the article is to get the article, as he had perceived it, on paper as rapidly and as enthusiastically as possible.

If, as he is writing, he finds that some of the methods of presenting the various units are not as effective as he had anticipated, he should change his outline as well as his first draft. He should check his outline to see whether that change will necessitate additional ones.

Writing the Conclusion. A good lead requires a good ending. Its function is: (1) to leave the reader with the impression that the writer wishes him to have; (2) to give the reader a feeling of satisfaction, or even gratification; and (3) to make an artistic conclusion, or finish, to the article.

No matter which type of ending one uses—summary or general

statement—the writer should keep one or more interesting facts for it. It may be an application of the facts, or an astonishing result, that proves the statement in the lead. Regardless of what facts the conclusion contains, the writer must take the reader back to the point of presumable interest, as illustrated in Fig. 4. By so doing, the semicircle is completed around the apex of the pyramid and makes the conclusion unified and artistic.

With the exception of writing the caption, the amateur finds that the first draft is now completed. He should give it an immediate reading, checking with the outline carefully to see that the paragraphs are in the best order and that nothing has been omitted. Some professional writers say that the revision comes easiest immediately after the writing of the first draft. The majority, however, prefer to put the article aside and revise it after they have had time to look at it from a detached point of view. No matter which method the writer finds best, he should give thought to his caption and write it, if possible, before typing the final draft. Ideas expressed in the caption may necessitate changes in the article.

Best Writing Conditions. With the completion of the first draft, the amateur will realize that he, like the professional, can write easier and better under certain conditions. Half of the difficulty of writing is overcome when the amateur has firmly made up his mind that he will start his first draft at a set time, regardless of what distractions there may be. No matter when he starts, or under what conditions, he probably will increase the business of the paper manufacturers by filling up his waste basket until he gets his brain cells and fingers limbered up. One will never be inspired to write until he has worked up an inspiration by writing. If possible, one should at least start his writing in a room free from distractions, to enable him to think clearly and concentrate earnestly. Some persons write better at night; some in the morning. Some cannot get started at their articles until they have had a brisk walk in the fresh air; others until they have had a short nap.

If one does not use the touch system on the typewriter, he will save time and energy by learning it immediately. Practicing an hour a day for three weeks, he will acquire some skill and speed. He should train himself from the beginning to compose on the typewriter as he writes. It is only the newest novice who writes out the article in longhand and copies it on the typewriter.

Professionals are divided upon the question as to whether it is better to outline the article and write the first draft immediately after the interview, when their enthusiasm is high, or to transcribe their notes and wait to outline and write until they have had sufficient time to think through the material and the methods of development. The majority of writers combine the two methods. They transcribe their notes in any order that they may interpret later. By this method they retain the ideas, expressions, and quotations that they acquired in their first zeal. The material is put aside and forgotten temporarily, but the subconscious mind is working away on the article. This process results in clearer ideas of methods of presentation and of development. This, after a little experience, makes for easier writing—and a first draft that will need but little revision.

If one has difficulty in making the passages clear or determining how to develop one of the outlined units, he may find that talking it off to himself will solve the problem. It will increase his enthusiasm and will aid his creative instincts immeasurably.

A young home economics teacher, after the completion of her first feature, exclaimed with considerable emotion, "Writing is hard work. I never worked so hard in my life. If I have to work like that, I am going to return to teaching, much as I hate it."

She was astonished to find that very few people "dash off" their articles. Most writers admit they work and struggle over every paragraph, every sentence, and every word. Of course, with experience one writes much more easily and smoothly, but even so, writing *is* work. However, it is fun, as the home economics teacher found out before the end of the semester. By that time her checks totaled $1,386. She also found that there is no satisfaction that equals that of creative work and the pleasure of seeing one's writing in print.

Analyzing Articles Aids Novice. For the beginner's convenience in studying the techniques of feature writing, a number of articles written by novices, and sold to periodicals of all kinds, have been reprinted at the end of some of the chapters. It is suggested that the tyro examine these student-written features to study the sources, the manner of presentation, and the style. The writer, amateur or professional, should include in his study current publications of the type for which he plans his feature, because fashions in features are ever changing. What was the vogue with an editor a year ago may be passé with him the next month or week.

Exercises

1. List three ideas that you could use for possible leads for your next feature article.

2. In which articles in your favorite magazine did the beginnings fail to meet the functions of a lead?

3. In chart form list the appeals used in the leads in the articles in the magazine of your choice.

4. Which lead is suggestive to you for ideas in the development of the lead for your next feature?

5. In three paragraphs of not more than fifty words each, describe the kinds of leads that each of the three possible markets, to which you are slanting your next feature, seem to wish.

6. In the second row of the chart started for Exercise 3, indicate any faults you found in the lead that the writer should have avoided.

7. In the third column of the chart, classify the types of leads that you analyzed for the sixth exercise.

8. In the fourth column of the chart, indicate the person in which each of the articles is written.

9. Hurriedly read one of the articles to ascertain the devices the writer used to keep the reader's attention on the interest-holding line, and list them.

10. Estimate the length of each article and record the result in the fifth column of the chart.

11. In the sixth row, indicate which structural units were used in each article.

12. Indicate in the seventh column the methods used in presenting the structural units.

13. For each article tabulated, make a rough estimate of the number of words in the average paragraph and place the figures in the eighth column opposite the article.

14. Estimate the average sentence length used in each article and record in the ninth column.

15. In the tenth column, write "yes" or "no" after each article listed, according to whether or not you think the vocabulary met the three requirements of words as listed in this chapter.

16. In the eleventh column, indicate which type of arrangement of material was used by each writer.

17. Indicate by "yes" or "no" in the twelfth column whether the endings meet the requirements of the function of a conclusion.

18. Make a diagram, similar to Fig. 4, in the previous chapter, of one of the feature articles.

19. Read through the leads of the articles in current periodicals and classify each according to the types listed in this chapter.

20. What structural units did you note in the articles that are suggestive to you for use in your next feature article?

21. List suggestions by comparing an original article with the same article as used in *Reader's Digest.*

Publication Analysis

Art, Dance, Music, and Theater Magazines

Analyze, by using chart form as illustrated in the Appendix, one magazine of each of the above types. Although these magazines are not numerous, some of them may be obtained at newsstands, from magazine dealers listed in the Appendix under "Aids to Writers," in library periodical reading rooms, or may be borrowed from artists in these fields or from subscribers. Some suggested magazines on art are: *Magazine of Art, Design;* on the dance: *Dance Magazine;* on music: *Musical Digest, Down Beat, Educational Music Magazine;* on the theater: *Theatre Arts,* or others of your choice.

Do not spend more than one hour and three-quarters on the preparation of this report.

  I. Identification: Name, publisher, editor, where published, price of each magazine.

 II. Make-up:
    1. What do you like about each magazine?
    2. What do you dislike about each magazine?

III. Advertising:
    1. What is the difference in the appeal in the advertising of the magazines?
    2. From the advertising, what kind of a reader do you visualize for each publication?
    3. One tip from the advertising of each magazine (four tips in all).

IV. General Policy:
    1. If you were editor, would you change any of these magazines in any way?
    2. Give reason for your answer to the preceding question.
    3. What types of articles could you submit to each magazine?

V. Feature Articles:
    1. What types of articles do you find in each publication, and to whom do they appeal?
    2. Analyze an article from each magazine, using Fig. 4, in Chapter 10, as a basis for the analysis.
    3. List five suggestions for improving the writing of your own feature articles, and for finding markets for them.

VI. Illustrations:
    1. List ideas you gained from this study for illustrating your own articles.
    2. What is the average number of pictures or drawings used for each article?

VII. Rates of Payment:
    1. Compare the advertising in general magazines with the ones analyzed for this report. Which class do you think pays the highest rates?
    2. Compare the rates as listed in the *Writer's Market* for the above periodicals. How nearly correct was your estimate in the above comparisons of advertising?

VIII. Four Tips—one from each magazine: Source, authority for the article suggested, and three possible markets for each one that were suggested by the study of this magazine.

CHAPTER 12

Composing the Title

▀▄

The Purpose of the Title. When the reader opens the newspaper feature section or the magazine, his eye is drawn to a particular article by the title or the headline, the illustrative material, or the name in the by-line. If the writer's name is unfamiliar to the reader, then only the caption and the pictures or other illustrative matter will attract. The purpose of the title is to make the reader want to read the article immediately. His first impression of the article is obtained from the heading, which gives him an idea of the content and arouses his curiosity. Its function is not only to catch the reader's attention but to advertise the content of the article and to aid in "selling it to the reader."

The writer gives thought to composing the caption of a feature as the copy writer does when he is planning a title for an advertisement. A challenging heading not only adds to the appeal of the article, but it frequently aids in "selling" the editor the idea that his magazine should have the article in a future issue. The novice must not be tempted to make it simply decorative. The purpose of the title is to attract the reader and to take him on down the interest-holding line to the lead. As the manuscript reader looks over the copy, his eye will be attracted by a good title and his favorable opinion will be carried to the lead and into the article. It is essential to give thought to the writing of the caption because the writer hopes not only to attract the reader but the editor.

Many writers consider captions as important as the article itself, or even more so.

Factors Influencing Form and Style. From the weekly or semi-weekly Publication Analysis one sees the great variety of form and style in which titles are written. The influencing factors are the size of the printed page and its "make-up" as well as the editorial policy. The tendency of the newspaper to use shorter headlines with fewer "banks" or "decks" has extended, with a few exceptions, to the feature section and to the magazine. Conciseness and terseness are required in almost any publication's captions because of the restrictions of the size of the page and the limitations of type. The beginner should analyze the form and length of the titles of the publication to which he is slanting, in order that his will fit the publication "style sheet." He will find that captions follow the fads of the time. Some are written all in capital letters, or with no capitals at all; others are a combination of capitals and small letters (or, as the headline writer says, "upper and lower case").

In examining the titles of the articles in current periodicals, one finds a great variety in style and in form. Alliteration, figures of speech, verbal balance, rhyme, jingles, quotations, parodies, and puns are all used by clever writers when, by so doing, they make the caption more effective and more attractive. Humor, if in keeping with the tone of the article, frequently can be used to advantage. The allure of alliteration, if not overused, is pleasing. The writer may use any device that will aid in making the title clear, stimulating, and appealing.

Elements of the Good Title. Since the purpose of a good title is to get the attention of the reader, it should be: (1) attractive, (2) accurate, (3) terse, and (4) concrete. Since the title is a concise, accurate statement of the content of the article, it makes the same appeal as the article does. But in the caption, not only the idea that is expressed, but also the way in which it is written, is important.

One must avoid sensationalism and exaggeration as well as misleading statement of fact. The title should be honest; it should portray the same spirit and tone as that expressed in the lead and throughout the body of the article; and it should be adapted to the taste of the reader. If the tone of the article is serious, so should the title be; if it is humorous, so should its caption be.

Some persons seem to be born with an aptitude for writing clever captions, as was a young woman who sold everything she wrote. Her features were not particularly outstanding, but the headings were. She had a way of giving a simple declarative sentence an unexpected twist that lifted it above the ordinary class. The ability to write a clever caption that will attract the reader is an art, but it is one that anybody may learn. Editors appreciate clever titles if they are informative and give the reader an idea of the content.

There can be no rule as to when one should write the title. An idea for a caption has probably been under consideration in the writer's subconscious mind ever since he selected the tip for the article. If a clever one has not occurred by the time he has completed the first draft, he should attempt to write it then, in order to get a detached point of view about it by the time he starts revision.

Space Limitations and Mechanics. Since the size of the headline type, the width of the column, and the size of the page of any periodical are fixed, the caption must be planned to fit the available space. Careful study should be given to the typographical style and to the space limitations of the captions in the particular publication to which one is slanting. Should the article return, it is a simple matter to retype the caption to fit the second periodical to which one may be sending an article.

Any type of mechanical arrangement that will add to the interest should be adopted. The novice will find that paradoxical, figurative, interrogative, or alliterative forms will aid in the attention-getting value, as will verbal balance or rhyme.

Word Selection Is Important. An attention-arresting vocabulary, which aids in giving a vivid picture to the reader, is important. One should not be satisfied until he has found colorful words that will call forth mental images and recall associations to the reader's mind. Concrete words are essential in the caption if the reader is to comprehend the meaning quickly. Because specific words are necessary to give the reader a clear-cut mental image, abstract words are to be avoided. The novice will find that picture-making nouns and action verbs used in declarative sentences will entice alike the editor's and the reader's eye. A verb, or an implied one, should be used in every caption to give it life.

An analysis of titles will show that they generally contain three or four important words, with the additional particles and connectives to complete the idea. The majority of titles, or "top decks," do not exceed at most seven words. Short, pithy words, rather than long ones, are to be preferred. They enable the reader to grasp the idea at a glance.

The Sub-title. Many publications use a second title to amplify the first which must be in sufficiently large type to attract the reader. This limitation makes it difficult to give an idea of the content in the very few words allotted. The sub-title's purpose is: (1) to give supplementary information, to explain the short compact caption; (2) to increase the reader's interest; and (3) to serve as a connecting link between the short caption and the lead.

In a well-written sub-title, the same tone is retained as in the title, but repetition of words is avoided. In some publications the title and the sub-title are combined to make a continuous statement. The average sub-title consists of from nine to twelve words, or even more if one includes the articles and conjunctions. As in planning the caption, one will write a more accurate and interesting second "deck" if he analyzes several sub-titles in the publication to which he plans to mail his manuscript. The nearer the style of one's heading approximates those of the possible market, the more confidence the editor will have in the manuscript and the more inclined he will be to think that the writer is a professional.

Classification of Titles. In classifying types of captions, one encounters the same difficulties of overlapping that he did in grouping the leads. This probably explains why many editorial offices classify the titles under the same names as they do the beginnings. Although publications may vary in the arrangement of the types, many offices, to distinguish between the kinds, use the following terms: (1) summary, (2) striking statement, (3) narrative, (4) descriptive, (5) quotation, (6) question, (7) direct address, and (8) alliteration.

Summary Title. This type of caption includes: (1) the label, (2) the simple statement of fact, and (3) "W" titles. The first type, which is most popular in trade and class publications, may consist of a single word or a few simple ones and may, or may not, have a sub-title to explain the first caption. The second consists of simple statement of facts. The third group contains the words *who, what, where, when, why,* and *how* in declarative form. The following are examples of the various kinds of summary captions:

(1)

(Today's Health)

FROZEN SLEEP

*New Hope
for Heart Surgery*

(2)

(The American Home)

TIRE TUBE SWING

*Here's an extra something for the kids—
and its a cinch to make*

(3)

(Fortune)

BUSTLING BANGKOK

(4)

(Popular Mechanics)

BATH ROOM GLAMOUR

*Careful planning and colorful fixtures and walls can
make a bath room as modern as any room in the house*

(5)

(Town Journal)

WINDOW DRESS-UPS

Striking Statement Title. A novel idea expressed in a unique way in the caption to arouse in the mind of the reader wonder, surprise, or astonishment is classified as striking statement heading. It is effective because it is a departure from the ordinary, but it must be brief in order to have the reader grasp the idea. All sorts of figures of speech are adaptable to this classification. Of such a type are the following:

(6)

(*The Atlantic*)

THE VALOR OF TEACHING

(7)

(*Woman's Home Companion*)

I WANT MY PARENTS TO GET A DIVORCE!

Her parents shunned divorce "for the children's sake" but no love could bloom in their divided home. This is a teen-age daughter's story of family tragedy and heart break.

BY A SEVENTEEN-YEAR-OLD GIRL
as told to Arthur Gordon

(8)

(*Natural History*)

SOMETHING NEW
IN OLD TREES

(9)

(*The International Review*)

JAPAN—HINGE OF DESTINY

(10)

(*Life*)

THE GLOW OF PARIS

It evokes a city's many moods.

Narrative Title. To tell the reader something in the caption by means of action words or any of their forms, or by words which imply action, is effective. As with the lead, any techniques used in fiction are appealing to the majority of the readers. Narrative titles are as follows:

(11)

(*Look*)

THE TRAIN THAT RIDES ON AIR

*Automotive and railroad skills are
creating a 100 mph train that may
solve the railroad passenger dilemma*

(12)

(*Ladies' Home Journal*)

THEY SWIM BEFORE THEY WALK

*"Ten days is a bit young,"
but these babies,
4 to 9 months,
take to water like tadpoles*

(13)

(*Outdoor Life*)

FOOT RACE
WITH A GRIZZLY

(14)

(*House & Garden*)

A KITCHEN PLANNED AS A SOCIAL CENTER
IS PERFECT FOR ANY ONE WHO LIKES TO
ENTERTAIN GUESTS WHILE COOKING

(15)

(*Dance*)

*Behind the scenes with
the force behind the
Marquis de Cuevas Ballet*

THE MARQUIS IS
A SHOWMAN

Descriptive Title. Just as the descriptive lead deals with producing images in the reader's mind, so does the caption. The purpose of the descriptive heading is to enable the writer to make the appeal to the reader by means of words with an emotional connotation. Figures of speech with vivid adjectives or implied ones predominate in this type of caption. Humor also is used to advantage. Here are some examples:

(16)

(*Living for Young Homemakers*)

NEW STORAGE SOLUTION

(17)

(*Holiday*)

MAGNIFICENT VERSAILLES

*The glorious old palace with its fabulous
gardens and fountains was the golden
nucleus where the Great of Europe gathered
for love and intrigue*

(18)

(*The American Home*)

MAYHEM IN THE SUPER MARKET

(19)

(*Harper's Bazaar*)

CUCKOO HOUSES OF HAITI

(20)

(*Field and Stream*)

COYOTE HUNTING IN HIGH GEAR

*Ranchers in western Kansas ride souped-up jalopies wired with
intercom radios and loaded with specially trained dogs to give
the coyote a run for his money*

Quotation Title. That fashion in features is as inconsistent as fashion in costumes is shown by the lack of quotations used as leads, although they are used in abundance as titles. A quotation with which the reader is probably familiar makes an appealing title, but if the application to the article is not evident, such a title will require a sub-title or might better be discarded for a new one. Well-known quotations paraphrased in a novel way are effective because of the psychological principles of recall and association of ideas. A title that "plays on" or assumes the form or likeness of a familiar quotation has strong attention value, because its familiarity and strangeness arouse the reader's interest. Examples of such titles are these:

(21)

(*Good Housekeeping*)

OUR DREAM CAME TRUE

(22)

(*Harper's*)

THE MAN WHO READS CORPSES

*Fatal accidents, suicides, and murders often look strangely
alike but in the laboratory of the Morgue, Alexander
has developed a battery of scientific tests that are making
homicide hard to conceal*

(23)

(*American Home*)

JUST PLAIN BEAUTIFUL

(24)

(*Sports Illustrated*)

TIP FROM THE TOP

*For golfers of all
degrees of skill*

(25)

(*Popular Mechanics*)

HOMES THAT LOOK AHEAD

Question Title. The interrogation attracts some readers because they are curious or they desire to be informed. It may be used as a challenge to the reader's knowledge. If a subtitle is used, it may consist of a second question, but the writer must avoid using it as an answer to the why or how of the question asked in the title. Because of overuse, the interrogative title is not so popular now as it was a few years ago. The following are typical:

(26)

(*The American Home*)

ARE YOU AN ATTIC STUFFER?

(27)

(*Natural History*)

WANT TO COLLECT
INDIAN RELICS?

*Finding mementos of the
ancient past adds unlimited zest
to outdoor rambling*

(28)

(*The Journal of Business*)

IS EXECUTIVE DEVELOPMENT COMING OF AGE?

(29)

(*Ladies' Home Journal*)

SHOULD *YOUR CHILD* GO INTO BUSINESS FOR HIMSELF?

(30)

(*The American Home*)

LIKE TO HAVE
A GREENHOUSE?

*New Metal Frame Models Merge
Low Cost, Easy Upkeep*

Direct Address Title. Direct address may be used or implied in captions as well as in leads, but it likewise should not be over-used and it should be employed only when the writer can avoid a dictatorial tone. A test of when it may be used is to ask oneself the question, "Is there any other type that may be used effectively?" If the answer is negative, then the writer may use it, as, for example, in the following:

(31)

(*Holiday*)

YOUR TRAVEL FUTURE

*Revolutionary, stranger-than-fiction
ways of getting
around are brewing,
and you'll be trying them out
sooner than you think.*

(32)

(*Flower Grower*)

*Raise your own perennials
from seed this spring*

BUILD YOUR GARDEN AROUND DAY-LILIES

Plan to have some varieties in flower every day of the season

(33)

(*House & Garden*)

PLASTIC POOL
YOU CAN SET UP YOURSELF

(34)

(*Lifetime Living*)

TAKE A TRIP INTO HISTORY

(35)

(*Better Homes & Gardens*)

Imagination Pays Off

PUT YOUR SALAD
IN A SANDWICH

Your salad sandwich is a breeze to fix, a picnic to eat. It's a natural for a cool lunch on the back yard table. Try one of these sandwich specials as a quick 'n easy answer to your what-to-eat problems.

Alliterative Caption. This title includes any of the others except it differs in word choice. Composing it may take more time and care than other types. Alliteration depends upon cleverness and skill in selecting words that will produce the same letter or sound at the beginning of words which succeed each other immediately or at short intervals. Some editors bar them; others use them at every opportunity. The following are alliterative:

(36)

(*Life*)

POTS, PANS AND PROSPERITY

*Boom Takes over Housewares As
U.S. Manufacturers Put On
Biggest Show*

(37)

(*Lifetime Living*)

FIGHTING FAT AT 56

(38)

(*Outdoor Life*)

CROUCH, CREEP, AND CRAWL

(39)

(*Field and Stream*)

CROSS-COUNTRY CAMPING

There is no better way to learn camping than on a cross-country trip on which you stop overnight at state and national campsites

(40)

(*Ebony*)

BIRMINGHAM'S BUSINESS BARON

Writing the Title. After the novice has analyzed the titles in the publication to which he plans to send his manuscript, he should jot down, as a first step, a number of "sample" headlines. From these he may ascertain the number of letters, units or characters as they are termed journalistically, that can be accommodated in the title and the sub-title. He should keep these "samples" before him as a "pattern." Accurateness in writing a title of the correct length and style will impress the editor with the writer's ability as much as the writing of a clever caption in tone with both the publication and the article.

A reference to the purpose of the article, which was written as a declarative sentence at the top of the final outline, is the second step. It will refresh the memory as to its aim, and it may be suggestive of a good caption. Before determining the content of the heading, the writer should ask himself, "What is the biggest thing in my story?" Further checking with the final outline will yield at a glance the high spots of the article. Any one of these may be suggestive for a title that will attract the reader and "advertise" the content of the article. These points should be written down as declarative sentences. A reading of the manuscript may suggest ideas for making the declarative sentences more vivid or alluring to the reader. If so, these should be added to the sentences.

With the idea, or ideas, for the content of the title on the paper before him, the beginner, in taking the third step, will analyze each caption-sentence that he jotted down, to see: (1) if it will serve as a connecting link between the policy of the periodical and the presumable reader interest as outlined in Fig. 2; and (2) that it is in harmony with the interest-holding line in Fig. 3.

The fourth and final step is to juggle the ideas by taking part of one of the declarative sentences and combining it with another, in order to adapt it to the style and length of those in the proposed market. When a combination is found that meets the requirements of a good title, the novice condenses the declarative sentence selected by finding shorter or more vivid or more colorful words. He should be sure that the title contains picture-making words that will enable the reader to know the content of the article as well as words that will have an association or that will recall something in his experiences. If the content of the article lends itself best to an interrogative type of heading, then the declarative sentence should be changed into a question to meet the requirements.

Constructing the Sub-title. In writing the sub-caption, the same steps are taken, except that one may have to amplify the declarative sentence instead of condensing it. One must remember that the purpose of the secondary title is to explain the first and to aid in the transition between the title and the lead.

Value of a Good Caption. The writer will be well repaid for his time and efforts in writing a clever title. It is a sort of tactful compliment to the editor that one knows just how his captions are written. Painstaking accuracy in trying to slant the article 100 per cent to his publication gives the editor confidence in the writer's manuscript. A clever heading serves as an ace salesman in "selling" the article to the manuscript reader and the editor.

A careful writer may have ten or thirty possible captions for one article jotted down if he has approached the problem from as many different angles as possible. From a large number, there may be one or more that the writer feels have attention values. If so, he should submit them all and let the editor choose the one to be printed.

If one is unable to obtain a copy of the publication to which he is slanting, he should keep his title short but see that it has a vivid verb to give it action. It is a good policy in writing a caption without a "pattern" to include a sub-title, for it aids in giving the manuscript reader a definite idea of the content even if the form of the titles and sub-title may not fit the publication's style.

The experienced writer generally does not set about in any formulated way to write the caption. Somewhere in the procedure of gathering, planning, outlining, and writing the article, one or several excellent ideas will flash across the mind. The professional jots it down immediately, wherever he is, lest it be lost to memory by the time he has revised the manuscript and typed the final copy of the article. But of course the novice may have to have considerable experience in writing before he will be able to have a clever and appropriate title pop into his mind.

Exercises

1. Turn through an issue of a magazine that you have not even glanced at heretofore. Look at each feature article. Jot down the caption and indicate which did, or did not, attract you.

2. List any unusual fads that you find in the titles.

3. Turn through the issue of a newspaper feature section that you have not seen. Note the headlines and what did, or did not, attract you.

4. Compare the form, length, and style of the titles in the two periodicals.

5. Write down the titles that did not contain all the elements of a good caption.

6. Make a list from the two publications of the words that you consider good title words.

7. What differences did you find between the sub-titles of the two publications?

8. Write down an example for each of the seven classifications of titles from the magazine and also from the feature section. What differences did you find for each type in the two publications?

9. List ten titles included in this chapter that you think will be suggestive in writing the caption for the article that you are working on now.

10. List the "pattern" titles from the publication to which you are slanting the article that you are now writing.

11. Copy the declarative sentence, from your final outline, that contains the purpose of your article.

12. Condense or amplify it to meet the requirements of your "pattern" title.

Publication Analysis

Hobbies, Home Craft, Mechanical, and Science Magazines

Analyze, by using chart form as illustrated in the Appendix, one magazine of each of the above types. They may be obtained at newsstands, from magazine dealers listed in the Appendix under "Aids to Writers," or in library periodical reading rooms. Some suggested hobby magazines: *Hobbies, Profitable Hobbies, Trains, United Hobbies, Philately, Modern Popular Photography, Photography, U.S. Camera;* home craft: *Mechanix Illustrated, Popular Mechanics;* science: *Popular Science Monthly, Science Digest, Science Illustrated, Scientific American,* or others of your choice.

Do not spend more than an hour and a half on the preparation of this report.

I. Identification: Name, publisher, editor, where published, price.

II. Make-up: Including typography, size, style, etc. What do you like about the magazines?

III. Advertising: To whom does the advertising appeal? Is there anything different about it from that in the other magazines studied? From the advertising, what type of material would you expect to find in the magazines? List at least one tip suggested to you by some advertisement in *each* magazine.

IV. General Policy:
   1. From the table of contents, estimate roughly the amount of different material used.
   2. What do you think are your chances of selling to these publications?
   3. What do you like about the magazines?
   4. If you were editor, what would you change in the magazines?

V. Titles:
   1. Why did, or did not, the titles in each publication attract you?
   2. Enumerate any novel ideas that you found in the captions.
   3. Distinguish the policies of each publication toward its titles in reference to style, form, and length.
   4. List the words that you thought were good headline words.
   5. What variances did you find in the use of sub-titles?
   6. Which one of the classifications of titles did you find used most often? Which least? Which not at all?
   7. What suggestions did you get for writing captions that will aid you in your own writing?

VI. Features:
   1. What feature articles could you have written for each of the publications?
   2. Which types of features seem to predominate?
   3. Analyze one feature article in each magazine in any way you wish, but do it from the point of view of what you can learn about writing your own articles. (Devote not more than thirty words to each article.)

VII. Illustrations: What ideas did you get for your own article for photographs or other illustrative devices used in the publications?

VIII. Slogan: Make a slogan for each magazine.

IX. Four Tips: Source, authority, and three possible markets suggested by this study (eight tips in all, including tips suggested by advertisements in III above).

CHAPTER 13

Revising First Draft of Manuscript

▛▀▙▀▜▀▛▀▜▀▛▀▜▀▛▀▜▀▛▀▜▀▛▀▜▀▛▀▜▀▛▀▜▀▛▀▜▀▛▀▜▀▛▀▜▀▛▀▜▀▛

Necessity of Revision. The majority of authors will agree that revision of the first draft is necessary, even for the professional. If anyone is to write freely and enthusiastically, he must write rapidly; and rapid writing does not permit time to think through the structure and simultaneously to polish up every sentence as it is formed. Amateur and professional alike will save time and energy in the long run if the amplification, correction, or deletion is done after the first draft is out of the typewriter. Literary excellence demands something more of the author than the bald recitation of facts. It is the difference between doing a thing and doing it artistically, in a way that will please the reader's aesthetic taste.

A novice may expect to make several drafts of his article before it is ready to be submitted. In feature writing, however, the beginner who has had training or daily practice in writing for print and who follows accurately the suggestions in planning, outlining, and writing the article, as given in the three preceeding chapters, may find little revision necessary, except to give attention to the elements of style and the touching up and the tightening of sentences and paragraphs.

Style of Writing Is Important. Style may be summarized

roughly as the way in which a writer does his work, or the manner in which thought or emotion is expressed in words. Each person's thought differs from any other's, and a writer must transfer the feelings of his own mind, mood, or emotion to the mind of the reader. Style is as essential in fact writing as in any other type of composition. It is an organic, integral part, and is written into the article. The elements of it may be improved by revision of diction and phraseology. But style cannot be used as a woman's compact to touch up the shiny or the bald places; it is fundamentally as much a part of the article as the facts are. It is the way the article is written that enables the writer to convey what he thinks, what he sees, or what he or others do in such a way that the reader grasps the author's thoughts and emotions.

Factors of Style. The market, the subject matter, its purpose, and the writer's point of view influence the style in which an article is written. Because of its importance, it should be given as much thought as the gathering, planning, and writing of the article.

Style affects the reader intellectually, emotionally, and aesthetically and is dependent upon the qualities of clearness, force, and good taste. The best style consists of transferring to the reader the exact words or the exact feeling that one has, in order to give him the exact idea. To do so, the writer must: (1) see exactly in his own mind what he thinks, or sees, or feels, and (2) have the words to express the shade of feeling or thought that he desires to express. The first requisite of style is its readability. Therefore, the writer must select words that will appeal not only to the reader's sight, but to his senses of sound, taste, smell, and touch as well.

It is not the purpose here to discuss the theories of style in detail. The interested student will find several excellent books listed in the Appendix, under the "Free-Lance Writer's Library," that will be informative and stimulating. It is suggested that the articles in current periodicals be analyzed in order to ascertain the elements of style used by the authors.

Growing Vocabulary Is Aid to Style. The writer's solution to the problem of style is to have a large, modern, and ever-growing vocabulary. Authorities have estimated that a minimum of from five to fourteen thousand words is required to read a newspaper, although the journalists use words that everyone will understand.* People with a high-school education or its equivalent are known to have a reading vocabulary of between nine and ten thousand words, sometimes even more. The effective vocabulary, it has been said, is one that is large enough to permit wise discarding.

Whether one is making writing an avocation or a career, he should strive to have the best diction possible. Anyone writing regularly can easily use words over and over again. Constant reference to dictionaries and a thesaurus for specific words will enable a writer to get into the habit of using them in place of abstract ones. Thus may he inject life into his articles and lift himself above the amateur class.

As the rhetoric books explain, the elements of style are: (1) words, (2) sentences, (3) paragraphs, and (4) figures of speech. The theory of style is an old subject to anyone who has had a composition course; yet it takes on new interest to the novice about ready to revise the initial draft of his first feature.

Function of Words. The word-tools used by the writer to bring forth the reader's images and emotions depend, for their efficacy, upon the nature and experience of the reader. If he cannot comprehend, he will not respond. The novice should choose: (1) only those words with which the average reader is familiar; (2) concrete words, to aid in giving the reader definite ideas; (3) words that will have an association for the reader, or that will enable him to recall ideas out of his own experiences; and (4) words that are up-to-date. Yesterday we wrote *trailer camp,* today, we write *mobile home in the court;* tomorrow, we may have a new word for it since $100,000 "parks" are often constructed for the portable dwellings.

The beginner should select usual words—but not commonplace ones—and combine them to give the reader a vivid picture, to stir the reader's imagination, or to take him back to his own

---

* Smith, S. Stephenson, *The Command of Words,* p. 1. New York: Thomas Y. Crowell Company, 1940.

experiences. When it is necessary to use an unfamiliar term, it should be explained the first time it is used. The most forceful words are short ones. If it is necessary to use trite, antique words, the writer may give them new life by using them in phrases or clauses with little-used ones.

Language is a vital force in writing. Some words that are full of life and meaning to us may carry no significance whatever to others, and vice versa. On the other hand, certain words and phrases have the power of stirring everyone. Success as a writer depends upon ability not only to say what one wishes to say, but to transmit to the reader the impression the writer desires him to have.

Advantage of Specific Words. To make the phraseology specific, avoid excessive use of adjectives and adverbs by substituting active verbs that will take the office of the modifier and at the same time denote action. Beginners usually feel that an adjective adds something to a noun; but it may also cut off some of its possible meanings. When one writes of the *placid sea,* he may decrease the reader's possible impressions conveyed by the single word *sea.*

In narrative and descriptive sentences particularly, the words should not only produce pictures in the reader's mind but should enable him to have all the sense impressions of taste, sight, sound, touch, and smell as well. Active verbs should replace passive ones, in order to make the reader feel that the event he is reading has just happened.

By analyzing published features, the writer observes how the professional constantly creates concrete pictures in the reader's mind by using active verbs that call forth vivid images. When one writes the sun "came" in the window, the reader does not know what time of day it is; if the writer says the sun "is creeping" in the window, the reader not only feels that the article is about the present, but he knows that the writer refers to the early morning sun. The word "broncho" yields a different meaning to the reader, as contrasted with the abstract word "horse." As one revises his manuscript, he should strive to substitute specific words for abstract ones, and active verbs for passive ones. By giving thought to the fine distinction between words as well as their emotional value, the novice will improve his style.

Word Position Is Important. In revising the manuscript, the writer is able to survey the position of the words in the sentence, to see whether the style could be improved by changing the word order. The rapid reader's eye is attracted by the first group of words at the beginning of the sentence. Sentences may be made more effective by rearranging the words to have the important ideas near the beginning.

Improving the Diction. In order to add to the effectiveness of the phraseology, the writer should exclude: (1) unnecessary words, (2) general words (by substituting specific, colorful ones), (3) unfamiliar terms (unless he explains them), (4) words not in keeping with the tone or pace of the article, and (5) words used in hackneyed phrases and figures of speech.

By constant reference to a thesaurus and the dictionary, a writer not only develops his vocabulary but clarifiies his meaning and stirs the reader's imagination.

Skillful Use of Sentences. If the hurried reader is to grasp the meaning of the sentence, the relation of each part to every other should be clear and definite. Grammatical structure must be evident to enable one to grasp the meaning immediately, even in the short sentence.

The structure of the sentences determines the tempo of an article even more than the choice of words. It also effects the harmony between the movement of style and the ideas advanced. Whatever the rate of movement, it should be appropriate to the content. Thus, the writer is enabled to adjust the tempo to the nature of the material. Although the tone of the article is produced more by word selection than sentence structure, it is influenced by the latter. Both tone and tempo may vary according to the material.

Sentence Variety. Next in importance to vocabulary is sentence variety. It is attained by diversity in sentence length, structure, and form.

The length of the sentence is influenced by the short line in the newspaper and magazine column, as pointed out in Chapter 10. The narrow measure makes sentences and paragraphs appear longer than they are and suggests that the novice should guard against too-long sentences, which are a handicap to clearness. In revising, he must check to see that the sentence length is varied. He should see that a short sentence contains fifteen words or less; a medium length one from fifteen to thirty; and a long sentence thirty or more words. All lengths should be used to attain variety and contrast. A short sentence should be used to give clearness and emphasis to a passage. It also speeds up action and serves as an excellent means of transition. The mid-length sentence should be used to present average thought. A writer should avoid excessive use of it, because it tends to become monotonous. Because of its length, the long sentence is excellent to present a series of details or a summary. It offers contrast to the short, rapid sentence, because its structure impels it to move slowly and deliberately.

A variety of the various types of structure will prevent sameness and will aid in holding reader-interest. The periodic, the balanced, and the parallel sentences are aids to easier reading and to arresting attention.

The form of the sentence gives opportunity for variance. A simple sentence may be used for emphasis, to attract attention, or to serve in making transition from one paragraph to another. The compound sentence aids in making contrast; the complex in summarizing details. In revising the manuscript, the writer will give variety to his style if he makes use of the three forms.

Revising Paragraphs. The novice must keep in mind, in his task of correcting his manuscript, that paragraphs are to a sentence what the latter is to a word. Before revising them, the novice should refresh his memory on paragraph requirements by reference to Chapter 11. If paragraphs run the same length consistently, they should be amplified or pruned down to give variety. To attract the reader, the average newspaper or magazine paragraph runs from two to five sentences. Some should be longer;

others should be shorter. Attention should be given to coherent connectives to see that they fit their tasks.

The reader may often glance over an article before beginning to read it. If he sees long solid paragraphs, the chances are that he will not bother to read the article. The beginning of the subdivision, like the beginning of the sentence, should be emphatic. If it is not, it should be revised to arrest the reader's attention as his eye goes down the page. Each paragraph should be scrutinized to see whether it can be improved—whether it sounds natural and logical.

Figures of Speech. Derived from feeding thought with imagination, figures of speech have been called the romance of composition. One author says figures of speech are devices, both comparative and mechanical, used for the purpose of beautifying, clarifying, vivifying, energizing, and picturizing language.* They serve: (1) as a departure from the ordinary way of writing, for the sake of greater effect in phraseology; (2) to arrest attention; (3) to stimulate the imagination; and (4) to appeal to the emotions. In improving the style of a manuscript, the novice should use only such figures as the reader can best understand. Although the feature article lends itself to literary treatment, just as the short story does, the writer should never use a figure unless it contributes to the effectiveness of expression. Figurative language cannot be used as an adornment nor as jewelry of literary style.

The psychological devices of association and recall may be adapted to figurative phraseology. The author may make it easier for the reader to comprehend the new by comparing it with the familiar by means of a simile, or by implying the likeness by use of a metaphor. Often references to literature and to language will give the reader the effect, even if he does not know the story to which the writer refers. For further discussion of this particular aid to style, the novice should examine some of the books on the subject referred to in the "Free-Lance Writer's Library," in the Appendix.

* Opdycke, John Baker, *Get It Right,* p. 78. New York: Funk & Wagnalls Company, 1935.

The Novice Revises His Manuscript. Desired results in any form of art depend as much upon leaving out as upon putting in. Sometimes skillful trimming or cutting counts for more than perfect technique. To put in too much is bound to result in confusion and lack of reader-interest; to leave out every non-essential increases clarity and heightens interest. Cutting is more of a problem than padding—and it is more necessary, because the beginner must make every word work. Editors pay by the word, and every word should be worth its price. If one writes anything of which he is particularly proud, he should delete it—or at least cut it in half. Learning what to leave out is learning how to write what will sell.

As psychology points out, an individual can think effectively of only one thing at a time. For that reason, the beginner should go through his manuscript several times, each time seeking to improve a different element of style. He will save time if he gives attention to: (1) the general organization, to see that the relation of paragraphs is effective and that the first six words of each contain a striking idea; (2) the grammatical structure of each sentence, to see that the modifiers are related to one another in just the right way to clarify the meaning at a glance; (3) the length and type of sentences, to see that they are varied; (4) the length of the paragraphs, to see that they give variety in appearance; (5) a scrutiny of every sentence, word by word, to see if better words may be substituted, and if clauses may be reduced to phrases, and phrases reduced to single words; (6) elimination of errors of grammar, spelling, punctuation, and capitalization; (7) the tempo and tone, to see that they are harmonious throughout the article; (8) the lead and conclusion, to see that the reader is left with the impression the writer desires by repetition in the ending of the words or the idea expressed in the beginning; and (9) the title, to see that it has an active verb, or an implied one, to give it life, and that its tone and tempo are harmonious with that of the article.

Good magazine writers work cleverness into their articles by revising several times. Many of them prefer not to revise until a period of time has elapsed after the completion of the first draft.

They feel that the interim enables them to look at their manuscripts with a detached point of view and to become keener self-critics. Every minute spent in revision will increase the opportunities for sales, as will constant study of the articles of other writers to learn the secret of the success of their style.

With experience, the beginner, like the copy reader on the news copy desk, will be able to detect several or more faults at one reading and will then find it necessary to go over the manuscript only once or twice instead of nine times to find the specific faults.

Errors Common to Beginners. In the course of handling many manuscripts written by amateurs, editors find a number of mistakes that they all make in common and that crop up constantly. Generally these are due to: (1) neglect of checking the outline for omissions and (2) failure to punctuate accurately.

Articles may have to be revised because the beginner fails to fulfill the purpose he had in writing it. In others, the young writer could not resist the temptation to "preach" or editorialize, forgetting that the reader is not interested in his opinions and that he should leave himself out of the article. Or he may fail to keep the article addressed to the same reader. Frequently the authoritative sources that would give confidence to the statements are omitted, as may be proof to back up drastic statements. Statistics may be given in terms too large, or too many at a time, for the reader to grasp them clearly and quickly.

Failure to make use of opportunities to refer to events in history or literature, or to use appropriate figures of speech, keeps the articles in the mediocre class that editors return "with regrets." Important information may be omitted and sentences may be incomplete in meaning because the tyro has not learned to see his own shortcomings in writing. Too often a beginner fails to keep in mind that the subject matter must be timely six months in advance for magazines and from three to seven weeks for newspaper feature sections. Or he may write and revise the manuscript without checking to see if the length falls short or is beyond the limits of the publication to which he is slanting.

Typographical style presents a problem to the amateur who is inclined to be careless. Capitalization, punctuation, and spelling may not be uniform. He may have failed to follow the typographical style of the publication for which he is slanting, either through his own carelessness or through his failure to examine an issue to ascertain the style. Many first manuscripts abound with punctuation, particularly dashes, parentheses, and exclamation marks. This fault is most commonly found in articles written by young women, although young men have it too. Dashes should be used instead of commas only when the expression so set off is thrust into the sentence and does not have a close grammatical connection. Printers object to the use of dashes, except when necessary, because they break up the artistic appearance of the printed page. Many writers neglect to start a new paragraph for each new and separate quotation; others fail to put end quotation marks at the end of quotations. Thought and care in checking the manuscript before typing the final draft may prevent a rejection slip. To read the article aloud enables a beginner to hear mistakes that his eye fails to catch.

Determination Will Bring Success. If one is sincere in his desire to write, if he wants to write more than anything else in the world, he will not find the details of revision discouraging. Determination to succeed is an important factor in writing. Probably more than half of the well-known writers of today would never have succeeded had they not been filled with dauntless resolution. They, too, had to give much attention to the details of revision before they were able to take their place with other successful magazine writers.

Those who follow the suggestions in these chapters will learn to write successfully, as have thousands of beginners before them who have followed this so-called "formula" for writing and selling articles. In the process they developed the true writing instincts, by means of which they learned to command words, phrases, and sentences to do their bidding, and to marshal the elements of style in such a way that readers across the land were guided, informed, and entertained by their articles. Beginners who fail are those who feel that what they write is too good to change in any particular.

They refuse to revise their manuscripts. "Writing, revising, and keeping at it" supply the secret of successful free-lance writing.

Many beginners who have been painstaking with their revisions have been rewarded, not only with checks, but with letters from editors commending their writing. Such a letter is shown here:

Mr. Harry E. Wood,
Madison, Wis.

Dear Mr. Wood:

In preparing our August schedule, which is to contain your article on how to make a sea horse, I have just read over the manuscript again and cannot refrain from expressing my congratulations upon the skill displayed in its wording. It is a vivid, lively piece of writing and a remarkable demonstration of what can be done with a subject which in most hands would be tepid and matter of fact.

Sincerely yours,
Arthur Wakeling,
Home Workshop, Editor
Popular Science Monthly.

A careful survey of published articles will reveal that originality in the presentation has been the winning point, rather than anything particularly new in the content. "It is the way it is written," the results of thoughtful revision, that has influenced many editors to buy articles from writers they did not know were beginners. If the novice will give the editor and the reader something out of the ordinary, a check will be forthcoming.

Exercises

1. Select some piece of writing, preferably your first feature article, that you did some time in the past and list suggestions for its amplification, correction, and deletion.

2. Which factor do you believe will be the most important in influencing the style of your next article?

3. Make a list of ten words and their synonyms that you think you will find it necessary to use in your next article.

4. Write a 100-word summary of your reading in one of the books pertaining to words, writing, or style listed in the "Free-Lance Writer's Library," in the Appendix.

5. Write a summary paragraph of 100 words for each of five books listed under Vocabulary Aids in the "Free-Lance Writer's Library." In-

clude in each paragraph the help that a writer should expect to find in the book, according to the preface.

6. Select an article in a current issue of a newspaper feature section and one in a current magazine and make a table listing the average number of words in a short, medium, and long sentence in each of the two articles.

7. Write down an example of periodic, balanced, and parallel sentences taken from each of the two articles. Analyze them to see why they are, or are not, effective in the style of these particular features.

8. Which of the three forms of a sentence predominate in each of the two articles?

9. What is the average length of the paragraphs in the two articles?

10. Which length predominates?

11. Do you find any paragraph lead sentences in either article that are not emphatic and attention-arresting? If so, copy them down to read in class.

12. List the most effective figures of speech that you found in each article. (A list of the figures of speech will be found in any of the books on style listed in the "Free-Lance Writer's Library.")

13. Did you find any paragraphs, sentences, or words that could be deleted in either of the articles? If so, list them.

14. Select one of your own manuscripts and read over the first five pages seeking to improve the style in the nine ways suggested.

15. Check the first five pages selected for Exercise 14, to see if there are any errors that are common to beginners.

Publication Analysis

Civic, Health, Travel, and Religious Periodicals

Analyze, by using chart form as illustrated in the Appendix, one magazine of each of the above types. These publications may be obtained at newsstands, from magazine dealers listed in the Appendix under "Aids to Writers," or in library periodical reading rooms. Some suggested civic publications: *Elks, Kiwanis, Lions, Rotarian;* health: *Life Today, Today's Health, Your Health;* travel: *Buick, Caravan, Everywhere, Flying, Ford Times, Highway Traveler, Holiday, Lincoln-Mercury Times, Motor News, Traveler, Travel Magazine;* religious: *Christian Century,* the *Christian Herald,* the *Living Church, Presbyterian Life,* the *Sign,* the *St. Anthony Messenger,* the *Victorian,* or others of your choice.

Do not spend more than one hour and a quarter on the preparation of this report.

I. Identification: Name, publisher, editor, where published, price of each magazine.

II. Make-up:
    1. What do you like about each magazine?
    2. What do you dislike about each magazine?

III. Advertising:
    1. What is the difference in the appeal in the advertising of the magazines?
    2. From the advertising what kind of a reader do you visualize for each publication?
    3. One tip from the advertising of each of the four magazines analyzed (four tips in all).

IV. General Policy:
    1. If you were editor, would you change these magazines in any way?
    2. Give reason for the foregoing answer.
    3. What types of articles could you submit to each magazine?

V. Feature Articles:
    1. What types of articles do you find in each publication and to whom do they appeal?
    2. Analyze an article from each magazine, using the pyramid as a basis for the analysis.
    3. From the articles make a list of ten words that you feel give distinction to the style of writing.
    4. List three figures of speech from the features in each publication and discuss their effectiveness.
    5. Did you notice in any article a lack of completeness, or did the writer anticipate the answers to your questions?
    6. List five suggestions for improving the writing of your own feature articles.

VI. Four Tips (one from each of four magazines): Source, authority for the article suggested, and three possible markets for each one that were suggested by the study of each magazine.

CHAPTER 14

Preparation of the Final Manuscript

Professional Appearance Aids Sales. After the free-lance writer has carefully revised the manuscript, he is ready to start copying the final draft to send to the editor, its prospective purchaser. As has been pointed out in earlier chapters, one's manuscript competes with hundreds, or even thousands, of others in the editorial offices of a large publication. Therefore, the article must be submitted in a neat form that will attract the manuscript reader's eye immediately as the work of a professional. The reader detects the work of the amateur at first glance by the manner in which it is prepared. Naturally, he will have more confidence in the manuscript that obviously is written by an experienced writer. He will be inclined to give more consideration to an article that is carefully and neatly prepared in the professional manner.

The way in which a manuscript is submitted may mean the difference between an acceptance and a rejection. The novice must take great care to prepare the copy carefully, just as he would give thought to the details of his dress and manner if he were applying for a position. The editor's first impression of the writer's accuracy and dependability is formed when he looks at the manuscript for the first time. Many beginners fail to sell because they lack pride in the "physical" appearance of their articles. If they used "corrasable" bond paper, their erasures would not be obvious. Editors say that Americans are more careless than foreign writers in the preparation of their manuscripts. A well-prepared manuscript will make for an immediate friendly feeling toward the author on the part of the manuscript reader or editor as illustrated by the following letter:

AMERICAN RESTAURANT MAGAZINE
Patterson Publishing Co.
5 South Wabash Avenue
Chicago 3, Illinois

Mr. Kenneth C. Wagner
807 Oakland Avenue
Madison 5, Wisconsin

Dear Mr. Wagner:
We liked your story. It will make a nice human interest feature in our magazine. You will be advised when it runs, and we will send a copy of the issue carrying the story.
I am enclosing our check for $50.00 to cover the article and photographs you sent with it. I am not sure that we can use all these photographs—in fact, I don't think that we will, but I don't know at this time which photographs the Editors will want to use, so I am keeping the entire set.
I would like to compliment you on the neatness of your manuscript. You should see some we have submitted to us!

Cordially yours,
AMERICAN RESTAURANT MAGAZINE

MWilson/NM
Encl.

Method of Preparation Is Uniform. A writer should give every possible consideration to the manuscript reader or editor who has to read his article and determine whether it will be accepted or rejected. Professional writers follow, on the whole, a uniform style in drafting the final copy. They are anxious to prepare it in the editor's accustomed way and to do everything that will make the reading of the article easier.

If a manuscript is typed on paper that is too thin, or is written on both sides, or is single spaced, or is written in longhand, or is without page numbers, the editor will classify the novice with others whose manuscripts are physically unattractive to him.

Some authors submit well-prepared thick manuscripts on first-class bond paper, but instead of sending them flat, they fold them twice and mail them in business-letter envelopes. The editor has to take time to straighten out each page—which is most annoying. Others use the same typewriter ribbon for years, with the result that the letters are blurred and difficult to read, and this will exasperate any editor.

Before beginning to type the final copy, one should plan to include: (1) a cover sheet; (2) the typed article; (3) a back cover sheet; (4) pictures or drawings (the preparation of which will be discussed in the following chapter); (5) cardboard for packing; (6) a self-addressed postal card to acknowledge receipt of the manuscript; (7) a large manila envelope for returning the manuscript; (8) adequate postage stamps, attached by means of a wire clip, for the return of the manuscript; (9) a still larger manila envelope in which to mail the manuscript, and (10) sufficient postage for first-class mail.

Every person who writes for publication should check his manuscript on the following points to see that he has not omitted any of the requirements of a professional manuscript.

Manuscripts Must Be Typed. Every person who writes, even as an avocation, should learn to use a typewriter. Until the writer has learned to type accurately he will have to have a typist copy his manuscripts.

A good typewriter with type kept clean and with a black ribbon in good condition will produce neat, legible copy. An editor will usually read such a manuscript with some degree of interest and will feel kindly disposed toward the writer.

Unruled white bond paper of good quality (not too heavy) in standard typewriting size, 8½ by 11 inches, should be used. Good paper not only looks well but stands more handling and saves retyping of manuscripts when they are returned, because it will be less worn and "dog-eared." It is cheaper to buy paper by the box.

The professionally prepared manuscript is typed on only one side of the paper. It has a margin of at least an inch on the left-hand side, at the top, and at the bottom of all pages except the first page, which should have a margin of three or four inches at the top. The copy is double spaced to allow room for editorial corrections, changes, or subheads between the lines.

A businesslike writer makes a carbon of everything he writes for print: one copy for the editor, the other for his own files. If the original is lost in the mail or in the editorial office, the writer may replace it easily by retyping the carbon copy. If the article is accepted, the carbon also serves as a check to see how the printed copy was changed; or it may be of further service to the writer at some later date, even after the article is printed. One should have a sufficient supply of good carbon paper to insure clear copy.

Preparing the Cover Sheets. If a writer wants to sell articles, he should have a front cover sheet to serve as an introductory salesman in meeting the buyer—that is, the editor. If it is properly prepared, it tells the editor: (1) the purpose of the article, (2) the identity of the writer, (3) the source of the material, (4) the number of words, and (5) the kind and number of illustrations.

In the upper left-hand corner the writer should type the statement: "to be paid for at usual rates," etc., as shown in Fig. 5. The market should be indicated in the upper right-hand corner, as should the date of mailing the manuscript.

The author should type the title on the cover sheet about one-third of the way down the page, in order to leave sufficient space for the editor to change the caption if he wishes to. If the publication to which the article is slanted uses all capital letters, so should the author. If capitals and small letters are used—or, as a journalist would say, "upper and lower case" letters—the author should use them too. If the publication uses a second deck, or subtitle, underneath the caption to further explain the content of the article, so should the writer.

Two lines beneath the title the writer should type his name, or "by-line." If he has "ghosted" the article, he should use the name of the celebrity on the "by-line" and, two lines lower down, type his own name on a second "by-line," preceded by the words "as told to."

The note to the editor should be started three or four lines below the "by-line," as shown in Fig. 5. It contains the salesman-

```
To be paid for at usual            Written for Today's Health
rates, or to be returned
with the eighteen (18)             Mailed Oct. 8, 1958
cents in stamps enclosed, to

Robert E. Neprud,
740 Langdon Street,
Madison, Wisconsin.




                    MILK--FROM DAIRY TO DINNER TABLE

                                by

                          Robert E. Neprud



        (Note.  This article is based on an interview with
                Dr. L. C. Thomsen, an associate professor of
                Dairy Industry, College of Agriculture,
                University of Wisconsin, and on material
                from government bulletins concerning milk
                consumption. It contains 1,850 words.)


        Two (2) photographs are enclosed, as follows:

                1. Rinsing the Milk Bottle Under the Faucet
                2. A Clean Cold Place for the Milk

        Two (2) drawings are enclosed, as follows:

                1. The Housewife Should Know Her Dairyman
                2. Milk Ranks at the Top as a Food
```

Fig. 5. A Cover Sheet for a Manuscript.

ship points and guarantees the goods, or, in other words, assures the editor of the authority for the content. One or more plausible reasons should be listed why a given article has reader interest, and it should convince the editor that he ought to read all of the

```
                                        Place
                                        Date


    To Whom It May Concern:

                        I have read this article
    and it is scientifically (or technically) accurate
    The quotations are just as I made them.
                        Yours respectfully,

                    (signed)_____
```

Fig. 6. Approval Sheet to be Signed by Interviewee.

manuscript. The full name and identification of the interviewee or other sources that will aid in "selling" the manuscript to the editor should be included.

However, the note does not serve as a means of telling the editor how to run his publication or what his readers want to read The youthful amateur in his enthusiasm and in his desire to "sell" the editor often offends rather than convinces. It is important that one give thought and care to writing the note. A tactless note is worse than no note at all.

The number of words in the article should be listed at the end of the note. That is where the editor is accustomed to find such information. A quick and fairly accurate estimate may be made by counting all the letters and spaces, or "units," in one average typed line and dividing by 7 (the number of letters in the average word). The result is the number of average, or seven-letter, words to a line. By counting the lines on an average page and multiplying by the average number of words to a line, one knows the average number of words to the page. Multiplying the number of average words to the page by the number of pages in the manuscript gives a fairly accurate estimate of the total number of words. Or a writer may use a character counter. See Free-Lance Writer's Library.

In the note to the editor the author may explain his reason for writing under a pseudonym by saying "that for obvious reasons I am writing under an assumed name." Or an author may not want to use his own name because the interviewee may be a member of his family. Or the article, particularly if it is a confession, might be too personal. If a nom de plume is used, it should be written in parentheses after the real name in the upper left-hand corner of all the pages, in order to insure mail delivery of the acceptance or of the rejected article. If the article is accepted, this practice enables the business office to write the check out in the writer's own name rather than in his assumed one.

The number of photographs, drawings, or other illustrations should be listed three lines below the end of the note. The captions, or "cut-lines," of the illustrations should be listed as well as the number, as shown in Fig. 5.

Before inserting the completed manuscript in the envelope for mailing, a blank sheet of typing paper should be placed at the end of the manuscript to serve as a "back" cover sheet. It, like the front cover sheet, will aid in keeping the manuscript from becoming grimy and soiled as it is passed about from one manuscript reader to another in the publication office.

At least the cover sheet and the first page are read in most offices. From those pages the manuscript reader judges whether or not the article will have enough interest for the publication's subscribers for him to read all of it. A writer can see how important it is to prepare the cover sheet and the first pages with extreme care if he would impress the manuscript reader favorably.

Approval Sheet May Aid in Selling. If an article is of an extremely scientific or technical nature, or contains facts that the editor may doubt, the writer should ask the interviewee to sign a statement that he has read the article and that it is accurate or scientifically correct, whichever the case. The writer should type on a separate piece of paper the form illustrated in Fig. 6. The signed approval sheet is placed just under the front cover sheet when the article is assembled for mailing.

Summaries Are "Boxed" on Separate Page. Some publications have a policy of occasionally using a summary, a list of directions, recipes, or a check list by "boxing" or indenting the material and placing it at the beginning of the article, or at the end, or perhaps in the center of the printed page. Since the writer does not know where the make-up editor would like it placed or whether he will want to use it at all, it is advisable to type such material on a separate page.

Lines may be drawn about it to form a "box," or the word "box" enclosed in a circle may be written at the upper left-hand corner of the page. If the writer knows that the publication's policy is to indent rather than box such material, he should write the word "indent" enclosed in a circle at the upper left-hand corner.

In arranging the manuscript for mailing, the sheet containing the boxed or indented material should precede the first page of the article. It follows the cover page and approval sheet (if there is one).

Typing the Final Draft of the Manuscript. The upper half

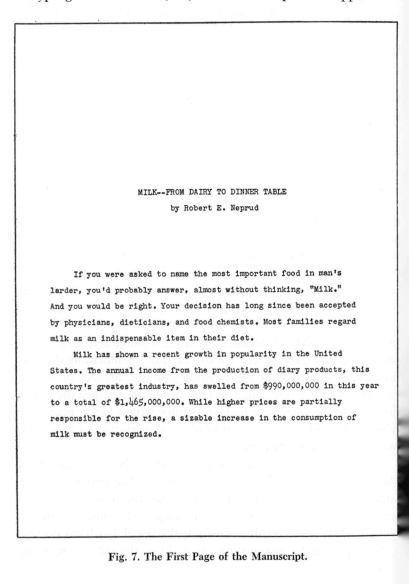

MILK--FROM DAIRY TO DINNER TABLE

by Robert E. Neprud

If you were asked to name the most important food in man's larder, you'd probably answer, almost without thinking, "Milk." And you would be right. Your decision has long since been accepted by physicians, dieticians, and food chemists. Most families regard milk as an indispensable item in their diet.

Milk has shown a recent growth in popularity in the United States. The annual income from the production of diary products, this country's greatest industry, has swelled from $990,000,000 in this year to a total of $1,465,000,000. While higher prices are partially responsible for the rise, a sizable increase in the consumption of milk must be recognized.

Fig. 7. The First Page of the Manuscript.

of the first page of the article should be left blank, in order that the editor may write a new title and subtitle if he so desires. The title, subtitle, and author's name should be repeated on the first page exactly as they are on the cover sheet. The article should begin three lines below the "by-line," as shown in Fig. 7.

At the left-hand side and as close as possible to the top of each page after the first should be placed the author's name, followed by a dash and the title of the article. The pages should be numbered clearly and consecutively in the upper right-hand corner, thus:

Neprud—MILK—FROM THE DAIRY TO THE DINNER TABLE —2—

Unnumbered pages may be dropped, scattered by a breeze, or even lost in the editorial office. Pages without numbers may cause the manuscript reader trouble and annoyance, which will not make him any more appreciative of the article than he is compelled to be.

Each paragraph should be indented five spaces on the typewriter. A sentence should be started two spaces after the period of the preceding one. An end mark, or double cross (#), should be put at the end of the manuscript to indicate that there are no more pages.

Any last minute corrections that cannot be made neatly on the typewriter should be made legibly in ink. Every omission or error in the typing should be corrected either on the typewriter or with a pen. A writer cannot expect an editor to think well of a manuscript if he himself does not respect it enough to make it as nearly letter perfect as is possible. One should remember that carelessness is the earmark of the amateur.

Lightweight cardboard about a quarter of an inch larger than the size of typewriting paper will be needed in mailing to prevent the manuscript from becoming worn and to prevent damage to photographs, drawings, or other illustrations.

Postal Card Serves as Receipt. A government two-cent postal card, self addressed, should be enclosed with the manuscript. The other side of the card should contain a statement acknowledging receipt of the manuscript, as illustrated in Fig. 8.

The postal card, along with the stamps, should be clipped to the envelope enclosed for the manuscript's return. In this way the writer is provided with an acknowledgment that the publication has received the manuscript. The returned card should not be destroyed until the manuscript has been accepted or returned. In

```
                              250 Park Avenue,
                              New York City,
                              October ____, 1958

Miss Lois Brock,
2421 Sunset Drive,
Denver, Colorado.

Dear Miss Brock:

             This is to acknowledge receipt

of your manuscript, "Meet the Co-Founder," which

came in today's mail.

             (signed) _____
                              Editor, Collier's
```

Fig. 8. Postal Card Receipt.

many offices the envelopes are opened by a clerk or an office boy, and the card may not come to the immediate attention of anyone with the authority or interest to mail it. Since the idea of the postal card receipt originated in a journalism class room, a large number of publications have adopted the practice of mailing out their own cards acknowledging receipt of the article.

Manila Envelopes for Mailing Manuscripts. Two sizes of manila envelopes are needed. They must be large enough to contain all manuscript material without folding the paper or breaking the pictures. The larger envelope, in which the article is sent to the publication, should be 13 by 10 inches. The smaller one, for the return of the manuscript, should be 12½ by 9½ inches. If one cannot obtain the two sizes, he will have to fold the envelope that he encloses for the return of the article. The author should check to see that the smaller return envelope has his correct address and that his return address is written in the upper left-hand corner of the large envelope, which is sent to the editor. In case the publication no longer exists, the manuscript will be returned. "First Class" should be written on both sides of both envelopes to aid the postal clerk in correct sorting.

Postage Stamps. Before one writes in the amount of postage on the cover sheet, he should include all material to be mailed—manuscript, pictures, drawings, return manila envelope, and return postal card—and it all should be weighed on a postal scales. Stamps should be attached, along with the postal card, to the return envelope with a wire paper clip. Stamps should not be pasted on the return envelope. If the editor buys the article, he buys the stamps along with it.

Following the Accepted Typographical Style. Before typing the final draft of the article, a writer should analyze several issues of the publication to which he is slanting to ascertain the typographical style. He should list the publication's peculiarities of typographical form and follow them. However, if the style is extremely different or freakish, it is better to write the final copy according to the commonly accepted rules of capitalization, abbreviation, punctuation, hyphenation, and the use of figures. If the manuscript is returned, it will not then need to be rewritten because of its unusual typographical style before it is mailed out to another publication.

In typing the article, the writer should remember that each page should end with a complete sentence—if possible, a complete paragraph. The copy then can be divided between several operators for setting in type. If the page ends in the middle of a sentence or paragraph, it is more difficult to break up the manuscript.

Correcting Typographical Errors. Manuscripts should be typed as nearly perfect as possible. If errors slip in here or there, the novice could correct them in ink. The following are copyreading marks accepted by all editors and printers.

Three lines under a letter or word indicate that it is to be set in capital letters; thus, united states = United States.

Two lines under a letter or word indicate that it is to be set in small capital letters; thus, Kansas City Star = KANSAS CITY STAR.

One line under a word indicates that it is to be set in italics; thus, Gone with the Wind = *Gone with the Wind*.

An oblique line drawn from right to left through a capital letter indicates that it is to be set in lower case; thus, Feature Article = feature article.

A circle around a numerical figure or abbreviation indicates that it is to be spelled out; thus, ⑤feet and three⑪ = five feet and three inches.

A circle around a word or figure spelled out indicates that it is to be abbreviated or that numerical figures are to be used; thus, ⓟPresident⦆J. D. Jones is⦅six⦆feet in height = Pres. Jones is 6 feet in height.

A caret is placed at the point in the typed line where letters or words written above the line are to be inserted; thus, One should never

    a letter
write‸to the editor = One should never write a letter to the editor.

Short curved lines indicate that two words or two parts of a word are to be run together without space between them, in order to make one word; thus, cran‿berry = cranberry.

A vertical line between two words indicates that they are to be separated by a space; thus, An amateur should never|query an editor = An amateur should never query an editor.

A small cross or dot within a circle indicates a period; thus, U⊗S⊗or U⊙S⊙ =U. S.

Small half-circles around single or double quotations indicate whether they are beginning or end marks; thus,⟆Ten cents a quart is much too high⟆ he said.

A curved line under one word and over the next indicates that they are to be transposed; thus,⦅article⁀feature⦆ = feature article.

A paragraph mark is used to indicate a new paragraph; thus,
|They are as follows; or   ¶ They are as follows:

A line is used to connect the end of one line with the beginning of another when both are to form a continuous line of copy; thus, The check came by messenger on Monday afternoon in a long, brown envelope,~~a long one~~ with nothing else in it.

Sending the Manuscript. Postal regulations require that all written matter must be sent as first-class mail at the same rates as letters. The pages of the manuscript should be clipped together with a paper clip before inserting it into the envelope. The latter should be sealed. Both envelopes should be marked on both sides "First Class—Handle With Care." Delay in the delivery of the article because of insufficient postage may be prevented by weighing the article on an accurate postal scales. Stamps to cover the postage for the article's return, in case it is rejected, should be attached along with the post card receipt to the return envelope with a wire clip.

Even though one knows the editor's name, it is advisable to address the outer envelope containing the manuscript simply to "The Editor." If the article is going to a newspaper, it should be addressed to the "Article Editor" or to the "Sunday Feature Editor." If one addresses the outer envelope by using the editor's name and it reaches his desk when he is away, his secretary may think it is personal and not open it. Unnecessary delay would result.

Manuscripts, even those of a few pages, should be mailed flat with a sheet of cardboard a little larger than the paper, to prevent the article from becoming crumpled and the photographs bent or broken. Select cardboard heavy enough to afford protection but not so heavy that it adds to the postage expense unnecessarily. If large photographs or drawings are sent, two pieces of cardboard should be enclosed to assure protection. As previously pointed out, a manuscript is an article of merchandise to be sold to a customer—the editor. Needless to say, he will not be interested in buying one that is not neat and professional in appearance any more than he would want to buy a suit of clothes that was wrinkled and shopworn. A folded piece of paper used as a tab underneath the paper clip which holds the pages together will prevent telltale marks. A cardboard backing placed inside the *return* envelope will insure better return if the manuscript comes back. Office boys often fail to return cardboard packing, with the result that pictures are broken and the manuscript is crumpled. It is important then that careful attention be given to "packing" the manuscript, in order to have it arrive on the editor's desk in the best possible condition.

A careful writer, before putting the manuscript in the mail, will check again to see that he has included all the material to be mailed: manuscript, pictures, drawings, and the return manila envelope, with postal card receipt and sufficient return postage clipped to the envelope.

If the manuscript is a bulky one or the photographs so large that the package cannot go as first-class mail, it should be sent by express or air mail.

Mailing Manuscripts to Foreign Markets. English, Canadian, Australian, and New Zealand publications offer a wide variety of opportunities to all writers since the advent of global air mail. But before submitting articles to publications in foreign countries, it is best to write to the publications in which one is interested and obtain sample copies, if they are not available on newsstands or in the local library. Many authors could add to their revenue by selling second rights to manuscripts that they have already sold in this country.

Often writers do not know how to obtain foreign stamps for return postage if the article is not accepted, and they defer the day of mailing manuscripts to foreign publications for that reason. Return postage may be secured by writing to the postmaster in any city in the foreign country (no further address is necessary), who will send stamps in exchange for an international money order. Or, better still, one may obtain at his local post office an international postage coupon, exchangeable in any country belonging to the Universal Postage Union for postage stamps representing the amount of postage needed for an ordinary single-rate letter destined for a particular foreign country, which may be sent with the manuscript for return postage. Though more expensive than foreign stamps, it has the advantage of being obtainable at one's local post office, and it therefore saves time. The same method may apply to other foreign countries which belong to the Universal Postal Union. A non-resident tax is deducted from sales in a foreign country, by that country.

The Manuscript in the Editorial Office. A record is made of the manuscript by most publications as soon as the huge mail sacks are opened in the mailing room and the manuscripts are sorted and delivered to the various editors. Some offices make the record on a card, others use ledger-like books. The name and address of the author, the title, the type of article, the number and nature of illustrations, and the time of the article's receipt are entered. The amount of postage on the envelope and the amount clipped to the return, or "inner," envelope is noted on a card. The estimated number of words is also recorded. If the photographs or drawings are damaged, that, too, is noted.

The manuscript and illustrations, with the record, are sent to the editor's, or the assistant editor's, secretary. She sorts the manuscripts as to assignment to assistant editors, records on the card the name of the department or the assistant editor to whom the article is to be given, and files the record card under "Manuscripts Received."

If the editor or manuscript reader to whom the article was delivered rejects it, he clips a rejection slip to it. If he "almost accepted" it, he may write a letter to the author. The secretary takes the card from the "Manuscript Received" file, stamps the date on it, and places the card in the case marked "Manuscripts Returned." The secretary or the office boy puts the manuscript with the rejection slip and photographs in the return envelope, and, if sufficient postage was enclosed, sends the manuscript to the mailing department. However, if the writer did not send an adequate amount of postage, as many amateurs do not, the manuscript is held in the publication office. Some offices send a postcard to the author asking for postage sufficient for the return of the article; others destroy the rejected article if it lacks return postage.

Some publications send out a form letter explaining to the contributor why the article was rejected. Others send a personal letter of rejection and may suggest another market to which the manuscript might be acceptable. Or an editor may suggest revision of an article with merit and ask that it be submitted again.

If the manuscript is accepted, the associate editor notes on the card the suggested payment for the manuscript and for the illustrations and sends it to the editor. If the latter approves of the article, he may raise or lower the price indicated on the card, his action depending upon the author's rating or ability, the authority contained in the article, and the probable reader interest in the subject. He approves of the associate editor's judgment by endorsing the card. It, along with the manuscript, is returned to the reader who recommended the purchase. The card then goes to the secretary, who stamps it paid, and it is then filed under "Manuscripts Paid." In some offices from four to six associate editors must approve of an article before it is accepted.

A few publications submit galley proofs to the author for correction and for any necessary changes he desires to make. Only necessary alterations should be made, however, in order to avoid delay and expense of resetting type. The author should return the proofs promptly.

The Length of Time for a Reply Varies. The efficiency and the size of the editorial staff determine the length of time it takes to inform an author concerning the fate of his manuscript. Some offices reply within a week; others within a year or even longer. However, the better established offices do not hold a manuscript longer than three or four weeks and they pay promptly. They realize that the free-lance writer has to pay his bills and that prompt consideration and prompt payment win friends. The result is that they have a larger number of manuscripts submitted by free-lance writers, which enables them to choose their manuscripts rather than to take what they can get.

Plans and Methods of Payment Differ. Publications vary in their systems of payment as well as in their methods of handling a manuscript. Some pay once a month, whereas others pay once a week. Many pay upon acceptance, but the majority pay upon publication. And a few pay only when the author threatens exposure of the publication's inability or lack of interest in paying.

Some publications pay as little as $1.50 for an article, whereas others pay from $100 to $500. If the contributor is well known, he may be paid several times that amount.

In the majority of publication offices, rates of payment are based upon a certain amount per word. Others pay so much per article, regardless of the number of words. Rates per word vary from a quarter of a cent to five cents per word to unknown writers, whereas established authors are paid more than the minimum rate by most publications. Some editors require a statement that a manuscript is original, or that by accepting the check the writer gives certain rights to the publication. These rights will be discussed in Chapter 16.

The present tendency is toward prompt payment and also toward payment on acceptance.

Successful Writer Keeps a Manuscript Record. Keeping a record of one's manuscripts is most important, because it enables one to know: (1) where his articles are, (2) where they have been, (3) how long it takes the editor to make a decision, (4) the rate of payment, (5) the time of payment, (6) the cost of photographs, art work, paper, envelopes, and postage, (7) the total cost, (8) the hours spent in gathering the material and in writing it, and (9) the profit. Such a record is a necessity when making out one's income tax. The form for such a record is shown in Fig. 9.

The professional writer, by examining his manuscript record sheets, or cards, knows how soon he may expect a decision from most publications to which he submits articles. If an article depends upon timeliness for its interest, he cannot risk sending it to an editor who takes several months to consider a manuscript; otherwise, if it is rejected, it will be too late to send it elsewhere. By surveying his manuscript record, the writer will note the publications that give prompt decisions; by sending his article to one of those, his chances of selling will be infinitely better.

Checking Up on Unheard-from Manuscripts. Manuscript records should be filed by the dates upon which a manuscript was mailed out last. A check-up then can be made easily to ascertain the articles that have been out a month or more. The writer should send a note or postal card of inquiry as to the manuscript's whereabouts. He should phrase his note tactfully by insinuating

Article No. 9. Title *Taming Wild Pasture*

No. of Photographs 3. No. of Drawings 2. Date Article Was Written *October 3, 1958.*

Publication	Date Sent	Date Ret'd	Date Accept'd	Amount Paid	Photo Cost	Art Cost	Paper Cost	Envel. Cost	Post-age	Total Cost	Hrs. Spent	Profit
1. *Farm Journal*	10/ 5	11/ 2	.....	.....	$2.00	.07	1.60 (Box)	.10	.18	3.70	8	.....
2. *Success. Farm*	11/ 3	11/25	.....	.....	......	......	......	.10	.18	.28	.....	.....
3. *Capper's Farm*	11/26	.....	12/18	100.00	......	......	......	.10	.18	.28	.....	$95.74
4.												
5.												
6.												

Fig. 9. Form for Manuscript Record.

that he is afraid the manuscript has been lost in the mails, since he sent it on the date a month previous and has heard nothing concerning it. He should suggest that if the manuscript has not been received, he will be glad to send another copy. If the editor ignores the inquiry, the writer should follow it up with another every week until he does get a reply.

Some professional writers use a "top front" cover sheet of salmon pink or red paper, which is placed on top of the regular front cover sheet to call the manuscript reader's attention to the immediate timeliness of an article. If the writer does not hear within ten days about a timely manuscript so prepared, he should send a postal card inquiry to the editor to call his attention to the fact that he has not taken any action. If nothing is heard within a week thereafter, a letter to the same effect, asking for the return of the manuscript or its definite acceptance for publication, should be sent. The writer can explain tactfully that because of the very timeliness of the article, his work in gathering and writing it will be lost if the article becomes outdated. Needless to say, the red cover sheet and the ten-day follow up should never be used except for extremely timely articles. If the red cover sheet is overdone, it will fail to catch the manuscript reader's eye, just as the cry of "wolf" by the boy in the fable failed to get attention when he really needed it.

Writers deplore the long time it takes editors to make a decision concerning a manuscript. But the fault often is with the writers themselves for not following up manuscripts systematically and periodically. Of course, the follow-up notes must be phrased tactfully. Many editors are overworked and are even more aware of the delay in replying than the contributor is. Remember that the editor is the free-lance writer's best friend and should be so treated.

Resending Manuscripts to Market. Many writers have received rejected manuscripts in the mail only to realize that they must be retyped before they could be sent to other prospective purchasers. The pages were battered and wrinkled from careless handling in the editorial office or by hurried mail clerks. Much as an author may begrudge the time spent in retyping, it is time well spent. A fresh, crisp, unwrinkled manuscript that bears no traces of prior journeys to other publication offices invariably will be given the editor's first attention.

Retyping is slow and costly in time, and to a person with creative instincts it is apt to be boring and monotonous. An electric iron and a soft gum eraser will save hours of time for the free-lance writer. Many have finally sold articles that have been out four or five times by ironing page by page over a thick magazine placed on an ironing board until the entire manuscript looked fresh and crisp. One must take good care that the iron is not too hot or the paper will be yellowed or scorched. If it is necessary to retype a few pages, they, too, should be pressed, in order that they will have the same yellowed appearance as the other pages.

If the edges of the sheets are soiled, they may be cleaned with a soft gum eraser. The pages should be straightened, until they all are even, and then they should be "riffled" in order to spread them apart at the edges. The manuscript—with the pages still a little apart or offset at the edges—should be put on a flat hard surface so that the edges of the pages will project like miniature stair-steps. The gum eraser may be rubbed over the page edges that project, and they will thus be cleaned in surprisingly quick time. By treating the four edges of each page—both front and back—with the eraser, a manuscript can be made to present a fresh and untraveled appearance with very little effort.

Some writers find that dusting powdered pumice such as stationery stores use on the soiled surface and brushing it off with a soft clean brush or cloth is superior to other methods of erasure. Others run the point of an eraser over fine sandpaper a few times before erasing. The result is a thoroughly clean erasure.

New cover sheets—front and back—should replace the old ones each time an article is remailed. But remember to press the fresh pages, in order that the color will match the rest of the manuscript. The time saved by not retyping the article may be spent in gathering material and writing another. The more one writes, the more he sells.

Writer May Syndicate Articles. A writer may add to his earnings by sending copies of an article to several newspapers for simultaneous publication. This method is termed "syndication" in newspaper parlance. Newspapers circulate only in certain areas or localities. For example, Kansas City papers are not read in

To be paid for at usual
rates, or to be returned
with the twelve (12) cents
in stamps enclosed, to

Robert Anderson,
Shorewood Hills,
Madison, Wisconsin.

Written for Milwaukee Journal
(Exclusive for the Journal's
circulation territory. This
article is also being submitted
to the Detroit News, The
Kansas City Star, and the
Los Angeles Times.)

Release for publication,
Sunday, November 8.

Mailed October 15.

MANY PUPILS IN WISCONSIN TAUGHT

TO TUNE OF RADIO SPEAKERS

Instruction in Music, Drawing, Conservation, and Geography

Given to 50,000 School Children

by

Robert Anderson

(Note. This article is based on interviews with Harold B.
McCarty, director of Station WHA, Prof. E. B.
Gordon of the School of Music, University of
Wisconsin, and Wakelin McNeel, 4-H club leader,
all of Madison, Wis.
It explains the methods and relates the results
of class room radio instruction as conducted by
this educational radio station. It contains 2800 words.)

Three (3) photographs are enclosed, as follows:

1. Education Is in the Air for Wisconsin Pupils
2. Professor Gordon Instructs His Unseen Pupils
3. Wakelin McNeel, Known to His Radio Classes as
   Ranger Mac.

One (1) drawing is enclosed, as follows:

1. A Radio Student Draws Rip Van Winkle

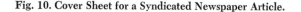

Fig. 10. Cover Sheet for a Syndicated Newspaper Article.

Detroit or Minneapolis; thus, the feature sections of these papers could publish the same article on the same day.

One cannot syndicate his articles to a number of magazines, however, because their circulations overlap, and magazine editors buy only exclusive articles. A subject may be written in two or more ways, to make entirely different articles, which may then be submitted to different magazines. Different pictures should be obtained for each article for a magazine, but in syndicating to a newspaper one would need only duplicate sets of the same pictures. Unless one knows absolutely that a publication's circulation is sectional, he should never send the same material or illustrations to two or more publications simultaneously.

In syndicating feature articles one must: (1) ascertain that the newspapers' circulations do not overlap; (2) make as many clear copies as he intends to submit; (3) obtain separate sets of photographs for each copy; (4) indicate that the article is syndicated by writing in the upper right-hand corner of the cover sheet, "This article is exclusive for your circulation territory. It is also being submitted to . . . ," and then name the other publications to which it is being sent; (5) indicate the date upon which the article may be published, by writing, for example, "Release for Publication, Sunday, Oct. 4"; and (6) mail the articles out at least three weeks in advance of the release date, to enable all Sunday editors to arrange for engravings for the pictures and for publication of the articles on the release date.

It is almost futile for the beginner to attempt to submit articles to a syndicate company, as pointed out in Chapter 9. He may be quite successful, however, in "syndicating" his articles directly to several newspapers. A student wrote a feature concerning a student equestrian club. He sent copies of the same feature to ten different newspapers in ten different sections of the United States and Canada, because the home cities of the student club members were in the circulation territory of the ten newspapers to which the articles were submitted. He received ten checks from the newspapers in addition to that for the original feature, which he had written for a national equestrian publication. His sales for the original article and ten syndicated ones totaled $140.

Understanding the Editor's Problems. Novices are continually protesting against ill-treatment by magazines. They forget that the editors did not ask them to offer their manuscripts. They entered the most highly competitive market in the world of their own free will. They must realize that they are the sellers and that they must accept the buyer's offer. If the editors mess up the script, they should not complain. He did not ask them to send their articles to him.

Editors are not disagreeable. With marketing experience, the beginner will find editors very human and willing to help those who show promise in mastering the craft. They are the best friends a writer can have, if one will work with them instead of against them. Treat your editors as friends and they will treat you the same way.

If one would attain success in writing, he must not be discouraged every time an article does not sell. A young woman who tried writing features was discouraged every time an article was returned. But she often rejects all of the many dresses that she tries on in the shops without ever thinking that the saleswomen might feel hurt because she did not buy. Shopkeepers cannot afford to take offense when their customers do not buy; neither can free-lance writers. The writer must take the attitude of the merchant who, when he does not make a sale, consoles himself that there are others who will buy. No one is likely to succeed at writing unless he is fair-minded, patient, tactful, and willing to meet editors half way in an effort to gain mutual advantage.

Membership in a writers' club, subscriptions to writers' magazines, and a review of textbooks on feature writing will aid the novice who is easily discouraged or irritated at rejection slips to adopt a cheerful friendly attitude toward the editors to whom he hopes to sell. By these means he will acquire an understanding of the editor's problems.

Exercises

1. After checking your supplies for writing features, make a list of additional ones you need before starting to write your final draft.

2. Make a tentative headline schedule for your first article by analyzing the "style" of captions used in the publication to which you are slanting your first article.

3. Make a tentative "style sheet" by listing all unusual style usages found in analyzing three features in the publication to which you are slanting.

4. Make a tentative "style sheet" for the cut-lines used in the publication.

5. What is the average number of pictures used for each article in the publication?

6. What is the average number of drawings used for each article in the publication?

7. What is the average wordage of articles in the publication?

8. How long are the short ones? The long ones? The mid-length ones?

9. Is the content of your article of such a nature that you will need an approval sheet?

10. Is there any material in your article that would lend itself effectively to being "boxed" or indented?

11. Would the content of your article lend itself to syndication?

12. If so, to what newspapers would you submit copies of it?

13. To which of the writer's magazines listed in the Appendix—"The Free-Lance Writer's Library"—do you plan to send a subscription? Give reason for your choice.

14. Which market book listed in "The Free-Lance Writer's Library" do you plan to buy with money earned by writing feature articles?

15. Before submitting your article to your instructor or before mailing your article, check it on all the points enumerated in this chapter in reference to preparation of a manuscript. List the points that you had failed to include in the preparation of your article for market.

Publication Analysis

Nature, Outdoor, Recreation, and Sport Magazines

Analyze, by using chart form as illustrated in the Appendix, one magazine of each of the above types. They may be obtained at newsstands, from magazine dealers listed in the Appendix under "Aids to Writers," or in library periodical reading rooms. Some suggested nature magazines: *Frontiers, National Geographic, Natural History, Nature Magazine;* outdoor: *Field and Stream, Fur-Fish-Game, Outdoor Life, Sports Afield;*

recreation: *Bowling, Motor Boating, Ski Illustrated, Yachting;* sport: *All-American Football, Athletic Journal, Popular Sports,* or others of your choice.

Do not spend more than one hour on the preparation of this report.

   I. Identification for each magazine: Name, publishers, editors, where published, price.

  II. Make-up: What to you, as a future magazine editor, are the interesting things about the make-up of the four magazines analyzed? Give reasons for your answers.

 III. Advertising:
1. From the point of view of what you know about advertising, do you think the copy in each publication will appeal to the reader?
2. What did you like about the advertising in each publication? Give reason.
3. What did you find different about the advertising appeal in each publication?
4. What tips were suggested to you by the advertising?

 IV. General Policy:
1. To what types of readers do the four publications appeal?
2. Why should you as a free-lance writer know these magazines?
3. What features might you have written?
4. Do you find any difference in the appeals here from those in your last study of magazines? What ones?

  V. Features: Read a feature in each of the four magazines and list five suggestions for each feature read that will enable you to write better features (20 suggestions in all).

 VI. Illustrations: List suggestions concerning illustrations for these types of publications.

 VII. Slogans: Write a slogan for each magazine.

VIII. Four Tips: Source, authority, and three possible markets suggested by this study.

CHAPTER 15

Illustrating the Feature Article

▄▀

Writer's Hobby Will Bring Profits. Since many psychologists advise everyone to have a hobby, the feature writer finds himself in a fortunate situation. He may select a hobby that not only will be interesting but will add to his success in his avocation or career. It will help him to sell his manuscripts, it will pay its own expenses, and it will bring in profits. The hobby is photography. The development of engraving and photography, and the increasing popularity of the camera, have been important factors in the growth of magazines and the use of illustrations—color transparencies as well as black and white.

With a little study and practice, writers can take photographs that will aid in telling the stories of the articles and that will reproduce for printing as well as those taken by professionals. The writer-photographer may take pictures how and when he wishes. He will decrease his expense account and will increase his sales. Unconventional pictures add to the reader interest of an article and are in great demand by editors.

The processes of developing films and making prints and enlargements are even more interesting than taking pictures. They, too, will serve as a means of reducing expenses on the manuscript record. However, it is advisable not to attempt taking or making pictures until one has had some photographic experience. Courses are offered in night school and adult-education classes. Self-help books are listed in the "Free-Lance Writer's Library" in the Appendix. Analyses of pictures in the picture magazines will be suggestive.

The Value of Illustrations. The writer learns to think in terms of pictures because readers have become picture-minded. Editors desire illustrations in their publications. Pictures show graphically what otherwise would require description in hundreds of words or even pages of type. They convey facts so effectively that entire magazines as well as entire sections of newspapers and magazines are devoted to pictures.

Readers are attracted by illustrations and frequently, because of them, are lured into reading the article. Illustrations give an authoritative tone to the written word and add to the attractiveness of the page make-up. They serve as a universal language and aid in sales of manuscripts. An editor of a well-known trade publication says that if, for example, a contributor sends an article on how to paint a house, he probably rejects it. But if the writer also sends pictures to illustrate the article, he generally buys both. Another editor finds that approximately one writer in forty submits an illustrated manuscript; the other thirty-nine articles go back promptly. Writers cannot sell their manuscripts if they are not illustrated.

Photographs Must Be Twice Slanted. Photographs add to the value of the manuscript only when they are twice slanted. In preparing the article, as described in Chapter 9, a writer should consider carefully the number and character of photographs, kodachrome transparencies, or drawings necessary to add to the interest of the manuscript, as well as the kinds of photographs that fit the publication's art policy. One publication may desire the artistic variety, with shadows, color, and bright highlights; another may prefer the straight news picture, without any pretense at artistic photography. The successful writer will increase his sales by studying illustrations as diligently as he studied the features and advertising.

Sources from Which Photographs May Be Obtained. One

of the most difficult things for the amateur to overcome, in his attempt to become a free-lance writer, is his lack of willingness to learn about and to obtain illustrations for his articles. Many novices fail to sell because they do not realize that purchasing illustrations, hiring photographers, taking their own pictures, or having drawings made is a part of their necessary expense and their stock in the business of writing. In one large course only one student in the last ten years sold an article that did not have pictures. They willingly pay large fees to take courses in writing, or they buy expensive typewriters, but they begrudge spending a cent for pictures or investing in a camera. They do not realize that editors reject articles because illustrations are lacking.

Photographs may be secured from photographers who have suitable negatives taken for other purposes. For a small charge these photographers will sell prints from negatives. If a writer desires a picture of something in a distant community, he may refer to a directory of photographers or contact a photographer there by addressing a letter to "Photographer" at that place. If the postmaster does not wish to deliver the letter, it will be returned, provided the writer has requested a "return in three days" (the minimum allowed by postal regulations). If a reply does not come in a few days, one might refer to a newspaper directory for the name of a newspaper in that community and ask its art editor or news editor to recommend a photographer to whom one could write. Perhaps the newspaper art department might be willing to sell a print if it had a suitable negative.

A writer unable to obtain prints from photographers should not hesitate to have pictures made if there is no other source from which he may obtain them more cheaply. In arranging to have either photographic or art work done, a writer should always be businesslike. He should discuss prices in terms of the total fee, rather than on an hourly basis, before contracting to have the work done. Direction and rates should be given in writing to the photographer for "glossies." The charges for such services in most communities are about three dollars per picture and up, depending upon cost of supplies and time spent. Although several such photographs add considerably to one's expense, money spent for illustrations is money well spent. Pictures not only add to the size of the check, but in many instances will help to sell articles. One may be able, however, to have the work done by commercial photographers whose prices will possibly be less, because they are equipped and accustomed to giving such service. Their names can be found in the classified section of the telephone book or in the city directory.

Picture syndicates, listed under that subject in "The Free-Lance Writer's Library" in the Appendix, will furnish suitable illustrations on almost any subject, generally at a cost of a few dollars for each print. Many Federal, state, and city government departments and agencies will supply a writer with mimeographed lists of good photographs that they have available on various subjects in their departments. From the list, a writer may select the ones he thinks will be suitable; the pictures usually cost twenty-five to fifty cents apiece. A beginner obtained pictures from the United States Signal Corps in Washington to illustrate an Armistice Day feature; another used pictures from the United States Department of Agriculture for an article on better farm housing; and a third got excellent photographs from the office of his state conservation department for an article on reforestation.

Many commercial institutions, industries, travel agencies, advertising agencies, museums, house organs, and publicity departments have pictures that they will supply for a small fee. In some cases they will give them to a writer free of charge, because they are anxious to create a demand for their commodities, or they desire to make their clients better known. The advertising departments of concerns manufacturing silver, china, bedding, furniture, and other products often will send large photographs for a small charge. The writer, however, when making the request should suggest, of course, that he is willing to pay a reasonable amount for the pictures if he can use them. Sometimes the interviewee or the authoritative sources for the material in the article will provide pictures at a reasonable price or will give them to the writer.

Qualities Desired in Photographs. The writer must give thought to the pictures for his articles, whether he takes them himself, has a photographer take them, buys prints from a photographer, or gets them gratis. In the first place, each picture must tell a story and tell it at a glance. Its composition, or arrangement, is affected by the time of day. Light and shadow become a part of the photograph. There should be but one central or dominating point of interest in a picture. Highlights, shadows, masses, and lines should be arranged according to principles of balance, symmetry, and harmony in art.

The photograph must be pleasing to the eye, artistic, and fascinating. Two bright spots or two darks spots should not be of the same importance. The center of interest, or the dominant part, should be just a bit away from the center of the picture. The horizon line in a landscape should never divide it into two equal parts. Meaningless backgrounds should be avoided, since pictures should utilize their space to advantage. In planning the picture, one must remember that the camera is a device for making drawings with reflected light; one should utilize the highlights and the shadows to accentuate the meaning the picture conveys. Clarity, detail, and contrast are essential in a picture for reproduction.

Careful thought should be given as to the most advantageous point of view in order to avoid too much or too little detail. The items to be photographed should be placed as close together as the telling of the story (or the process) and the principles of good art permit. The idea of size in a photograph may be presented by including a person, a hand, a finger, or some object the size of which is familiar to the reader. If one is showing a picture of a machine, he should show the operator working it, to give life, action, and human interest to the photograph.

Since the successful development of the new color films, many periodicals now use kodachrome and ektachrome sheet transparencies. The writer should make a note of the magazines using color which faithfully exhibits all the hues of the original scene. In submitting manuscripts to them, he should send transparencies, if the subject lends itself to this method.

Testing the "Suitability" of a Photograph. If any one of the details is obscured by heavy shadows, this part may appear black in the half-tone illustration. The "suitability" of any part may be tested readily by covering up all of the print except the small area that appears black. If it is the subject's face that is somewhat obscured by the shadow, one should cover up all of the photograph except that part of the face. If that small area can still be recognized as a part of the subject's face, it is fairly safe to say that the picture will reproduce satisfactorily when the half tone is made.

Good Photographs Find Markets. There are only three reasons why editors reject photographs: (1) technically, they may be poor and inadequate; (2) they may not illustrate properly the subject the writer intended; and (3) they may not be slanted to the editor's particular publication. But a good photograph will find a market if it has: (1) originality, (2) human interest, (3) broad appeal, (4) good composition, and (5) subject matter that helps to tell the "story" of the article.

Photographs Must Conform to Necessary Requirements. Pictures to be reproduced by means of the half tone must conform to definite requirements. A ferrotype print, or "glossy print," as it is better known, is made by drying it on sheets of metal to produce a smooth shiny surface. It is more readily adapted to the engraving process than are photographs made on rough papers; therefore glossy prints are required by editors. The picture on single- or double-weight glossy paper should be unmounted; if it is not, the print has to be removed from its mounting.

Size of Photograph Is Important. Since engravers can produce better half tones, or "cuts," by reducing the picture at least one-half, one should have photographic prints of the standard size. Photographers—professional and amateur—should have negatives for illustrations in the sizes of 5 x 7, or 8 x 10 inches. The smaller ones are accepted by a few publications, but 8 x 10 are preferred by most editors. Should a free-lance use smaller photographs, he must have them enlarged to 8 x 10.

Photographs May Be Enlarged. Enlargements may be made from negatives if they are clear and sharp. They must be rich in "velvety" blacks and crisp in clear highlights, or the gloss print will not reproduce satisfactorily. As editors pay space rates for illustrations, it is profitable to have them enlarged as much as possible, and it saves considerable money. Engravers say, however, that even with all the modern equipment, it is more difficult to get a clear distinct half tone if the negative has been enlarged. Most editors will accept transparencies 4 x 5 although they prefer 8 x 10. They cannot accept 35 mm. transparencies because they will not reproduce colors satisfactorily.

Rates of Payment. The usual allowance for black and white photographs to illustrate articles is from $3 to $10 or more apiece. In many offices a completely illustrated article will bring more per word for the article than the words sent without illustrations. If the editor has to find the illustrations by sending messengers scurrying around among photographic syndicate files to find six or more adequate and appropriate photographs for the writer's article, he does not buy the manuscript. An idea, or picture story, when completely worked out with words and photographs and other illustrations, is a real article of commerce that an editor is only too willing to pay for as generously as he can.

Periodicals vary in rate of payment for transparencies as they do for black and whites but the former help sell articles and as a rule the writer is well paid. Most magazines pay from $25 to $100 for transparencies to be used with articles. If a transparency is selected for the cover of a magazine the writer-photographer is paid even more.

Developing Camera Technique. Like every good thing in life, picture taking and picture making require study, observation, and painstaking care. If they did not, photographs would not bring attractive prices. A good camera is an essential part of a writer's equipment for feature writing. It will pay its way many times over if used with knowledge and thought. By simplification, and by improvement of cameras and the development of new types of films, successful photography has become so simple that every writer should take it up, not only as a hobby, but as part of his profession, because it reduces expenses and aids in making sales.

A journalist may acquire a good camera for any amount from fifty to one hundred dollars. If one desires to purchase a camera and knows but little about them, he should seek the advice of an expert before determining the kind of camera he wishes to buy. The important factors that a writer should consider in selecting one are: (1) the kind of pictures that he wishes to take, (2) the best shape and size, and (3) convenience in carrying. Many writers use a press reflex type of camera equipped with the fastest type of lens and shutters. It is particularly useful in taking subjects in poor light or in taking rapidly moving objects.

As soon as one finds that he has developed a fair camera technique, he will be anxious to learn to do his own finishing. He will find excellent guidance by reading the stimulating books and magazines on the subject listed in "The Free-Lance Writer's Library." He may be appalled at first at the seemingly intricate directions, but if he will follow an instruction book accurately, he will find it all quite simple. He should be content with small beginnings at first; when larger checks result from his combined labors at the typewriter and in the dark room, he may try more pretentious photographs. Nine-tenths of the fun of photography is in planning the composition and in the developing and printing. Some writer-photographers have had Polaroid backs placed on their press cameras for less than $100 which enables them to see the print in a minute. If it is not what the author wants, he can snap the setting again.

The amateur photographer will find photographic silhouettes, or shadow pictures, an aid in illustrating ideas. They can be made indoors very easily by the novice if he follows the instructions closely. A young woman wrote an article on posture and illustrated it with silhouette photographs.

Amateurs Should Use Professional Methods. Too many

writer-photographers are content to make "satisfactory" pictures, with the result that they fail to add to their incomes as much as those who make exceptionally good pictures. The ambitious amateur photographer who wishes to do professional work gives study and thought to: (1) focusing the camera on the main point by measuring rather than guessing distances; (2) timing the exposure, under the given light conditions, as correctly as experience and the exposure-meter allow; (3) avoidance of faster exposures than the motion of the subject requires, by using a tripod and making a slow automatic snapshot or even a time exposure in order to get sharpness and depth, the quality much desired in editorial offices; (4) having people in the pictures give life and action; (5) making the pictures clear by giving more light to objects close to the lens and less light to those farther away; (6) making the pictures sharp in detail by cutting down the lens opening and giving it a longer exposure; (7) giving more exposure to objects dark in color than to the same objects if they are white; (8) avoiding horizontal or vertical lines, because they will cut the picture in two; (9) viewpoint and balance; (10) learning how to reduce overexposed negatives, intensify underexposed ones, and increase or decrease contrasts by the use of proper chemical solutions; (11) the use of different color transparencies and filters, diffusion disks, photoflood lights, portrait attachments, films, and papers in control of natural and bizarre effects; and (12) taking interesting photographs and writing articles around them as well as writing interesting articles and taking pictures to illustrate them.

Using Drawings to Illustrate Articles. Pen and ink sketches, diagrams, floor plans, and working drawings often are necessary to explain and illustrate elements in a feature. Even though the writer may have excellent photographs, drawings may show the detail that the camera fails to emphasize.

If a writer has even a little skill in drawing, he may prepare rough sketches that will enable the staff artists to catch the idea to be illustrated and make the finished drawings. However, if a writer has any training or even some ability in making pen and ink sketches, he may prepare his own illustrations. The books listed in "The Free-Lance Writer's Library" will be suggestive. Publications pay for acceptable art work as well as for photographs. Even beginners have used simple skeleton lines, or pictographs, representing the human figure, or rough sketches to explain an idea or a symbol. Typewriters may be used to represent figures by filling in the desired spaces with the letter x. Translucent paper may be used for floor plans and maps.

Line drawings, such as pen and ink sketches, are made into zinc etchings for reproduction and show no gradations in tone. Photographs, in order to show all the gradations of light and dark, are reproduced by the half tone. Drawings and pictographs should be made on fairly lightweight bristol board with black India or drawing ink. They should be at least twice or even three times the size intended to be when published.

Charts, Graphs, and Tables Add to Reader Interest. Many articles, particularly those slanted for the business papers or farm and home magazines, make use of other devices than photographs or drawings to clarify, condense, or explain points and to give a tone of authority. Editors use them because they build good will toward the publication. Subscribers appreciate having information in a concise form that they can clip and file. Some publications devote pages to recipes, household, and budget problems in chart and table form for convenient filing. Even the novice may, with the aid of the books listed in the Appendix, use these devices.

All lines, printing, and lettering should be done in India ink on bristol board. Statements or figures on record sheets or blanks intended for reproduction should be typed with a fresh record black ribbon.

Preparation of Illustrations for Mailing. A carefully planned caption, or "cut-line," adds much to the interest of the illustration and of the article. Periodicals vary in the style of their captions as much as they do in the style of the titles of the articles. If the caption is not appropriate, the editor will have to rewrite it. Before writing a "cut-line," one should analyze those in the periodical to which the article is slanted. Some publications use long

statements as "cut-lines"; others use short ones. Some are humorous; others are serious. Whatever style of captions the publication
uses, it should serve as the pattern for the novice. One should also
count the number of units, characters, or letters, in the "cut-line"
selected as the guide and use that number as a measuring stick
for his own captions on pictures, drawings, charts, or graphs.

With a little practice and a great deal of thought, one will find
it easy to write "cut-lines." The beginner should jot down the
"story" of the picture or drawing in one sentence. After one finds
the right idea to explain the illustration, he can give attention to
word selection and caption length. He should keep in mind that
every "cut-line" will be more effective if it has an actual or an
implied verb.

"Cut-lines" for glossies should be typed on a piece of paper and
with rubber cement pasted on the back lower edge of the illustration in such a way that the "line" will extend down under the picture or drawing, as shown in Fig. 11. With a pair of scissors, its
edge should be trimmed off so that they are even with those of the
illustration. If the illustration has been obtained from a source
that desires credit in lieu of payment, credit should be given by
adding a credit line, such as, for example, "Reproduced by permission of the Alabama State Historical Society."

One should never write the identification on the back of the
photograph. A sharp pen point or pencil point may ruin it for
reproduction. The writer may type his name, address, and the
title of the article which the photograph or drawing is to illustrate
on a small piece of paper and rubber cement it on the back of the
illustration—photograph, drawing, or chart. Some writers prefer
to use "Scotch" tape rather than cement or paste. If the quality is
poor, talcum powder dusted on the "right" side of the tape or
paste will prevent its sticking to something to which it is not sup-
posed to stick. A wire paper clip should *never* be used to fasten
the illustrations together. If the illustrations are small, enclose
them in an envelope so marked.

Rubber cementing or "Scotch"-taping the edge of a sheet of

We Are Ashamed of Ourselves Now

Fig. 11. Photograph with Cut-line.

very thin paper on the back and at the top of the illustration, so
that the paper folds over the face of the illustration, will prevent
the surface of the photograph or drawing from becoming
scratched or marred. Such an "overlay" tissue, or "flimsy," should
be trimmed to the size of the picture it protects.

In preparing color transparencies, number the kodachrome or
ektachrome slides. Then list the numbers with their cut lines on a

separate sheet of paper because the slides are put in a lantern to be reproduced.

Some writers who sell many pictures place a reservation of rights on photographs submitted for publication. Using a rubber-stamp, they indicate on the back of each print the following: "WARNING. License to reproduce this photograph, on which a copyright is pending, will be granted upon acceptance of the terms quoted. If purchased, it is for your publication only, and must not be syndicated, rented, loaned, nor used for advertising purposes without written permission."

Since the writer mails the manuscript flat, all illustrations— photographs, transparencies, drawings, charts, graphs, and tables —may be mailed in the same envelope. They must be protected with additional cardboard packing. One cardboard may be sufficient to keep the manuscript from becoming damaged, but there should be cardboard on both sides of the manuscript and illustrations, because the latter are damaged easily. A large number of transparencies may have to be sent in a strong pasteboard box under separate cover. If so, be sure to so indicate on cover sheet and include a duplicate list of transparency "cut-lines" with the enlarged transparencies.

Accepted Photographs Are Not Returned. If the manuscript and the illustrations are purchased, they are not returned. For that reason, writers never promise to return illustrations that they obtain for an article. If persons furnishing them request that they be returned, the writer should have copies made from the originals. If one cannot get the negatives to have duplicates made, he may have the photographs rephotographed.

Examples of Articles Built Around Pictures. As suggested earlier in this chapter, frequently one can build a short article around a picture or can assemble a number of pictures into a "picture story." The first of the following examples was "built" around a single picture of the "smithy" at work and sold to the *American* magazine. The writer-photographer attracted readers by drawing on childhood recall of the well-known poem. The second story, selected from *Outdoor Life,* illustrates how travelers whose hobby is photography can let the camera practically write their articles. This story was illustrated with 17 glossies size 8 x 10, which told the story. Students often find picture stories among their films.

(1)
Rubber-tired Blacksmith*

BY SUSAN AMMANN MCLANE

The one-time village blacksmith doesn't stand under the spreading chestnut tree any more. He drives right up to it in his truck, takes out his forge, and gets to work. Typical of the new streamlined smithy is John Mulcahy, of Madison, N.J. John's forge is a prewar truck and he covers the garden state, traveling sometimes as much as 100 miles a day and shoeing horses all along the route. The son of a blacksmith, Mulcahy has been shoeing horses ever since he left St. Vincent's School in Madison. He has become so well known up and down the state that famous racing stables as well as farmers wait for John to do their shoeing, no matter how long it takes him to get there. Working 6 and sometimes 7 days a week, John usually can manage to reshoe a dozen hayburners daily. Married, John lives with his wife and mother in the house that his father built. His old forge is still out in back, but mostly all the shoeing that John does is on the road. A collector of horse pictures and a sure-fire David Harum when it comes to a horse trade, John usually swings around the horse-fair circuit looking over withers and stifles and buying an occasional horse.

(2)
Week-end with Wings†
An Outdoor Life Picture Story

BY ROB F. SANDERSON

We braced ourselves as the sturdy Fairchild 24 seaplane gunned Lake Michigan near Sheboygan, Wis. Then the ship lifted gracefully and gained altitude. Shadows of the wings raced northward; over

* Reprinted by permission of *The American* and Susan Ammann McLane.
† Reprinted by permission of *Outdoor Life* and Rob F. Sanderson.

cities and wooded terrain toward Ontario's waters, where scrappy fish rise from the cold clear depths.

That was the start of the flying fishermen's week-end. Dr. John A. Tasche was in the cockpit of his plane. Dr. Leslie W. Tasche, Konrad Testwuide Jr., and I were his guests. Our destination was Frank Kinahan's trapping camp on Belle Lake.

That Aubinedong River country, eastward from Lake Superior, is a tough three-day trip overland. But by skybuggy it's only five hours away.

It was early spring and we winterstarved anglers were eager to feel the throbbing strike of big trout and wall-eyed pike. We yearned for the sights and sounds, the exhilarating air of the great Canadian wilderness.

Besides tackle and gear, I took my camera along. Here, in brilliant detail, is a lens-eye view of three days' flying and fishing in real wilderness country. . . .

Exercises

1. Examine the publication to which you are slanting an article to see how many of the pictures are formal, informal, black and white, kodachrome, or ektachrome.

2. Are there any illustrations in the issues examined that were not well slanted—either to the article or to the periodical? If so, why not?

3. Classify the illustrations as to artistic and news types. How many of each did you find?

4. Are there any sources indicated for the illustrations used? If so, list them.

5. Did you find any illustrations that lacked the desirable qualities listed in this chapter? If so, what qualities were missing?

6. Selecting some photograph or snapshot with heavy shadows that you have, apply the test for "suitability." Can it be reproduced?

7. Talk with an expert and write a 300-word report on "A Good Camera for a Feature Writer."

8. How many drawings did you find in the publication to which you slanted your feature? List them as to kinds.

9. How many charts, graphs, or tables did you find in the periodical? List them as to kind and number.

10. Analyze the "cut-lines" or "over lines" as to length and style and record your findings in a table-like form.

11. Write one "cut-line" for each of the five or six illustrations that you have planned for your article.

12. Inquire the price from a local photographer for rephotographing a photograph.

13. What would he charge for making an 8 x 10 picture of a garden?

Publication Analysis

Aviation, Automobile, Motor, and Service Magazines

Compare, by using chart form as illustrated in the Appendix, one magazine of each of the above types. They may be obtained at newsstands, from magazine dealers listed in the Appendix under "Aids to Writers," or in library periodical reading rooms. Some suggested aviation magazines: *Air Facts, Air World, American Helicopter, Skyways;* automobile and motor magazines: *American Motorist, Automotive Digest, Motor News;* service magazines: *American Legion, Anti-aircraft, Combat, Foreign Service, Infantry Journal, Leatherneck, Link, Marine Corps Gazette, Our Army, Our Navy, V.F.W.,* or others of your choice.

Do not spend more than 45 minutes on the preparation of this report.

  I. Identification for each magazine: Name, publishers, editors, where published, price.

 II. Make-up: What to you, as a future magazine editor, are the interesting things about the make-up of the four magazines analyzed? Give reasons for your answers.

III. Advertising:
   1. From the point of view of what you know about advertising, do you think the copy in each publication will appeal to the reader?
   2. What did you like about the advertising in each publication? Give reasons.
   3. What did you *not* like about the advertising in each publication? Give reasons.
   4. What tips were suggested to you by the advertising?

IV. General policy:
   1. To what types of readers do the four publications analyzed appeal?
   2. Why should you, as a free-lance photographer, know these magazines?
   3. What photographs might you have submitted?
   4. Are there any illustrations of special interest in these publications?
   5. Look at the illustrations in each magazine analyzed and list three suggestions for each that will enable you to select better pictures (12 suggestions in all).

 V. Slogans: Write a slogan for each magazine.

VI. Four Tips for illustrations: Source, authority, and three possible markets suggested by this study.

CHAPTER 16

Legal Rights of Manuscripts

▰▰▰

Writers Should Know Something of Their Rights. Although free-lance writers of feature articles do not need to be concerned greatly about the legal rights of their manuscripts, since publishers copyright their periodicals, such knowledge will benefit them financially. It also may save them worry about what they can or cannot do legally concerning their manuscripts.

A movement to revise the copyright law in the United States has been going forward for years, sponsored by both writers and publishers, who find much that is objectionable in the present law. Customs and practices are important in influencing interpretation of the law as it is now. There is a constant tendency to make the laws concerning literary property more liberal. Bills for revision of the copyright law are introduced from time to time in sessions of Congress, because the present law is outdated in many respects.

Literary Rights Protect Author's Work. A feature writer who gathers facts from other sources for an article does not own the facts. Legally they are considered public property. But he does own his mode of expression, or literary style; in this he has literary rights. Legally the word "rights" means the right to use or sell elsewhere, and "American" rights means the right to use or sell

304

in the United States. One's original ideas, even if they are copyrighted, are free to the public. But the manner, arrangement, and combination of words—the style of one's writing—is the writer's own property. Although the laws concerning literary rights sound simple as one reads them, cases involving their infringement often are extremely involved.

Serial Rights Cover Wide Range. The majority of publications purchase "first magazine rights," or "first serial rights." The word "serial" in connection with rights in a manuscript refers to its publication in a magazine or newspaper that is published serially—weekly, daily, or monthly—and not to a fiction serial. The term came into use to distinguish the right to publish articles in a periodical from the right to publish a book manuscript. Although an editor accepts an article, he does not have to print it unless there has been an agreement to publish. The only redress the author has for a long delay in publishing an unpaid manuscript is to demand its return. If the "first serial rights" are sold to a magazine along with the manuscript, the author retains all other rights.

"Second serial" or "syndicate" rights permit publication of a manuscript in some publication other than the one in which it first appeared. In addition to selling unpublished articles to foreign magazines, as suggested in Chapter 14, it is possible to gain additional income by selling second rights to manuscripts that already have been published in American magazines. The author should submit the manuscript in typewritten form, however, because it is easier to handle in the editorial office and the composing room.

As a rule, a feature writer is not concerned with the other rights —dramatic, photoplay, book, foreign, and translation. He may be interested in "all rights," since a few magazines—but only a few—do buy all rights, even on fact articles. Their publishers generally are willing to pay somewhat in excess of what they would be willing to pay for merely the first serial rights.

Authors May Indicate Rights They Wish to Sell. It is advisable for an author to know what rights a magazine wants to buy.

Today most magazines buy first American and Canadian serial rights. An author may retain all other rights by typing on the cover sheet, in the upper right-hand corner, "First American and Canadian Rights only for sale." The majority of feature writers do not include that notation, since most feature articles do not possess value for other than first serial rights.

Endorsement of Check Transfers Right. An author's writing and style are his own property until he sells or gives his property rights to another with or without restriction of rights. But if the writer sells his article and endorses the check for its payment, he always gives up his rights to the publication that bought them.

Many magazines do not have formal contracts of purchase. They do have printed notices on the check for payment of the article, however, and these state that endorsement of the check by the writer transfers specified rights to the publication. The notice may include the right of the new owner to make a minor revision. A writer should read the check carefully to see what rights he is transferring. A few publications enclose vouchers with the check, explaining the rights they wish to retain, as in the following:

ESQUIRE

The Magazine For Men
919 No. Michigan Ave.
Chicago

ARNOLD GINGRICH, *Editor*

April 18.

Mr. James F. Scheer,
216 North Carroll Street,
Madison, Wisconsin.

Dear Mr. Scheer:

Enclosed is check for $150.00 in payment for North American magazine rights on your manuscript, CHEATERS VS. EXAMS, including pocket-size digest rights for which you will receive full compensation, if and when sold.

Cordially,

HELENE RICHARDS
Secretary to Mr. Gingrich

HR:ef
Enc. check $150.00

Copyright Law Reveals Rights and Liabilities. A copyright insures to the writer or to a publication, which may buy and copyright the manuscript, full protection against its reprinting in whole or in part for a period of twenty-eight years. This copyright may be renewed within one year before the expiration of the original term for another period of twenty-eight years. No further renewal can be made after the expiration of the fifty-six years. Copyright protects only the literary style and not the content of the manuscript. It is merely a registration of property rights; the copyright notice states that these rights have been registered and reserved by the copyright holder. If the manuscript is reprinted and sold without the latter's permission, he may bring suit against the infringer and recover damages if he can prove in court that he has suffered.

Arrangements can be made with a publisher to copyright a manuscript, either in the name of the author or in the name of the publisher. In the latter case, the publisher will agree to transfer the copyright for a nominal sum to the author if he so requests. Although transfer, or assignment of copyright, is a simple process, it is impractical to ask that it be done unless there is a real need for it (e.g., republication of the manuscript in book form), because most magazine publishers would rather not buy a manuscript than to go to all the bother over the various technicalities involved. The publisher's "blanket copyright," protecting each issue as a whole, affords ample protection to a feature writer.

If a writer wishes to secure protection under the copyright law, he must send a complete and exact copy of the published manuscript to the Register of Copyrights, Library of Congress, Washington, D. C. It must be accompanied by an application for copyright on the correct official form and a postal money order for $4 for the fee. The former interpretation of the law required the payment of the fee, the giving of the notice for copyright, and the depositing of the requisite copy or copies before the copyright became valid.

Few writers apply for copyright in their own names. As a rule, publications are honest, and it is not necessary for the writer to take out copyright in his own name; thus, few bother to make the application.

Most free-lance writers never are tempted to violate the law of copyright. The source of their material is available as public records. They may interview authorities, but if an interviewee asks a writer not to make public or not to print certain information given him, the latter is liable to damages if the interviewee can show that the printing of the forbidden material has affected him financially.

Writer Has Legal Right to Use Facts. An author is permitted to make use of ideas expressed or facts presented in any published writing, whether or not it is copyrighted. If the material is not protected by copyright or if the copyright has expired, an author legally may take as much material, word for word, as he so desires, without giving credit.

If the factual material is protected by copyright, he may take whatever content he desires, as long as he does not copy nor imitate the literary style or the manner in which the ideas are expressed. The encroachment of copyright lies in saying the same ideas in the same words as the author from whom one is taking the material.

Common Law and Other Rights. An unpublished manuscript, except certain classes of material such as lectures, sermons, and unpublished plays, cannot be copyrighted. The common law protects an author's rights in an unpublished manuscript, but this protection ceases upon publication.

If a writer has acquired information entirely by his own efforts, as does the scientist who makes a discovery, he can take legal action to prevent another writer from using his material by suing for damages under the laws of unfair competition. The right to defend original work against plagiarism by an appeal to the laws against unfair competition holds whether or not the work has been published.

Libelous Statements Must Be Scrutinized. An author is liable for damages if he makes any statements that injure a person's character, reputation, or ability, if he cannot prove that they are true, since, in a civil suit for libel, the facts must be proven by the defendant. A suit for libel cannot be instigated unless the material said to be libelous is printed, or if the person said to be libeled cannot be identified, or if the defamatory words are not in themselves actually malicious or the circumstances do not make them malicious.

Even a beginner, if he has a high regard for accuracy and ethics, is not endangered by libel suits. He will ascertain the truth before he writes anything that might be construed as libelous.

In order to establish a lack of malice in using a fictitious name that might be the name of an individual, publications or authors explain that "All names used are fictitious and resemblance to or duplications of the names of living persons is coincidental." But even this statement printed in the book or periodical, or explained in the feature article, does not entirely protect the publisher. A writer may say the most unpleasant things about the work or the results of the work of "people who offer themselves for public approval." Legally authors, actors, singers, public speakers, and candidates for public office (but not always public officials) are included in the group seeking "public approval." A writer is not permitted, however, to make uncomplimentary statements about the personal life of "people seeking public approval."

Since libel laws are not the same in all states, a writer will do well to keep his writing free of statements that might be said to be libelous anywhere concerning private individuals or groups of people.

Biographers, novelists, and short-story writers are more likely to write material consciously or unconsciously that may be considered libelous.

The right of "qualified privilege" gives a writer authority to print, without evil intention, true reports of public and official proceedings (but only public and official), and it prevents publications from being sued for printing such matter.

Using Quotations. Novices frequently ask how much material may be quoted from publications without obtaining permission. Legally the use of a single sentence may be considered a violation of the law of copyright. Short quotations, however, generally are made without asking for permission. Although a short quotation has not been defined legally, many writers and publishers consider that a maximum of fifty words from one publication may be used without permission if full credit is given to the author and publisher.

Material first published in a government bulletin is in the public domain.

If a book printed in Great Britain does not contain a copyright notice, it does not mean that it is not copyrighted. British law does not require a printed notice in the book. The British copyright term differs from the American, in that it is for the life of the author after publication and for 50 years following his death.

Plagiarism and Piracy. Plagiarism, in its broadest sense, may be defined as the act of taking the language or the style elements of an author and using them as if they were one's own. It involves moral rights rather than legal. Thus, the author of the material said to be plagiarized may have no redress in the courts. Piracy is an unauthorized reproduction of another's production, word for word, idea for idea, or the essence of the writer's work, and therefore is in violation of either his common law rights or his statutory copyright, whichever is applicable.

Manuscripts May Become Public Property. If a writer makes mimeographed or other duplicate copies of his manuscript and distributes them to a number of persons, he may make it public and lose his rights to the manuscript. If any one else so desired, he might be able to submit such a manuscript to a publication and accept payment for it without legal encroachment of rights. If a manuscript is delivered by its author as a speech before a public gathering, he makes it public property, but he loses no rights in it, since oral delivery of a speech, lecture or sermon does not throw it into the public domain.

Photographs May Be Copyrighted. The writer-photographer may have photographs that he believes will have a varied market and that will lose their value if not copyrighted. Indiscriminate copyrighting of photographs for articles is unnecessary and expensive in the long run, although copyright may be secured for a fee of $4.00. There can be little if any advantage in having a photograph copyrighted if the owner believes that he will never be able to sell it to more than one publication.

Some writers who sell pictures, as discussed in Chapter 15, place a reservation of rights on photographs submitted for publication by stamping on a "warning notice." Unless one really is going to have the copyright registered, he should not stamp on a copyright notice. The copyright law, Section XXIX, states that "Any person who inserts a false note of copyright with fraudulent intent . . . shall be guilty of a misdemeanor, punishable by a fine of from $100 to $1,000."

Writers Should Read Law on Author's Rights. The courts do not accept ignorance of the law as an excuse for violation of laws. Amateurs and professionals both must be well informed on the protection afforded authors and their manuscripts. They should be posted on the liabilities as well as the rights. This chapter, because of space, cannot cover the subject in detail. When in doubt about a serious question of law, the writer should consult a lawyer. Informative books on the subject are listed in the "Free-Lance Writer's Library" in the Appendix, and they may be obtained in any city or state library upon request.

Exercises

1. What have you read recently in the newspapers, writer's magazines, or other professional publications concerning changes in the law of copyright?

2. Do you recall reading recently in the newspapers or magazines for writers of any cases in the courts concerning the violation of literary rights?

3. List two publications in which you found notices of serial rights of any kind, and include the caption of the article and the kind of right listed.

4. What statement will you look for before you sign the checks that you will be receiving for your feature articles?

5. Go over your feature articles to see if you have violated the copyright law. List any point that you think violates it.

6. What is the law of "unfair competition"?

7. Check your manuscripts carefully for any libelous matter. If you

find any material that you think could be said to be libelous, how could you prove the truth of your statements?

8. What is the libel law in the state in which you live?

9. Go over your manuscripts carefully to see if you have violated any rules concerning the handling of quotations. If so, what rules?

10. List the cases of plagiarism or piracy of which you have heard or read.

11. List the photographs that you have taken which you think you might want to have copyrighted, and tell why.

12. If the photographs which you have taken for publication have persons in them, did you get the subjects' permission to use them?

13. List five points concerning author's rights that you have read in one of the books listed in the "Free-Lance Writer's Library." Give the title and the author.

14. How does Great Britain's copyright law differ from that of United States?

Publication Analysis

Intellectual and Quality Magazines

Compare, by using chart form as illustrated in the Appendix, four magazines of the above types. They may be obtained at newsstands, from magazine dealers listed in the Appendix under "Aids to Writers," or in library periodical reading rooms. Some suggested magazines: *American Mercury, American Scholar, Atlantic Monthly, Current History, Harper's Magazine, Saturday Review,* or others of your choice.

Do not spend more than 30 minutes on the preparation of this report.

I. Identification: Name, publisher, editor, where published, price.
II. Make-up:
  1. What do you like about the make-up of the magazines?
  2. What do you dislike about them?
  3. What changes would you make if you were editor of each?
III. Advertising:
  1. If you were placing advertising in one of these magazines, what appeals would your copy have to have?
  2. In glancing through the advertising, do you think that the advertiser gets returns from his copy?
  3. Give reasons for your conclusion.
  4. List a tip suggested by the advertising in each magazine.
  5. If you were editor, what changes would you make?
IV. Feature Articles:
  1. What types of articles do you find and to whom does each one appeal?

2. Analyze any article that you wish and in any way that you wish, but include the pyramid form of analysis.
3. What do you think are your chances of selling to these magazines?

V. Illustrations:
   1. What illustrations did you find?
   2. If you were editor of each of these magazines, would you use pictures?

VI. Literary Rights:
   1. What statement does each magazine carry concerning its copyright?
   2. Did you find any notice of serial rights of any kind in any of the magazines?

VII. Four Tips: source, authority for the article suggested, and three possible markets for each tip suggested by the study of these magazines.

Part II

ADVANCED MAGAZINE WRITING

Training for a Career As Contributor or Staff Member

CHAPTER 17

Training for a Career in Magazine Writing

Amateur Becomes a Writer. The beginner who has successfully completed his training for free-lance writing by applying the content of Part I, doing the exercises, analyzing publications; slanting, outlining, writing from four to six articles; and submitting them for publication can now be more professional in his approach to the writing of fact articles.

Such a student, working either in an advanced class in magazine writing or at home alone, may now begin to consider himself, or herself, less of an amateur and strive to become more the specialist, if he desires either to continue free-lancing, becoming a regular contributor, or eventually to seek employment as a staff worker on a publication. With these purposes in mind the following chapters were planned to give three-fold guidance.

Training for Magazine Career Varies from That for Free-Lance. This section of the book, Part II, presupposes: (1) a recent and careful reading of that part of the Preface which concerns the course in advanced magazine writing, or training for magazine staff work; (2) a thorough knowledge of the first part of the book, which deals with writing and selling free-lance articles; (3) careful analysis of various publications to determine

317

possible markets; and (4) some experience in writing and sub-mitting feature articles.

The advanced student in magazine writing will observe that in Part II the weekly written analyses, or research reports, assigned are not analyses of publications each week as previously, but rather are concerned with research work. Instead of being listed at the end of each chapter as in Part I, the weekly Research Reports for the advanced student will be assigned by the instructor. A report is planned for each week of the semester, to be due on the day the instructor selects. If the course extends over a full year, the instructor may either require reports on alternate weeks only or may assign additional ones. The Research Reports were primarily designed for a second semester course following the beginning course in feature writing.

Carbon copies should be made of the weekly research reports, to enable the student to have his material at hand for oral class reports even though the instructor has not been able to return the originals. The student in a class or working at home alone will also want carbon copies for his files, since the original copies, which the instructor returns, will later on be bound in a project book to be handed in at the close of the semester.

The professional writer will volunteer in class to subscribe for one of the writer's publications listed under the "Free-Lance Writer's Library" in the Appendix. If a number of students take the same periodical, the instructor may appoint a chairman for each "professional reading group" who will assign articles of interest to the others in the group. Each will report orally on points that will interest his classmates. A group of writers not members of a class could adopt the same plan for its informal meetings.

The person studying at home alone may apply the suggestions in the following chapters as thoroughly as if he were in a class or taking the course by correspondence study.

Experienced Writer Queries Editor. As previously explained, amateurs should not query editors, but after a writer has sold a few articles, he should analyze the markets, select the ones that might be interested in his idea for an article, and write to the editors of several publications that he thinks will be interested in seeing the article when it is written. An intelligent, carefully worded, neatly typed, concise, one-page letter enthusiastically explaining the idea of the article, or giving a brief outline, will be sufficient to enable the editor to decide whether or not he desires to see the completed article. An editor may even give the writer some suggestions about the development of the article, but of course such encouragement does not mean that the editor has agreed to purchase the manuscript, even though he knows the contributor's ability from previously purchased articles. Needless to say, the writer should enclose a stamped self-addressed envelope when making a query.

An editor may reject an article for many reasons, even though he replies to a query favorably. But an encouraging reply to a query does aid one to write with more enthusiasm, inasmuch as it shows that an editor is interested in the proposed subject, even though such an expression of interest is not a contract, nor an agreement, to purchase the manuscript.

It is encouraging for the contributor to know that the present trend is toward the purchase of more free-lance articles by editors, as well as toward the enlarging of editorial staffs.

Although one submits articles to only one publication at a time, the professional writer may query several editors simultaneously concerning the same proposed article in order to save time. If several editors ask for the article, the clever writer will develop it for each editor in a different way, as illustrated by examples in this chapter. Just as the writer keeps a carbon of each article submitted for publication, so he should keep a carbon of each letter of query. He should set up letter-size folders in his files, one marked "Queries Now Out," one, "Queries Returned—Favorable Reply," and one "Queries—Rejected." With such a system, the writer will not be embarassed to find he has queried the same editor twice on the same subject.

Purpose of Training for Research Work. Everyone uses libraries, but the majority of people who have used them throughout high school and college are not as aware of the many valuable aids they offer the researcher as are the trained magazine research workers.

Research, or getting facts, is of two types: (1) applied, and (2) pure. The latter is the kind done by the scientist because he is interested in a particular activity or the results of an activity, in its ultimate aspects, whereas applied research is defined as that engaged in for immediate use.

From the scientist's point of view, one does not engage in research unless he makes a contribution to knowledge by discovering new principles, facts, norms, or laws. But from the writer's point of view, research consists of garnering the knowledge which others have already uncovered. As the term is used by magazine editors, research begins with searching out and interpreting the knowledge which others have found, then giving these facts garnered from many and sometimes difficult sources to the readers of the magazine in terms that they can understand.

The writer's research includes specialized and thorough investigation of available written material on a subject, to which he adds information acquired by his own interviews, observations, investigations, questionnaires, or correspondence with experts in the field. The fact writer engages in academic as well as social research, but he must be constantly on his guard not to violate laws of copyright, as explained in Chapter 16.

Most professional writers get their first and probably their greatest help from the library. They make use of both primary and secondary sources. The former includes books, manuscripts, diaries, letters, journals, and original manuscripts of published works. The latter, or secondary sources, include many kinds of printed material, particularly reference works and periodicals which report and analyze the findings of scholars, technicians, and scientists.

Qualifications Necessary for Research. The writer, like the scientist, approaches his research with a high regard, if not love, for accuracy and truth. He uses scholarly care in taking his notes. He is persevering because he realizes that he cannot give up the search for even one important fact.

The successful research writer is impartial and is not influenced by his emotions and prejudices, nor by mental biases. If he were, he would not read broadly, but would neglect facts and interpretations contrary to his own beliefs. Research requires a trained scholarly mind which will not confuse facts with prejudices.

A writer uses his native detective-like instincts and is forever on the alert for inaccuracies, just as is the laboratory scientist. If one would be a research writer or magazine staff worker, he will make use of both primary and secondary sources. He will find the research reports in technical publications—which are based upon the findings of laboratory tests and experiments carried on by manufacturers, industrialists, and commercial concerns—of real value in suggesting ideas for articles for the general reader as well as material for them. Above all, the fact writer must have enthusiasm to carry on the search for facts if he is to attain success.

Learning Research Techniques. The professional writer, contributor, or staff worker learns to use a library skillfully before he accepts assignments or a staff position, because not all publications have well organized research departments, as do the *Saturday Evening Post* and some other magazines. He should be able to do his own research efficiently in a library. Only a person without intelligence would attempt to pilot a plane through modern-day crowded airlanes without instruction; neither should one attempt research without knowing the techniques of using a library and realizing the great wealth of material and services available in it.

Skill in finding sources and material for the article is as important as slanting, organizing, and writing it. In addition, a writer should know the short and direct methods, because he cannot waste time browsing, as does the amateur. He should acquaint himself with the other services which a library supplies that aid the writer in many ways. But although there are suggestions to help, and reference librarians to aid, there is but one way to develop research technique, and that is to do research.

Detailed Plan for Advanced Magazine Course. Because so many teachers of journalism, aspiring contributors, and potential magazine staff workers have expressed interest in the advanced course in magazine writing offered by one school of journalism, with reporting and feature writing as a prerequisite, the weekly assignments of that course are discussed here.

Many of the students who performed these assignments have since contributed to markets paying $100 and up for their articles. Upon graduation many of them have gone directly to work on staffs of magazines and specialized periodicals. Many others, who added to their qualifications by first taking newspaper, public relations, radio, or advertising jobs, later accepted positions on magazines. Still others became regular contributors.

Students working together in the Advanced Magazine Writing class or working alone far from a university campus have applied the content of the following chapters before writing their articles, and thus produced manuscripts that were thorough, accurate, and enthusiastically written, as was evidenced by the willingness of editors to pay for them at considerably more than their "usual" rates.

Anyone who will read and apply the following chapters carefully, and will then work out the planned Research Reports assigned in class, too, will succeed. Those working alone at home will be equally successful if they apply the suggestions in the following chapters and work out the Research Reports at the end of each chapter the same as do the students in class.

Examples of Articles By One Training for a Career. Because a young zoology major knew just what he wanted to do after graduation, he elected magazine writing courses in a journalism school. In high school he decided he wanted to write and to work with photography and wild animal life because they interested him. Upon graduation from the university he found a place where he could satisfy his combined interests. You have probably read about him in magazines containing articles on the true animal-life pictures Walt Disney produces—pictures that make the animal kingdom better understood by young and old alike. Because of limited space only a few of the articles that he wrote while a student in class and for which he was paid almost $1800 can be reproduced entirely or even in part. Probably his number of sales was due not only to his splendid, concise writing but to the generous number of pictures which he took, processed, and submitted to illustrate his manuscripts.

Fig. 12. The Milwaukee "Journal" Used an Article on this Student's Sales.

(1)
Wildlife in the Rough*

By Tom McHugh

A motorist from Massachusetts, dreaming of Beacon Hill, ancestors, and cod, for the moment forgot that he was driving in Wyoming. His return to reality was conditioned by the abrupt appearance of a herd of 70 elk.

"Home," he said, applying his brakes, "was never like this."

He was of course referring to his own home. For the home of the elk herd had always been "like this"—exactly like it, which is one of the chief features of Wyoming's Jackson Hole Wildlife Park.

Jackson Hole is a great natural bowl of lush forest and meadowland, surrounded by mountains, of which the Tetons are most famous. The park itself embraces 1,500 acres. Four hundred of these acres are surrounded by a fence, cunningly placed behind small hills, or running through densely wooded areas, so that it remains almost completely invisible. It is this naturalistic area which has been stocked with 125 large game animals, including buffalo, mule deer, whitetail deer, moose and elk. Geese, ducks, sage hens and grouse live on the swamps and meadows, and the clear lakes are stocked with trout.

Passing directly through this region of the natural zoo, U.S. Highway 287 provides ready access to the big game. For a still closer look, the motorist can drive through more of the park through a secondary road, and may even find himself in the midst of a herd of buffalo!

No animal in the park creates more interest than the buffalo. Perhaps it is because the story of this animal is so closely interwoven with the settlement of America. As near as naturalists and historians can figure, there must have been at least 70,000,000—civilized man has never seen a greater aggregation of animals anywhere on the earth.

* * *

With such a wealth of wildlife, the Jackson Hole Wildlife Park has recently initiated a biological field station for scientific research in the Rocky Mountain area. Although field scientists have made long-continued studies of the important needs of wildlife, there is still much to be learned if this natural resource is to be preserved intelligently. The park is a vast laboratory where scientific workers can operate effectively—and where the animals can say—with security: "Home was always like this!"

* Reprinted by permission of *Ford Times* and Tom McHugh.

(2)

Big Game "At Home"
to Visitors*

BY TOM McHUGH

America's first natural wildlife park was recently opened to the public near Moran, Wyo. The Jackson-Hole Wildlife Park, as it is called, has earned this distinction by displaying big game in a vast, apparently unfenced area.

An "invisible fence" is the unusual device used by the park to enclose more than 100 big-game animals. The fence has been so well camouflaged that it remains almost completely hidden. This was accomplished by concealing it in wooded areas or behind hills.

Buffalo, antelope, elk, moose and deer can be seen by the motorist as he drives through the park amidst herds of these creatures. The beasts seem to be little bothered by their intruders and carry on as if they had complete freedom. Last summer they produced more than 20 young in the park.

*   *   *

Moose are the only animals that can jump over the seven-foot fence surrounding the wildlife park. Since ponds inside the park are so attractive to moose, a few of these large antlered animals can always be seen.

With such a wealth of wildlife as a background, the Jackson-Hole Wildlife Park has also launched a biological field station that will search the Rocky Mountain area for new facts about our wildlife. Thus, the park is serving conservation both by displaying wildlife to the public and by uncovering new data to aid in wildlife preservation.

(3)

On the Trail of the Bat†

BY TOM McHUGH

Fred Greeley and Dr. James Beer of the University of Wisconsin are working on a mystery which may prove more exciting than any

* Reprinted by permission of *Popular Mechanics Magazine* and Tom McHugh.
† Reprinted by permission of *Popular Mechanics* and Tom McHugh.

Scotland Yard case. They are trying to find where more than one million bats vanish each winter.

Before dawn in subzero weather these men drive off in search of Wisconsin caves on their bat-banding expeditions.

Leaving the car, they plow through snow-covered fields seeking holes, from which thin vapor trails rise, indicating caves below. There the temperature remains about 42 degrees the year 'round.

Bats stream into these caves when cold weather cuts off their food supply of insects. In hibernation they pass the winter, hanging upside down by their hind feet. In fact, one observer estimates that bats spend five sixths of their lives hanging head downward in the dark.

*   *   *

Another misconception is that bats carry bedbugs, lice and numerous other parasites. That may be partly true, but these parasites are quite particular and won't live on humans.

Nor do we have any blood-sucking bats in the U.S. These bats live only in the tropics, where they bite sleeping animals or men, then lap up blood from the wound.

These are some known facts about bats. There are many other facts still unknown. Scientists, like Beer and Greeley who are following the trail of the hibernating bats, will some day solve the mysteries of the winged mammals.

(4)

Photographing
Wildlife at Jackson Hole*

*The Second Part of This Interesting Feature Describes
How to Photograph Small Animals with a
"Photographic Cage."*

BY TOM McHUGH

Photographers interested in the wildlife at Jackson Hole may be seriously handicapped if a small group of influential Western stockmen fulfill their desire to abolish the Jackson Hole National Monument. Not only has this selfish group introduced bills to wreck the Monument, they have also strangled the development of the Monu-

* Reprinted by permission of *U.S. Camera* and Tom McHugh.

ment for the public by prohibiting the National Park Service from spending any money on the Monument for the past five years.

* * *

The commonly occurring mountain storms can often be advantageously used by the photographer. Immediately following such storms the air is so clear that distant peaks can be photographed without the use of filters. The last few clouds that enshroud the snow caps after a storm are the raw materials for pictures that show the unstable weather conditions in the mountains. The haze preceding the storm is of great value in adding a third dimensional quality to the picture. If properly photographed it can give a feeling of distance to the mountains and aid in giving depth to the valleys and canyons in the picture.

As a further device to add depth to the picture, some object should always be included in the foreground. This could be a frame of foliage, a person, or a nearby tree or rock. In any case, this foreground interest should not dominate the picture—rather, it should lead the eye into it by being as much a part of the scene as the mountains.

(5)
Little King
of the
Underworld*

So Completely Is the Mole Adjusted to Life in His Lightless Labyrinths That He Even Goes through the Motions of Digging in His Sleep.

By Tom McHugh

The sod cracked and heaved upward. First one side and then the other of a small ridge were pushed up. Nothing stopped the work of this subterranean earth-cleaver as he forged on through the soil. Stalked plants fell over on their sides and small roots were torn apart with a faint crunching sound.

My curiosity could wait no longer, and I quickly plunged a trowel through the ridge to trap the animal in the blind end of his

* Reprinted by permission of *Natural History* and Tom McHugh.

tunnel. But even that was not enough to corner him. By the time I had brushed away the top of the ridge, the only remaining sign of the creature was a patch of velvety fur and a little pink tail. I rapidly seized the tail and started pulling, but pulling on that organ was about as successful as trying to uproot a small tree—it just didn't work.

Finally, by removing all the earth around him, I succeeded in pulling out all seven inches of a gray furry mass. With its broad, spadelike feet and pointed pink snout, it gave every indication of an animal that was truly "king of the underworld." Few animals have become as specialized for a narrow existence as this common mole.

* * *

With man's occupancy of the land the value of moles as cultivators ceases. Their natural process is much too slow. But in the uncultivated areas of the earth, the little king of the underworld still remains a useful citizen—the symbol of one of Nature's most complete and successful ventures into the realm of subterranean darkness.

(6)
Outsmarting Birds*

Bird Photography Is a Game of Wits. Here Are Some Pointers That Will Help You Bring Home Good Pictures.

BY TOM MCHUGH
with photos, except as noted, by the author

Have you ever watched a robin bathing in your backyard? Or peered into dark foliage to glimpse a nestful of chittering fledglings? For nearly everyone birdlife holds a special fascination and for the camera-minded it's natural to want to record such scenes on film. Patience, ingenuity, and a camera equipped for synchronized flash are the only prerequisites.

Unlike other forms of wildlife photography, you won't have to go far for your bird pictures—perhaps to your neighborhood park if you are a city dweller. Since birds are timid creatures, however, some lure must be used to draw them in front of the camera. This may be a feeding station, water bath, or nest. Picture making at the nest is

---

*Reprinted by permission of *Modern Photography* and Tom McHugh.

most successful, for the parents will nearly always return to feed and care for their young.

*   *   *

With these instructions and a share of patience, you can add some remarkable wildlife photos to your collection. When friends ask how you got so close, keep it a secret—you can fool them just as you deceived the birds!

Exercises

1. List the feature articles which you wrote in your course in Feature Writing last semester or last year.

2. Which articles did you sell? To which periodicals?

3. What was your total income from your free-lance articles?

4. Approximately how many hours did you spend writing them?

5. What was your average hourly rate for the writing done in the Feature Writing course?

6. In looking over the articles which you wrote for the course, but which have not sold yet, what do you think you can do to make them marketable?

7. Which ones do you think it would be a waste of your time to re-write, or reslant for mailing? Why?

8. List the suggestions in the Preface for using Part II of this book.

9. For which writer's periodicals do you plan to subscribe?

10. After writing a practice letter querying an editor, ask your instructor to have the letters read in class. Each student should list suggestions for improving the letters of query.

11. What system will you use in keeping your records on queries you send to editors?

12. After surveying all available libraries, list the specialties of each.

13. What other services does your library, or do other libraries, offer?

14. List the special libraries, departments, or rooms in the libraries in your community.

15. What help could you expect to obtain from your state's traveling library?

16. List libraries of private citizens in your community or of associations such as your city's advertising club or merchant's association which might be helpful in a specialized field.

Research Report No. 1, due first week of second semester.

SELECTING A FIELD IN WHICH TO SPECIALIZE

(Purpose of this Research Report is to investigate one or more specialized, technical, or scientific fields briefly in order to determine which will offer the greatest opportunity in obtaining material, markets, interviews. Students should have read or skimmed Chapters 18, 19, 20, 21, 22, and 23.)

Testing Field: After checking possible fields by means of questions under "Factors to Consider in Selecting a Field," Chapter 20, page 377 and "Beginner Tests Tentative Field," Chapter 23, page 442, the field offering the greatest opportunity for me is:

_____

_____

Discarded Fields: _____

_____

Reasons for Choice: _____

_____

_____

_____

Etc. Etc.

CHAPTER 18

Doing Research for
Magazine Writing

▪▪▪

Library Systems of Organizations. Many students go through high school and college with but a superficial acquaintance with a library, but the magazine writer has more than a casual knowledge of its organization and the material it contains. The feature writer will recall from previous experience that library materials are classified as call and reference. The first classification includes special books and periodicals; the second classification, reference, covers general and much used authorities, or reference books and handbooks.

Although a librarian will look up information on request, a professional writer should know the classification systems of libraries in order to find his own material, because it will save time in the long run. There are two systems of classifications: the Dewey Decimal system, which is used in most public libraries, and the Library of Congress system, which is better adapted to scholarly and university libraries because of their enormous collections. The Dewey Decimal system has ten main classes, each of which has subdivisions; the Library of Congress system has twenty. Except that the latter prefixes letters of the alphabet to arabic numbers, the two systems are similar.

It is not absolutely necessary to memorize either classification, for one knows that 2 comes after 1 and N comes after G, but more exact knowledge will increase one's efficiency. In larger libraries one will find diagrams showing the location of each classification; in others, the contents of the shelves are listed at the end of each stack, or set of book shelves, in the stack rooms. The numbers on the books, as one recalls, indicate the shelf location of the volumes.

If possible, the feature writer should obtain permission to use the stacks, not only because of the time saved, but because it will enable him to find material that he might otherwise miss.

The main classes in the Dewey Decimal system are:

> 000 General Works
> 100 Philosophy
> 200 Religion
> 300 Sociology
> 400 Philology
> 500 Natural Science
> 600 Useful Arts
> 700 Fine Arts
> 800 Literature
> 900 History

The main classes in the Library of Congress system are:

> A General Works
> B Philosophy, Religion
> C History
> D Foreign History
> E, F American History
> G Geography, Anthropology
> H Social Sciences
> J Political Science
> K Law
> L Education
> M Music
> N Fine Arts

P Language and Literature
Q Science
R Medicine
S Agriculture
T Technology
U Military Science
V Naval Science
Z Library Science, Bibliography

Card File Is Key to the Call Department. A librarian has likened the card catalog to a port of entry to the library, and the periodical guides to gang planks on which the journalist may make a landing. But teachers are always finding students who are not familiar with this invaluable aid. As every one knows, the card file contains drawers full of 3 by 5 cards, which are in alphabetical order. Each book and each periodical in the library is listed on a card. Each is cross-indexed and may be located by its (1) author, (2) title, or (3) subject.

The card gives (1) the number of the book in reference to its location on the library shelves in the stacks, (2) the full name of the author and his dates, (3) the full title and subtitle, (4) place of publication, (5) the publisher, (6) the date of publication, (7) the length of the book in number of pages, and (8) frequently, the table of contents. The feature writer will be able to judge the value of the book for his purpose by this information. The card files with their subject entries in reality constitute a bibliography on every subject listed.

The fact searcher copies down on "call slips" supplied by the library and always placed near the card files the name of the book, the author, and the call number. If he has access to the stacks, he gets the book and may see other books that will aid him. If the stacks are closed to the public, he asks a librarian at the "Call" Desk to get the book for him. It is because the writer "calls" for the books that that department is known as the Call Department. In the meantime the writer has copied the information, and any other he desires, from the card file upon his own 3 by 5, or 4 by 6 cards, or half sheets of typing paper, listing each book on a separate card or sheet in order that he may place his cards in alphabetical or any other desired order. These cards are the beginning of the writer's bibliography. If a librarian reports that a book is out, the writer may have it reserved. Clues from reference books and periodicals will next be added to the writer's personal file or bibliography.

Reference Division Provides Fun of Treasure Hunt. The feature writer will find looking through the encyclopedias, handbooks, yearbooks, atlases, gazetteers, biographies, bibliographies, dictionaries, and indexes to periodical literature, which are found on the shelves of the Reference Room, to be as much fun as any game. He will become fascinated by the ever growing list of sources and up-to-the-minute, concise, accurate, concentrated information found between the covers of the books.

In using these volumes, one should read the introductions for explanations, instructions, and abbreviations. Because these authorities are constantly used in the Reference Room, they cannot be checked out, as may books from the Call Department.

The best way to make the acquaintance of the books in the Reference Room is to consult one or all of the following:

I. G. Mudge's *Guide to Reference Books,* published by the American Library Association; John Minto's *Reference Books,* similar to Mudge's, but listing only English books; Louis Shore's *Basic Reference Books,* also published by American Library Association, but simpler than the Mudge book.

Encyclopedias Provide Ideas for Tentative Outline. As every school child knows, an encyclopedia brings together in one volume, or a set of them, all knowledge, in which each branch of learning is discussed in a separate article. The writer will consider the encyclopedia valuable only as it gives him an outline of the selected field and a starting point for his subject. A list of references at the end of the article in the encyclopedia will suggest more books for the research writer's bibliography. These volumes are kept up to date by publication of revised editions, supplementary volumes, or yearbooks.

Writers will recall that there are many kinds. The *Encyclopaedia Britannica* is the oldest, most authoritative in some respects, and the most scholarly. The *Encyclopedia Americana* is good in the fields of applied sciences, business, and government and has an American viewpoint. The *New International Encyclopaedia* with its new *Yearbook* is valuable for Latin-American biography. *Columbia Encyclopaedia* is useful when brief articles are sufficient: it consists of only one volume, with a new supplement.

In addition to the general sources listed above, the research writer will next examine some of the special encyclopedias which are more thorough and detailed than the general ones. He will find specials for aeronautics, agriculture, American biography, American government, American history, art, banking and finance, Catholicism, chemistry, education, education research, engineering, Jewish life, literature, medicine, music, political science, religion, social science, and other subjects.

Encyclopedias become dated rapidly, but the *New International,* the *American Annual Year Books,* and *Britannica Book of the Year* give recent information. The special yearbooks include the *American Statesman's Year Book, Statesman's Year Book, Statistical Abstract of the United States,* the *United States Commerce Department Year Book,* the *United States Agricultural Department Year Book,* the *American Labor Year Book,* and many others.

Almanacs, such as the *World,* the *Chicago Daily News,* and *Whitaker's* (British), are also published annually and contain a great amount of detached information which saves hours for the feature writer when verifying facts.

Biographies Are as Interesting to Read as to Write. A journalist is not like the boy in the oft-told tale who spent hours paging through *Who's Who* for a sketch of George Washington, because the writer knows that only if he is writing a biography of a living person does he use *Who's Who* and magazine and newspaper articles. If the person is not living, a writer will refer to special encyclopedias and to one or more of the four other sources for biographical sketches in addition to the encyclopedias:

the *Dictionary of American Biography*, the *Dictionary of National Biography*, the *National Cyclopaedia of American Biography*, and Webster's *Biographical Dictionary*. The research writer will find other lesser known sources of biography in most Reference Rooms. *Who Was Who* is also suggestive for sketches of those no longer living.

When writing sketches of living persons, one will find that *Who's Who*, which is published annually in England, *Who's Who in America, Current Biography, American Women*, and *America's Young Men* are valuable sources. Among the various specialized sources are: *Who's Who in American Education, Who's Who in Art, Who's Who among the Clergy, Who's Who in Medicine, Who's Who in New York, Who's Who in the Theater, Twentieth Century Authors, American Authors, Dictionary of Music and Musicians, Scientific Encyclopedia, Dictionary of American History, American Men of Science, Congressional Directory, Leaders in Education*, and lesser known ones in other fields, such as *United States sectional Who's Who*.

Now that going around the world is a matter of hours, the magazine writer's knowledge of people will need to be global. For information concerning the British nobility and aristocracy, he may wish to refer to *Official Baronage* or *Burke's Peerage;* for European aristocrats, *Almanach de Gotha;* and for American blue bloods, the *Social Register*.

Bibliographies Serve as Writer's Short Cuts. Various lists of books or other material assembled with unity of subject or of purpose are available to the magazine writer on many subjects. Those concerned with earlier publications are *American Bibliography, Dictionary of Books Relating to America, Bibliotheca Americana, American Catalog*, and *American Catalog of Books*. Special bibliographies are available on many subjects.

For more recent book listings, one will refer to the *Cumulative Book Index*, which until 1928 was known as the *U. S. Catalog*.

One may save time by checking his bibliography before he starts his reading with the *Book Review Digest*, which gives the opinion of the book world on almost any book published. It is issued annually and in monthly supplements and gives plus and minus ratings on books listed.

Dictionaries and Word Books Are Writing "Tools." As every writer strives to find the right noun, verb, or adjective in order to put the "picture which he desires in his readers' minds," he will make constant use of one or more of the following dictionaries: The *New English Dictionary* (formerly known as the Oxford), Webster's *New International Dictionary, Second Edition,* Funk and Wagnalls' *New Standard Dictionary,* Roget's *Thesaurus* (Mawson's revision), and Fowler's *Dictionary of Modern English Usage.*

Other helpful books are Webster's *Dictionary of Synonyms,* Fernald's *English Synonyms, Antonyms, and Prepositions,* Allen's *Synonyms,* and Crabbe's *English Synonyms.* For references to well-known lines in literature, the writer uses Bartlett's *Familiar Quotations,* or Stevenson's *Home Book of Quotations.* To check important days and anniversaries, which, incidentally, suggest timely feature tips, there is Douglas' *Book of Days* or Hazeltine's *Anniversaries and Holidays.* Concordances for the Bible and famous authors are also useful.

Atlases and Gazetteers Aid Verification. Since so many men and women readers once served their country in many foreign lands, the magazine writer has to be exceedingly careful in presenting geographical facts and statistics. Not only will he find the Rand-McNally *Commercial Atlas,* Shepherd's *Historical Atlas,* and Lippincott's *Gazetteer* helpful in verifying information, he will also discover excellent "tips" for articles when turning through the pages.

Periodical Indexes Are Writer's Gold Mines. Because of the very nature of magazines for which fact writers write, the magical indexes to periodical literature are useful in several ways. First, they enable one to know before starting his article whether similar ones have already been published and if so, where, which will save time and postage. Second, successful and well-known writers find the indexes useful sources of ideas for articles for general or class publications, and the staff writer will find material which he can slant to his own publication. The majority of articles in general reader magazines originated in the technical or specialized periodicals. Third, looking at lists of titles of current features will suggest hundreds of "tips" to the writer. Fourth, it reveals the sort of material editors are purchasing, and even beginners in feature writing know that there are fashions in features as in clothing.

These indexes include *Readers' Guide to Periodical Literature,* Poole's *Index to Periodical Literature, International Index to Periodical Literature,* and the *Magazine Subject Index.*

The special indexes are concerned with periodicals devoted to Agriculture, Art, Biology, Catholicism, Chemistry, Drama, Education, Engineering, Law, Industrial Arts, Internationalism, Public Affairs, and Psychology. Newspaper indexes are for the London *Times* and the New York *Times.* The latter is published twice monthly. It is on 35 mm. microfilm and is available for the years from 1851. This yearly index service may be obtained at a library since its cost makes it prohibitive for the average writer. The most recent articles will be listed in the supplements to the indexes.

Publications Are in Great Demand by Writers. Current publications in large libraries are obtained in the Periodical Room. The bound volumes, which are listed in the card catalog, may be found in the Periodical Room, the stacks, or in special rooms, as the "Magazine Room" and the "Newspaper Room." If one cannot obtain the desired periodicals in the library or borrow them from friends who are specialists in the field, one may be able to purchase them from a magazine distributor or broker or from the circulation department of the publication itself, or the library may arrange for a loan from some other library, or one may pay a library research worker at some library or magazine office for a digest of the requested article. It will aid the librarian to have a copy of the writer's outline.

Fact writers are familiar with the many journals of technical and learned societies. Some are difficult for people who are not experts in those fields to understand, but the majority of such periodicals are well worth the effort of the magazine worker to comprehend, because of the unlimited ideas and material which, if interpreted in articles for the general reader, would be of interest to him. The *Journal of the American Medical Association,* the *Journal of Applied Psychology, Proceedings of the American Institute of Electrical Engineers,* or the *Public Opinion Quarterly* are only a few of the hundreds which the "magazinist" will find helpful.

Fig. 13. Research Workers in New York City Library Periodical Room.

The periodicals of the trades and business institutes and associations are equally suggestive to the investigator, as are the "house organs" of commercial and industrial firms.

The Periodical Room in the New York Public Library provides more than 40,000 periodicals, which are in great demand by authors, journalists, reporters, staff writers, editors, publishers, and advertising copywriters. They are continually at work abstracting material. The Chief of the Periodical Division says that as many as a thousand magazines are asked for in a day. So great is the demand for trade and technical publications that many are worn out in a short time and have to be replaced.

Directories Are Most-Thumbed Volumes. Writers use the directories almost constantly, and they are found not only in magazine research departments but in the free-lance writer's personal library. Among the most usable ones are N. W. Ayer & Son's *Directory of Newspapers and Periodicals,* Ulrich's *Periodical Directory, Writer's Market, Writer's Yearbook,* and Standard Rate and Data service.

Document Catalog Is Source of Numerous Checks. The Depository Library, or Document Room, as some libraries term it, contains government bulletins, pamphlets, and miscellaneous publications that are almost as valuable to the research writer as are the periodicals. The *United States Document Catalog,* which is kept up to date by the *Monthly Catalog of United States Documents,* lists all government bulletins. Two other aids are the *United States Government Publications as Sources of Information,* and the *United States Reference Publications.*

In smaller libraries these bulletins, or documents as the librarians term them, may be in the Periodical or the Reference Department.

Writers Should Browse in Special and Departmental Rooms. If one is writing in specialized fields, he should acquaint himself with the special and departmental rooms. Whether it is the rare books room, or the genealogy room, or the state collection, or the museum, there are "tips" and information for every writer.

Universities also have special or departmental libraries housed in the various departments, such as agriculture, education, journalism, sociology, commerce, and others. Here student writers, if they are alert to their opportunities, will find many checks awaiting them for a little time spent there, if they add information obtained from interviews.

Many Journalists Overlook Library Services. Although a research person may not find the material he desires in his local library, inter-library loans make any book available, if the borrower pays the postage. The local librarian can write to any of the libraries which list the book in their catalogs, or to the state library, and obtain the requested material in a few days. The catalog *Special Libraries Resources* lists the books in about a thousand special libraries of large manufacturers, associations, and learned and technical societies to which the local librarian may request a loan if the borrower pays the postage. By the same method a writer may borrow from such libraries as the Museum of Modern Art, the Army Medical Library, Massachusetts Institute of Technology, and the Pan American Union, which are also listed in *Special Library Resources*. Many university libraries have an author-card catalog for books in the Library of Congress in addition to their own, and they can obtain the books on its four hundred miles of shelves through the Inter-Library Loan. The Library of Congress will send photostat copies of any magazine or book pages covering any information a writer desires for a nominal charge. Its library personnel will aid a writer in locating information he needs if he writes clearly as to what he wants. Or one may ask the local library to make the request.

Other local library services include inexpensive microfilming and the making of photostatic copies of material in newspapers, documents, and rare books. If a library cannot provide such services, the librarian will tell one where these services may be obtained.

Professional Writers Know Research Reference Books. A research worker can never know too much about a library. There are numerous and helpful aids, such as *Using Books and Libraries, A Research Manual, How to Do Research, How to Locate Information, Preparing the Research Paper, Research and Thesis Writing,* and *Newspaper Reference Methods,* as listed in the appendix under the "Free-Lance Writer's Library."

Successful Writers Spend Much Time in Library. One of the best-known and highest-paid magazine contributors, when asked how he attained his success, replied:

"I never spend any time at amateur mutual admiration societies, known as writers' clubs, and I have attended only a few of the best writers' conferences. Instead I go where I will meet people who know things I don't know; I write about people and their activities, not about writers!"

This writer's by-line is well known because he keeps regular working hours and spends them at the library doing research for his articles, except for time spent interviewing and writing. He has spent anywhere from one day to nine days and evenings on research for short general articles, and for the more important ones for the class magazines he spends as much as two months on research alone. He points out he can afford to do so because of the generous-sized checks he receives for his manuscripts.

Magazine editors employing the idea of "group" journalism—several of the many staff members working on various phases of the same article at the same time—think nothing of having the staff working two or six months on one article. For example, several members of *Fortune* staff assigned to the Hearst article spent more than six months assembling material for it, and an article on the New York Central Railroad took two months' time of the staff members assigned to that subject.

Even the busiest researcher makes friends with all of the librarians and knows them by name, because efficiently trained librarians not only save a writer's time but are generous with their ideas and their help. The fact writer who is equally generous with his expressions of appreciation for their help is the popular library "guest."

Writer in Remote Area May Do Research at Home. A feature writer who has access to a public library as well as the writer who lives a hundred miles from even a small one should likewise acquire a private specialized library to suit his field of writing. Books that researchers anywhere will want to own are the current *World Almanac;* Mawson's edition of Roget's *Thesaurus;* Fowler's *Modern English Usage;* one or two of the unabridged dictionaries, Webster's *New International* and Funk and Wagnalls' *Standard Dictionary;* the *Columbia Encyclopedia,* and *The Writer's Market Book,* all of which can be ordered through any book store. Although such an investment amounts to about $75 or $100, it will repay the writer in the time saved, for to the researcher, time is money.

If one lives in a rural community far from a library, he will find the *Readers' Guide to Periodical Literature* indispensable, because it informs the subscriber of the service of the subjects in the current periodicals. He should query the publishers as to its exact price, which probably will be about $15.00. After learning the contents of the periodicals from the *Guide,* one may write to the magazines to purchase the desired issues.

A letter of inquiry to Standard Rate and Data service would provide information as to which of the special sections would be helpful and also the price of each. A similar letter to N. W. Ayer & Son would give information as to the price of the *Directory of Newspapers and Periodicals.* If the isolated writer can afford them, they will aid in slanting to the correct market and will soon pay for themselves because of the increase in checks. Their addresses, along with those of firms which send out helpful free mailings, may be found in the Appendix.

For a postage stamp any writer may secure library service from his state's extension traveling library located at the State Capitol, which in turn may be able to secure the privileges of the Inter-Library Loan. Many foreign countries provide similar inter-library loans. Extension divisions in some state universities will provide, upon request, a clipping service, or one may pay a fee for clippings on particular subjects from commercial clipping bureaus.

Doing Research by Mail. Requested printed matter from government bureaus, whose bulletins are listed in the *Monthly Catalog of United States Public Documents,* may be slow in reaching one, but a letter to the writer's congressman or senator, asking for the material, will be given prompt attention for obvious reasons. If not in a hurry, one may address the Superintendent of Documents, Government Printing Office, Washington 25, D. C. The *Catalog,* which sells for a nominal fee, lists bulletins varying in price, but even the most expensive costs only a few cents and will add immeasurably to one's personal research library. The *List of Selected United States Government Publications* may be obtained free upon application to the Superintendent of Documents. Remittance for bulletins must be made in advance, either by coupons, twenty for a dollar, which are good until used; or by check, money order, or a postal note payable to the Superintendent of Documents.

One may receive factual help from other Federal departments as the Children's Bureau, Bureau of Mines, Bureau of Entomology, and so forth. Information bureaus which syndicate newspaper columns, such as the Haskin Service and other research syndicates; Science Service; and Union Library Association—all of which are listed along with others in the "Free-Lance Writer's Library" in the Appendix—may be able to answer inquiries. Book stores, foreign government public relations bureaus, and information services often will respond to writers' requests for information and material. Frequently they are able to supply "glossies" for a small fee. Advertisements in almost any magazine will suggest fruitful sources for acquiring information, illustrations, and "glossy" prints, if one uses his initiative.

State offices, large corporations, associations, chambers of commerce, commercial organizations, manufacturers, advertising agencies, and insurance companies having public relations offices or publicity bureaus often can provide by mail the material and pictures the remote writer, or a writer anywhere, needs.

Accepted Plans for Note-Taking Are Suggestive. The research writer does not summarize his notes as does the freshman, because he wants specific facts, ideas, and pertinent statements that will enable him to interview intelligently and to write accurately.

As one recalls from his rhetoric, the note-taking systems are the *précis,* a brief summary; the *rough summary,* which as its name indicates is more of an outline style; the *paraphrase,* a restatement of the passage in the research writer's own vocabulary; and the *quotation,* which is an important form to the writer, because he uses it when in doubt as to whether he will want full or abridged notes. The practiced fact searcher finds a combination of these methods most usable.

System Is More Important than Method. Methodical note-taking saves times and adds to the writer's efficiency in magazine research. He should work out some plan and then form the habit of: (1) labeling every sheet or card in the upper left-hand corner as to subject matter and the division of it; (2) numbering or lettering the sheets to correspond to the position of the material in the outline; and (3) indicating every source by giving the authority's surname first, followed by his given name or initials, the title of the book, chapter number, and page number. Or, if a magazine, its name, volume number, issue number, and page numbers should be listed, in case the writer may wish years later to use it again, or may desire permission from the copyright holder and the author to quote a passage, and so will want to cite them.

Many of the sources a writer skims; in others he finds the material relevant or the authority an expert, and so reads with care, taking full and complete quotations if he has the slightest expectation of using the material, after obtaining permission to do so. If one has to check sources later, it is like looking for the proverbial needle in the haystack, for nothing is as elusive as the source of a quotation, even a few hours later.

The professional avoids taking worthless notes or notes not relevant to the subject, but he is equally careful not to omit anything that he thinks will be useful. He develops a uniform note-taking system, selects wisely, classifies, and arranges materials to appeal and to hold the reader's interest.

Experienced Writers Develop Own Note-Taking Methods. The majority of writers prefer to use half or whole sheets of typewriting paper, or paper pads, or cards about 6 by 8 inches in order that the notes on each phase of the sub-topic of the tentative outline will be on separate sheets or cards. The professional writer transcribes or dictates the notes as soon as possible in order that a carbon copy may be made. He files one copy and cuts the other to organize his notes to follow his outline. The structure of the article can then be roughly built by sorting the sheets to conform to the tentative outline; with the insertion of material from other sources, such as interviews, the notes become the first draft of the article. If his notes become confused, the writer can refer to the "file" copy.

Credit to sources is given in feature articles by means of either direct or indirect quotations, rather than by use of footnotes, but the writer must be as accurate as the historian, even though his method is different. Omission of words or phrases is indicated, as one recalls, by "ellipsis points" or three dots or periods in addition to a period at the end of the sentence. To indicate interpolation—for example, of a noun to clarify a pronoun—one uses brackets: He [John] found the quotation.

Even though the writer develops short-cut methods, he will always take notes accurately and in a legible form, because he may use the same notes years later in a different way for a different purpose. Or if he is one of the prolific writers who employ a staff of research workers, he will require them to work in a scholarly fashion for the same reasons.

Accuracy and Honesty Necessary in Research. The searcher for facts must constantly be aware of the limitations of his rights as an author, as discussed in Chapter 16, because phraseology is individual personal property. One violation of the copyright law may bring disaster to the magazine writer's career.

Note-Taking for the Article Begins in the Encyclopedia. Efficient researchers with their stack of cards of all available sources start the actual work of note-taking for the article by first looking up the subject in encyclopedias.

When taking notes from books or periodicals, it is advisable to get only a few books or periodicals at a time, because others may desire to use the same references at the same time. Then, too, the task does not look so huge. Before closing a reference, a careful writer verifies the facts for errors in copying, and also indicates by a check mark on his source card that it has been read.

Keeping the Purpose and Point of View in Mind. After the note-taking is completed, the writer determines the main purpose in writing the article and his one conclusion, point of view, or angle, before he does any interviewing. As he writes, he keeps these two points constantly in mind, or better still, jots them down on a card which he keeps on his typewriter desk. In case, when brain-weary, he is in doubt as to whether to use certain material, a glance at the card will enable him to determine whether to retain or discard.

Notes should be transcribed as soon after they are taken as possible. They may be "scissored," notes from interviewees or other sources included, sorted in order, pasted, edited by substituting better vocabulary, adding to, or deleting, with the result that the treasure hunt for facts is concluded and the first draft of the article is completed.

Research Techniques Determine Writer's Success. The difference between the amateur and the professional writer is that the latter is as much, or more, a research worker than he is a writer. Some would-be writers find research of so much interest that they seek employment in the research departments of the well-known magazines, rather than magazine staff positions as manuscript readers, copy editors, writers, or associate editors.

The latest trend in magazine staff work points toward more opportunity to do research. The demand for writers with such training and ability is greater than the supply, because only a few amateur writers without research training bother to get themselves out of the beginner's class and too few journalism schools offer courses in advanced magazine writing in which research work is emphasized.

Any alert and ambitious writer, in a class or working alone at home, who will follow the suggestions given in this chapter and read the books listed under "Free-Lance Writer's Library" in the Appendix can train himself in research which will increase his skill as a magazine contributor, though he lives a thousand miles distant from publication centers, or will enable him to become a member of some one of the 8,220 magazine staffs as listed in the Appendix under "Opportunities to Sell Feature Articles."

Learning to do research, like learning to write, can be done in only one way—by doing it, whether in a magazine class or working alone at home.

Exercises

1. List five magazines that you might later wish to query after you have completed an analysis of research sources for your selected field of writing in this course.

2. Suggest a plan for a questionnaire that would supply material for your selected field of special writing which you plan to do in this course.

3. List three local experts or authorities in your selected field whom you could interview.

4. Name two sources which you could contact by mail for printed material for your chosen field.

5. Suggest two names of authorities whom you could interview only by mail, include their addresses, and tell why you chose them.

6. After making a survey of your library's primary sources, list any that you might be able to use for the articles you plan to write in your selected field this semester.

7. For each of the secondary sources in your library list at least three departments that you will probably use in doing research.

8. List any prejudices you now have concerning your field of writing and how you plan to overcome them.

9. Which system of classification does your university library use?

10. Which system of classification does your city library use?

11. Select five sources from the card file that you probably will use for research for the articles you plan to write later this semester.

12. Consult one or more of the guide books to references. List one reference which you think you may use for each type found in the Reference Room.

13. Enumerate the references for your subjects which you found in the encyclopedia which you consulted.

14. List references found in the yearbooks for your selected field.

15. What information for your field did you find in an almanac?

16. What information did you find in the biographies of any of the living experts in your field, whom you might later wish to "interview" by mail?

17. What estimate did the *Book Review Digest* give concerning the books you selected in Exercise 11 for sources for your field?

18. Which dictionary do you find most useful for your field of writing?

19. What help did you find in recent atlases or gazetteers for your articles?

20. List three articles suggested to you in one of the *Guides to Periodical Literature*.

21. Which special index to periodical literature had articles for your research?

22. Which technical or learned publications will be suggestive for your field of writing?

23. Which directories will aid you in your research?

24. List bulletins found in the *Document Catalog* that you can use as source material.

25. In what special or departmental libraries can you find source material for your field?

26. Enumerate the services your local library or libraries offer. Which ones can you use for your field?

27. List the librarians you can call by name. In which departments are they?

28. List bulletins which you requested from your congressman or senator.

29. What research do you plan to do by mail?

30. What is your present system of note-taking? Explain orally in class.

31. List any suggestions you can for improving your note-taking methods.

32. What are the purposes of each of your articles and what point of view do you plan now to give them? Why?

33. What phase of magazine work do you now think you would enjoy doing most? Why?

34. Go through a feature article in an issue of *Saturday Evening Post, Life,* the *Atlantic Monthly,* or any others assigned in class or obtainable, and list the evidences of the writer's research. List the sources you think he used.

35. Now that you are training to become a professional writer, to which of the writer's magazines will you subscribe? Why?

36. To which of the publications for magazine editors and staffs will you subscribe? Why?

37. When you receive the check for your next article sale, which books will you purchase for your personal writer's library?

38. List the research which the writer did for any one of the five articles used as examples in Chapter 20.

39. Indicate the types of sources used for each kind of research which you listed in Exercise 38.

40. Do you have any suggestions to add to the Research Report assigned by your instructor now that you have completed the library research for your articles? Make them to your instructor and to the others in the class.

Research Report No. 2, due second week of second semester.

OPPORTUNITIES IN SELECTED FIELD

(Purpose is to survey opportunities in more detail of chosen field, now that a final selection has been made. If, for some reason, the field does not seem adequate, the student may select another, and so on until he finds a satisfactory one.)

Articles on Subject Listed in *Readers' Guide to Per. Lit.*: Title	Periodical	Vol.	No.	Mo.	Date	Year
1.						
2.						
3.						
4.						
5.						
6.						
7.						
8.						
9.						
10.						

Etc. Etc.

Will Subject Be Timely 6 or 24 Months from Now?

_____

_____

Availability of Research Sources: (Chapter 18)

_____

_____

_____

New Developments Not Yet in Print: (Based on Inquiry.)

_____

_____

Authorities to Be Interviewed and Why Selected:

_____

_____

New Angles to Appeal to Readers:

_____

_____

Twelve Suggested Tips for Selected Field of Writing (Only Three Articles Will
  Be Written.)

1. _____

2. _____

3. _____

4. _____

5. _____

6. _____

7. _____

8. _____

9. _____

10. _____

11. _____

12. _____

Tentative Ideas for Illustrations of the Three Articles:

_____

_____

_____

_____

CHAPTER 19

Surveying Magazine Markets

▪▪▪

Writer Surveys Markets Before Starting Research.
As pointed out in earlier chapters the modern successful writer is,
first of all, a practical alert business executive, not a starving
daydreamer as were the writers of yesteryears. One must have
executive qualities, either innate or acquired by training, or hire
some one who has them, if he is to succed as a magazine contributor.

The latter, like the executive, must be able to plan, to sense
the reader's interest six or more months ahead, and to make exhaustive investigations into opportunities to sell his ideas. This
ability must be in addition to the ability to do library research in
order to ferret out facts which enlarge his store of ideas and
which enable him to interview intelligently. If he is not of a practical nature, he will have to acquire the services of an agent, who,
like all other agents, is interested in placing articles only for
writers who have made names for themselves in the magazine
world.

Contributors free-lancing to many periodicals do their market
surveys before they even start the research for an article. The
businesslike writer is constantly surveying markets and filing the
information acquired in order to know hundreds of periodicals

and to have the information available in his files for immediate use.

A well-known contributor, whose by-line is seen in a number of "top" class magazines every month, knows, not several markets, but hundreds in every conceivable field almost as well as each editor knows his own periodical. Another writer, equally well known and as financially successful, has made three hundred general magazine tabulations and has surveyed more than 500 periodicals that use articles or have departments or special sections devoted to the field in which he is a specialist.

These professional writers believe that the time spent in market research is just as important, or more so, than the days or months spent in research on the article. Their opinions on the value of market surveys are valuable because they are at the top of the magazine writing profession.

Libraries Are Sources for Market Research. Even before the experienced writer queries an editor, he will have completed the research necessary for a market survey. The practical contributor obtains his market information from several sources. First, he examines the most recent writer's market book listed in the Appendix, which lists many magazines, trade journals, and syndicates. The writer's magazines, too, will be suggestive, because they include information on markets; some announce the founding of new periodicals and the discontinuation of old.

In surveying markets in magazine and feature sections of newspapers, one will find the N. W. Ayer & Son's *Directory of Newspapers and Periodicals* informative. *Editor and Publisher International Year Book* is also helpful, because it gives current information concerning newspapers, advertising agencies, newspaper department editors, syndicates, foreign language press, correspondents, news services, newspaper advertising, and circulation rates.

The professional examines the latest listings of the Standard Rate and Data service, which are issued in four different sections: (1) Magazines, Farm Papers, Transportation, and Advertising; (2) Business Papers; (3) Newspapers; and (4) Radio Stations.

The section concerning periodicals gives the contents and the coverage of articles. The above market sources are listed in the Appendix under the "Free-Lance Writer's Library."

Other Survey Material Available. For the writer far distant from a library as well as for the person who lives in its shadow, other sources are available until he can purchase source books for his own library. For a two-cent postal card, one may get his name on the free mailing lists for catalogs of the various subscription agencies and magazine distributors, whose addresses may be obtained from the various trade publications for magazine editors and writers, as listed in the Appendix under the "Free-Lance Writer's Library."

If one cannot obtain one or two issues of a certain periodical to examine, he can write for a sample copy of the publication. One's knowledge of a periodical will be more accurate if he can examine several issues, but even one copy is better than none. One may be able to borrow, or at least examine, certain specialized publications from experts in the fields they cover, such as dentists, physicians, scientist-researchers, and others.

If one does not have access to technical, trade, and business publications, he may borrow from firms which subscribe for them by introducing himself to the owner or manager, presenting one of his business cards bearing his address and telephone number, explaining the purpose of his call, and asking permission to examine the specialized periodicals. The subscriber will probably tell the writer that he may take the magazines home, in which case the professional writer assures him that he will return them promptly. This he will do, because he may want to borrow other publications again from the same source. Subscribers value their professional and trade journals and usually keep files of them, clip them, or have them bound because of the ideas they contain, so experienced article writers are extremely conscientious about the return of borrowed magazines.

Unusual magazines which cannot be obtained from a library or from one's "loaning friends," may be found in the second-hand magazine or "back-number" shops which are available in some cities. A free-lance should acquire the addresses of these shops, because from such a shop, for a few cents, he may obtain a copy of a particular magazine which even the publisher is not able to supply if the issue has been completely sold out.

Methods of Market Research. The practical contributor acquires his knowledge of markets much as does the advertising space buyer in an advertising agency—by investigating all the phases of the magazine: circulation, advertising, and editorial content. He, too, is accurate, scholarly, and exacting in recording and filing the various phases of information he obtains from the directories compiled for the journalistic profession. He, too, as do the advertising research people, saves time by using forms upon which he tabulates his survey information. Each writer soon develops his own system in gathering and assembling market information. Until one becomes accustomed to doing market surveys, he may find it easier to follow the plan of the form of the Research Report at the end of this chapter, or one suggested by the instructor. But soon, he will be able to gather the needed facts easily from each source for the different phases of the survey as he is examining each source of information.

Circulation is Research Key to Reader Identity. Invaluable short cuts to market information, because they give the writer an insight as to whether the circulation is mass or class and just who reads what, are the latest editions of the N. W. Ayer & Son's *Directory of Newspapers and Periodicals,* the *Editor and Publisher International Year Book,* and Standard Rate and Data service. The first includes the circulations of all periodicals published in the United States and its possessions and some of the British Dominions. It gives the circulation for agricultural papers, foreign language periodicals, fraternal publications, general magazines, Negro periodicals, religious journals, trade, business, technical and class magazines. The second, *Editor and Publisher Year Book,* is valuable in surveying the magazine sections of newspapers.

If the local library cannot provide a recent edition of these source books, any daily newspaper, no matter how small, and almost every weekly newspaper will have them. The newspaper librarian or the editor, if approached tactfully, generally will permit a writer to use the latest editions of either reference.

The third, Standard Rate and Data service, one recalls, is a national authority and is issued in sections which not only give the names of the magazines, circulations by year and by single copy, the subscription price by year and price per single copy, but also the dates the periodicals were established. This information gives some insight into the dependability of the publications. Too often new periodicals spring up which have little or no financial backing. They accept articles, publish them, but are unable to pay the contributor before publication is discontinued.

Material in Source Volumes Varies. A writer needs to have access to all these source volumes, because no one of them lists all periodicals, as they were compiled with different purposes in mind. Since the *Directory* and the *Year Book* are available in nearly all libraries and newspaper offices, a writer can get along for a time without copies of each in his personal library. Not all of the sections of the Standard Rate and Data service may be obtained in all libraries, but an advertising agency might occasionally permit a writer to use its sections, although they are much in demand in an agency. Of course one would be embarrassed to impose on such an agency often. The experienced writer, as soon as he can afford to do so, acquires all of the market source books, as well as a file case—even if it is only a portable pasteboard one—in his own library. The total expense for all, including a market book, would probably be somewhere between $50 and $100. But the professional does not object to such an expenditure in his chosen career if the investment in a source library and a file case will save him time. Time to a research writer is money, and a well-equipped library is as essential as a typewriter and carbon paper.

Circulation Survey Reveals Who Magazine's Readers Are. An amateur would probably feel that such an exhaustive investigation would not be worth his time, but the professional realizes that one must know who the readers are, mass or class, if he is to write to them interestingly. (For example, *Saturday Evening Post*, has, at the time this was written, a total net paid circulation average of 4,597,987 copies each week. Thus a writer slanting an article to the *Post* knows that it must have mass reader appeal.) The writer must know the reader's reading habits, whether he buys at the newsstand or subscribes by the year. This information is enlightening if the writer is to get and hold the reader's attention.

The price and type of a subscription indicates somewhat the kind of reader—whether he is one who plans ahead or one who buys on impulse, or because he is influenced by an attractive newsstand display. The surveyor notes not only the circulation but the subscription price of a magazine and multiplies the one by the other to get an estimate of the magazine's income from circulation. He jots these figures down for further consideration as a key to the periodical's ability to pay.

If the writer knows all he can about the reader's reading habits, he will be better able to slant an article which even the newest and least experienced manuscript reader will feel is something that he should pass on to a senior manuscript reader, who, too, will probably feel that the article should be sent to the editor for final decision. It is to attain this information that the professional writer studies the four sources previously listed, which enables him to see in his mind's eye the reader, just as the editor of the periodical does, and to write to him, or to slant accurately.

Advertising Survey Introduces Writer to Reader. Every writer knows that advertising agencies spend millions of dollars annually in order to learn just who reads the publications in which they place their clients' advertising copy. They are not content with knowing who the readers are. Through their surveys, they know what the reader's income is, the kind and amount of investments he has, the kind of home, furniture, color schemes, car, television, clothes, hobbies, and what his recreations and cultural interests are.

How do they learn all this? They have large research staffs who obtain these facts by interviewing a cross section of the subscribers of the periodical which is being surveyed. The results of similar research are assembled in Standard Rate and Data, but reveal facts about the periodical, rather than the reader, which also are necessary to a professional writer.

Survey of Advertising Reveals Periodical's Reliability. The professional again finds the Standard Rate and Data sections another short cut, for in a few minutes he obtains from them all of the information he desires—information which it took research staffs months to assemble.

He turns to the index and finds the publication he is considering. He observes that the advertising rather than the editorial address is given, but he probably has already obtained the latter from a market book or from Ayers' *Directory,* or from the publication itself when he began the survey. He jots down the advertising rates per page, back page rates, any other interesting listings concerning advertising rates, and the number of pages devoted to advertising.

By simple arithmetic he roughly estimates the income from the advertising per issue by multiplying the average income per issue by the number of issues a year and records that for consideration later.

Of course a writer is aware that estimated income from circulation and advertising does not represent clear profit, because the business of printing and publishing, at any time an expensive one, in recent years has increased in expense manyfold. Even though one does not know the expenses of a publication, the total estimated incomes, derived from circulation and advertising, do, to a certain degree, indicate the periodical's financial ability to buy manuscripts.

Investigation of Advertising Shows Purpose of Magazine. The surveyor notes anything about the magazine listed in Standard Rate and Data which gives insight as to what the periodical likes or does not like, as the advertising policy reveals the editorial policy. He observes whether the publication does not accept advertising or which ones have unusual advertising contracts. One publication, for example, may indicate that it does not accept alcoholic beverage advertisements. A writer would then know that the magazine would not be in the market for articles concerning the mixing of alcoholic drinks or the selecting of appropriate types of cocktail glasses.

Another reason that the professional glances over the advertising contract is to discern any clues to reasons the publication is different in some respects from other magazines, and just what that difference is. This in turn may explain why the circulation is small or large, as the case may be. Too, he learns how the periodical rates as an advertising medium, and although as a writer he is not interested in placing advertising copy, he acquires information as to the periodical's ability to pay for thorough, complete, well-organized, and interestingly written manuscripts accurately slanted to it.

Examination of Editorial Content Is Necessary. Although the Standard Rate and Data service sections include a brief enumeration of the contents and coverage of articles in each periodical which adds to the writer's knowledge of the magazine's distinctive policies, yet there is nothing as valuable as the actual examination of the editorial matter in the publication. A cursory examination of magazines may reveal new publication policies that were incorporated after the directory and market book listings. The writer must keep up to date in order to slant carefully. In addition to turning through periodicals, the professional skims the writer's magazines for information on markets. The following announcement from a magazine editor in a writer's publication aided two students in an Advanced Magazine Writing Course to slant their articles and receive checks from that editor:

> The Kiwanis Magazine is in need of factual articles from 1500-2500 words on current, general interest subjects. Its policy requires that the articles must be packed with facts and a variety of interesting examples as evidence of the facts. Only articles based on thorough research and mature thought will be considered.

No matter how experienced a writer is, time spent in analyzing publications as suggested in the earlier chapters and as outlined in the Research Reports at the end of each chapter in Part II and in glancing through the writers' publications will be time well spent because one's market knowledge must be added to and kept up to date or he will be like the amateur, "shooting in the dark."

Policy Concerning Illustrations Is Important. The more aware a writer is of a publication's policy concerning illustrations the better able he is to include ideas concerning them when he queries the editor. In some cases where the editors think the material important enough and the photographic opportunities warrant it, the magazine sends a staff photographer to work with the contributor in getting the illustrations.

The best source for this part of the market survey is to turn through at least three or more issues of the publication under consideration, checking the kinds, sizes, and anything individual or unusual about the different types of illustrations.

Writers Study Markets as Editors Study Their Readers. By knowing the markets, the writer knows the readers. It behooves the professional to study periodicals constantly, watching for changes in editorial policies, since magazines are always changing their appeals in order to be up to date, to get new subscribers, and to hold those they have. The editor, through his surveys, studies the readers and their interests and tries to develop a "book," as magazines are termed, which will continue to hold that interest. At best the magazine reader is a fickle person. Each publication has many competitors, any one of which may lure the subscriber to cancel his subscription and subscribe to another periodical.

Editors find that first of all each reader is interested in the utterly fascinating subject of himself. Subscribers like the so-called art-of-living, self-help, or uplift type of articles above all others. Health—either directly or indirectly—is fourth in interest, as many reader surveys show. The many articles appearing in autumn issues about the common cold are evidence of the health interest. Other ailments make just as popular reading. Personality sketches are fifth in demand in many publications, because again the reader sees himself or measures himself, as it were. Although the past world wars have broadened the reader's interest immeasurably, articles concerned with science, government, and world problems of the day rate only sixth in appeal in general magazines. It is true the reader does have a better comprehension of how an event in China or Russia or elsewhere may affect his health, his happiness, or his income, but editors regret that the average subscriber still finds too little interest in such subjects. However, interest everywhere is greater in social progress, as is the interest in articles concerning welfare, which rates seventh in many general periodicals. The ratings in class publications, of course, do not fall in the above order.

Reader-Interest Surveys Aid Writer. General magazines with mass circulation are read less thoroughly than are the specialized publications for specialized readers, as shown by reader-interest surveys. These reveal that older people read much more than younger people. Readers who are annual subscibers read less of the same periodical than do the newsstand buyers; however, the yearly subscriber is more interested in the factual content while the purchaser of the single copy is more interested in the entertainment appeals.

Surveying Markets Becomes a Habit. Although professionals continually add to their market research files, because magazines are constantly changing, it soon becomes a pleasant and profitable habit, if not a hobby.

Just as something is difficult in every profession, one finds writing is not easy work. But it is a fascinating career if one likes it, because writers stay alive and alert and, unless mentally ill, are never too old to continue their writing. Their creative work may not be classed as art, but it is high craftsmanship.

The continuous and careful market survey makes possible a successful writing career with an income in proportion to the business judgment applied to the work of the survey, the research, and the writing. As in other professions, the specialist makes his rewards what he will: just so with the writer.

Need Is Great for Expert Writers. Editors of magazines agree that they have difficulty getting a sufficient amount of quality material.

A well-known editor said he was unable to name twenty-five writers who sell regularly to the high-pay markets. This shows that the writing field is not crowded at the top. If asked the reason for this scarcity, any editor would reply that too few writers survey markets from a practical point of view and too few of them spend time on exhaustive investigations of differences among magazines.

These same editors point out that the writers who are surveyors of markets and researchers of material as much as they are writers, and who approach their writing from a practical and businesslike point of view, know what to sell and where to sell it. This they learn from their research and their market surveys. When writers know what to sell and where to sell it, their by-lines are seen on pages of many periodicals each month.

The things that irritate editors are the lack of thoroughness of writers in getting facts, or the failure to cover the material completely, or the neglect of slanting, because each publication tries to have a different purpose or a different appeal. As one editor said: "Too many writers would rather buy postage stamps and shoot without aiming than to make a detailed market study and know what the editor wants before starting research for material or writing the article."

When journalism students in advanced magazine writing classes go forth trained to make market surveys and to do research, or when writers working alone at home will train themselves to do research as suggested in these chapters, editors will not complain of the lack of qualified contributors or staff workers.

Professionals Use Blank Forms for Market Research. Surveys of markets which writers compile from their businesslike research are as important to them, or more so, than their files of research notes for the articles they write. Market information can be of service to the free-lance for many articles. This is particularly true if a professional is a specialist in some one of the many fields of writing.

He devises a form which he can fill in easily and rapidly, whether he is a student in a course or a professional, and has it duplicated several hundred times by mimeograph, or has it printed, on typewriting-size paper in order to fit his files conveniently. One should not have too many copies of the form made at first, for each person has his own system of surveying and may wish to add more items. The pages can be stapled together with a little staple machine obtained at a ten-cent store or stationery shop, leaving the blank sides for additional notations, which should include the source and the date of the new information.

Such a plan enables a contributor to record his market survey information permanently, to keep it up to date easily without having to transcribe the figures and conclusions, and always to have the surveys in his files, where they may be checked in a moment without wasting time, for in a free-lance career, as in any other, time is money. The system permits filing alphabetically, by subject, by type of publication, or in any other way the surveyor desires.

A typical and suggestive survey form for the use of student or professional contributors will be found at the end of this chapter.

Exercises

1. List five fields in which you think you would like to specialize this semester and in which you think there will be sufficient reader interest six to nine months from now, or at the time the articles will probably appear in print.

2. After investigating the opportunities in the five fields, which one did you select to write in? Why?

3. Make a list of from 10 to 25 possible markets for your selected field.

4. Indicate, by writing "WM" after the periodicals on your list, which were suggested to you by your survey of the most recent *Writer's Market* book.

5. Indicate, by writing "A" after the periodicals listed, which were sug-

gested to you by the survey of the most recent N. W. Ayer & Son's *Directory of Newspapers and Periodicals.*

6. Indicate, by writing "EP" after the periodicals listed, which were suggested by the survey of the most recent *Editor & Publisher International Year Book.*

7. Indicate, by writing "SRD" after the periodicals listed, which were suggested by the survey of the Standard Rate and Data service.

8. List, by writing "S" after their names, the publications which you could not find in the periodical room of your library, city library, or local firms, but to whose circulation departments you are writing for sample copies.

9. List periodicals and the names of the firms permitting you to examine their specialized or technical publications to which they subscribe, but which you could not obtain in the library or at the newsstand.

10. What periodicals did you find in second hand or "back-number" magazine shops in your city that might be possible markets for your specialized field? Suggest other sources of obtaining back numbers.

11. What suggestions can you add to those given in this chapter for the Magazine Market Survey at the end of these exercises?

12. List the circulation for each of the magazines which you listed in Exercise 3 and indicate the source by writing the letter abbreviation for the source—for example, "A" for Ayer & Son's.

13. From Standard Rate and Data service, list the page advertising rate for each of the publications which you have selected, as in Exercise 3.

14. List the subscription prices, yearly and single issue, for each periodical you listed.

15. After examining the feature articles and the advertising in the last three issues of each periodical on your list, which ten do you think offer the best market for articles concerning your selected field?

16. List from Standard Rate and Data service any unusual advertising or editorial policies which will aid in slanting your articles.

17. After examination of the periodicals, list any information concerning use of pictures, drawings, charts, or graphs.

18. Indicate to which age group each of the ten publications will appeal.

19. Indicate whether reader-appeal of each is to masses, classes, specialized, business, technical, or scientific groups?

20. For each publication, list the ones with well-known by-lines.

21. What do you think will be your opportunities in competing with the "big-name" by-lines? Why?

Research Report No. 3, due third week of second semester.

MAGAZINE MARKET SURVEY

Student: _____ *Key to Source of Information:*
(to be indicated after each item)

Course: _____ A: *Ayer's Directory*

Date Survey Made: _____ EP: *Ed. & Pub. Year Book*
SRD: *Standard Rate & Data*

Time Spent: _____ WM: *Writer's Market*

Instructor: _____ M: Magazine examined
WP: Writer's Periodicals

Name of Publication: _____ Dates of Three

Issues examined: _____

_____

_____

Published: weekly_____bi-weekly_____monthly_____Date established:_____

Size of page: inches _____ number of pages _____

Circulation: annual_____ single copies _____

Subscription price: yearly $_____ single copy _____ cents.

Territorial distribution of circ.: _____

_____

Estimated income from subscription: $_____ (circ. times rate)

Conclusion as to reader interest: _____

(judged by circulation)   _____

Advertising: rate by page $_____ back page $_____

No. of pp. devoted to advertising: _____

Estimated income from advertising: $_____ (pp. times adv. rate)

_____

_____

Unusual Adv. Copy Requirements: _____

_____

_____

Unusual Contract Requirements: _____

_____

_____

Conclusion as to Type of Reader, Judged by Adv.: _____

Conclusion as to Possible Rate of Pay, Judged from Adv.: $_____

Editorial Address: Ed. or Feature Ed. _____

Editorial office _____

City _____
zone   state

Rate of Pay by Word for Article (WM or WP): _____

Comparison of Rate of Pay for Art. with Adv. and Circ.: Excellent _____

Good _____

Poor _____

Editorial Content: (by exam. of mag., SRD, and WM)

No. of fact articles: _____

No. of fiction pieces: _____

Kinds of departments: _____

No. of poems: _____

Subject matter of editorials: _____

_____

_____

Feature Articles:

(in estimated No. of words)

Length, short _____ medium _____ long _____

Style: 1st person _____ 2nd person _____ 3rd person _____

Uses interviewee as authority _____ Does not use _____

Vocab. Appeal: simple words _____ long words _____

Differences of Style: _____

_____

By-lines: Known _____ Unknown _____

No. of Each Type: *Subject Matter*

Interview _____   _____

Utility _____   _____

Experience _____   _____

Confession _____   _____

Personality _____   _____

Narrative _____   _____

Specialized _____   _____

Business _____   _____

Technical _____   _____

Scientific _____   _____

Purpose of Publication: _____

Reader Appeal: children _____ youth _____ young _____ older_____

Class of Reader Appeal (judged by name-brand products advertised):

mass ____ middle class ____ class ____ spec. ____ tech. ____ sci.____

Rate of pay: WM _____ WP _____ Estimate from Adv. & Circ. _____

When payment is made (WM): upon acceptance _____ upon publication _____

Suggestions for Slanting: _____

_____

_____

Illustrations:	Average No. per Art.	Size	Rate of Payment
Transparencies	_____	_____	_____
Photographs in color	_____	_____	_____
Photos in black & white	_____	_____	_____
Color pictures	_____	_____	_____
Photostats	_____	_____	_____
Drawings	_____	_____	_____
Charts	_____	_____	_____
Diagrams	_____	_____	_____
Graphs	_____	_____	_____
Blueprints	_____	_____	_____

Size-up as General Market: _____

Size-up as Market for My Specialized Subject of _____:

_____

_____

Additional Future Notations to Aid in Slanting (always include source and date):

_____

_____

_____

_____

_____

_____

(Continue notations on back of page if necessary.)

CHAPTER 20

Writing in Specialized Fields

▗▖

Contributors and Staff Workers Specialize. Even a cursory survey of current magazines shows that nonfiction writers have changed American reading tastes from fiction to fact articles. Astute editors and keen business managers now emphasize facts in their periodicals, rather than fiction, to attract readers and advertisers. Schools of Journalism are just beginning to follow the trend, although a few have had advanced magazine courses since 1935.

Writers who receive checks in large figures usually are regular contributors or staff workers on top-pay periodicals who have found, as did the lawyer and the physician, they could increase their income if they trained themselves, or were trained in Journalism schools, to specialize in one or more writing fields. Of course, these specialists do write articles in other than their own fields—for variety—but those who pay big income taxes specialize in one or more subjects. A well-known contributor writing in the field of medicine has recently turned, after haunting libraries instead of hospitals, to writing articles on architecture, farming, and mining. He has established so many contacts and knows his sources and markets so well that he is assured a regular income from his medical writing. Through investments he became interested in writing in the other fields, which he terms his "side lines."

The magazine writer is much like a newspaper reporter, in that he should be able to write in many fields. Or, if he is on the staff of a class or special publication, he should be able to write on many phases of a subject. The staff beginner, or "trainee," should be versatile, but if he trains himself to be an expert in the field, or fields, in which the publication is interested, he is just that much more valuable to the editor. Unless one has an independent income or has attained success and become regularly established as a contributor to one or more publications, he should not resign from a position to specialize, because writers have to pay the grocer, too. If one makes his living at something else and contributes as a "side line," he probably can find marketable material in his own profession or business which will save hours of research and interviewing.

Qualifications for Specializing. The specialist has advantages over the amateur, or even over the general contributor, because he has been trained, or trains himself, to become a thorough researcher, a global postal interviewer, and an expert in writing on particular subjects. These skills enable the specialist to narrow down his competition greatly, because too few are willing to train themselves and only a very few schools have included such training in their curricula.

The willingness to attain: (1) all available knowledge by accurate library research; (2) skill to interview by letter, which is more difficult to do successfully than the face-to-face type; (3) thorough market information by surveying periodicals; (4) ability to follow clues as would a detective; (5) facility in writing with initiative, resourcefulness, and enthusiasm; (6) dexterity and courage to be a leader in presenting new ideas rather than a follower; and (7) his own specialized library, as well as to know thoroughly the near-by public ones, will enable the contributor or staff worker to move ahead rapidly and successfully.

Demand for Specialized Articles Is Increasing. With the great growth in the number of periodicals during recent years, the increased reader popularity for the factual article, and a better-educated and more intelligent reading public to read magazines, editors are finding it difficult to obtain sufficient well-written contributions. It is true that many not-too-successful fiction writers and poets have given up their struggles and have turned to writing features, and this has increased free-lance competition. But persons trained, or self-trained, in the technique can avoid competition by specializing, and editors, trying to supply excellent articles to their readers, will welcome the manuscripts of these experts.

Turning to the tables, "Opportunities to Sell," listed in the Appendix, one will find, if he subtracts the number of general magazines and newspapers with their total annual issues from the total opportunities to sell articles, that the specialist has 93,148 annual issues of 7,587 magazines to which he may submit manuscripts and which are in the market for superior or even good articles. This number is actually greater, because even the general magazines and the newspapers will use some specialized articles. Examining the market sources as suggested in Chapter 19 will provide abundant markets for thorough and expertly written articles.

The Specialist Is His Own Literary Agent. The experienced writer certainly does not need the services of an agent, because in order to slant accurately he knows markets from the detailed surveys which he makes before beginning to write. As pointed out in Part I, agents do not wish clients whose names are not well known. The majority of them charge a reading fee, unless the writer comes highly recommended or has been successful in selling. If an agent places an article for a specialist, his fee will be at least ten per cent of the author's gross receipt.

If a writer, after he has made a name, consults an agent, he should investigate the agent's reliability and dependability from some fellow writer who knows the agent from experience. The successful, experienced agent does not need to advertise nor to run correspondence schools. It is true that agents just beginning do have to advertise, but writers must use caution before signing contracts.

Techniques Vary with Fields and Markets. Even though one specializes, he does not do so in the narrow sense, but rather to gain competence in the field of his choice. Through research, as suggested in Chapter 18, he reads everything available on the subject. He ascertains who the leaders in the fields are and he knows personally as many as possible either in person or through correspondence. As his knowledge of his specialty increases, so does his enthusiasm.

The experienced contributor knows much more about the topic he writes upon than he includes in his articles—which is one reason the specialist's manuscripts are in demand by editors seeking thorough and accurate articles. As soon as they can afford to do so, some writers employ trained research workers who enable them to produce more articles and to become greater experts in their fields. The specialist, who applies the chapters on research and market surveys, is regarded as a magician by the amateur when he learns that the expert's output may be from five to ten articles a month and his profits, after paying his research staff, from one to three or more thousand dollars a month. Even though top-name specialists have research staffs, they continue doing some research, because from it they receive ideas for more articles and also see opportunities for new fields of specialization.

As one gains writing skill, he will be more businesslike in his methods. He will keep a "future book," much as does a city editor, by jotting down "tips" or ideas on 5 x 7 or even larger cards, or on sheets of paper. There will be room for notations suggesting sources, ideas from market surveys, addresses of markets to query, and ideas for interviewees and pictures.

If a favorable reply comes from a query, the specialist will jot down the date that the research for the article should be started and the date that the completed manuscript should be mailed. He will then file the answers to the queries in the proper folder as previously explained in Chapter 17. Because most individuals are inclined to procrastinate, the "tip" cards aid the professional to produce manuscripts steadily for editors who he knows are at least interested. The cards may be sorted in chronological order by the "start-work" dates. A well-known specialist, who averages ten or more articles a month, has all of the qualities of the good business executive. This specialist usually has many projects which he keeps in mind because his work methods are well organized. He has easy access to his plans, which are in his files and which enable him to see that each article is progressing as previously scheduled.

To give the article solidity and authority desired by editors, the specialist plans personal or "postal" interviews. He uses a different technique in interviewing by mail than when he is sitting across from the interviewee.

In the postal interview, the writer must phrase his questions to arouse the interviewee's interest so that his answers will be enthusiastic. But the questions must also be planned to provide sufficient material for generous quotations. If the experienced writer explains in his letter of request that he is a professional writer, names magazines in which his articles have appeared, tells why he wants the desired information, gives the name of the publication which he has successfully queried and for which he plans to write, and suggests that the "postal interviewee's" information will help, guide, inform, or entertain the readers, since the interviewee is an outstanding authority whose name will carry real influence, the latter not only will feel grateful to have the opportunity to be of help to the writer but will be pleased that he was selected.

The flattery must be subtle and the entire tone tactful and appreciative to secure the desired information, because authorities are busy people whose time is valuable.

To know and read all the periodicals concerned with the particular field will acquaint the specialist with an over-all picture of the problems as well as the opportunity to increase his list of "tips" for articles. The professional subscribes to as many of the specialized publications as he can. Some even take two subscriptions to each periodical, in order to cut and file, regardless of what is on the back of each clipping. In one issue he cuts the even-numbered pages and in the other, the odd-numbered. If one is not interested in reading the publications in one field regularly, then he is not interested in writing in that field and should select another.

As a writer continues to specialize, he will develop his filing system, which will include his research notes, clippings, bulletins, notes which he takes from his own observations, and notes from interviews. Thoroughness is the specialist's chief asset.

While working at one's research, a writer will save time if he begins listing technical words and phrases on cards, later to be alphabetized. Not only will he familiarize himself with the phraseology, but he will acquaint himself with the distinct shades of meaning of technical words in order to write with an accurate terminology. The vocabulary cards may be kept by the typewriter for reference. Writers, however, may become so much the experts that they forget to explain technical terms to their readers, who may not be as expert. The professional checks his material to see that it is not a "rehash" of his research. If the material is extremely technical, he checks it with an authority. He stresses, not only the important, but the significant.

Specialized Fields Are Unlimited. As mentioned earlier, market surveys show that articles are more factual, shorter, more numerous, and have more illustrations than a year ago. Analyses of classes of publications indicate that they have increased manyfold during the last decade. These factors increase the opportunities for the writer who wishes to specialize. The atomic era seems to be the "golden" if not the "platinum" age for the research writer who specializes, because there are as many fields as there are periodicals.

The specialist may write on making a living, being happy, being wealthy, being healthy, or being wise. He may specialize without stirring out of his home, if he is ingenious. He may travel, making the articles he writes about the trips not only pay for them, but produce an income above the expenses, after he has become well-known.

But whatever field is selected, the specialist, to be successful, must exhaust every source, cover every angle, and then write sincerely, accurately, and enthusiastically for the queried market.

Professional Avoids Poor-Paying Fields. Since the modern specialist writes for security as well as pleasure, he checks his market surveys, market books, and writer's periodicals to avoid writing on subjects that are limited in reader appeal and for markets which do not have sufficient circulation and advertising to enable them to pay well for articles. While all the world "loves a humorist," when that humor is in cold print, it must be clever indeed to hold the reader's interest. Almost every beginner thinks he was born to be a writer of humor, because flattering friends overcredit his ability. Humor, like genius, is nine-tenths hard work, even when one has real aptitude for it.

Sectional periodicals and some of the quarterlies will use material which may be easy for the expert to obtain. But because of the magazines' limited sectional or class circulation, which in turn limit their advertising incomes, the specialist will do well to leave those poorer paying manuscript markets to the amateur and the general writer.

Specialized Fields Offer Great Variety. A writer desiring to specialize in particular fields has a great variety of choice and a good future financially. The educational field, which is seldom considered along with the professions, businesses, trades, and associations, although it might well be for it has many similar problems, is always a good field, because of its universal appeal. Its subject matter includes the preschool through university and adult school administration. In this, as well as in other fields, the writer may be able to arrange for a series of articles when he queries.

The current popularity of regional articles offers an opportunity to point out the essential differences—economic, social, climatic, topographical, and historical—and their environmental influence on the people. Newspaper files, diaries, letters, regional histories, and books provide rich sources for research. As with any field, one should survey possible markets carefully before selecting regional feature writing, because too often the payment is small unless the writing is for periodicals with national rather than sectional appeal.

The 683 religious periodicals with their 8,196 annual issues offer a great variety of fields. The religious press, like the agricultural press, serves the family, widens the reader appeal, and creates a larger demand for all types of articles. One creed has so many periodicals that there is a market book devoted to its publications. Some of the church magazines pay but little; others pay well; but all of them buy a great quantity of articles and a writer will soon recognize which ones can afford better remuneration. Some of them pay as well as the general class magazines. General magazines use religious articles, too. Some church writers have become nationally known syndicate writers.

The historical article has enjoyed a revival of reader interest. One specialist combined history and religion and sold a series of articles on historical characters—presidents and generals—to two general class magazines. She is now writing a series on famous historical women.

Self-interest is another profitable field, because readers are first of all interested in themselves. Special magazines and general ones provide liberal paying markets for the endless list of subjects that one may write to appeal to "yourself"—your reader.

Appealing to those with wanderlust are the travel magazines. The library, travel information booklets from travel agencies, and some travel experience will provide unlimited material. The successful writer, recognizing their many-sided appeals, uses the descriptive powers and the narrative style of the fiction writer to give an enthusiastic tone to travel articles. He keeps his ear to the news in order to know where travel interest will lie six months or a year hence. If a spot is much in the news now, the specialist avoids writing of that locality, because six months later it may not hold the interest of either the armchair or the suitcase traveler. Motor car manufacturers publish travel magazines. They pay exceptionally well for short articles illustrated with many kodachrome as well as black and white "glossies."

An ever popular field is that of the home, with all of its various interests. The household, its management, equipment, decoration, textiles, design, needlecraft, foods, nutrition, health, family welfare, child management, personality adjustment, gardening, and housing, are phases all in great demand by editors if the articles are thorough and well written. An agile mind and a keen eye will see the unique and the new.

Ideas, information from research, interviews, and illustrations enabled a student majoring in magazine writing to sell 14 articles, for which she was paid from $50 to $150 a piece. She was not a home economics major, but a journalism major. A young woman specialized in the same field after she married and resigned her job, because her income from writing was more than $5,000 a year, although she didn't even have the services of a housemaid. She found that in addition to long articles, short articles on household helps and gadgets sometimes brought in an extra $100 per month. Checks from the latter came from home, farm, and mechanics' periodicals.

Since young people have become a force in modern life and have their own periodicals, the specialist finds several fields appealing to the readers of these new magazines which hold their interest. Library research and careful analysis of the style of the youth magazines will enable even a very mature writer to produce articles that will appeal to this newer reading group. One writer enlarged her field of teen-age articles to include a syndicated column which is used by more than 50 newspapers. Because of her writing she is a well-known lecturer and advisor on teen-age subjects.

Editors found during World War II that men needed their own periodicals, and a number of good ones changed their content to appeal to men exclusively. Others were started to catch masculine attention. Most of them have continued and prospered because the ex-G.I. continues to read them. As with the youth magazines, the writer for men's publications must analyze the style as well as masculine interests before he slants his material.

Fraternal publications offer a good opportunity for the specialist. One publishing house, at Mount Morris, Illinois, alone publishes more than 100 periodicals mailing out more than 150,-000 copies a day, so that a nonstaff writer can see unlimited opportunities in that field, with its 146 magazines which buy unsolicited manuscripts for their 1,752 monthly issues.

Although nature, outdoor, hunting, fishing, and sport magazines are numerous, their editors have difficulty in finding the kind of thorough, well-written, scientifically accurate, and interesting articles they would like to buy. These fields are fascinating and are well paid. A student "specialist" in the outdoor field received $450.00 for an article accepted by *Sports Afield*. A good writer and nature lover or sports enthusiast can ferret out data from a library and from federal and state government bulletins successfully only if he knows his subject. But then, that holds true for any specialized field. The number of really good nature and sports writers is appallingly small.

One could go on enumerating fields indefinitely. But since a writer's best specialties should be those in which he is most interested, if these fields are lucrative and if there is opportunity to get material, he will have no difficulty in finding fields in which to specialize, because they are endless.

Factors to Consider in Selecting a Field. From the thousands of fields suggested in the market books and directories enumerated in Chapters 18 and 19, a professional writer will select one, or several in which, not only is he interested, but in which, from his research and market knowledge, he is confident there is and will continue to be a lasting reader interest.

The magazine student, or "trainee," regardless of whether he plans to become a contributor or a staff writer, in selecting a field for his course in journalism school or working alone at home, will save time and energy if he gives himself the following test:

1. For my writing, what subjects interest me most?
2. Why does each of these subjects interest me?
3. Will each one interest others who read magazines?
4. Why will each of my choices interest readers?
5. Are these subjects timely now?

6. Will they be timely six to twelve, or even twenty-four, months from now?

7. From the above survey, which subject appears to be best for my specialization?

8. Am I sufficiently interested in the subject to continue to be enthusiastic about it?

9. Is there sufficient material available in this community?

10. Judging from the card catalogue in the library, will I be able to obtain sufficient research material?

11. What are the other sources from which I may obtain material, either in person or by mail?

12. Whom can I interview as authorities?

13. Whom may I interview by letter, if necessary?

14. What class of publications will "my" readers read?

15. In what age group will these readers be?

16. Which sex will be most interested in the field?

17. Will the field be of more interest to readers of one religion than another?

18. What periodicals, listed in some one of the guides to periodical literature, have had articles on the subject, and with which phase was each article concerned?

19. What new angles or phases will be most profitable for my articles?

20. Where can I obtain pictures for the field?

21. What suggestions do I have for taking pictures for the field?

22. What other illustrations suggest themselves to me?

23. What are the best possible markets for this field?

If the specialist-to-be answers the test to his satisfaction, he should work out a tentative analysis for each of the fields under consideration until he finds one that appears to be adequate in every respect. He then is ready to work out a permanent and more detailed analysis of his selected field. If he finds the subject is too broad, he may narrow it, as did a beginner in advanced magazine writing who selected the subject of rheumatic fever. As her survey for the field progressed, she found it advisable to limit the subject to the symptoms and care of the child with rheumatic fever.

Recent reader-interest surveys, conducted by magazines or advertising agencies, may reveal information for the specialist.

They are limited in number, but when the results are announced, one will find them "digested" in the writer's periodicals.

After the field is selected, if the specialist "trainee," either in the magazine class or in his study alone, will apply the suggestions in these chapters and complete the Research Reports at the end of the chapters, he should be able, as a beginning specialist, to contribute successfully, or to find a magazine staff position.

Specialist Uses Many Illustrations. Ferrotype prints or "glossy prints" and kodachromes or "transparencies" have just as much to do with selling the specialist's articles as with selling those of the amateur. In fact, the editor of a periodical using pictures would doubt that the writer were experienced if his articles did not have numerous "glossies," transparencies, drawings, charts, graphs, or tables to illustrate the article—whichever type the magazine uses.

Time spent on this phase of the magazine survey will assure the writer of the type of illustrations desired. If one is in doubt, he may ask for photographic instructions when he queries an editor concerning an article. Editors want pictures with only one center of interest. People in the pictures should be doing something related to the article. In planning a Research Report on Illustrations one should review Chapter 15. He also will find unlimited guidance in books on photography, drawing, charts, and graphs, as listed in the "Free-Lance Writer's Library." Even though the writer is not skilled, his work can be polished up or done by the staff artists if the idea is presented clearly.

Rewards of Specialization. The magazine specialist—contributor or staff writer—does not live a narrow or monotonous life. One's specialty may require presenting two sides, or six, or eight, of a subject. It may take one to widely divergent places, as it did the writer whose article, "The Vanishing Professor," appeared in a recent class magazine. This writer visited the universities to gather his material, as well as doing research in the library.

The research writer may be led into other phases of writing. One woman who specialized in three fields—careers, foods, and fashions—became a magazine department editor of foods on a class publication; directed a fashion television program on fashions in her own community; and wrote a book on choosing one's career. She now is much in demand as a public lecturer on these and related subjects. She says the latter activity necessitates keeping up to date, which in turn provides her with more ideas for articles, TV programs, and nonfiction books. One agrees that the specialist's opportunities are not limited; but like the magician, he, or she, seems to be able to do anything.

Specialists not only enliven their own lives by meeting interesting, successful, happy people but enrich the lives of others by guiding, informing, or entertaining through their sepcialized articles. Getting one's name known among editors who hire writers or buy articles will insure security; may bring requests for articles which generally are paid for at higher rates than queried ones; or may be the means of one's becoming an associate editor. After the specialist becomes established and knows editors prefer his articles, he may suggest that he no longer can accept the "usual rate," if the "usual rate" is not to his satisfaction. One specialist found that a similar suggestion resulted in a cent increase per word which provided an annual total increase of more than $300 from one periodical.

The monetary reward cannot be ignored. If a trained or self-trained specialist gives the same energy, intelligence, thought, and skill to his work as does the successful physician or lawyer, his income will be comparable. The difference between a $100 article and a $1,000 one is exactly a matter of how much research has been done and how much market knowledge has been acquired. In other words, it is a matter of how much the writer really knows and writes about his subject. His income may be from $5,000 to $25,000, or, if he reaches the top, it may be $50,000, or even a $100,000.

"The two engaging powers of a writer are to make new things familiar and familiar things new," wrote a man of letters years ago. He must have been envisioning the specialist contributor or the magazine staff writer of the present day.

Examples of Specialized Articles. The first two of the following articles, written by a well-known authority in her field were selected from the Seattle *Times* and the St. Louis *Globe-Democrat*, two of the many daily newspapers carrying the writer's syndicated column. They were selected to show how one may widen a specialized field to include syndicated articles in addition to magazine articles. The third article, from *Fur-Fish-Game* and illustrated with two pictures, was selected from outdoor articles in which the author specialized. He succeeded in his chosen specialty because he was successful in making the reader recall his own hunting experiences and in giving him interesting information. The fourth article from *Motor News* and the fifth one from *Outdoor Life* could be classified as other types, but they were selected for this chapter because both writers specialize in this phase of outdoor and adventure experience. The fourth article had several excellent pictures and the fifth article had one map and nine pictures. The fifth author, whose other hobby in addition to writing is photography, has several cameras. Each hobby aids the other in getting articles printed in well-known outdoor magazines.

(1)
Teen Etiquette:
Tips Given for Better
Relations with Father*

*Common interests encourage closer relations between a father
and his children. Henry Haggard, 846 E. 83rd St., helped
his son, Gary, with his golf game. Gary is a pupil at
the Cornish School of Allied Arts.*

BY KITTE TURMELL

How can you get closer to your Dad?

That's what quite a few teen-agers ask or wonder. It's elementary, family counselors say, if you view it this way: He's your Dad; he's the one of his kind for you. Enjoy him, accept him for all he is and wants to be.

* Reprinted by permission of the Seattle *Times*, *Teen Etiquette* syndicate, and Kitte Turmell.

Here are some pointers on how to have better relations with this important man around the house:

Introduce him to your friends as "Dad" or "My Father." To use the title, "Mr.," in introducing or speaking of your father to friends, even if he's a V.I.P., is not correct. But it is respectful to address him, or any older man, as, "Sir."

Bring him into the conversation by starting to talk about things he likes to discuss.

Avoid troublemaking topics at meals or when he comes home weary.

*   *   *

You can't wave a wand and say: "Presto, chango! Perfect father, model son, ideal family." Dr. C. Wilson, a family expert, says:

"It takes time to bridge the gap between the adult male and the boy who never has felt close to his father.

"You can't force it by insisting that Dad gallop off with his son to a picnic or ball game. It seems to me that the tender deep-rooted feelings between father and son come with the slow growth of better understandings.

"For a good beginning, it is well to find things you like to do together, or want to talk over. To share ideas and experiences helps them to know each other."

(2)
Teen Etiquette:
Proof That You Are Growing Up*

To prove you are "growing up," ready for more teen-freedom, you can do things around home every day in a more mature way as does Gail Carson, 7668 Lindbergh Dr., who shares household tasks with mother cheerfully.

By Kitte Turmell

"How can I get my mom to quit treating me like a little kid?" Johnny asks. "When can you convince parents that you are old enough to drive a car, date or go steady?" teen-agers want to know. "Why can't grown-ups see that you are growing up?"

* Reprinted by permission of the St. Louis *Globe-Democrat, Teen Etiquette* syndicate, and Kitte Turmell.

"Why don't you act your age, skip the kid tricks, to prove you can be trusted with more freedom?" some parents snap back. That's the bugleblare for many a family battle.

Let's roll up the sleeves, to wrestle with this age-old problem.

What if you want to find ways to prove you are not a "child," so parents will begin to treat you like a young adult, after mid-teens?

Here are some suggestions from Dr. Norman Q. Brill, noted psychiatrist and medical educator at the University of California at Los Angeles.

*   *   *

"Think of growing up as something that should be a gradual thing," says Dr. Brill.

To rush growing up is "kid stuff." "What's so rough about being a teen-ager, living at home, going to school, having fun with friends?" adults wonder. "You'll never be so free from responsibility! The seven years from 13 to 20 are short. Enjoy the advantages of your age, from birthday to birthday. Wait until you're ready to date, drive a car, be on your own in due time."

(3)
Twenty-Five Dollar Pheasant*

Your Wife May Tell You Hunting Is Expensive: But—
Does She Really Know Why?

By Don Huibregtse

Remember the last time you had a brace of cock pheasants for your Sunday dinner? How much did the main course of that meal cost you? Not much, you say. All right, so you shot the birds on opening day last year and they cost you almost nothing—excepting the initial outlay for hunting equipment.

Then you probably won't believe that those birds actually cost you, as a taxpayer, about $50. But it's true: they cost about $25 each. Conservation departments all across the country have plenty of sound proof to show that it's true.

Here's the situation. If those birds you shot wore a leg band put on by your state game department, and the chances are good that they did, then it actually cost about $25 to put each one in front of your

* Reprinted by permission of *Fur-Fish-Game Harding's Magazine* and Don Huibregtse.

gun. That band means that the birds were raised artificially; and incidentally your game department would like you to tell them the details of where and when you shot them.

* * *

Your state conservation department knows how to increase the pheasant populations to provide better hunting for you. However, its hands are tied as long as the hunter groups and the farmer groups are not willing to cooperate.

Next time you shoot a cock with a band on its leg remember to stop and consider how much that bird actually cost. Twenty-five dollars is a conservative estimate. Think what that same twenty-five dollars could do if it were used to improve the pheasant's habitat so the native stock would be able to carry its share of the load.

Twenty-five dollar pheasants are downright wasteful. Let's stop that waste by getting behind our conservation officials and help them to improve pheasant habitat. That's the best answer to our nation-wide pheasant problem.

(4)
Vacation
in a
Volcano*

*Move into the shrouded past 70 million years
and watch as Mount Mazama
blows her top.*

By Charles E. Edwards

IMAGINE yourself seventy million years in the past. The earth is rumbling and lacy fingers of gray smoke and vapor writhe from the gaping "wounds" in the crust of the newly-formed Cascade Mountain range in southwestern Oregon.

Periodically, shiny tendrils of molten lava spill over the brims of the coneshaped mountains and etch paths down the sides of the graceful, yet violent, volcanoes.

Before you, rising in majestic splendor, is Mount Mazama, one of a band of "fire mountains" that blaze their beacons along the Pacific shore.

* Reprinted by permission of *Motor News* and Charles E. Edwards.

Suddenly, without warning, the entire sky seems to ignite, and you stand spellbound as the mighty mountain, Mazama, explodes before your eyes.

Streams of lava shoot out from the sides of the volcano and spread glassily toward the foothills. The anguished rumbling has grown to a roar and the sky is dark with smoke and acrid fumes.

Peering through the smoky haze, you search for the slender spire of the volcano; but, where only a few seconds before you saw the peak stretched longingly toward the sky, there is nothing. The top of Mazama has disappeared, leaving behind jagged lava edges silhouetted against the crimson sky.

Dr. R. L. Laudon, professor of geology at the University of Wisconsin, says: "It has been estimated that about 17 cubic miles of the upper part of the mountain was destroyed by the explosion. The top of the mountain fell in on itself."

*   *   *

Since then, Deep Blue Lake has come into its own. Its name was changed to Crater Lake in 1869, and, in 1902, Judge William Gladstone Steel realized his hopes of seeing the lake preserved for all to enjoy. Crater Lake was established as a National park. The results of that momentous explosion seventy million years ago were made available to all who searched for rest, recreation and beauty.

Thousands of visitors from New York, the Middle West and the Deep South now include Crater Lake as a "must" vacation spot.

They've fallen in love with the majestic beauty of this calm, mysterious lake with the chameleon-like colors. They're charmed by Wizard Island, a small volcanic cone that has grown out of the lake near the west shore. They're intrigued by the Phantom Ship, a ship-shaped island that rises 169 feet above the waters of the lake. They're awed by the massive beauty of Llao Rock, an immense lava cliff, upon which, an Indian legend says, an ancient god lost his life.

But there's more to Crater Lake than its unbelievable natural beauty.

With anglers in mind, the National Park Service of the Department of the Interior has stocked the lake with fish. Rowboats are available to the visitor and no fishing license is needed for you to match wits with the rainbow trout and silverside salmon.

Four free public campgrounds have been set aside within the park for those who want to "rough it." Ghosts of the past are conjured before the campfire in the evenings. You'll be entranced as you hear the legend of Llao Rock.

This Klamath Indian legend tells of Llao, an ancient Indian god who ruled over the mountain range and kept giant crawfish in Crater Lake. You'll feel a thrill of excitement when the account of Llao's death is told—the tale of how Llao was captured by a rival god while walking atop the impressive lava cliff (Llao Rock)—of the battle that followed and how Llao's body was dismembered and thrown to the giant crabs.

Wizard Island, the legend says, is actually Llao's head, which the crawfish recognized and refused to eat.

The park remains open the year 'round so visitors may enjoy the scenic beauty and participate in winter sports amid a fantasy of snowy splendor. The gentle slopes are excellent for skiing, and the lake retains much of its summer appearance. Because of the year-'round high temperature of the water, only skim ice forms around the lake's edge during winter months.

Paved state highways connect with the roads of the park at all of its entrances, which gives you a chance to enjoy the scenery of the National Forest, within which the park is located.

Crater Lake has become "Stop number one" for thousands of vacation-bound people throughout the nation. But this is understandable, for where else can you enjoy a vacation in a volcano?

(5)
Curse of the Witegoo*

BY ROB F. SANDERSON

This is the story of a fishing trip to northern Ontario where a demon Indian god guards a wilderness lake filled with mackerel-sized trout.

It all began in the summer of 1946 when Dr. John A. Tasche, my fishing and flying side-kick, intercepted an end-of-the-rainbow tale. Rumors whispered that a bush pilot and his prospector landed on this lake and, fishing from the pontoons with a hand line and bacon bait, tied into five-pound brookies by the bushel. The lake was called Sutton. After that one day's fishing, the pilot moved to British Columbia, and the prospector never came out of the bush. That's as far as the rumors went. We had a name but no lake. A close search of maps of the area showed no lake labeled Sutton. We began making

*Reprinted by permission of *Outdoor Life* and Rob F. Sanderson.

guarded inquiries of everyone we knew who was familiar with the territory.

Finally the fur-trade department of the Hudson's Bay Company located it. They said Sutton Lake is the source of the short Button River, which drains into Hudson Bay between Cape Henrietta Maria and Weenusk Post. We got a more detailed map of the territory, but it didn't help much. It showed a straight line for the river and a generalized ellipse for the lake. Vague hachures indicated a narrow range of uplands about the lake. For many miles south of these, the map was a vacuum of white sparsely veined with dotted lines for rivers. The whole set-up was potent stuff for our imaginations, as good trout waters are generally believed to end at the southern edge of the muskeg wastes.

"An entirely new trout country," John enthused. "Maybe hotter than the Nipigon of 1910. Maybe a new world record." Swearing each other to secrecy, we vowed to make the trip as soon as better maps would permit.

In March, a new chart, W.A.C. No. 181, was issued, but the word UNRELIABLE overlay vast empty spaces. It was two years later before a chart giving sufficient detail to warrant planning the trip became available. That winter we assembled a pared-down outfit that, when spring came, proved too heavy a load for John's Fairchild 24W monoplane.

*   *   *

We speeded across the lake to the Cree village, where the entire population stood around one group of tents. We were escorted immediately to the patient. After a short examination, John announced that the girl had died minutes before our arrival. We assembled in front of the tents for an informal inquest, interpreting through Johnny Yesno, the financial wizard of the Treaty Indians, who reputedly has amassed a fortune as an independent trader, trapper, fisherman, and general wheeler and dealer.

"Possibly a cerebral hemorrhage," John diagnosed. "Without an autopsy, it's impossible to be more definite."

"Witegoo—that's what Cree people say," said Johnny. He pronounced the word "Wit-ee-goo," drawing out the last syllable in a moody sigh.

"What's a witegoo?" I asked.

"Evil spirit," Al explained. "Maybe you've heard it called windigo, which is the Ojibway name. The Indians here-about have more evil spirits than you Americans have television sets."

"Bad spirits all around," Johnny said soberly. "Catch Indian any-time not careful—maybe white man, too."

We had a short, interesting visit with Johnny, and asked him about the lake we intended to visit. "Plenty trout," he told us. "But Bad country. No like men."

*   *   *

We were ready to say farewell to Sutton. But as the plane vaned into the wind prior to take-off, John loosed his seat belt, hopped out onto the float, and returned to the cockpit with a pocket cup filled with lake water. He held the cup high.

"To the witegoo," he cried, and, with the air of satisfying a long-contained repression, drained the contents at a gulp.

Our lightly loaded ship lifted quickly and hastened skyward. Off either wing tip lay the silent wilderness which might hoard the record trout of our hopes, but now this country was farther beyond reach than ever. We ruddered the nose to the course, climbed above the muskeg, and leveled off at 6,000 feet. John adjusted the mixture control to economize on fuel.

Mottled clouds moving southeast across the desolate wastes below warned us to expect no assistance from the wind. But the engine gauges read normal, we flew through the magnetically disturbed zone without confusion, and the flight proceeded under control. But we faced one big problem, and it stuck in my throat like a fishbone.

This was the essential transfer of fuel from the fuselage tank to the left wing tank. Fuselage fuel could not be fed directly into the engine, and tank-to-tank transfer was impossible while the receiving tank was feeding the engine. To transfer fuel by stopping somewhere along the way would be to risk a crackup on the notoriously treacher-ous waters of some shallow muskeg lake. Several gallons of our price-less gas would also be consumed in take-off and climb afterward. Finally I thought of a method which both of us hoped would do the trick.

When the left gauge read nearly empty I began pumping fuel from the fuselage to the empty—and leaky—right tank. As I did so I saw droplets of leaked gas gather on the trailing edge of the right wing and vanish into the slip stream. But just before the left tank went dry I switched the engine to the right tank and began pumping gas furi-ously into the left.

Either the transfer was too slow, or the leakage too great, but be-fore the fuselage tank pumped dry the right tank began sputtering. The starved engine coughed and spurted, and the ship lost altitude.

I pumped frantically as the altimeter unwound: 5,500, 5,000, 4,500. At 4,000 feet the pump sucked air and the transfer was complete. The engine cut in, smoothed, and we purred along thankfully at 4,000 feet until Eabamet Lake appeared in the distance.

The gas gauge still had a wiggle in it as we descended in a wide arc over the trim white buildings of Fort Hope, creased the blue water, and rode to shore on wings of spray. Al threw us a line and we made fast for refueling. As the left wing tank swallowed two twelve-gallon kegs with room to spare, Al remembered something.

"The old man who plays Ouija with the witegoo asked about you this morning," he said. "He told me not to expect you if your ship didn't fly in today."

I glanced at John, who was nursing the last drops from the gas hose. Silently I wondered what awful things might have happened had we stayed on at Sutton for additional fishing following John's defiant toast to the witegoo. Would we have discovered giant trout? Or would we have met our end, as the leathery old Indian predicted? Did my good-luck cap or our drinking the spring water have anything to do with our fate?

Further speculation will have to be done by someone else. John and I, more than ever, are strictly trout men. Record witegoos aren't in our line.

Exercises

1. Enumerate the advantages of specializing in one or more fields of writing.

2. List disadvantages of specializing.

3. In what ways are magazine staff writers similar to newspaper reporters?

4. List the advantages the specialist has over the general contributor.

5. Note the trend of feature articles in this or last month's periodicals which you have examined.

6. What is the number of periodicals to which the specialist may contribute and how many of them do you know?

7. How does a beginning specialist work?

8. What methods do the "big-name" specialists employ?

9. Enumerate the advantages of querying an editor.

10. Why is the "postal interview" more difficult than the face-to-face type?

11. Read your vocabulary of words for your specialized field to the class.

12. What are the advantages of writing for the business and trade fields?

13. What are the advantages of writing for the other specialized fields?

14. List 10 fields in which one might specialize profitably and successfully that are not enumerated in this chapter.

15. Discuss the results of the self-test for selecting a field.

16. Why should an experienced specialist have more than one field?

17. Why should a beginner be content with one field?

18. To what sources would you direct a free-lance writer to find ideas for special fields, if he felt he were experienced enough to start specializing?

19. List five fields in which you now think you would be interested in specializing.

20. What additional rewards, supplementing those listed in this chapter, can you list for the specialist?

21. Skim through the preceding examples, jotting down for each one read or assigned the points you learned in reference to writing specialized articles.

22. What changes would you make in each article had you been a manuscript reader on the editorial staff of a magazine?

Research Report No. 4, due fourth week of second semester.

SURVEY OF SELECTED FIELD

(Purpose is to see what periodicals have used subjects selected, and to get background material for the three articles required for the course.)

Sources: *Readers' Guide to Periodical Literature* _____

Research Sources as Suggested in Chapter 18. _____

Bulletins, Documents, etc. _____

Bibliography: List of sources from which later you will want to take notes for Report No. 5, due the fifth week, based on Chapter 19. (Bibliography to be listed on cards or typewriting paper, as suggested in Chapters 18 and 20.)

_____

_____

_____

Interview Plans: List of possible interviewees, phases of subject, or field which you think now that you will want to interview authorities on. (Interviewing will not be done until Research Report No. 6, due sixth week.)

_____

_____

_____

New Research: List any new research or new ideas or new angles of the selected field which have not appeared in print. (This part of the report probably will contain the new ideas that will help to sell the three articles to be written for the course.)

_____

_____

_____

_____

_____

_____

Plans for Illustrations: Photographs, color pictures, photostats, drawings, charts, diagrams, graphs, blueprints.

_____

_____

_____

_____

_____

_____

Additional Ideas: Any other ideas or plans that you wish to include in this survey.

_____

_____

_____

Suggestions for the Future: _____

_____

_____

CHAPTER 21

Business Writing Offers Many Opportunities

▪▪

Business Field Covers Wide Range. Business writing can be broken down into six categories, all of which offer the writer variety and opportunity. Five of these six types are writing for the publications in the business field: professional, business, trade, association papers, and house organs. The sixth category, writing about business for general magazines, has expanded and gained in importance during the last decade. Business periodicals, as well as articles concerning business in the general magazines, differ in appeal from other publications and articles because the emphasis of the appeal in each category is to its particular group. The readers of business magazines, or articles concerning business in general magazines, have a common bond based on their professions, businesses, trades, or membership in their business associations.

The newest angle of business writing—writing about business, not for the business press but for the general magazine—includes articles for the general reader on (1) business information, (2) business transactions, (3) success in business, and (4) revelation of bad business practices. The latter is not a new phase but is in part a mild revival of the "muckraking" articles of the late '90s when a small group of newspaper writers turned to writing magazine articles revealing bad business practices. That period was followed by articles and even entire magazines which related success stories in business designed to inspire the reader and inform him about better business practices. Books listed in Free-Lance Writer's Library in the Appendix tell the fascinating history of business writing. Every business writer should know something of the background of his profession.

Definition of Business Writing. The business press consists of specialized publications which inform or guide special groups of people in business or general readers who desire to know about business. The business magazine's aim is to aid business people by suggesting easier, more efficient, more profitable, and newer methods for operating their businesses. These publications are a sort of "bible," or textbook, for the readers of professional, business, trade, and association periodicals, and company-sponsored employee and consumer publications, or "house organs." The business press is not written *about* the people in the business world but *for* them.

Variety of Readers Widens Field for Writer. Professional publications are of interest to lawyers, physicians, dentists, and teachers. Business magazines appeal to people in all kinds of business. They consist of two kinds: the "horizontal," covering all types of business in one field; the "vertical," covering only one phase of a field. Trade papers aid shopkeepers in operating their trades. Company-sponsored house organs build good will for the company either by means of the "internal" or employee paper or the "external" or consumer periodical. Association magazine editors buy articles that they think will interest the organization's members.

Editors of all these types of publications pay well for free-lance articles that show evidence of careful thinking, thorough research, effective organization, and clear, terse writing. As an example, *The American Rifleman,* the magazine for members of the Association of American Riflemen, pays as much for articles it buys as do some of the popular general magazines. One does not have to be well known to receive top pay if his manuscripts measure up to the standard required by these excellent periodicals. A student, who sold the articles he wrote for the magazine course offered to people in service by the United States Armed Forces Institute, found his sales totaled more than $2,500 for articles he wrote as a soldier correspondence student. His work in the service had made him an expert in the field about which he wrote.

The official publication of the United Commercial Travelers, *The Sample Case,* and other association magazines buy free-lance articles. Even many business writers do not realize the opportunities of writing for the association press. One should ascertain from manuscript market books which periodicals pay. Those supported by membership only, rather than by subscriptions and advertising, are not financially able to buy manuscripts.

General Reader Desires Business Information. Well-organized and carefully written business articles sell, not only to their respective professional, business, trade, and association papers, but to all sorts of periodicals. Even the general magazines and daily newspapers buy business articles because, directly or indirectly, business touches the lives of all readers.

Second class magazines, so rated because their incomes from circulation and advertising are not large enough to enable them to pay as much for articles as first class ones, also buy business articles. Their subscribers are concerned with articles on sound business methods and are interested in articles about new developments in the business world. Such articles appeal to men, women, home owners, church groups, farmers, and other similar groups.

Articles concerned with business, written by well-known writers or experts, appear in the *Saturday Evening Post, Reader's Digest,* and other popular magazines. They are not written for the business world but for the general reader. Many smaller general magazines buy articles for the same reason though they cannot pay top prices unless the writer is well known in the field.

Business Writer Has Many Opportunities. Business periodicals, like the businesses they serve, have increased in number during the last decade. If they keep up with the growing business world, the number of periodicals will continue to increase. However, if the United States has a financial "recession" at some future time, in all probability the publications will decrease in number.

If one checks the current directory of *Standard Rate & Data* or other business paper listings, he will find about 200 different classifications. One publication may have from 100,000 to 5,000,000 readers. A professional or business person generally subscribes to one or more papers in his special field. Many subscribers, depending upon the scope and size of their specialities, may take from 5 to 25 publications in their fields because of the special information that may be obtained from them.

Business Press Is Important in Moulding Opinion. In the public library reading or periodical room one will find many of the 4,749 business periodicals with their 56,988 annual issues, many of the 6,000 company-sponsored house organs with 72,000 issues, and the 1,068 agricultural and farm publications with 12,816 annual issues. The many publications in even a small library reading room will convince a writer that these magazines have expanded in number and appeals just as the professions, businesses, trades, and associations, for which they are edited, have expanded. These periodicals with their modern content and interesting factual style of writing have become powerful moulders of opinion during the last decade. They represent not only a bigger but a better paying field because they demand more thorough and better written articles. The business press, through the professional, business, trade, and association periodicals, is concerned with other topics besides business. It reports activities in politics, government, and education. It analyzes the effects of new cultural and mechanical advancements. All of these activities affect business.

The writer should never forget that these magazines cover the interests of everyone, in one way or another. Either directly or indirectly these publications are concerned with aiding their subscribers to obtain more business, make more money, solve more problems, or give better service, not in one locality, but everywhere, since most of the magazines are national, or at least sectional in their appeal to their readers. Their articles concentrate on unusual situations, the solution of problems, or new ways to serve their clientele, customers, employees, or association members.

Sources of Materials Are Numerous. Not only Main Street but the side streets everywhere provide the writer with ideas and material for articles if he is an astute student of the business world. As in all types of fact writing, sources of ideas for business articles are everywhere as students learned in Part I. One of the best sources for business "tips" is the local daily newspaper.

Another field that offers interesting sources for business articles is that of government—municipal, local, state, and national. An article on government may be written for the business press, then the facts reslanted to appeal to readers of general magazines. Writer's market books and writer's magazines list a number of government business periodicals. Many government business papers will buy articles if the interviewee's name is used as author with an "as told to" (giving the writer's name) instead of the usual "by" line.

Conventions and conferences of business people provide a splendid source of ideas and material for the business writer. In attending them the writer learns the special vocabularies used in specific fields, meets his potential readers, and becomes acquainted with business editors. By studying the needs of businessmen, as revealed in their convention speeches and discussions, he can tell readers how to be more efficient in their professions, businesses, trades, or associations and enable them to make more profits and to give better service.

Covering Conventions Is Profitable for Writer. Dates for the convention of a particular type of business may be obtained from its own periodical, from the listings at the Chamber of Commerce, from businessmen's association secretaries, or from public relation directors listed in the back of the telephone directory. By querying editors in advance, setting forth one's qualifications, and requesting, if he receives the assignment, instructions as to special angles to be included, editorial policy to be followed, pictures to be obtained, and deadlines to be met, the business writer not only adds to his growing list of ideas for articles but may obtain material and interviews during the convention. He, or she, will be well paid for the assignment.

The business writer assigned to "cover" a convention contacts, by telephone or letter, the association secretary, or the convention director, or a member of the arrangements committee to obtain advance copies of the program. The latter will enable the writer to obtain advance copies of the speeches for the advance convention story. Even though the writer has the advance copies of speeches, he always checks with the speakers at the convention to see that the speeches are not changed in content. At that time he may obtain ideas or material for additional articles. Advance arrangements may be made for convention pictures. Because speed and accuracy are important in convention stories, it is well to make three copies of each. If one is lost, then another may be mailed immediately or filed at the telegraph office without the writer having to recopy it or to use his own file copy.

The real value to the business writer of covering a convention is not the reporting but the opportunity it gives: (1) to add to the list of ideas or "tips" for articles to be written in the future, (2) to popularize ideas for general magazines, and (3) to interview authorities who are attending the convention. As a rule, it is at conventions that the first announcements are made of the results of research, the findings of new discoveries, and the developments of new techniques and methods.

Business Writers Always Query Editors. Because some periodicals have 50 to 75 "string men" or correspondents throughout the United States, or employ regular contributors, the free-lance business writer always queries the editor. He includes an outline or a brief letter explaining the points of the story that he thinks would interest the editor's readers. If the magazine has a correspondent who has submitted a manuscript on the same subject, the free-lance will not waste his time or kodak films.

In addition to "selling himself" to the editor by querying, the free-lance should relate briefly his experience, his facilities to obtain the story and pictures, and the business magazines to which he has sold.

When querying an editor the free-lance writer should ask for specific instructions concerning photographs. Some business magazines and association periodicals, such as *The American Rifleman,* upon request will supply free a "Writer's and Photographer's Guide." It would be helpful to editor and free-lance writer alike if all magazines had similar information prepared when they have definite requirements.

Requirements for Successful Business Writing. Writing skills in this field do not differ greatly from those of other types. Perhaps it does, however, take more skill to ferret out the information, to recognize what is unusual from the reader's point of view, to employ business discernment and good judgment in investigating new trends, and to gain the confidence of the interviewees so they will talk freely. Needless to say, research, slanting, outlining, writing, and illustrating the article should be of the same high standard as for first class general publications. The subscribers are thoughtful readers who do not "skim" but read thoroughly every page of their business magazines. The writer studies the advertising as well as the articles in all of the business magazines in the field or fields for which he writes.

A business writer should be able to use a good camera because "handout photographs" given by the interviewees often do not help tell the story. Of course the writer can hire a photographer whose charges, however, may take most of the profits. Business editors buy only clear photographs. If they are small the writer should have them enlarged to size 8 x 10 inches. Business editors, as well as editors of general magazines, cannot use 35mm. kodachromes or transparencies but require 4 x 5 enlargements in order to obtain satisfactory color reproductions. Even a beginner's good photographs will be paid for at a rate that repays the writer, and they are an important factor here, as in other kinds of writing, in helping to sell the article.

Test for Checking Business Manuscripts. Checking one's own copy for business magazines involves the same steps as those used in specialized writing explained in Chapter 20, with the addition of asking one's self:

(1) Have I insulted the reader's intelligence by explaining the obvious to the business subscriber who knows the field thoroughly? (2) Have I checked all ideas for authority and all facts for accuracy? (3) Have I included generalities, outdated figures, or other information which will only bore my readers? (4) Have I "read copy" and substituted words that will add to the clarity, and will ease and speed the job of reading for the subscriber? (5) Have I shown how the ideas can increase skills, make money, and save time and labor? (6) Have I clearly shown how the reader may incorporate the ideas in his business to provide better service, better products? (7) Have I covered the subject thoroughly? (8) Do the photographs or art work help explain the subject? (9) Have I slanted it to fit this particular specialized group of readers? (10) Have I checked the facts to avoid inaccuracies?

If the answer to each question is yes, the retyped manuscript will claim an editor's attention because thorough and well-written business articles are in demand by editors of these magazines.

Business Writer Makes His Own Future. As in any type of writing, but particularly in the business field, the rewards for the writer are many. As a free-lance he is his own employer. If he desires to become a staff member or an editor in this field, opportunity will come if he succeeds in his free-lance business writing. He is aided by the fact that the number of business publications is large. Another advantage is the good chance he has to make from $6,000 to $25,000 or more a year if he is energetic and ambitious. Many of the better writers and editors in the field make this much and more by directing the articles they write and read to the average subscriber of business magazines.

One successful business writer says he spends one half of the day reading newspapers and current business periodicals relating to the business fields for which he writes. He clips and files the ideas by geographical location. He indicates in his cross reference file the subject and the location of the clipping. When he plans a trip to gather material, he lifts the geographical folders out of his file and is on his way. If he wishes to widen the reader appeal when he returns to his office or study to write the articles, he refers to the cross reference file to locate clippings on the subject to tell what is being done in Maine or California or some place in between as well as in the locality which he has just "covered." Another well-known business writer, whose home is in Chicago, says he spends about one half of his time reading, one fourth interviewing, and one fourth writing. Another business writer says that for recreation two evenings a week he processes the pictures he has taken to illustrate his articles. By having an office, the business writer will procrastinate less and will get more work done in a professional atmosphere.

Most all cities offer opportunities for editorial staff positions because even smaller cities have business publications edited in their communities. Larger cities—New York, Detroit, Chicago, Kansas City, San Francisco, and others—each have a large number of these magazines. Opportunity awaits for those who search it out.

Examples of Business Articles. The first of the following articles was suggested by a little news story in a daily newspaper. An interview with the state police radio supervisor and the initiative to develop the article brought a check from *Law and Order*. The second, which had two charts and a picture, was written by a medical expert, a beginner in the feature writing course given by the United States Armed Forces Institute. His total sales to the association magazine, *The American Rifleman,* amounted to $2,500. With the exception of one other article, this was the only one he wrote in the course that was based on his medical background. The third and fourth articles, revealing modern business methods, were selected from *Reader's Digest* and the *Saturday Evening Post* respectively. Their authors, once free-lance writers, are on the staffs of first class periodicals. Because of limited space, the articles had to be "cut" as indicated. With the exception of the third article, each article had from one to five pictures and drawings, maps, or charts to illustrate the facts.

(1)
New Airs for Wisconsin
Law Enforcement*

BY EARL B. DUTTON

Law enforcement in Wisconsin is putting on new airs. Microwave, a modern electronic miracle, will soon play a leading role in reducing crime in the Badger state.

On the top floor of the State Office Building in Madison, carpenters, painters, electricians, radio men and state law enforcement officers are hard at work, readying several rooms for the installation of microwave equipment which will connect the capital city with all state-owned police radio-equipped vehicles.

When the project is completed by July 1, Wisconsin will be the first state to have a state-wide police radio network operated by microwave relays from a central point. Throughout the state, towers are being erected to carry the narrow radio beams. This network of towers will tie Wisconsin's eight state police radio stations together.

*   *   *

As modern as all this is, the Wisconsin microwave system is the result of one man's dream and devotion. He is Raymond Hoffman, the state police radio supervisor at Madison. By getting the backing of the Motor Vehicle Department Commissioner and the Governor, Hoffman convinced the legislature to appropriate $254,000 for the project.

It has been estimated that depreciation costs of the microwave system will run to about $40,000 a year. However, Hoffman believes the new system will save about $50,000 annually in manpower, overtime and rental expenses.

To effectively maintain the present police radio system in Wisconsin, 31 dispatchers are needed. By using the new microwave system all eight stations can be manned by 17 dispatchers working around the clock in Madison.

Hoffman says that microwave can and will possibly be used for

---

* Reprinted by permission of *Law and Order* and Earl B. Dutton.

civil defense. Sirens could be set into operation in cities throughout the state by merely pushing a button in the Madison control room. Plans are being made to connect the radio-equipped vehicles of the state traffic patrol and conservation department, federal wild life service, FBI, and state crime laboratory cars with the central control.

Test signals on the new microwave system are already passing between Madison and Milwaukee. But Hoffman and his associates want the change-over to be gradual, so they are working on a do-it-yourself basis rather than hiring the manufacturer to erect the system.

Other states are studying the prospects of using microwave in their police communications. A great deal will depend on the success of the Wisconsin venture.

(2)

Eye Sight*

(Conclusion of Series)

By A. M. LIBASCI, MD

If you have eye trouble, an examination is in order. Should you go to an optician, an optometrist, or an ophthalmologist? Let's unscramble these four-dollar words.

The *optician* is the 'manufacturer' of our trio. He grinds lenses, makes spectacles, and dispenses them according to prescription, as does the pharmacist with drugs. He does not examine eyes.

An *optometrist* is a professional man with a degree in optometry. He is a specialist in refraction examinations and is licensed to practice optometry by the state, as are doctors.

An *ophthalmologist* ('oculist' is practically synonymous) is a doctor of medicine who specializes exclusively in diseases of the eye. He is qualified to do eye surgery. He is the eye specialist par excellence.

Any of the three can cope with your eye troubles. Your choice depends upon your needs.

Shooters who must wear glasses need not despair. Many of our finest shooters have refractive errors. Remember, quite a few of our topnotchers are over forty and the majority of them are likely to be farsighted.

*   *   *

Another important factor in the care and preservation of the eye-

* Reprinted by permission of *The American Rifleman*, Official Journal of the National Riflemen's Association of America, and A. M. Libasci, MD.

sight is the matter of adequate lighting. A properly lighted place for reading at home is more the exception than the rule.

Most of our homes and places of business are poorly lighted. Here are the minimum requirements. Borrow a light meter from your light company and test your surroundings.

For severe prolonged reading such as newsprint, bookkeeping, or fine type, a minimum of 50 to 100 foot candles is recommended. For ordinary prolonged reading of ordinary type such as this, 20 to 50 foot candles is required. For occasional reading, 10 to 20 foot candles is sufficient.

Do not read in a darkened room with only one light source over your chair. Do not work at a bench with only one light source over it and the rest of the room dark. Do not shoot in a darkened range with lights only at target. Under these conditions your pupils are alternately dilating and contracting as you raise your eyes and lower them.

People with uncorrected refractive errors sometimes compensate by using stronger light. If you find yourself demanding stronger light than those around you, suspect eye trouble.

A final word: Your efficiency as a wage earner, your safety and welfare, and your happiness depend largely on your ability to see clearly and quickly. Don't be a victim of false pride. If you need spectacles, wear them. Don't give up shooting if you have defective vision. You can still be a champion if you have your troubles corrected properly.

(3)

The Shocking Truth
About Our National Parks*

Have we forgotten their original purpose?

By CHARLES STEVENSON

One out of three persons in the United States will visit some part of our national-park system during the coming season. To these visitors I must pass along a warning: Your trip is likely to be fraught with discomfort, disappointment, even danger.

This warning, the result of a year-long investigation which included an 8000-mile inspection tour, is borne out by the director of the

---

* Reprinted by permission of *Reader's Digest* and Charles Stevenson.

National Park Service (NPS) himself, Conrad L. Wirth. Says Mr. Wirth:

"It is not possible to provide essential services. Visitor concentration points can't be kept in sanitary condition. Comfort stations can't be kept clean and serviced. Water, sewer and electrical systems are taxed to the utmost. Protective services to safeguard the public and preserve park values are far short of requirements. Physical facilities are deteriorating or are inadequate to meet public needs. Some of the camps are approaching rural slums. We actually get scared when we think of the bad health conditions."

*   *   *

Conditions in the major parks are appalling. Drive to Yellowstone, as my wife and I did late last summer, and the moment you enter you are in a big-city traffic rush. Speed limits have been raised to 45 miles an hour, the better to hurry you through a preserve dedicated by law to the leisurely appreciation of nature. Pause to look at sights you've come thousands of miles to see, and cars pile up bumper-to-bumper a quarter of a mile behind you. If a Park Ranger is around, he compels you to move on. "I hate to do it," one of them told me, "but we've got to break up traffic jams."

Tourists must compete for food and sleeping accommodations in congested centers where concessionaires' hotels and cabins and free campgrounds are jammed up together. You buy a ticket to stand in line at the restaurant of Yellowstone's Old Faithful Inn; you breathe down the neck of some diner at the coffeeshop counter until he relinquishes his seat. I heard the hostess at this counter say to two young men, "Get up, you. You're only drinking coffee. You can't take up seats all evening just for that."

A 25-watt bulb hanging from the ceiling provided our $11.50 room at the old Lake Hotel with the dark mystery of a cocktail lounge. We were lucky, though. While still 200 miles from Yellowstone we had phoned and reserved a room. Less fortunate tourists couldn't get rooms even in the vast cabin colonies.

The cabins, grimly brown or sickly yellow-green, are actually shacks, overpriced at $1.50 per night for two persons if they bring their own bedding, up to $4.75 if they don't. Deployed around a central toilet house, they form slum-like cityblock groups that cover acres often devoid of trees, shrubs or grass, and with cindery dust underfoot. Many still in use were condemned before World War II as unfit for human habitation.

We should charge fair fees to cover cost of special services which visitors want. Admission to our parks should be free because the natural wonders belong to all Americans. But the idea that this right should extend to their cars makes no sense. Automobile fees should be realistically revised upward. If motor visitors to Yellowstone during 1954 had paid just $1.27 each toward what they received instead of 75 cents, and those to Yosemite 95 instead of 62 cents, they would have paid the entire annual cost of the two parks.

Let's concentrate on maintaining and repairing current facilities in the parks instead of launching new developments. New roads should be built only when there is a need for traffic to reach an essential destination. Even then, the realization that every road is an encroachment upon the wilderness must be kept clearly in mind, or our parks will soon be turned into the equivalent of drive-in movies.

If such changes in policy and practice can be carried out, we'll reestablish our parks as the sanctuaries they were intended to be: retreats to which harassed modern folk can flee from the congestion of cities, and learn again how to walk, relax and contemplate.

(4)

The author takes you along on his recent—and risky—trip, prowling
the lush new Caribbean gambling dens. Take Havana, where
American gangsters-in-exile clip tourists for millions, with
outrageously crooked games. Sometimes the customers
squawk, but there are plenty of

Suckers in Paradise*

By Lester Velie

The time is New Year's Eve; the place, the Gran Casino Nacional in Havana, Cuba, and our hero is a perspiring, elderly American gentleman—let's call him "D.J."—who is learning why Havana is called "one of the last of the world's sinful cities."

Outdoors, where a tropical moon turns the casino garden's hibiscus and bougainvillaea to flaming color, roistering Americans battle their way noisily into the casino driveway, bumper to bumper. Inside, in the bar, the laughter rises in pitch as midnight and the New Year nears. And in the great, high-ceilinged ballroom the brassy blare of the rumba band blends with the gabble of the dancers into an insistent roar.

But in the gambling room, our D.J. is oblivious of all this. His

* Reprinted by permission of the *Saturday Evening Post* and Lester Velie.

world has suddenly narrowed to the pitchman's table with the green-baize, numbered squares, the eight dice in his hands, and the small fortune of house money before him that draws him on. The dice cup rattles, and the dealer's flying fingers count and whisk the tumbled dice away before the player's swimming eyes can tally them.

Back home in New England, D.J. is an insurance executive, respected for his solid judgment. But here in Havana, in a game he's never seen, D.J. has lost in three minutes what his secretary earns in a year. The impassive-faced credit man on the high stool beside the pitchman's table notes another $1000 on his pad, bringing the player's debt to the house to $4000. D.J. hesitates.

"Shame to quit now," says a kibitzer to his left.

*   *   *

So many Americans had been fleeced that their cries had been heard by the American embassy and Cuba's Tourist Commission. Among the victims was a honeymoon couple who lost the $500 they had saved toward furnishing an apartment. Another was the mother of four children who paid her losses with five checks, predated against her husband's weekly salary. A third created an international incident. He was Dana Smith, Los Angeles attorney and a sponsor of Vice-President Richard M. Nixon's senatorial expense fund. He gave a $4200 check, thought better of it and stopped payment. Sued in an American court, Smith won with a defense that the game he had played was fraudulent and illegal in Cuba. All this caused Cuba's minister of the interior to proclaim on the radio that gambling was suspended by government decree.

Since Cuba's gambling is illegal and runs only on a protected basis, the decree was a curious one. And since it was aimed at American hoodlums, it had no chance. For the *Yanqui* racketeer, with his teeth in a good thing, knows his way around abroad as well as he does at home. So, by evening, the decree had been modified to bar only "illegal games." By nightfall, as any reporter could see by making the rounds, the razzle con artists were as busy as ever. And by dawn many a saddened American was wondering gloomily whether he had enough money in the bank to cover the check he had given to some bust-out joint "for value received."

*   *   *

I called on the president of Cuba's Tourist Commission, Marcial Facio. A retired sugar millionaire, still vigorous at sixty-five, Facio talked freely and indignantly about the defiance of his government's order.

"The roots of these racketeers have gone in deep," the tourist chief said unhappily. "In a wink a man loses a thousand dollars at this cheating game. So we ordered them out last November. Two months later they're still running behind my back."

* * *

"Puerto Rico's gambling," John Scarne told me, "gives the player as good a break as he'll find in any casino anywhere."

Yet, even in this lily-white atmosphere, the wheels and dice work—in the long run—only for the house.

"We caught hell from the opposition when we plunged $7,200,000 into a luxury hotel (the Caribe Hilton)," Gov. Muñoz Marin said. "But we're making twelve per cent on our money." (The insular government, as owner, takes two thirds of the profits, the Hilton Hotels Corporation, as operator, takes a third.) The decorously run carpet joint on the hotel's mezzanine, where American Cabinet members, movie stars and magnates rub shoulders with thrifty package-tour travelers, is responsible.

Puerto Rico's gambling law shrewdly grants casino licenses to hotel keepers who spend at least $350,000 to build new facilities or to refurnish old ones. So, the happy example of the Caribe Hilton's prosperity has encouraged native owners of the Condado Beach Hotel to spend $1,000,000 on face lifting. A luxury hotel, designed by Miguel Ferrer, Jose Ferrer's cousin, has bloomed at Barrangquitas, fifty miles from San Juan by hairpin roads. The promoter, Waldemar Lee, the former tourist director, expects to fly guests there by helicopter.

"With a gambling joint in the place, how can we lose?" he asks.

The answer is, the house can't lose. It earns a steady percentage of the total play—as low as 1.4, if honest. If dishonest, as high as 100 per cent on a skin game like the razzle. For a casino operator never gambles. He runs a business as solid and about as risky as the Bank of England. He leaves it to the sucker to take a chance with his money. And suckers' money circulates fast these days. Although the birth rate is the same—one born every minute—he's traveling now.

Exercises

1. From the Business section of your city telephone directory, select five businesses about which you now think you might be able to write five articles, for their respective business papers, if you had time to "study"

each business, interview, and read several business publications pertaining to each of the five fields.

2. Find five businesses from the Business section of the telephone directory that you now think might be sources for five articles on business for general reader magazines.

3. Indicate for each of the above "tips" how you now think you would develop each tip according to the four types of business articles for general magazines.

4. After reading the required qualifications that a business writer should have, check yourself to see which qualifications you should develop to be a success in this field of writing.

5. What will you do to develop your weaker qualifications?

6. Make a list of the advantages enjoyed by the free-lance business writer.

7. What do you think the disadvantages are?

8. Look at five business periodicals in your library and list what seems to be the trend in the types of articles that each one uses?

9. How does the beginning business writer work?

10. How do successful, experienced business writers work?

11. Of the business articles you recall seeing in general periodicals, indicate which ones you think were written by staff writers and which ones were written by business writers?

12. Give reasons for your choices in the above exercise.

13. Why should the business writer always query the editor?

14. Why should the business writer query the editor in reference to illustrations for his proposed article?

15. Work up a vocabulary for any field of business writing.

16. What professions in your community do you think might produce ideas for articles in professional publications?

17. Make a list of "tips," one for each phase of business writing, which would make interesting subjects for articles.

18. List five business fields in which you now think you might find it interesting and profitable to write.

19. If your answer to the above exercises is blank, explain why you cannot "sell yourself," or interest yourself, in this type of writing.

20. "Skim" through the five types of business magazines, jotting down the subject matter of the articles and the points you have learned about them in this chapter.

21. What changes would you have made in the preceding examples of articles had you been a manuscript reader on the editorial staff of a business paper or on the staff of a general magazine using those business articles?

Research Report No. 5, due fifth week.

NOTES ON PRINTED MATERIAL READ

(Purpose of report is to gather material, by library research, taking accurate notes in a systematic way, and to hand the notes just as taken in to the instructor, who may make helpful suggestions concerning the methods of note-taking used. Each student may discuss and exhibit his method in the pro-seminar so that he, or she, may get suggestions from other students as well as from the instructor. The notes will serve as the background material for the three required articles to be written during the last half of the semester.

Fasten notes together securely with rubber bands or clips and place in envelope before handing them in to the instructor. On the first sheet of paper or card explain your note-taking systems, except the content. The notes are the content.)

Form: Follow instructor's directions or, if working alone, follow those in Chapter 18 or devise your own. On first sheet or card of notes explain form as well as the following items.

Method: Use any method suggested by instructor, or, if self-taught, those in Chapter 18, or devise your own, but explain method used on first sheets or cards of your notes.

Content: Apply suggestions in Chapter 18. Your notes are the content.

Sources: Indicate accurately and in detail sources of material, either for future reference, or to give credit, or to obtain permission to use quotations in copyright, as suggested in Chapter 18.

New Ideas: List suggestions for better note-taking that you gained from your experience in taking notes.

Suggestions for Future: _____

CHAPTER 22

History of Science Writing Aids Writer

■.

Laboratories Gave Impetus to Science Writing. In order to understand problems in writing about science and technology that may arise even in this modern day of more readable science and technical articles, science and technical writers may benefit by knowing something of the history of writing in these two similar fields. For the sake of brevity, since the techniques used in writing about science and technology are so similar, the term science writing will be used to describe the writing on both subjects.

Science writing developed on a university campus. College laboratories continue to be one of the best sources for scientific or technical "tips." Another excellent source is found in commercial laboratories. If the writer looks back into the origin of science writing he will understand why the scientist of the past feared newspaper and magazine writers. He will understand why today's trained journalists prefer the term "readable science" or "non-technical" to the former one, "popularized science." He will be sympathetic with, rather than antagonistic to, the scientist's attitude.

The Atomic Bomb Also Bombed the Scientists. As periodical readers sat safely in their comfortable homes reading in awed silence of the great destruction of Hiroshima on that sixth day of August, 1945, consciously or unconsciously they realized what might happen to them if an enemy had that weapon.

Immediately they wished to know the *how* and *what* and *when* and *why* and even the *who* of nuclear energy. They wanted to know why half an atomic bomb is safe but a whole one is devastating.

Although readers have always been interested in science that is written in a way they could comprehend, the scientists, probably because of their objective training and experience, formerly were not interested in having their knowledge given to the general reader. They were willing to write of their discoveries in "reports" or "papers" for other scientists to read in the learned journals. But beyond that, the majority of them still had the attitude of the educated person of the middle ages and refused to write of their research for the general reader—even refused to be interviewed by writers. They maintained that "if their discoveries were written so the common person could understand them, they would no longer be science."

Not only did the atomic bomb bring an earlier end to World War II, but it forcefully convinced even the most conservative scientist that his work was not finished when he had completed his laboratory research. Only a few scientists remain who have failed to keep step with the modern viewpoint. The present-day science writer, in his interviewing, finds the majority of scientists more co-operative than did the writers of yesteryear.

The Sensational Press Irritated the Scholars. Even though the reader does not always understand the scientific processes, he has long been interested in science news. It was the sensational press of the '90s that first exploited this interest. Those writers were trained in the school of experience of the "yellow press," and they wrote only exaggerated, pseudoscientific articles. Because of the great reader appeal, other periodicals imitated the exaggerated accounts, until thoughtful and intelligent readers could not believe what they read concerning science, even though it was interesting reading.

These sensationalized accounts of laboratory research irritated the scholar working with his test tubes. The majority of scientists had been trained or had come to believe that they lived and worked in a mysterious world beyond the comprehension of the average person, not a fellow scientist. With distrust for the newspaper and magazine writers and with a feeling of superiority, or so it seemed to the lay writer, the majority of them retired into their laboratories and became aloof, if not brusque, toward writers, trained or untrained.

Scientists Became Public Relations Writers Almost Overnight. Just as "the man on the street" became an even more avid reader of science after the bombing of Hiroshima, the scientists immediately became aware that they must learn the techniques of interpreting their knowledge to the public, or of translating it to trained and skilled writers who might write readable articles to explain the significance of nuclear energy.

Of necessity scientists realized almost overnight what they had avoided for years. They saw they must become public relations men in addition to being scholars. Because of the misunderstandings and superstitions which were growing like wildfire, scholars were called upon to give speeches over the radio and to write articles about the atomic bomb for the general reader rather than for their fellow scientists. They even worked through Congress and the President of the United States in order to overcome the dangers to mankind of ignorance or half-knowledge. They had forgotten the lessons learned in overcoming, through "popularization," the public's prejudice against vaccine and similar discoveries which resulted in saving thousands of lives. Although the scientists did not have the time nor the skill to write of their own research, they saw they must co-operate with writers who had the training and ability to write with precise accuracy in terminology that would hold the reader's interest.

University Press Bureaus Developed Accurate Science Writing. To know the history of readable science writing will enable one to cope better with problems which may arise when interviewing scientists and technicians.

Probably credit for the earliest work in persuading the scientists to co-operate in popularizing their research belongs to some of the first university directors of public relations, or "editors," or "publicity directors," as they were termed in that period.

These helped pave the way for the remarkable institution, *Science Service,* by making the scientists willing to have their research interpreted. When *Science Service* was planning its first publication, it sought the co-operation of the scientists, but found that battle had been won by the university press bureau directors before the plan for "dissemination of science" was made.

Among the first of these university public relations men who had the idea of a university press bureau which would send out news accurately written was the late Dr. Willard G. Bleyer of the University of Wisconsin, who later became Director of the Wisconsin School of Journalism.

He obtained permission from the university president, Charles R. Van Hise, to write up a series of articles about the University's Jubilee in 1904 for the newspapers in the state. Since he was an experienced newspaper writer, the stories were so well received that what is said to be the first university press bureau in the world grew out of these Fiftieth Anniversary news releases in 1904. Dr. Bleyer was its first director. By 1913 his time was so occupied with teaching that he turned the press bureau over to a nonacademic publicity writer. But the latter antagonized the scientists and revived their dread of "popularization" of their research.

The university administration realized that, if the press bureau were to be of value again, a director must be obtained who had advanced degrees, as did the scientists, and equal academic rank as a faculty member. Grant M. Hyde, then an assistant professor on Professor Bleyer's staff, was persuaded in 1915 to become the third director of the press bureau. He formerly had been a writer of a science column for the Chicago *Tribune,* assistant editor of *Popular Mechanics,* and managing editor of *Popular Science.*

Bureau Editor's Precise Accuracy Won Scholars' Confidence. In the University of Wisconsin, Mr. Hyde saw a gold mine of unwritten science news. From his previous experience he knew how to overcome the difficulties of interviewing scientists. He set as his goal the complete coverage of science on the campus. But to attain this goal, he needed the confidence of the scientists. Accordingly he had every article checked for accuracy by the scholar interviewed. If the latter did not wish the story printed, he did not release it to the press, but "killed it" as the newspaper writer would say.

From the point of view of director of a university press bureau, Mr. Hyde saw an even greater need for popularized science stories. The financial support for the research and for the scientists themselves, as well as the other faculty members, came from the state's taxpayers. If more financial support was to be obtained to continue research, the taxpayers must know what the scientists were doing to help the commonwealth and its citizens, who, through their taxes, supported the university.

Professor Hyde succeeded in gaining the confidence of the scholars because he realized that their only "stock in trade" was their reputations. Formerly they had been afraid to trust that reputation to unknown, and, often at that time, untrained writers. They were more willing to co-operate with their academic colleague, because he wrote of their work with precise accuracy and aided them in upholding their reputations as scientists. After twelve years of service as director of the press bureau, Mr. Hyde resigned to devote his time entirely to teaching and textbook writing. Upon the death of Dr. Bleyer, he was the Director of the Wisconsin School of Journalism until he resigned to devote his full time to teaching and writing.

Untrained Writers Often Misinterpreted Research Results. Professor Hyde relates an incident to show how the untrained writers antagonized the scientists and often misinterpreted or exaggerated the results of the research:

"One of the scientists on the campus conducted experiments with rabbits to see if their young were affected by an alcoholic diet of various degrees fed the parent-rabbits. A trained writer would emphasize that the research and conclusions applied only to rabbits. But a newspaper writer of the 'sensational school' rewrote the story and went a step further than the scientists saw fit to do. The writer, out of his imagination and desire to sensationalize the story, applied the results to human beings, drawing the unwarranted conclusion that children of drunkards had a bad start in life. Of course this was offensive to the scientist. Such incidents reaffirmed the scientists' prejudices against 'popularization.' "

Agricultural Press Bureaus Followed the Wisconsin Plan. The first agricultural college to adapt Wisconsin's idea of a university editor and of the "popularization" of science articles was Iowa State College, which, records show, issued a bulletin dated December 1904. Its example soon was followed by the College of Agriculture at Wisconsin, which established its own bureau to translate the research in agriculture for farm readers. The idea spread, leading to the establishment of other university and agricultural press bureaus, whose editors developed co-operation of scientists with writers and also evolved the science or technical article written with precise accuracy.

Science Service Added to Impetus of Science Writing. The history of the development of science writing is not complete without proper credit to that great institution, *Science Service*. It is the largest and most influential unit today in giving knowledge of science to the nonscientists and the common people.

Some of the writers relating the development of *Science Service* either did not know or overlooked the pioneer work of the early university and agricultural college editors in creating precisely accurate and readable techniques in science interviewing and writing. They attribute the origin of each to the plan of E. W. Scripps, the late newspaper publisher, a patron of the sciences from childhood, although he did not have a formal scientific education.

As a successful publisher of one of the largest newspaper chains in the nation, Mr. Scripps believed that "the only way to make democracy safe is to make it more scientific." He felt that nonscientists, classes or masses, must have some understanding of science if they were to vote intelligently. He thought newspaper readers should have a knowledge, even if a limited one, of what science was doing directly and indirectly for mankind, if the nation were to survive.

"Dissemination of Science" Plan Was Drafted After Press Bureau. Mr. Scripps, aided by Dr. William E. Ritter, a scientist, drafted a plan under the date of March 5, 1919, for the "American Society for the Dissemination of Science," according to the former's biographers.

One notes that this plan was dated four years after Professor Hyde began developing the readable science story based on the co-operation of the Wisconsin scientists. The files of the *Science News Bulletin* reveal that the first issue appeared April 2, 1921. Dr. Edwin E. Slosson was the first editor chosen by the Board of Trustees. Mr. Scripps fulfilled his promise to endow *Science Service* liberally by a most generous bequest to start it, a bequest which enabled it to continue and expand. Originally, it was to have included both natural and social science.

Before starting the work of editing the *Bulletin,* Dr. Ritter and Dr. Slosson arranged for a conference with the up-to-date scientists at Wisconsin, recalls one of the outstanding scholars on the latter campus, who is well known for his own ability in writing readable science books.

"We called Professor Hyde into the meeting because we felt that he knew more about writing to the general reader and the techniques in obtaining the confidence of scientists than any of us. The *Science Service* men returned to Washington feeling that Mr. Hyde had given them many practical suggestions of which they made continued use and for which they expressed their appreciation to us and to Mr. Hyde."

The Organization Binds Science and the World. In taking science to readers in all the states, not in just one, as each of the university press bureaus had to do, *Science Service* has become "the liaison agency between scientific circles and the world." Its Board of Trustees consists of six journalists and nine scientists from the leading national organizations of sciences: the National Academy of Sciences, National Research Council, and the American Association for the Advancement of Science. The journalists are selected by the journalistic profession.

Valuable Aid Is Given Science Writers by Science Service. Under the direction of Dr. Watson Davis (who upon the death of Dr. Slosson followed him as Director) and his staff, *Science Service* has become, not only a remarkable, but a most influential institution for popularizing science by its many projects.

Its activities include, for the newspaper: (1) "highlights of science" sent by leased wire; (2) advance wire releases sent by mail; (3) science news reports sent by mail; (4) a complete science page including photoprints of half-tone pictures and mats of illustrations; (5) a tri-weekly health column; (6) a column on the oddities of nature; (7) science shorts, a daily release of seven-sentence paragraphs on scientific subjects; and (8) a monthly map of the stars which enables the layman to enjoy the night skies.

Its other services include: (1) *Science News Letter,* a weekly summary of current science for scientists and nonscientists; (2) *Chemistry,* a magazine devoted to simplifying the terminology of chemistry and related fields; (3) the editing of scientific manuscripts for book publishers and magazine editors, and the writing of scientific articles for magazines; (4) participation in television and radio programs on science; (5) *Things of Science,* samples of new products of scientific research; (6) *Science Fundamentals,* experimental kits of educational value for school or home; (7) aid in organizing more than 10,000 science clubs in high schools in the United States and in 18 foreign countries; (8) a retail book-order service; (9) *Science Talent Search,* a contest for high school students; and (10) translations of scientific books for Latin-American republics.

Each service is supplied to writers for a reasonable fee. Subscription rates may be obtained by using the address of *Science Service* as listed in the "Free-Lance Writer's Library" in the Appendix.

Science Writers Owe Much to the Pioneers. Without the readability, or popularization, of science made possible to newspapers and magazines by these pioneer agencies, a large section of the adult population would have little or no comprehension of the world of science and its application to their lives. The common man and the scientist alike should be eternally grateful to the great vision of Professor Hyde and the other university and agricultural press bureau editors in aiding to develop readable science; for the endowments of Mr. Scripps which made *Science Service* possible; and for the valuable services given the world first through Dr. Slosson and now through the far-reaching plans of Dr. Watson Davis.

The work of the scientists would be limited in its value to mankind were it not for the skill of men and women in another field—an equally important one—journalism. They are trained and proficient in the art of writing precisely accurate and readable science articles for the readers of the world. What the writers of the past had not been able to accomplish with the ultraconservative scientists, the atomic bomb did. It blasted the scholars into having a sincere appreciation of and a high regard for the value of readable science for the general reader.

The science writer of today, likewise, is grateful to those pioneering groups and to nuclear energy, which together have made the task of interviewing the learned authorities in their laboratories a pleasant one and have as a result created a demand for more scientific articles than the writers can supply.

Social Scientists Are Co-operating with Writers. Most of the natural scientists have learned that trained writers can write with precise accuracy even though what they write must be, and is, interesting to the reader. It took writers more than forty years to build up that attitude. However, the majority of the social scientists have not caught up with the natural scientists in co-operating with trained reporters.

Some, however, like the outstanding, progressive natural scientists, realize their studies will be of but little benefit to human beings if they are not understood by the general reader. The outstanding scientists in either field making the greatest contributions to the world are those who are willing to translate the translatable things in their laboratories or to give interviews graciously to experienced writers who know the techniques in writing readable science articles with precise accuracy.

Modern Scientists Have New Attitude toward Journalists. The influence of accurate and intelligible articles by trained journalists upon readers has resulted in the technician or scientist interviewees discarding their mantles of aloofness, superiority, and mystery, with the exception of a few "old fogies." The modern ones donned cloaks of cordiality and friendliness, and even of eagerness, in their willingness to co-operate in telling the world of their knowledge and research through skilled writers. They realize that if their laboratory research is not applied to humanity, it is of little or no benefit to mankind. Readers will not accept their new theories and facts unless they can comprehend the science back of them.

Universities Have New Concept of Science Teaching. Not only are the scientists becoming aware of their obligations to humanity to share their knowledge in writing, either their own or that of journalists, but in a few midwestern universities courses are offered for nonscience adults in extension and evening classes on "contributions of science to the modern world." The administrators publicize the fact that "the new science frontiers of medicine, industry, engineering, agriculture, and human welfare will be explained in *nontechnical language,* with a résumé of the part that scientific methods and research are playing in the aspects of modern life." But it took forty years of constant work by university press and *Science Service* directors and finally the atomic bomb to attain such a changed attitude upon the part of the men and women of science.

Magazines of Many Types Use Science and Technical Articles. Publishers of periodicals have benefited by serious, factual, and clearly explained science and technical articles. They have increased their subscriptions and their advertising space because of this newer reader interest. Even readers with grade school or possibly high school educations, as well as the educated nonscientists, are eager for practical information that is related to their daily activities at home or to their vocations. Relatively few people read books after their formal education is completed. As adults they turn to newspapers and magazines, as pointed out in Part I, as their chief sources of information and education.

Even those who turned, in the past, to books found difficulty in understanding the language of the scientist or technologist. Some forward-looking publishing houses have produced attractive, readable science books for children. These explain the scientific phenomena in terminology which the little people can understand—if they can get the books away from their parents in order to read them. There was a greater increase, the American Library Association reported last year, in requests for books on inventions, research, and new medical techniques than there was in those for fiction.

Many magazines are adding sections devoted to science features. *Better Homes and Gardens* was one of the first specialized periodicals to add a "limited number of articles concerning science, medicine, mental health, social and personality problems." Other magazines in limited fields have added similar departments.

Science Writing Has Come of Age. This has been termed the age of science. In the periodical world, it is the "age of science and technical writing." A writer is much better paid for interpreting the science or technical news of peace or war, industries or professions, politics or economics, science or religion, medicine or human and social welfare, than for other types of articles, because the former require more research. They also are in greater demand, because readers wish to know what is going to happen next.

Maturity has come to science writing. Its youth was delinquent, because it was tainted with sensationalism, exaggeration, and inaccuracy. Trained and conscientious writers converted it into an adult who is welcomed by the scholar and the world. Science is not only democracy's, but the world's, best hope.

Writing Readable Articles Is Difficult for Scientists. Even the scientists and technologists themselves, at the meetings of their various associations, deplore their lack of ability to write interestingly. They realize that in their own journals the "reports" are so obscure in meaning that even other scientists cannot understand many of them.

Their training has made them objective, but it neglected to give them the subjectivity of the successful journalist. More than a century ago, Gergonne, a French mathematician, said scientists should not think they had completed their research until they could explain it to the "man on the street." Dr. Slosson, a chemist as well as *Science Service* editor, told scientists they wrote as if their thinking were "muddled," because they "bungle language deplorably." He thought they overstressed efficiency, yet showed no regard for the effective use of the dictionary or typewriter.

The scientists are the only people who have anything important to say, according to James M. Barrie. But he criticized their education, because it had failed to teach them *how* to say it. The modern scholars realize that the day is gone "when they may write like scientists." Perhaps the science student in the future will have as one of his requirements for graduation a course in "the art of writing readable science," or perhaps he will be required to elect enough journalism courses to acquire the technique of "writing interestingly, like a trained journalist."

Some Scientists Are Self-Trained Writers. A scientist, as some have, may train himself to write subjectively if he: (1) knows and likes people enough to know how science should be written to appeal to them; (2) has the courage to ignore his jealous colleagues when they say "it isn't science if the general reader can understand it"; (3) learns to consider the effects of his research on the life about him; and (4) acquires the technique of incorporating human interest and the personal element into his manuscripts by visualizing how the results of his research may affect the readers or their families or friends in the future.

The very aloofness of the scientist in the past tended to make him jealous of his colleagues' successes and reputations. Scientists who do not write, for one reason or another, often charged the more popular scholars who do write with "seeking publicity" or with "writing frivolous popularizations." Then the colleagues were afraid to try to write interestingly and even tried to be dull. Fortunately the atomic bomb blasted this attitude into history, so that the scientist writing in the future does not have to contend but little with such petty jealousies. He will succeed in writing readable articles if he will learn the art of simplification.

Science Writing Appeals to the Research Journalist. The magazine writer training for a career either as a contributor or a staff writer will find unlimited opportunities to apply his knowledge of library research methods and his techniques in the art of interviewing through selecting the fields of science and technology for specialization.

The writer, like the scientist, cannot expect to know all the sciences. If his formal science training was limited, he may overcome this handicap to writing readable science by diligent and accurate library research, as suggested in Chapter 18, before he begins his interviewing. No one today can keep up to date in any of the fields of science or technology, because the speed of their advancement is terrific. *Webster's Collegiate Dictionary, Fifth Edition, 1940,* contained the following entry: "In-fran'gi-ble (ĭn-frăn'-jĭ-b'l), *adj.* I. Not capable of being broken or separated into parts; as, *infrangible* atoms."

Under the caption of the single word *Eh?*, *Harper's Magazine* used it as a "filler joke" at the bottom of a page in its July, 1946, issue to indicate the speed of scientific progress. Textbooks are often obsolete even before they are published, but magazine articles can bridge the gap. The great scientific meetings are covered by writers more seriously than are the halls of Congress.

Even the experienced science writer finds that the average scientist is not easy to interview. The latter has not developed a news sense, and he still is afraid of being quoted inaccurately. If he reveals too much, another scientist, who may not have worked on the research as long, may gain information that will enable him to attain the desired results first. The writer must protect his interviewee by guarding against revealing anything that should not be released, even if the scientist does not sense the danger. A willingness to let the scientist check the article for accuracy will open the way for future articles and will win the scholar's confidence.

The careful science writer never thinks that an article has to be "miraculous or revolutionary." Research results often are a sequence of logical facts which develop into unusual results. Human interest and the personal element will always add to the readability of cold facts, if presented in a way to make the reader see how the discovery will affect his life, or that of his friends and neighbors. The fact writer never overlooks even the smallest discovery. A little mold may become a great story to readers, because of the saving of thousands of lives.

Journalists Organize National Association of Science Writers. As the special writers on newspaper and magazine staffs traveled from one science association meeting to another, a spirit of comradeship developed in spite of the natural journalistic rivalry. These recognized writers had the confidence of the science researchers. Many of the writers believed that an organization might establish their status for reliability when they met scientists to whom they were unknown. The charter members announced the organization of the National Association of Science Writers, September 14, 1934.

The organization has grown in numbers as more editors have sent staff writers to cover the meetings of the learned science associations. The group has done much to make science more understandable.

Editors and Readers Are Eager for Science Information. Modern scholars and modern trained writers of science and technology are each improving. One is willing to tell and the other is willing to try to understand and to be precisely accurate by having his manuscripts checked for scientific accuracy. Too many scientists still are not willing to check writers' manuscripts. But by doing so, they could prevent the writers from making their publications appear careless and could save themselves from being made ridiculous in the eyes of their colleagues and other scientists.

Alert writers watch for the impact of science upon the lives of their readers, since that is the reason subscribers read science articles. The public is eager for scientific information, since World War II gave it a great impetus. Man is surrounded by scientific marvels—the jet plane, helicopter, radio, television, radioactivity. Editors cannot obtain enough precisely accurate and readable manuscripts to supply their periodicals' needs.

Interpreting Implications of Science Appeals to Journalists. Subjective training in journalism courses, or self-taught ability to do journalistic research and writing, an inquiring mind, and an innate urge to help mankind enable the feature writer to begin his first science or technical article with confidence, if he has had some experience in slanting and writing general articles. The beginner who has never written for periodicals should not attempt to write science or technical articles until he has mastered the techniques of feature writing as suggested in Part I and the preceding chapters in Part II.

The writer of readable science or technical articles has, or acquires, in addition to having all the journalistic abilities: (1) the love of the hunt, because verifying one item may take not only time, but ingenuity; (2) the skill to extract news out of clouds of technical phraseology in his library research or in his interviewing; (3) the talent to translate scientific terminology into simplified, exact words that are familiar to the readers; (4) the ability to understand clearly each step of the processes by which the researchers arrived at their conclusions or obtained the results; (5) the facility of expression to explain the research, that the readers, too, may understand; (6) the honesty of purpose to discuss the future effects without the exaggeration employed by writers for the sensational press; (7) the insight to see the research from the scientific viewpoint; and to co-operate with the scientists; and (8) the aptitude to write pleasantly readable and precisely accurate articles acceptable alike to the scientist, the editor for whom it was carefully slanted, and the reader.

In his attitude toward his work, the science writer will be as much the scholar as is the scientist, because of his intellectual interests. Although he strives to have his manuscript authentic in every detail, he writes it for the reader, who not only will be able to understand it but will find it pleasant as well as interesting reading. Without exception the science writer will practice the journalist's code of ethics. This type of writing appeals to the alert journalist with much or little science background. He interprets science and technology, or learns to do so, to point out not only its practical applications, but also its cultural and philosophical implications. Even the manner of presenting the results of the scientists' work to the reader is not routine, because the technique of reader appeal has much to do with the response from the public.

Opportunities for Science Writers Are Increasing Rapidly. A writer, if he has the qualifications and aptitudes, should not hesitate to specialize in science and technology. Of course writers cannot keep up with all the phases of science; even the scientists cannot. But therein lies the journalist's opportunity. Natural and social scientists constantly are obtaining new research results or arriving at new conclusions which are important to the readers' welfare. They also are important to the periodical world. The writer may specialize in one field; he may vary his work by writing in many. One popular periodical devoted entirely to science of interest to scientists and nonscientists alike listed in its table of contents for twelve issues articles about the following subjects: agriculture, anthropology, architecture, astronomy, atomic energy, automobiles, aviation, biology, chemistry, new designs, economics, electricity, electronics, engineering, geology, health, household mechanics, new ideas in science, inventions, manufacturing, medicine, metallurgy, meteorology, metrology, mining, nature, physiology, physics, new processes, jet and rocket propulsion, psychology, radio, sociology, and zoology. The subscribers enjoy the great variety of the precisely accurate and readable articles.

The tables in the Appendix list 6,959 periodicals that frequently use science and technical articles. There are 6,875 periodicals—trade, agricultural, business, and professional—which always use one or more science and technical articles an issue. There are approximately 20 publictions which contain only natural science articles. About as many are concerned entirely with social science. The possible markets for technical articles number 4,749 periodicals. A total of 18,623 markets are available to free-lance science and technical writers.

Administrators in the professions, businesses, and trades realize the value of scientific research for their purposes, and many have established their own research laboratories. In doing so, they created another opportunity for publicity writers. The learned professions which once abhorred publicity or "popularization" also employ science writers to direct the publicity for the meetings of the scholars. Other journalists are editorial consultants on manuscripts for science and technical periodicals, and still others are associate editors who contribute science articles on contract or over a given period of time.

One of the national weekly periodicals had an interesting series of medical articles which it contracted Steven M. Spencer to write. The magazine's constant research into its subscribers' tastes revealed that the readers liked medical articles better than all others. The editors attributed the popularity of the medical pieces largely to their "dual attraction," or their reader appeal to both sexes. A student in an advanced magazine writing class sold an article on migraine headaches to a new department in a popular home and garden magazine. When he received a check for $100 for his first science article, he thought headaches were of value after all. A four-day conference attended by 600 scientists to discuss the use of isotopes in biology and medicine attracted science writers from many types of periodicals, as do all science and technical meetings.

Business and industry is science applied to the financial welfare of man. The former regards science as a "frontier of economic progress." The latter is the basis of modern life and the fabric of culture. Industry alone has a research and development budget of more than $600,000,000. Men and women in the professions, businesses, and industries are avid readers of science, because without it there would be no progress in their fields. They also see advantages for their fields and benefits for mankind in having their stories from their research foundations and laboratories told readably and accurately in print.

Even the magazines of hobbies and of entertainment use science articles to interest their subscribers. It has been estimated by survey studies that thirty per cent of the readers of popularized science periodicals are adult males who have science hobbies. The aged, the middle-aged, the young, even the children in this post-atomic age find science as fascinating as a mystery thriller.

Not only the comforts and luxuries, but men's very lives, since the atomic bomb, are in the hands of the scientists and technical experts. It has been said that America's future is controlled by the investigator, the interpreter, and the administrator. There may be an ample supply of administrators and investigators. But there is a shortage of trained interpreters who can explain the scientists' and technicians' research in a precisely accurate and readable style. This field offers unlimited opportunity for writers.

Science Writing as a Career or Avocation. Since science writers are paid better rates for free-lance or requested articles, and the editorial science consultants on publication staffs are paid better salaries, one is well rewarded in choosing science writing as a career or as a side line.

The science writer works hard, but so does every one who is a success in his profession or business. He, or she, meets interesting people, has the fun of thinking and continuing to learn. To interpret the work of the investigator is fascinating and oftentimes thrilling. It is always stimulating and satisfying, because the writer informs and helps the magazine readers. The science journalist knows that his work is important, worthy, and deserving of the best efforts that he can give it.

Scholars in the field of science find writing a lucrative side line, not only from a financial point of view, but because it adds materially to the scientist's reputation in the eyes of his professional or business superiors. As an expert, it is a gratification to be able to express one's self and to present information interestingly to educate and to aid humanity.

Every article has several angles: one for the general reader, one for the technical worker to read in his technical periodical, and one for the scientist to read in his learned journal. The reward for the latter, generally, is honor only.

Rates of payment by general magazines for science articles range from $100 up to $200 for the successful beginner. The well-known and experienced science writers, with some science background, are paid from $1,000 to $2,000. The exclusive requested science article carries even higher rates. The professional science writer may have at the same time from ten to twenty articles on magazine editors' desks, depending on the size of his research staff, if he follows the suggestions as presented in the following chapter.

Other sources of income for the experienced science writer may include writing instruction booklets for advertising agencies or industrial companies or contributing regularly to several periodicals as an associate editor on the staff of each.

The Future of Science Writing. Along with the demand for readable science articles and the scientists' realization that their work, to be of benefit, must be interpreted, has come the need for competent, trained science writers. With the present rapid development of science, it is safe to forecast that future research may bring achievements even more far reaching than the present ones. In the years to come there will be a greater need for interpreters who can translate the language of the laboratories into interesting, readable, and precisely accurate articles.

As science develops, so will the art of writing it. Schools of

Journalism are training students to write science articles with precise accuracy. The scientists are sending their students to take feature and magazine writing courses to have them learn to write readable articles. Each group learns much from the other; both groups are learning to write science manuscripts that editors buy gladly, if they are written professionally.

The writer of the future will analyze science articles in current periodicals to note the recent trends in reader appeal and readability in this type of writing. As the general readers become more informed about science and the scientists become even more co-operative, the interpreters will devise new techniques of writing and illustrating facts. The scholar is a scientist as long as he has test tubes and a laboratory; the science writer continues as a student of techniques in science writing as long as he can obtain magazines.

Professional writers are avid readers of the scholars' many learned journals published by their respective learned associations. They list the names of the journals and their addresses, and as many become familiar with them, they indicate those which provide the best sources for ideas and background material for interviews. The names and addresses of the journals are obtained from Ulrich's *Periodical Directory,* N. W. Ayer & Son's *Directory of Newspapers and Periodicals,* or the *Handbook of Learned Societies* published by the Carnegie Institute, as listed in the "Free-Lance Writer's Library" in the Appendix.

The future is bright for writers and scientists learning the art of interpreting the research of the investigators. It is exacting, but it is the most satisfying field of writing for those who are willing to learn and who are interested in humanizing the work of the scholar and the expert. The rewards are many now; they will be greater in the future.

Examples of Science Articles from College Laboratories. Because advance magazine writing students are so close to science laboratories and are familiar with which ones yield the best sources for readable science articles, only three examples are used to illustrate how campus laboratories, as well as commercial laboratories, provide material for science writing. The first one, which sold to *Field & Stream,* was selected to show how an alert student combined his interview with a zoology research assistant, his observation of the experiment, and his sense of humor. He took several pictures to illustrate the experiment. The second article, with a full page picture, sold to *Today's Health.* It appeared in the same issue with an article by one of the author's classmates. As the reader can see, this article uses the knowledge gained in the author's social science course in psychology and his skill in making the reader see and understand the problem.

Every science or technological laboratory is "uranium" to the writer if he applies, as did the following authors, what he learns in the next chapter.

(1)
Fish Can Smell*

BY EDWARD A. LEHOVEN

When the old boy who was fishing off the pier was asked how he managed to catch so many fish, he smiled. "It's easy, those perch just like the way I smell," he explained, and I laughed right along with him.

Now that I look back to that day, I wonder if we might have laughed a little too soon. At the Lake Mendota Experimental Station directed by the Department of Zoology of the University of Wisconsin, Theodore J. Walker is proving that fish can smell, and has already presented a paper on the subject before a recent meeting of the Wisconsin Academy of Science.

Down in the basement of the laboratory, Ted, who is a research assistant in the Zoology Department, has ten tanks, each containing six bluntnose minnows. They are all two-year-old males, a ripe old age for the species. Minnows are being used because of their value as a forage fish, and their small size.

Each of the fish in the tank has identifying beads on its back which were fastened with rustless tantalum wire after the fish had been anesthetized. These beads, besides aiding in identification of the individual fish, help to give each a sporty look topside.

---

* Reprinted by permission of *Field & Stream* and Edward A. LeHoven.

In performing the experiments, the zoologist has taken all possible precautions against his fish using anything but the sense of smell to obtain the food which he places in the ends of the tank for them. The minnows have been chemically blinded, which doesn't seem to bother them a bit. In fact, they are better off in the testing tanks, being free from the predatory fish which they encounter in their normal environment. These blinded minnows use a method similar to an underwater radar system to keep from bumping into obstacles. It is their lateral line or "far distant touch organ" which runs lengthwise along their sides. This enables them to feel underwater pressures and vibrations which vary as they near an object.

In proving that fish can smell, Ted uses the odors of the underwater plants—coontail and water milfoil. These aquatic plants seem to be the favorite hangout of the microscopic plants and animals on which the minnows feed.

* * *

Although it took two and a half months for the entire group to learn the association of odors with a reward or punishment, Ted says that some fish with a high I.Q. can rate a diploma after only two weeks. Even among minnows there are geniuses and dunces, just as in any group.

Ted became interested in fish while in the U.S. Navy, and through his reading of the studies and research of Professor Karl von Frisch of Munich, Germany. Ted praises much of the work of von Frisch and his students. In experiments just after the end of World War I, the German scientists established that individual fishes use tiny nostrils on both sides of the snout just in front of the eyes. A little scoop-like structure of the fish helps to force the water through the fish's nostrils as he swims, enabling him to identify the different underwater odors.

Von Frisch has proved also that each species of fish—as some say do the races of mankind—has its own odor. Another interesting thing he found is a "danger-alarm" system with which nature has provided fish that travel about in schools. When one of the school has been wounded or bitten by a predatory fish, the open wound gives off an odor that alarms the mates of the wounded fish, and they swim to safety.

The fact that fish can smell will probably open up a whole new field to the manufacturers of lures, baits and, perhaps, the perfume interests. Heaven help the fisherman if the perfume makers ever turn their copy writers loose! Imagine thumbing through FIELD &

STREAM and finding ads for "Flowers of Frog" or "Parfum de Porke Rindee."

But, enough of that—and enough of this article. Can fish smell? You bet, one of them in the frying pan is taking me away from this typewriter.

(2)
Are You Afraid of Heights?*

By Howard C. Custer

The young football player's strong tenor led all the voices. They were singing, "Oh, What a Beautiful Morning."

The morning was precisely that, he thought as he walked along, a gay companion by his side, a small troop of other couples hiking with them under a blue and white sky.

They were gaining altitude rapidly. Grassy lowland became wooded slopes. The singing petered out, so the climbers might husband their strength.

But Dick, the football player, continued to sing from time to time. He was too happy to be quiet, and as he assured them, "This is a breeze for me, after football workouts."

Then happened what he had dreaded. The trail led around a slope. At first the drop below them was only a few feet, but even that was enough to take the joy out of Dick's day. They had not gone far up the cliff before his stomach was swarming with butterflies. He bore as close to the hillside as he could, but the trail grew narrower and the drop ever more impressive. He was heavy with sweat.

Finally he turned in desperation to his companion and blurted out, "I'm sorry, Ruth, but I've got to go back." His pride made him walk back down, but he walked feverishly. He yearned to run. When he got past the precipitous part of the trail, a great relief welcomed him, but it was the relief of a boxer who is knocked out and no longer has to take a beating. He felt thoroughly washed out.

Dick is a typical sufferer from acrophobia, the medical name for a morbid fear of high places. An open window more than a few floors up is a frightful place for him. A walk across a high bridge takes all the spirit he can muster. Stairways with open wells, towers and domes

*Reprinted by permission of *Today's Health* and Howard C. Custer.

with open steel stairs, catwalks, galleries, mountain peaks, ladders: anything that presents a sudden drop frightens him and, after a certain point, unnerves him.

* * *

In the case of most simple fears, the proper remedy is a judicious and firm disregard of them, after recognizing them for what they are: helpful warnings of danger.

An automobile driver turning into a stream of traffic from a side road may well fear being hit by an oncoming automobile. But if he lets that fear cow him so that he doesn't ease out into the traffic until there are no automobiles coming from either direction, he will be increasingly unhappy in traffic and will spend much of his time getting nowhere. On the other hand, if he forces himself to move out, carefully and surely, he will have made the crucial step in mastering such situations.

As Dr. Harlow remarks, "In the case of adults, fear is often a symptom of some more basic personality problem. The inactive, brooding person with time on his hands, no outside interests and only himself to think about is more than likely to worry about personal appearance, panic, insanity or death. For those individuals the cure for fear is not cure of a particular fear, but activity and appropriate outlets for their pent-up physical and mental energy."

Firmly established fear complexes and phobias cannot be so casually dismissed. We should not underrate their seriousness or advise anything for them but the most painstaking, studied and patient treatment. It would be thoroughly ill-advised to tell Dick to disregard his fear and go at once and climb a dizzy tower. If he did, he would suffer one more shock to augment the others. He would be worse off than ever.

To make headway against his besetting fear, Dick will have to use his newly found understanding of it, and of fear in general—and his friendly and professional help from others—to do two things: (1) set up a routine that will gradually accustom him to increasingly high places, and (2) follow that routine without fail.

Each time he achieves a greater height without being unnerved, that height will tend to become familiar and natural to him, and he will enjoy the satisfaction of accomplishment.

Reverses are bound to occur, but with perseverance Dick is sure to overcome his fear to a reasonable degree. That is, there will be few times in his day-to-day work and play when fear will make him unable to go where he is needed or wants to go.

True, his innate tender-mindedness and his childhood conditioning will almost surely keep him relatively sensitive to high places. He'll probably never climb the Matterhorn, or even the Capitol dome in Washington. It would take too long to recondition himself to that degree of casualness, and he has little need or desire to do so.

For, as he says, "After all, you don't have to be a human fly to live a long and happy life."

Exercises

1. Selecting a Sunday feature section of a sensational newspaper of your choice, list the feature articles which you classify as "pseudo-scientific."

2. Did you find any articles written by scientists in the sensational newspaper's feature section?

3. Did you find any articles in which the writer had interviewed the scientist and used direct quotations?

4. Why should a science writer know the history of the readable science article?

5. Who originated the first university press bureau? When? Where?

6. Who developed the readable science story for the press bureau? When?

7. What methods did the first university science writer use to win the co-operation of the scientists?

8. Which agricultural college was the first to adopt the idea of the agricultural editor? When?

9. What was the "Plan for the Dissemination of Science"? When was it drafted?

10. What part did university scientists and a university press man have in helping to organize *Science Service*?

11. Who made a bequest which made *Science Service* possible?

12. How is *Science Service* organized?

13. Who is the present director of *Science Service*?

14. Select a metropolitan newspaper and check it to see how many of the *Science Service* activities the newspaper uses.

15. What *Science Service* activities did you not find in the newspaper analyzed?

16. Which activities of *Science Service* do you think would be helpful to the beginning science writer?

17. How does the modern scientist's attitude toward writers differ from those of the earlier scientists?

18. How many "hours" or "credits" of science are required at your university? Do you think it should require more science? Why?

19. Examine the table of contents of three general magazines. List the readable science articles you found there.

20. Examine five science books for children in the children's room at the library or in a book store. What impressed you most about them?

21. What magazines now use science articles which you think did not use them before 1947?

22. Why are science articles in the learned journals so poorly written?

23. How may a scientist train himself to write readable articles?

24. Why are scientists still difficult to interview?

25. When was the National Association of Science Writers organized? Why?

26. List eight qualifications in addition to journalistic training for writing science articles.

27. Why do many journalists like science writing?

28. In which field of science do you now think you would be most interested in writing? Why?

29. What are the total number of markets using science articles?

30. Why are medical science articles the most popular with general readers?

31. List the names of magazines that you know use science articles.

Report No. 6, due sixth week of second semester.

INTERVIEW NOTES FOR THREE ARTICLES IN SELECTED FIELD

(Purpose is to do the interviewing for all three articles at one time, in order to save time for the interviewer as well as for the interviewee. Apply suggestions in Chapters 3, 19, and 20.)

Interviewee's Background: Include information obtained in talking to others about the interviewees as well as from research and from the interviewees themselves.

Questions: Include a carbon copy of the questions which you memorized before you went to the interview as well as the additional questions you recall asking during the interview.

Interview Notes: Hand in the interview notes just as you jotted them down after you left each interviewee's presence, but indicate interviewees and the phase of your field upon which you interviewed each. Your instructor and classmates may be able to suggest additional methods.

Interview Problems: Enumerate difficulties and explain how you met them, or how you failed to meet them. Instructor and classmates may benefit by your experience.

_____

_____

_____

Suggestions for Future: _____

_____

_____

CHAPTER 23

Writing Scientific and Technical Articles

▪▪▪

Demand for Scientific and Technical Articles Is Large. The atomic bomb may wipe out the newspapers and magazines of tomorrow, but these periodicals, along with radio and television, have enabled scientists to tell their stories to the layman through simplified, accurate language that not only can be understood but is readable and interesting to people who are not scientists. The distribution of this knowledge may keep the bombs of the future from bringing an end to the world, because such information will replace superstition.

Because readers are better educated and more willing to learn, they soon grasp the meanings of unfamiliar scientific and technical terms. Writers have learned that it is not necessary to "write down" to today's readers. The more the writer helps the readers, not only to recognize but to be familiar with scientific and technical words, the sooner his manuscripts will be in demand by magazines.

Feature Writers Find Science a Great Adventure. A beginning science writer, in a story scientifically combating the common housefly, humanized Joe Housefly so cleverly, by building up in the reader's mind sympathy then hate for the fly's filthy habits, that, as the reader finished the article, she wondered whether the housewives' war would not completely extinguish the dangerous pest before the summer ended. The article was effective because of its personalized and human appeal. The explanations were scientifically accurate and the reading was teeming with human interest appeal because the writer made "Joe" a person.

To the science or technical writer, every "tip," every market survey, every research project, every interview, every outline, and every page rolling out of the typewriter is another milepost on the way to the greatest adventure—a science or technical article. The subject matter of both is as broad as science and technology; there is never a dull moment. The opportunities are what the writer makes them. The largest checks for manuscripts are paid to free-lance science or technical writers and, as a rule, the highest salaries are paid to the science or technical writers on magazine staffs.

The beginner soon realizes that writing science or technology is the most difficult of any type of magazine writing. But it is the most challenging. The keen and alert journalist finds it the most intriguing, because the science writer translates and reveals the mysteries and the magic-like skills of the men in the laboratories in universities, professions, businesses, and industries.

Sources of Ideas for Science Articles Are of Two Types. Instead of finding "tips" anywhere and everywhere, as for other types of feature articles, the science and technical writer finds the best sources for his work fall into two classifications.

The primary sources include those based almost entirely on interviews and observations, and on hearing papers discussed at conventions. The resulting articles may be written for either the nonscientist or "the man in the street." Sources and ideas for the interviews are found by attending meetings, conferences, and conventions of scientists or technicians. Many of the "learned societies" require that news of research results in science or technology may not be released for print until after the scientists have read their "papers" concerning their discoveries before the "learned associations." Once the facts are announced at the meetings, the capable writer gathers the facts for the article, or articles, he wishes to write by interviewing the scientists who gave their reports at the meetings. The writer remembers it is useless to interview a scientist or technologist until his research is completed.

The professional science writer obtains programs for the conventions or meetings from the association secretaries or reads them in the learned journals. If it is not possible or convenient to attend the convention, or "congress," he often may obtain the content of the papers by correspondence. In order to do the latter, the writer must have an adequate scientific background, because explanations in writing are more difficult to comprehend.

The secondary source of "tips" includes scientific and technical reports in the learned and professional journals published by or for the many associations; free bulletins from agricultural colleges and experiment stations; United States government publications, announcements of which are issued semimonthly by the Superintendent of Documents, as listed in the Appendix in the "Free-Lance Writer's Library"; bulletins from various departments of one's own state government, as suggested in Chapter 18, "Doing Research"; publicity releases from public relations directors of museums, laboratories, research divisions of the professions, businesses, and industries; "services" from *Science Service;* announcements from publishers who specialize in science and technical books; new books in the library and the book stores; and daily reading in the special periodicals and newspapers.

Conversations with friends who are experts in the field serve as a short cut to secondary and often primary sources. Ideas for articles will hound the science writer day and night, jump at him out of test tubes in laboratories, out of learned journals and daily newspapers. Every article which he writes deals with facts accumulated by someone's extensive research which may have been developing over years of time.

No matter how rapidly or efficiently the science or technical writer works, or how capable or large his research staff, there will never be time to translate all the research and technology for the reader.

Successful Writers Reveal Their Methods. A well-known technical writer says he gets most of his tips from his evening newspaper. If he reads that a new factory has started production, he asks himself what editors will be interested in the new factory plans, the new products it is making, the new efficiency methods it may be employing. He contacts the factory public relations office and arranges for interviews with the technical experts. The public relations office supplies "glossies," drawings, charts, graphs —often at considerable expense to the company, but then its purpose is to create good will. From one newspaper story he obtained ideas for articles on new principles in factory architecture, illumination, ventilation, personnel comfort, and safety. Concerning the new product, he wrote articles which sold to a mechanical magazine, a home magazine, a house-furnishing trade magazine, and a garden magazine. The total profits from the nine articles for this alert and experienced writer's reading of a short newspaper story were more than $1,500. This writer follows each technical announcement and surveys it for ideas for articles.

A science writer living in the shadow of a great university jokingly says he is a parasite, because he lives by means of the library and the periodical room. As a "parasite" he preys on the "hosts," the researchers, scholars, and authorities. He reads of their investigations in the learned journals of the natural and social scientists and technicians. These reports provide material as well as ideas for articles. Even back issues—as far back as fifteen years—may contain suggestive research reports. He interprets the papers reported in the periodicals, selects the salient facts, interviews the investigators or authors on the campus or by mail, and writes the information into readable, precisely accurate, or non-technical, articles. The scientists and technical experts are glad to co-operate with him, because the modern ones wish their knowledge to be applied.

His "unseen global research staff" includes thousands of researchers and scholars of natural science and technology working in universities, hospitals, foundations, laboratories, and industries, and the social scientists whose studies result in new concepts and theories of interest to readers because these concepts concern them.

Of course he, as do all professional writers, contacts the authors of the learned papers, compliments them on their discoveries, and explains that he would like to interpret the material for the general reader, who may benefit by the information. Frequently the writer and the scholar co-operate: the one clarifying the details for the writer; the other writing of the research for the general reader, but giving full credit for the new discoveries to the investigator. Even though one lives in a remote section far from libraries, he may subscribe to some of the more suggestive journals or secure single copies from the publishers or from periodical brokers.

Such a writer may classify himself as a "parasite," but he is as important to mankind as his "hosts." He, too, contributes to the world in making the expert's word understandable and usable to the reader.

Factors a Beginner Considers in Selecting a Field in Science. The beginner does not permit a limited science or technical background to discourage him in selecting science as a field for writing. Formerly universities had to require students to take a science course. But postwar students flocked into science courses. Their maturity and their experiences in the services enabled them to realize the value of these courses after graduation. The student, however, who for one reason or another has not studied more than the required sciences in high school or in college need not hesitate to choose a science or a technical field for his writing in an advanced magazine course, or to train himself in science writing at home alone without the aid of a magazine writing course.

The writer who has studied several sciences may find that his knowledge is not up to date. Even the scholars cannot keep up to date in all phases of their own science, much less in all the fields. If a writer has the background of even a little science, however, it will enable him to speak and to understand his interviewee's language. Many writers have turned to writing science who studied but little or no science in school. They were scholars as well as writers, and by their own efforts acquired the necessary background. It is as true in science and technical writing as in anything else that if one wishes enough to do so, he will attain the background to write intelligently and understandingly.

In selecting a field of science in which he wishes to write, the beginner will find it to his advantage to reduce the subject to some one phase of the science. Sometimes even a phase covers too much and must be reduced to some angle of the phase. A student who selected the field of medicine narrowed his selection to the "miracle" drugs. After making a bibliography, he further reduced the field to one of the "miracle remedies," and after he had queried some editors, reduced it again, writing four articles for the course on the angle of the dangers of just one "miracle" drug.

General magazines as well as scientific periodicals are using health and medical articles. The health columns, increased science news in the daily press, and better educated readers, who can comprehend medical terms by associating them with familiar words, are responsible for the increased reader interest in medical advances. Writers have learned that it is not necessary to "write down" to today's readers. The more the writer helps the readers not only to recognize but to be familiar with or to know scientific and technical words the greater the reader appeal will be.

As agricultural magazines—national, sectional, state, and specialized—have widened their range of interests, another profitable market for agricultural technology and science has developed. As technology and science develop so does the opportunity of writing about them.

Beginner Tests the Tentative Selected Field. The selection of a field of writing in which to specialize is perhaps the most difficult task for the young writer in an advanced magazine course. But in choosing a field, the student writer will find that the decision is not difficult, if he asks himself the following questions:

(1) Will the subject be interesting to periodical readers six months or a year from now? (2) Will the subject be interesting enough to me to write about it? (3) Even with diligent research, will I be able to understand the subject? (4) Is the subject adaptable to interpretation? (5) Is library research material available on the subject? (6) Are interviewees available, either in person

or by correspondence? (7) Are there a sufficient number of markets to query, and later to slant the articles for sale? (8) Will the rates of payment of the possible markets compensate me adequately for time spent? (9) Will I be able to obtain the types of illustrations that each of the possible markets use? (10) Do any of the possible markets have any restrictions concerning advertising copy that would prevent their consideration of my manuscripts on the subject?

If the first eight questions can be answered in the affirmative, the writer will find not only pleasure in the gathering of the facts and the writing of the readable articles, but also adequate compensation journalistically and financially. Science and technical writing can be a full-time career, or it can be an interesting side line.

Research Is Fun for Trained Science Writer. The gathering of facts by means of library research is as much fun as the old treasure hunt of childhood days, if one is trained in the techniques and knows the sources of material. As the writer gathers the facts, he keeps in mind the purpose of his article—to inform, to interpret, to explain, to apply it to life. He never forgets that he is to write with precise accuracy and to indicate to the readers the significance of the scientific discovery or invention in readable terminology. Even while gathering the material, the writer will be aided in his selection of interesting facts by having the potential readers of the article "sitting around in his mind."

The science or technical writer gathers the material on the basis of what he is going to explain to the reader. He selects the facts concerning the research in even more detail than for any other type of article in order that he may write clearly. He takes more notes than he thinks he will use when doing research and in interviewing until he has acquired skill in selecting wisely. He checks the research and interview notes to see that (1) the material keeps to the "interest-holding line" of the outline, as explained in Chapter 10; (2) the quotations are exact and that he has a sufficient number to quote adequately; (3) the sources are accurate and that he has the full names and titles of the authorities quoted or interviewed. Tracking down even one incomplete fact can change research for science articles from being an interesting and pleasant part of writing to drudgery. The work is a challenge: (1) to get information; (2) to keep up to date as much as possible; and (3) to win the confidence of the scientist or technical expert.

An inquiring and alert mind to gather and sift the facts is needed by the science writer just as much as by the science scholar. The two have much in common.

Planning the Science Interview. The success of an interview in writing a science article depends upon the writer's careful research, thoughtful planning, and ability to draw out the interviewee to speak freely. Interviewing is an art in any type of writing. But the statement is particularly true when applied to interviewing for science or technical articles. The differences in the methods of the training of the scientist and the writer—the specialized knowledge of the former, and the necessity of the latter clearly to understand every step of the research and to comprehend the future benefits or dangers of its results to mankind— make additional problems to those discussed in Chapter 3. If a science writer gives careful thought to the planning part of the interview, and if he is tactful in his approach, he should succeed in getting the whole-hearted co-operation of the expert, or experts, and in obtaining the desired information.

The plan for the science interview consists of five parts; each will follow in logical order. The first part is the preinterview.

It includes: (1) sending queries to editors of possible markets; (2) arranging the appointment for an interview through a brief and tactful letter enclosing a copy of the questions to be discussed and the name of the interested magazine queried; (3) doing accurate and thorough research; (4) taking to the interview a copy of the bibliography used for the research; (5) outlining the interviewee's biography, achievements, and their benefits obtained from library sources and from interviews with the expert's colleagues; and (6) including any human interest incidents to show that the learned scholar is human and likeable.

The tactful writer explains in the letter to the expert requesting an interview the reason for his selection. It may be that the scientist selected is the outstanding authority, that his new discovery will benefit mankind, or that his sharing his knowledge with the readers will be a real service to them. The writer should include in the letter some idea of the length of time that he estimates the interview will take. Even though most experts have secretaries, it is considerate also to enclose a stamped self-addressed envelope for confirmation of the time for the interview. If the writer has had previous interviews with the expert, perhaps the request for the interview may be made through the secretary over the telephone. Mailing the questions in advance gives the expert time to think about the answers. The more thinking the scientist does about the proposed questions, the more interested and co-operative he will be, and he will be less apt to answer merely "yes" or "no" at the interview. In this connection, Chapter 18 will be suggestive for the research necessary. A carbon copy of the writer's bibliography, particularly if he is just beginning science writing and his reputation for thoroughness is unknown to the interviewee, will instill confidence in the latter's mind and, too, may move him to suggest background sources unknown to the writer. The trained writer will weigh thoughtfully the comments about the interviewee's achievements made by his colleagues. Even scientists, with their objective training, have not all overcome the human weakness, jealousy. It behooves the writer to recognize jealousy as well as insincere over-praise prompted, perhaps, by an ulterior motive. The time that the writer spends on the preinterview will be time well spent.

Interview Questions Must Be Formulated Skillfully. The second division of the interview, planning the interview questions, is based on: (1) the research notes; (2) a survey of the interested queried market to know the editor's purpose and the readers' interests; (3) the trend of current events; (4) the effect that the research results will have on the lives of the readers; (5) the number of the scientific and technical terms the readers will understand without explanations; and (6) the most effective method of presenting the facts to hold the readers' interest.

The questions must be so phrased that the expert cannot simply answer "yes" or "no." They should be formulated carefully to instill confidence in the interviewee because he sees that the writer has adequate background, training, and experience. Without thoughtful preparation, the writer may find that he does not have sufficient quotations to explain the scientific processes with precise accuracy. If the writer does not understand every detail, he will not be able to write a readable as well as an accurate manuscript. Fortunate indeed is the writer whose interviewee speaks simply and freely. But carefully planned questions will give the interviewee confidence in the writer, and with confidence will come facility of speech to explain his research clearly to the writer.

The writer must know the interviewee's life history and achievements well enough to know what questions *not* to ask. If the interviewee is irritated by tactless questions, the interview may be a failure. With experience a sort of sixth sense comes to the writer to know when to interrupt and when to continue listening. If the expert gets off the subject, the alert writer tactfully swings back to the topic by asking a question concerning the process, but he avoids blunt remarks, such as, "To get back to the subject, Mr. Scientist. . . ."

Even though the writer has his questions well memorized, he must be able to change them when necessary. He must be alert to ask new questions about new angles of the subject which he had not anticipated.

Next to the last question, he will ask about pictures and other illustrations. If they cannot be obtained from the public relations office or its photographic department, he will make arrangements to have the pictures taken at the interviewee's convenience. The last question on the list will be a request for the interviewee to check the completed manuscript for scientific or technical accuracy. This point will be discussed in more detail in the post-interview part of the plan.

Developing a Co-operative Attitude at the Beginning of the Interview. The third step in the interview plan, establishing a co-operative attitude, is extremely important. But it is not difficult if one applies the techniques of the psychology of interviewing and ideas obtained from previous interviewing experiences. The writer will win the respect and confidence of the expert and, as a consequence, may in the future find frequent ideas for articles in the test tubes in the scientist's laboratory which will bring large checks.

The scholar, as pointed out earlier in the chapter, due to his way of life, may be reticent, because he may dread the taunts of his jealous colleagues who, he fears, will accuse him of "seeking publicity." The writer will be better able to put the scholar at his ease and lessen his dread of the criticism of his fellow scientists if he shows the learned man the importance of his helping mankind. This help can be given by making the news of a discovery available to readers through a precisely accurate article written in a readable style they can understand. The writer's own sincere enthusiasm about the expert's discovery will entice even an introvert into showing some interest in sharing his knowledge with non-scientists. The successful writer never forgets that enthusiasm is contagious.

In introducing himself, the writer will not attempt to impress the scholar with his own scientific knowledge or his success in writing. By his confident manner, the copy of the bibliography of his library research, which he gives to the interviewee, his intelligent questions, and his ability to comprehend the scientific explanations, the writer modestly shows that he has some background. Apologetically he may ask the scientist or technical expert for additional explanations of concepts, processes, or results of the research, because of his desire to present the facts to the readers with precise exactness.

The writer points out that he wishes to guard against misleading the editor and injuring his own reputation as a careful writer, and that, above all, he does not wish to make himself or his scientist-interviewee ridiculous in the eyes of other scholars by writing inaccurately. The expert probably will relax and feel that, at last, here is a writer he can trust.

If the journalist frankly explains to the expert that he is "just a writer and not a scientist" and that he will need the latter's help in understanding scientific terminology in order that he may write clearly for the reader, he generally gains the information in less technical language. If the expert continues to use scientific terms outside the writer's scientific experience, the latter should never hesitate to interrupt, laughingly explaining that he is "just a simple-minded journalist," and should ask for a simplified or more detailed explanation. The scientist, particularly if he, or she, is not skilled in writing, probably will be sympathetic and understanding about the magazine writer's problem. He may recall his own lack of confidence when attempting to write his scientific reports or "papers." Sincere appreciation expressed by the writer to the expert of the importance of the latter's research to humanity will increase the scholar's desire to be of help to the writer.

Part of the science writer's career is spent in persuading the shy natural scientists, or "pure scientists," as they sometimes term themselves, to become in part "social" scientists, by co-operating and aiding man's welfare through sharing their expert knowledge. It may take the writer's ingenuity and perseverance to obtain the interview, but a check of generous size may repay him for his efforts.

Interviewing Experts May Present New Problems. The fourth point in the plan is the interviewing of the interviewee. The beginning science or technical writer will profit by re-reading Chapter 3 to refresh his, or her, mind on the techniques of interviewing. In interviewing authorities for the science or technical article, the writer should use the following additional suggestions:

The science writer has a trained memory and does not need to take down notes until after he has left the scholar's presence. The reticent scholar, as discussed previously, may not talk freely if the writer is taking notes. However, if the interviewee is accustomed to being interviewed, he may respond with less hesitancy to the writer who takes notes during the interview. As a rule, both the interviewee and the writer are at a disadvantage if notes are taken during the interview. The latter may not have time for note-taking if he is to understand and to be alert to ask unplanned questions. He must be free to think as the interviewee talks.

Since the interview may concern material never before printed, the writer may not be able to recheck facts or processes which he does not understand completely—his part is a listening one. The interviewee may be the writer's only source of information. The latter must understand every step of each process before the scholar discusses the next. As the writer listens, he also makes mental note of new questions that come to his mind as the scholar talks. Thus he has two listening tasks at the same time.

To appeal to the scientist's imagination is more difficult than in interviewing nonscientists. The former's training and experience has made him objective and impersonal. But the keen journalist will use psychology of recall by suggesting experiences with which the scientist is familiar, or will get him to envision his family, neighbors, fellow townsmen, the nation, or even the world benefited or endangered by this new discovery. The scholar then will better appreciate the writer's mission.

The experienced writer weaves into his notes suggestions from Chapter 7 as well as from Chapter 3, in order to include the personalized and human-interest angle which increases the reader appeal of the article, particularly if it is to be slanted to a general-reader publication.

After checking his questions to see that he has all the desired answers and that he understands each, the writer discusses with the interviewee the arrangements for the illustrations for the article. These may be pictures, charts, graphs, or tables that will add to the precise accuracy and readability of the article.

A reputable science writer always asks the expert if he will be good enough to check the manuscript for scientific accuracy. The latter will be glad to have an opportunity to protect his reputation and probably will be more willing to co-operate with the same writer, or any writer, the next time an interview is requested.

In closing the interview, the writer sincerely thanks the scientist or expert for his time, his knowledge, and his help in explaining processes and terminology. The writer should not assume a begging attitude, but an appreciative one. After all, the writer is doing the scientist a favor by making his research known, just as the scientist did one for the writer by explaining the research and its impact.

An interesting interview is an inspiration to any writer, and to the reader of the resulting article, too, because it supplies "that extra something" to the article that aids in holding the reader's interest.

The Post-interview Is Important to Science Writer. The fifth and final section of the plan is the post-interview.

It includes: (1) the immediate transfer of the notes from the writer's memory to paper as soon after leaving the interviewee as is possible; (2) the "thinking period," consciously and subconsciously, which also may include more note-taking; (3) the detailed survey of the interested, queried magazine to slant the article to fit it, as suggested in Chapters 9 and, particularly, 19; (4) planning and outlining, as suggested by Chapter 10 and the magazine survey; (5) the writing of the article, making 3 copies, as discussed later in this chapter; (6) the obtaining and preparing for publication pictures, charts, graphs, maps, or tables; (7) the mailing to the interviewee of the third copy of the article and the illustrations to be checked for scientific accuracy, a large stamped self-addressed envelope for the return of the manuscript if approved, a small self-addressed envelope containing a note for the expert's signature, indicating the time he will see the writer to check the inaccurate statements which the latter may have made, and two approval sheets for the interviewee to sign; (8) necessary revision after the manuscript has been checked by the expert; (9) the mailing to an editor of the manuscript, including one of the signed approval sheets; (10) filing the carbon copy and the second signed approval sheet in the writer's files for his, or her, future protection; and (11) the sending of a note to the interviewee telling him the date when the article is scheduled to appear, or, even better, a copy of the magazine containing the article.

The experienced science and technical writer lets nothing interfere with his reducing the interview to writing in order to have precisely accurate quotations and detailed steps of the research. The "thinking period" permits time for the "subconscious mind" to do its work and for the writer to do more research or interviewing if necessary because of new ideas. The "thinking period" may extend over a day, a week, two weeks, or more, until the mind has a plan of presentation or an overdrawn bank account reminds the writer the "thinking period" must come to an end.

For the above steps numbered 3, 4, 5, and 6, the beginning science or technical writer may refresh his memory by reviewing the suggested chapters in Part I and Part II, relating them to the discussions on the following pages of this chapter.

Step number 7 is extremely important to the science and technical writer. No matter how experienced or how well informed, any writer may misunderstand some step or process of the research and make the scientist or expert appear ridiculous in the eyes of his fellow scientists and ruin his own writing reputation and the reputation of the magazine which buys the manuscript. The returned carbon copy checked for scientific accuracy and the two approval sheets signed by the interviewee will protect the writer against later criticisms of the interviewee or the editor.

Had a beginning science writer taken those precautions he would have had a defense when a certain scientist blamed him for inaccuracies which both the scholar and the writer had overlooked. In criticizing the young writer, the scientist insisted he had not approved the carbon copy of the article, although he had done so verbally.

Appeals to Use in Planning the Outline for the Science or Technical Article. As with any article, the writer gives careful thought to the plan of the outline. He incorporates into the outline any effective reader appeals that will enlist and hold the readers' attention. During the "thinking period," his subconscious mind probably works out a novel or unique lead with which to catch the reader's eye. To hold the reader's attention, the writer will recall from Chapter 10 and his own writing experiences that the writer must enable the reader to see himself identified with—benefited or endangered by—the new discovery or the results of the scholar's research. The experienced journalist includes in the outline the writing devices that will make the reader feel that the discovery does concern him or his friends personally; if not now, then in the future.

To show the reader the implications and impacts of the discovery on his daily living, his business, his nation, or his world, the science or technical writer makes points of contact with the readers throughout the article. By the use of the psychology of recall the writer appeals to the readers' previous knowledge and experience, a device which increases their interest. To present facts in a sequence will enable the reader to understand the scientific process more clearly. The modern writer avoids the sensational writer's overuse of reader-appeal devices, because the present-day readers of science and technical articles seek out factual material, whereas a decade or so ago their interest had to be caught and held.

Because of the nature of his material, the science or technical writer gives more thought to: (1) determining the limits of the article; (2) the scope of the treatment, and (3) the anticipation of what the reader may want to know. This process necessitates a thoughtful culling of his research and interview notes. As he plans the outline, he keeps his reader in mind, even more than when writing general articles, and he remembers his reader has intelligence, though he may not have a scientific or technical background. He follows the plan of the outline in Chapter 10, except that he substitutes "application to mankind" for the words "interest-holding line," in the pyramid construction. The subject matter may be planned to go from effect to cause, or cause to effect, depending upon the type of publication to which the writer is slanting.

In planning the outline, the writer remembers that understatement is better than overstatement and, like the scholar, he avoids holding out any false hopes to the readers. The well-organized science outline is the result of the writer's ability to visualize his readers, to hear them asking, why? how is it possible? how does it concern me, my family, my neighbors? will it make me healthier, wealthier, wiser, happier? what will be the consequences of this discovery on my children's lives? The experienced writer anticipates the reader's questions. If he does not do so, he will not have any readers, because he will not have an editor.

Writing the Science or Technical Article. The increased interest in science and technology during the last decade has influenced the style of the writing of science and technical articles. The modern writer regards them as adventure stories from a magic-like world of the scientist's laboratory. He keeps in mind the purpose—to interpret a scientific discovery and indicate its significance to mankind in a precisely accurate and readable or non-technical article. The writer's mission is to transform science from a thing of mystery into an enjoyable, understandable, and useful knowledge for the reader. The latter is too busy being an expert philosopher, advertising copy writer, bond salesman, mechanic, or home-maker to be an expert in science, but these readers wish to add to their knowledge of science and technology.

Of all the types of magazine writing, science or technology may seem more difficult, but to those interested in humanizing the knowledge of the scientist or the technologist, it offers many satisfactions. The scientists advance knowledge; the writer, interpreting that knowledge, advances development and progress. "Dual attraction" subjects, such as medicine, are of interest to readers of both sexes and are greatest in demand, according to a recent periodical survey.

In writing the science article, the beginner should refresh his mind by reviewing Chapters 11, 12, and 13. If he has been away from his writing for some time, he may find it of value to review Chapters 14 and 15. In addition to those suggestions, the writer will find others in the analysis of science articles as he makes the market surveys of the interested queried magazines.

The science writer, by injecting human interest and personal appeal into the article, will have no difficulty in holding the reader's interest. Constant references to the effect of the discovery on mankind will lure the reader on to the end of the article. The science writer, more than any other, must visualize his reader, sensing what he wishes to know as if he were asking the questions over the writer's shoulder as the latter sits at his typewriter.

The Lead Serves as Writer's Lure to Reader. As in any writing, the science writer avoids generalizations. That is why the pseudoscience and many of the popularized science articles of the sensational press are inaccurate. Their writers ignore the principle of precise accuracy. Interpreters of science regard their sort of writing as an exact science. They have the same attitude toward accuracy as the pure scientists. Facts are handled by science writers as carefully in writing as if they were atomic bombs. Every word is carefully selected and weighed to see that it puts the exact idea in the readers' minds.

In analyzing the articles written by the best science writers, the beginner finds that the first part of the lead starts with a definite situation, rather than an abstract idea. A situation in which the reader can see himself, or with which he is familiar, serves as the first part of the lead. The fiction part of the lead, or, in science writing, an "effect needing a cause, or a cause implying an effect," carries the readers' interest into the body of the article.

The first paragraphs of the modern science article are forward-not backward-looking. The science writer uses utmost care to use the familiar to explain the unfamiliar. He tells what he is going to explain in concise sentences. After writing the lead, the beginner will profit by checking "the faults to be avoided" in Chapter 11.

The technical writer, writing for technical readers, follows the same suggestions as does the science writer, except that he does not use a light opening or a fictional lead. He gets right into the subject in the first line of the technical article by using a simple, factual beginning. And of course he does not need to simplify as many technical terms as when writing to the general reader.

Writer Keeps in Mind the "Application to Mankind" Interest Line. Writing the body of the science article does not vary much from any other type of article except that the writer keeps in mind throughout the article that he must humanize science or technology by showing how the discovery affects the reader's life or the lives of his family or friends. The beginner in science writing must bear in mind that people are interested in people, and that first of all each person is interested in himself.

The modern science interpreter has given science a new meaning to the readers by showing them how the research or discovery will aid them directly or indirectly. General readers, for example, are not interested in isotopes, but when they learn how isotopes as "tracers" in elements may benefit humanity, they feel they know the word, because it means something to them. The appeal of the science article is in its application to the home, children, family, health, hobbies, trades, businesses, and professions. Nonscience readers are interested if they learn how the discovery may make them healthier, wealthier, wiser, and happier.

An informal tone adds to reader interest when the writer writes as if he were telling the reader the facts as they sit together discussing the discovery. He makes frequent use of anecdotes, hypothetical cases, personal pronouns, and familiar incidents.

In telling the reader of the various experiments and their developments, the science interpreter describes them in concise, unified paragraphs with concrete words. He writes clearly and with such precise accuracy that the readers cannot fail to follow each step. The writer quotes authorities frequently to make the subscribers feel that the facts are authentic and to keep the readers to the interest-holding "application to mankind" line of the article.

Only such details should be included as will help make the story more personal, more vivid, and more complete. If the writer overloads the manuscript with too many details—dates, figures, names, minute description of apparatus, and technical terminology beyond the reader's comprehension—he will lose the latter's interest.

Only those facts should be included that are significant. The successful writer assumes that the reader has no previous knowledge of the subject, yet avoids insulting him by defining every term used. If the beginner will examine articles written by experienced writers, he will find that they each relate the scientific discovery as if they were talking to a friend. One of the outstanding science writers points out that Kipling used many terms in his stories which were not in a dictionary, yet the reader caught the meaning and enjoyed the yarns. Scientific terminology, also, if it is not too technical, will not confuse the readers. Scientific articles can be dignified even though conversational. The news of the discovery gives the article the necessary dramatic effect.

Readable Science Article Is Result of the Style of Writing. Talent has but little to do with science writing. Skill (1) to get and to understand facts in order to explain clearly, (2) to narrate interestingly, (3) to describe vividly, and (4) to write with facility, is the important qualification. There are three types of science articles from the point of view of writing: (1) technical, written by scholars for the learned journals; (2) semitechnical, or semiscientific, for nonscience as well as science readers, written by scientists who have learned the art of writing readably, or by journalists who write with precise accuracy; and (3) readable science, or non-technical articles, written by journalists for non-science and general readers.

The style of writing in the readable science article is the result of about nine-tenths thinking. The successful writer gives thought to: (1) enlivening dry facts with human interest incidents; (2) breaking down statistical material into figures the reader can comprehend, as explained in Chapter 11; (3) simplifying by use of analogy; and (4) comparing scientific concepts to objects with which the reader is familiar.

Readable science articles are based upon the following qualities of style: (1) well-organized paragraphs, (2) varied sentence lengths, (3) application of principles of style, and (4) choice of words.

In science and technical writing, more than in any other, the writer avoids long paragraphs, because they are tiring to the eye and they make the writing look ponderous. As in any other writing, attention is given to making the paragraph beginnings forceful and eye-attracting. Unity, coherence, emphasis, and brevity are four principles of style to keep in mind in writing each paragraph.

Simple, vital, useful, and meaningful vocabulary is necessary for the interpreter of science or technology. He strives to write concisely but avoids overdoing it, because it may hinder the reader's grasp of the research steps as well as be too factual to be interesting. If the reader does not understand, he loses interest. Explanations and descriptions should not be wordy, but they must be clear to the reader. The interpreter selects words for their connotations as well as their denotations. He chooses simple, concrete, picture-making words—words that the reader can see, not abstract words nor the "mumbo-jumbo" of the learned scientists. He should have a large vocabulary to provide the right word in every instance.

The readable science writer uses scientific terms sparingly but includes informal definitions as he would in conversation. He also can explain by applying them to the reader's experiences. Airplane global travel is introducing many new words to readers and to radio and television audiences. Even grade school children use scientific terms correctly and have an insight into the problems of nuclear energy and other modern scientific discoveries. Old files of periodicals show that the writing of a decade or two ago was polysyllabic, ponderous, and dull. Today, science articles are readable, because they are written in simple terminology with words of fewer syllables. Readable effective science writing is hard work; easy writing is hard reading.

Precise Accuracy Is Necessary in Readable Science Article. "Accuracy Always," the journalist's motto, becomes "Precise Accuracy Always" in writing readable science. Using the new motto, the science writer gains the confidence of the scholars and of the readers alike. His opportunities for more articles and for more sales are increased if he is known for his precise accuracy. The ability to write with precise accuracy is due to an inborn desire never to misrepresent, or to scholarly journalistic training.

In his attempt to write with exactness so that those who do not know science will read and understand, the science writer must ever be on his guard not to write down to the reader nor insult his intelligence. The writer weaves into the article the necessary scientific background so that the reader can understand without looking up terms in a textbook or dictionary as he reads.

The experienced writer checks everything into which an error could creep. He checks titles, complete names, initials, positions, locations, facts, and dates. He re-reads the manuscript to avoid overstatement and "talking down" to the readers. The interpreter has a duty to the editor as well as to the scholar interviewee. He also checks to see that he has given credit to the investigators whose life work he uses. In indicating the source of his information in the note to the editor on the cover sheet, he indicates, if the source is from a scientific or technical journal, the name of the author, the name of the periodical, volume number, date of issue, and page.

A writer never fails to have his article checked by the expert interviewed for scientific accuracy and to have the latter sign the two approval sheets. Since the article was written through the scientist's or expert's co-operation in telling of his research work, the interpreter desires it to be precisely accurate to please the scientist, the editor, and the readers.

Checking the Science Manuscript for Readability. Just as the careful writer has his science manuscript checked for scientific accuracy, so also he checks it for readability.

Educators during the last fifteen years thought they had discovered "readability." The journalists, without the benefit of formulae, have been practicing readability principles for decades. The educators within the past few years have published several books on the art of readability. Interesting though they are, they have contributed little to the art of writing that the journalist has not been doing for many years, with the exception of working out intriguing formulae.

If the journalist used the formulae constantly, his writings would probably bore even the very young because of their monotonous simplicity. The educators maintain that "affixes, suffixes, prefixes, and inflectional endings make reading difficult." They are probably correct, if they apply the formulae to children only. But the journalist writes to intelligent, mature readers—intelligent even though they did not have the advantages of higher education. The unintelligent, to whom the formulae would apply, read little but the headlines of the sensational press. The general magazine reader is intelligent, and a few affixes, prefixes, or suffixes will not make an article difficult reading for him.

Readability analyses have spread rapidly. The journalistic critics of the educators' books say that the first purpose of writing is to tell the reader what the writer has to say. If a sentence of 17 or 25 words is not sufficient to say it, the best writers may use a 70-word sentence. Magazines and newspapers are not read by morons. The minds of the general readers are intelligent, not "dim-witted." Writers work with words to make a living. Their readers work with bonds, automobiles, shoes, real estate, foods, electric devices, or pots and pans and are as expert in their fields as are the trained and experienced writers in theirs. In addition, they do have an understanding of affixes or prefixes and are not discouraged at the sight of them on the printed page.

Science writing is practical, but it can be artistic. Long sentences as well as short ones add to the reading pleasure because of variety. Simple structure, carefully selected vocabulary, and psychology of recall all aid in making the reading easier.

In checking a manuscript for readability, the writer substitutes verbs or adjectives for nouns and Anglo-Saxon words for Latin because they are more forceful. Words that, as Walter Lippmann suggests, "put pictures in the reader's mind," or that appeal to his senses—suggesting sights, sounds, smells, feelings, tastes—aid in readability. Studies made by journalism scholars show that some of the digest magazines simplify articles by reducing sentence length from 25 words to 14.5 on an average. They also reduce affixes, but increase the use of personal pronouns, such as "you," "we," "us." They begin sentences with short, unaccented words instead of dependent clauses.

Every journalist knows that magazine articles depend on accuracy, brevity, clearness, coherence, and directness to hold readers. Brevity may be achieved by: (1) cutting out extraneous detail; (2) eliminating unnecessary use of the articles a, an, the, and that, when used as a conjunction; and (3) avoiding long, complex, and periodic sentences, as well as parenthetical expressions.

If the writer followed the suggestions of the formulae of some learned scholars in education, his life would be as dull as his writing; his manuscripts would not be read by readers, since the editors would not buy them because of their deadly monotony. The educators overlook the fact that variety is to style and readability what seasoning is to food.

Testing the manuscript for readability will repay the writer for his effort. Reading it aloud to himself as well as having a nonscientist—wife, husband, or friend—read it to see if she, or he, understands every sentence is a good test. But applying and following the educators' formulae would make the readers, with the exception of little children, lose all interest.

The technical and scientific vocabulary and ponderous style of the scientist of the past did much to hinder scientific education of the general reader, but the university press men and journalists have developed a new, terse, and lively style of science writing. Scientific knowledge is no longer worshipped as a mystic cult but is understood by and has value to the general reader. Readers are not awed by scientific terms, as many scientists of the old school would like to think. Even the beginner's science manuscript will be readable, if he checks it for the journalistic principles of readability.

The world of technology and science realizes its need for trained writers. Some engineering corporations have editorial bureaus with trained technical writers to make their accomplishments known. These writers have organized writing groups to be better able to write readable articles that editors will buy. They include technicians, editors, and technical writers. Technologists have sections on writing at many of their Institutes and many university extension departments sponsor writing courses for technical writers who want to improve the reader appeal of their writing.

Illustrating the Science Article. Some of the better science magazines devote 40 per cent of their publications to illustrations.

Pictures, transparencies, graphs, charts, tables, or maps are all effective media for translating scientific ideas for science or non-science readers. The writer should avoid including illustrations merely for decoration, however.

If pictures do not clarify the processes or explanations, editors will not buy them. A picture for a science article should be striking, revealing, and dramatic. The details of the processes must be clear and sharp. As suggested in Chapters 15 and 20, a writer may obtain pictures from public relations departments of the federal and state governments, university photographic laboratories, or public relations departments of manufacturing and industrial concerns, if he writes to explain his needs.

If possible, always include a human figure, whole or in part, in a picture. For example, a pair of hands arranging the apparatus gives a human appeal to the picture. The photograph of the interviewee has more reader interest if he is shown at work in his laboratory rather than sitting at his desk. Use of color in pictures also adds much to the interest appeal.

Transparent wax-back sheets, which can be obtained in an art supply shop, are useful in making diagrams and maps. A photolithographer's film is best to use in photographing India-ink drawings. Blemishes, such as pin points, may be covered with opaquink. Science writers use bar charts for data by years to show comparisons or contrasts, and line charts to show trends over a period of years. *Science Service* uses the cartoonograph to present scientific facts in picture form. If possible, long lists of statistics should be omitted, for they kill rather than attract reader interest.

The science writer will study illustrations used with science articles in current magazines, for the fields of art and photography are developing almost as rapidly as science itself. What is new today is old tomorrow.

Examples of Scientific and Technical Articles. The first of the following articles was slanted to *Better Homes and Gardens*. When the instructor objected to the appropriateness of the market, the student-author explained he had just read in a writer's magazine that *Better Homes and Gardens* had announced it was in the market for scientific health articles. The instructor (who had not yet read the writer's magazine) approved. In a short time after sending the article the writer received a check for $150.00 for the "head ache." The second science article from *Sports Afield* brought its author a check for $250.00, a good reward for having analyzed the market carefully to see how the subject should be written to appeal to the magazine's readers. In reading the first two articles one sees that before doing any interviewing both writers did a great deal of research.

A new type of market, the external house organ, often contains technical articles written simply but with human interest appeal injected into them to hold the reader's interest. Such a type is the third example selected from *Ford Farming*. The fourth article, similar in some ways to the third but slanted to a more general type of publication, brought the technical writer another good-sized check from *Popular Science,* which has used several of his earlier articles. The fifth article originated from the writer's hobby of "trains" and his thorough study of the market to which he was slanting his skillfully written article. Note the detailed table that helped sell the feature to *Trains.*

All of the articles were generously illustrated because all the authors knew that pictures help sell features on science and technology.

(1)

Migraine—
It's All in Your Head*

It won't lessen the pain to know that you're probably above average in intelligence. But it will help if you're smart enough to calm down, take it easy.

By Kenneth G. Johnson

The attendant carefully replaced the gas tank cap, dusted desert sand from the back window, wiped his hands on an oily rag and

---

* Reprinted by permission of *Better Homes and Gardens* and Kenneth G. Johnson.

repeated, "Yes, I'm a Harvard law graduate. Could be making a lot of dough in New York. But I just couldn't take it."

He walked around the front of the car to check the water. "Don't have much business here. Traffic over the desert is rather slim. But I'm taking it easy and haven't had a headache since I settled here."

Migraine, frequently called "the disease of the alert mind" had disabled another highly intelligent and gifted person who could do so much for his family and the world.

But, unlike so many migraine sufferers, this man had learned early the secret of combating those painful, throbbing headaches so frequently followed by nausea and utter misery. Dr. Walter C. Alvarez, a senior consultant in medicine at the Mayo Clinic, has this to say about the only known cure for migraine: "The best way in which to get rid of migraine is to solve life's problems and to learn to live calmly and peacefully, free from conflict with self and others."

The typical attack of migraine begins with quick "flashes" and a darkening of the visual field. This is followed in about 20 minutes by a throbbing headache, nausea, complete misery, and perhaps vomiting. An attack may last for hours or several days.

Of course, not all attacks are typical. Sometimes the flashes are missing. Occasionally, the headache is so slight that it is hardly noticed. And many times the nausea and vomiting never develop.

With such a variety of symptoms, migraine has always puzzled doctors. Even today the nausea and abdominal discomfort are frequently misinterpreted as an intestinal or abdominal disturbance requiring an operation. Patients encourage this kind of thinking because they want action. They are desperately seeking relief. An operation is real. It is something they can see and believe in. Advice on how to live, on the other hand, seems vague and uncertain.

Everybody tells them to "get more rest" or "take it easy," so these words from a doctor merely echo what they hear every day.

But after 40 years of work with the sick, Doctor Alvarez reports, "I have never seen migraine cured by any type of operation."

"One never finds the 'cause' of migraine by any amount of searching thru the body. The cause is a hereditary peculiarity of the brain. It is 'built into' the brain and cannot be altered by operations."

Most patients would profit much more from seeing a psychiatrist, interested in the problems of the sane, than from surgical operations. They must learn to recognize that they will probably always have the tendency to the disease, that searching for a complete cure is futile.

An attack is a sort of "storm" that takes place in an overly sensitive brain. Almost anything unusual can serve as a trigger to spring the trap and bring on a spell. A party, a trip, an accident, a bad night's sleep, or worry can start an attack.

For example, a woman received a long distance call from Cincinnati. Before the connections could be made, she imagined all kinds of horrible accidents that might have befallen her daughter, who lived in that city. She became nervous. Beads of perspiration stood out on her forehead. Her heart began to pound. The call proved to be a business call for her husband. But the excitement of those few moments brought on an attack of migraine.

Altho migraine is not primarily an allergic disease, the reaction to an allergy may serve to trigger an attack. The allergy, then, is not the cause of the migraine, but one of a number of things that can make migraine active.

Most of the sufferers seeking medical help are women. While men normally get only the headache and are able to carry on, women tend to have a complete attack with all the related misery.

These migrainous women usually have a distinct temperament that is peculiar to the disease. Doctor Alvarez has observed that, "They are more alike than sisters, and their troubles are due to their unusual sensitivity, their nervous tension, and their easy fatigability."

"They are usually above average in intelligence and social charm. They are tense, quick in thought and movement, and idealistic. They like to get things done fast and just so. They are perfectionists. Most are hypersensitive to sound, lights, and smells, and this brings them much suffering. They fatigue and wilt quickly under any strain or excitement. They can get so tense even thinking of doing something that they get a headache before they start."

"Because of their great sense of responsibility and their good intelligence, they usually carry on their shoulders the cares and worries of the rest of the family, and this often leads to their undoing."

As a result of this temperament many migrainous women have marital troubles or fail to marry. They tend to be such perfectionists that only a door-mat type of husband, or one who is extremely kind and considerate, can tolerate their fussiness. They are frail and fatigue easily, can stand little social life. Yet most husbands seem to be content. As one expressed it, "I'm satisfied. I'd rather be married to a frail, sickly little woman who, when well, is a keen, delightful, and charming person, than to a strong, always healthy woman with no distinction or charm."

Doctor Alvarez points out, "Many of these women can help themselves greatly by avoiding conflicts and emotional storms, by being less fussy housekeepers, by getting a nap every day, by going to bed earlier, and by cutting down, at least for a time, on a lot of unnecessary activities outside the home."

For the husbands he suggests, "In many cases the husband could almost cure his wife by giving up such activities as gambling, drinking, or 'chasing,' which keep her upset, or by making life happier and easier for her in other ways."

On the other hand, an unhappy married life and thoughts of divorce are sometimes the exciting cause of an attack. Doctor Alvarez, in describing his handling of these troubles, says, "In some of these cases I almost cure the disease by getting the woman to see clearly that she isn't tough enough or heartless enough, or unkind enough to get a divorce. Then when she stops thinking about it, she stops having headaches and gets as well as she can ever be."

No drug is known that will safely prevent migraine attacks. Only proper mental hygiene can do that. But once the attack has begun there are two drugs that will usually stop it. Intramuscular injections of gynergen or a similar drug labeled DHE45 are effective in relieving an attack if given as soon as it begins. A patient who has frequent attacks must be trained to treat himself with these drugs since they may occur at any time, as at night when it is hard to get a doctor.

Better than drugs and far more effective than operations is the simple formula that has grown out of the experience of Doctor Alvarez, "The best way in which to avoid migraine is to live quietly and peacefully and sanely."

(2)
Trout Fishing with Electrodes!*

Don't get ideas, it's for fishery biologists only. But the new shock method of taking trout censuses will mean a lot in better fishing.

By Lloyd Soehren

When an angler tells you that "they're catching trout now by the electric shock method," don't label him too readily as a spinner of fish yarns. It's being done, and it works. The only catch is that it's not legal—except for the boys in the state conservation departments.

The idea of collecting fish by the electric shock method originated

* Reprinted by permission of *Sports Afield* and Lloyd Soehren.

in Austria and was first tested in this country in 1939. Now the conservation departments of many states, including New York, Pennsylvania, Michigan, Wisconsin, Minnesota and Iowa, are shocking their streams in order to take censuses of the fish population.

The stunned fish are not merely counted and tossed back into the water. Age, length and weight are recorded, and conditions in the stream are studied. Through the correlation of their findings in trout stream research, conservationists hope to improve streams and give fishermen better trout angling.

The work being done by the Wisconsin Conservation Department may be taken as typical of that in other states. Elmer F. Herman, area biologist at the Nevin fish hatchery, is in charge of the work.

*   *   *

Forest fires are bad for fish populations because they destroy the cover along the streams. Lack of cover causes the water temperature to rise. Forests provide deep mold, which holds water. This means a slower runoff with less silt going into the water. Other causes of inadequate shade are overgrazing and unwise cutting of timber. A good trout stream must have sufficient cover both in and out of the water. Cover in the water not only harbors abundant food organisms but offers fish protection from natural enemies.

"We haven't done enough marking yet of hatchery-raised trout to tell how many of the trout we take by shocking are natural and how many were planted," McCutchin continued, "but we get a rough idea. We mark young trout by clipping off a fin or putting a tag in the jaw. Say we take 130 fish with the electric shocker. We see how many are fish that we put in.

"We are finding that it pays to raise legal fish, which are seven inches long in this state. We plant some big ones—up to 10 inches long and a year or a year and a half old. We can make them grow large by feeding and could push them even faster, but such feeding is too expensive. We give them liver at first and later a lot of carp, supplemented by vitamins.

"Trout usually hatch in January, and we plant them the following spring. We are trying to find out the best season for planting, and so far we feel that spring is the best. We see the ratio of return to the creel on the three plantings—spring, fall, and winter—by asking the fishermen to co-operate in a creel census. Sometimes nearly 50 per cent of the catch is planted fish."

The stream surveys serve to indicate what varieties of trout to plant. A given stream will vary in character throughout its length, and it may also change from one year to another. As loss of cover makes the water temperature go up and increased erosion makes the water muddy, the brooks and rainbows may be driven out in favor of less fussy browns.

(3)
The New Ford
Tricycle Tractors*

BY BEN LOGAN

There used to be an old man out the Ridge from our place who didn't like progress. Every time he saw a new piece of machinery in one of our fields, he'd come over, walk around it a couple times, then look down his nose at it and say:

"I don't like it!"

He didn't like anything that was new. He darned near had a stroke the day he came over to look at the first tractor in the neighborhood.

"Them Ford people are trying to change things," he said. "I don't like it!"

Then back he went to his team. When the wind was right, you could hear him cussing out those mules of his like he was standing six inches away and hollering into your ear. Sometimes, on a warm and quiet Spring day, I can hear an echo of his cussing yet.

Old Will and his mules are gone. Maybe it's just as well. He'd work up to boil sure enough if he saw what "them Ford People" are up to now.

*   *   *

A whole new line of Ford Front-Mounted implements has been brought out for use with the Tricycles. The 2- and 4-Row Mounted Cultivators can be put on or taken off in just about the time it used to take to harness up a team of horses. The new Ford Planter, Fertilizer and Side Dresser Attachments mount directly on the Cultivator frame: In addition to cutting implement costs, this idea also saves a lot of machine shed space.

Anyone who now owns a Ford 4-wheel tractor will find that most of his present attached implements can be used with the new tractors. A few will need simple adapter kits.

There are more new implements and machines on the way. The

* Reprinted by permission of *Ford Farming* and Ben Logan.

Ford 2-Row Mounted Corn Picker, 1-Row Mounted Corn Picker and 1-Row Mounted Corn Harvester will all be ready for the fall harvest season.

I guess old Will would have gotten kind of steamed up about them, too. You see, the corn crop was another thing that made him mad. On bad years he complained about no feed for the hogs, and on good years he said it took him all winter to pick the corn.

He was a hard man to stump.

(4)
Industry's Private Detectives*

By John L. Kent

Anyone at the Frederick A. Bacon Laboratories in Watertown, Mass., can tell you about the mystery of the pink candles. The smart detective work which broke that case illustrates the efficiency of its engineer-sleuths. Similar problems are being solved every day at commercial research and testing labs across the country.

If you ever want a job that combines the adventure of detective work, the thrill of scientific research, and the satisfaction of proving to yourself that man is still superior to the machine, get yourself a position in a commercial testing laboratory.

You'll get a special kick out of working there if you have an inquiring mind and know that no contraption can make a fool of you. But take warning, now, some of them will until you track down what makes them tick—or prevents them from ticking—and you ring up another solution.

The industrial detectives who were put on the "pink candle case" admit it had them baffled for a while.

One of the laboratory clients who manufactures altar candles, traditionally ivory, found that every so often a batch of candles would slowly turn pink after coming out of the molds. Churches don't want pink candles. Engineers sent to the factory checked the quality of the raw material and took temperature readings, but found no variation which could account for the change in color. The chemist assigned to the job studied each component of the chest and discovered that the guilty item was sulphur in the glue used to fasten the flannel linings to the wood. Sulphur-free glue was substituted and the tarnishing problem was solved.

* Reprinted by permission of *Popular Mechanics* and John L. Kent.

Commercial testing laboratories are called in as fact-finders in some cases which are being prepared for legal action. Often the presumed guilty party is found blameless and the real culprit found.

Just after the hurricane in Miami, Fla., in October, the South Florida Test Service was summoned to inspect a number of buildings in North Miami Beach. The paint on the buildings was developing a serious discoloration following a flight in the area of an airplane which was spraying DDT. Residents complained that the spray from the plane was responsible.

Results of the investigation showed that only buildings painted with lead-and-oil paint were damaged. Further study showed that hydrogensulphide fumes generated in filled-in land adjacent to the buildings were the cause. High water during the hurricane resulted in deposition of seaweed on these filled-in lands and a few days later the gas started to generate as the seaweed began to rot.

In a Texas case, the death of several valuable dogs was blamed on an insecticide spray. The manufacturer was being sued for the value of the dogs.

At the trial, several dogs were sprayed profusely with the supposedly deadly insecticide in question, brought into the courtroom and made to sit near the jurors for the duration of the trial. The dogs seemed comfortable and left in good condition when the case was over. The jurors were convinced, and decided in favor of the manufacturer. A later autopsy of the stricken dogs showed they had died of worms.

A spectrograph owned by the Hornkohl Laboratories of Bakersfield, Calif., proved which gun fired a murder bullet. The spectrograph "breaks down" an element into characteristic rainbow colors which are the element's "fingerprints."

The body of a woman who had been missing for three weeks was discovered in a field. A bullet had penetrated her skull and continued out the other side. The victim's husband was picked up with a .38-caliber pistol and ammunition in his possession. A day later another man was arrested with his .41-caliber revolver and ammunition. By shooting both guns into a large block of wood and running spectrographs of the lead from the two pistols in contrast with the lead recovered from the victim's body, it was proved that the .41-caliber gun was the murder weapon.

The laboratories do considerable work for insurance companies. Before they settle doubtful claims, the firms often seek the help of the laboratories to find just what the facts are. When some insured cattle of an Oklahoma farmer died, the farmer suspected paint which was left in open cans by a contractor who had been painting tanks on the premises. The paint was analyzed and found to contain lead compounds which, of course, poisoned the cattle. The responsibility was established.

In another instance, the Oklahoma Testing Laboratories of Oklahoma City showed that someone had poured salt into a car's gasoline tank with the intention of ruining the engine. The interior of the engine was covered with a shiny salt glaze similar to that formed on clay pipe or tile during its manufacture.

There are close to 400 commercial research and testing laboratories in the country. They range in size from some with four employees to a few with staffs of 500 or more. Laboratories will work for anyone, not only industrial firms. If you have a problem which scientific investigation and testing can solve, they'll uncover the facts and evidence. The fees range from $5 for a routine report on a bottle of liquid to over $100,000 for extensive testing.

(5)

Sand Springs Railway's 10 miles of busy interurban has fulfilled its founder's wish to be . . .

Generous
to the Unfortunate*

BY WILLIAM D. MIDDLETON

Photographs by The Author

The late Charles Page—oilman, industrialist and noted philanthropist—was mad at the Katy. Newly wealthy in the Oklahoma oil fields, he had just started construction of his Sand Springs Home for orphans and widows on 160 acres of sand hills and tangled underbrush along the Arkansas River west of oil-booming Tulsa, Okla.

There were no roads and the only means of transportation to the city was the Missouri, Kansas & Texas Osage Branch, whose trains could be "flagged at a near-by stop." Irked by the Katy's undependable flag-stop service, Page decided to build his own railroad to the home.

Page's Sand Springs Railway to the home was completed by 1911. For the first few years the line was steam operated, with a pair of McKeen gasoline motor cars for passenger service. Soon, however,

* Reprinted by permission of *Trains* and William D. Middleton.

following the electric railway rage of the times, the line was electrified, although some steam operation of freight continued into the 1920's.

* * *

The Sand Springs Line's passenger operation in recent years had been characterized as much by a conspicuous lack of profit as it had been by a high volume of riding. Despite a passenger traffic of over a million passengers annually, which contributed some 20 per cent to the line's gross revenue, the take from the busy fleet of yellow interurban cars never went over the break-even point with operating costs.

Unlike many passenger carriers, the Sand Springs Line never believed in higher fares as the answer to poor passenger earnings. It's interesting to note that the line saw fit to raise fares only once in its 44 years of passenger operation—this was in 1953 when fares were

Sand Springs rolling stock

LOCOMOTIVES

No.	Type	Weight (tons)	Horse-power	Tractive force (pounds)	Builder & date
1001	B-B	50	400	25,000	Baldwin-Westinghouse 1913
1002	B-B	50	400	25,000	Baldwin-Westinghouse 1915
1003	B-B	50	400	25,000	Baldwin-Westinghouse 1918
1004	B-B	45	400	25,000	Baldwin-Westinghouse 1928
1005	B-B	43	300	25,000	Baldwin-Westinghouse 1920
1006					

Remarks: Former Niagara Junction Railway locomotives bought 1946.

PASSENGER CARS*

No.	Motors	Weight (pounds)	Length	Seats	Builder & date
68	Four 25-h.p. General Electric	26,000	40'6"	44	Cincinnati 1918
69-70	Four 35-h.p. Westinghouse	34,000	48'0"	48	American 1918
71-76	Four 35-h.p. Westinghouse	34,000	45'0"	48	American 1925

Remarks: 68. Former Cincinnati, Lawrenceburg & Aurora car acquired 1934. Used occasionally.

69-70. Former Oklahoma Union Traction cars purchased 1934.

71-76. Former Union Electric Railway cars purchased 1947.

OTHER EQUIPMENT

Number	Type	Remarks
A-4	Line car	
A-11	Snow sweeper	Former Chicago & West Towns Railway sweeper bought in 1948.

Nonpowered equipment includes four box cars, five flat cars, and three maintenance of way side dump cars.

* All passenger cars were taken out of service January 1, 1955; all nine have been dismantled and most have been sold.

boosted from the nickel-local and dime-interurban rates which had prevailed since 1911 to a still modest 11- and 15-cent level.

The Sand Springs closed out passenger operations with a fleet of nine boomer lightweight interurbans. Six had been picked up in 1947 from the Union Electric Railway at Coffeeville, Kans., when that system folded. Along with two similar cars acquired in the 1930's from the old Oklahoma Union Traction Company, these ex-Union Electric cars held down almost all Sand Springs' passenger rush. A lone survivor of the line's older cars, which in turn had been picked up on the secondhand market from the defunct Cincinnati, Lawrenceburg & Aurora Railway, was held in reserve for occasional use on lightly patronized owl runs.

*   *   *

The first-rate maintenance of Sand Spring's equipment is no haphazard operation. The line's large, well-equipped shops at Sand Springs are capable of almost any type of repair. Rolling stock is checked on a regular schedule under the experienced eye of Master Mechanic Frank Avery. A veteran railroader, Avery helped build the line and has been with it ever since except for a few years' time out running McKeen motor cars on the Union Pacific.

Soft-spoken, pipe-smoking Avery showed us through the shops where equipment was getting the routine maintenance, cleaning and minor repairs required to keep 30- and 40-year-old interurbans running dependably. A welder laid down a neat bead as he patched the side of one of the yellow interurbans. Replacement doors and window sashes were being turned out by the shop's skilled carpenter. In the carbarn a freight motor was readied for an afternoon shift.

The railroad's right of way isn't overlooked either, and it gets the benefit of the same kind of continuous maintenance program. The road employs 16 full-time gandy dancers who can always be found somewhere on the line putting down a lift of fresh ballast, laying rail, or placing new ties. A line car and truck are in use to keep the line's 600-volt overhead in top shape.

What's ahead for the Sand Springs Line? The question was asked of several of the line's officers and they expressed a strong feeling of optimism for the future. The Tulsa area is in the midst of a period of business expansion typified by the rising skeletons of new office buildings in downtown Tulsa. Business is good, too, among the industries along the Sand Springs Line—many are expanding and new firms are constantly locating in the area. Plenty of choice industrial sites are still available which—coupled with the aggressive promotion practiced by the road's traffic department—should bring still more shippers to the Sand Springs Line.

Motive-power-wise, the Sand Springs plans to continue all-electric freight operation at the present time, Vice-President Babbitt says. It's no secret, however, that both officers and employees look with favor on diesel motive power, and it's a good bet the future will see the change when the time comes to retire the railway's present stable of 30- and 40-year-old electrics.

By reason of survival alone, the Sand Springs Line ranks as a rarity in this age which has seen the virtual disappearance of the electric interurban. Even more remarkable is the strength with which the line faces the future. For happily, the Sand Springs' management has energetically gone about developing a freight traffic that guarantees the line's future, as well as that of the unusual charity which owns it. Just about any way you look at it, this Sand Springs Line is a rare and remarkable electric railroad.

Exercises

1. What opportunities on your campus are there for science articles from each of the two sources?

2. What ideas for your own writing did you gain from reading how successful writers work?

3. What field of science have you selected for writing feature articles?

4. How will you narrow or limit the field for your science articles?

5. How do you plan to do your research for your selected field of science?

6. List the steps of the pre-interview which you have completed.

7. Read your interview questions to your classmates and ask them for suggestions for improvement of the questions.

8. Sketch briefly the life history and the achievements of the scientists you plan to interview.

9. How do you plan to develop a co-operative attitude in your interviewees?

10. How do you plan to interview the experts?

11. What will your post-interview plan include?

12. What appeals do you plan to use in developing your first science article?

13. What idea do you think now you will use for your lead?

14. What devices will you employ to keep the reader on the "Application to Mankind" interest line?

15. List the technique of style that you plan to use in your first science article.

16. Has your interviewee agreed to check your article for scientific accuracy?

17. Why are you having the interviewee sign two approval sheets?

18. What changes have you made in your article after checking its readability?

19. What pictures have you planned for your first article?

20. What illustrations other than pictures do you plan to use?

21. In analyzing general magazines, list the names of science and technical writers and the fields in which they seem to specialize.

22. What new ideas have you obtained from analysis of science or technical articles in general and semitechnical or semiscience periodicals?

23. Using the directories enumerated in this chapter, list five learned journals published by five learned societies.

24. List one idea from each learned journal for a science article and indicate from which journal you got the idea.

25. Suggest a semiscience or semitechnical market for the ideas listed in the above exercise for science articles.

26. Test one of the articles included in this chapter for readability. What devices did the author use?

27. In one of the articles list the research which the author did.

28. How many personal pronouns are there in the article of your choice?

29. Did any of the authors humanize the technical information for the reader?

30. Enumerate the methods used to interest the reader in an article of your choice.

31. Do any of the articles suggest tips for articles from any science courses which you have had?

32. What tips can you find at your university or college that suggest practical articles that you could sell to farm publications?

33. Do any of the articles suggest any particular treatment of science articles which you plan to write in the future?

34. List suggestions for rewriting one of the articles for general readers.

35. List two suggestions for rewriting technical articles to appeal to the general reader.

36. Rewrite a scientific or technical article for a general magazine which uses articles of between 250 and 1,000 words.

37. What sources did the author use? Enumerate the devices he used to make it readable as well as precisely accurate.

Report No. 7, due seventh week. Tentative outlines for all three articles.

CHAPTER 24

Magazine Production Is a Huge Industry

Magazines Influence American Way of Life. The huge billion-dollar magazine industry is the nation's distributor of "durable news" as contrasted with the "perishable news" presented by the radio and the newspaper. Magazines provide readers with information and the opportunity to re-read, study, and debate the facts. Periodicals unify thinking and aid in creating understanding throughout the world as well as the nation. The reading matter influences habits, sympathies, emotions, biases, prejudices, and interests of millions of readers in the United States and, in the last decades, the lands across the seas.

A career in magazine writing and editing is a constant challenge because periodicals are a growing power as a social, economic, and political force. The thousands of publications contribute to the development of public opinion as do the newspaper, the home, the school, public discussion on the television, radio, the pulpit, and the speaker's platform. The modern reader wishes to be informed honestly that he may do his own thinking and be able to discuss intelligently the things going on in the world.

The bases of the reader's opinions are the things he hears, sees, and reads. The influence of these factors may be determined by where one lives, how old he is, what he does, what his interests and hobbies are, how prosperous he is, and so on. These in turn may be conditioned by one's biological, physical, social, and psychological heritage. These factors probably explain why so many different types of magazines can compete with one another and yet succeed in spite of that competition.

Periodicals Aid in Forming Public Opinion. It is still the fashion with a certain kind of critic to assert that periodicals have in them little or nothing of reliable information or admirable literature. But however much the fair-minded critic may abhor certain faults and failings of periodical literature, he must, when he considers the great extent of its actual dissemination and the high quality of a part of it, recognize the great importance of the magazine in the formulation of public opinion.

Many believed that with the advent of television and radio the home, the school, the church, the lecture platform, the newspaper, and the magazine, in the future, would have little or no influence. But television and radio, along with their many advantages, still must struggle with the frailties of the spoken word and the human eye or ear. Anyone who has ever worked in a newspaper office knows how often listeners who heard something wrong, or heard it in part only, or cannot believe their eyes or ears, telephone the newspaper to get the facts. The influence of the school, the platform, and the pulpit in molding opinion is likewise lessened and for the same reasons.

Because the day's news is increasingly complicated, readers turn to periodicals where specialists discuss various aspects of it and interpret it in more detail than can the daily paper, with its limited time and space.

Important Services Are Performed by Magazines. The importance of the American magazines rests upon the services which they perform.

They provide a democratic literature which is sometimes of a high quality. They must keep their reading matter close to their reading public or subscriptions will not be renewed. One only needs to look back in old files to see that they have printed literature of excellent quality. Everyone is familiar with those early magazine features, the *Spectator* and the *Tatler* of eighteenth-century England. Moreover, it would be difficult to find a prominent author in the last hundred years who did not contribute more or less to the magazines, as did Tennyson, Dickens, Bryant, Longfellow, Mrs. Stowe, and others. William Dean Howells wrote some six decades ago that most of the best literature in print is in the magazines, and most of the second-best appears first in book form.

The magazines have had an important part in the economics of literature since 1840. Before that, the writer starved and wrote in his attic home; today the successful, modern contributor sits at his typewriter in his penthouse or his country estate.

Periodical files furnish an invaluable contemporaneous history of their times and aid the researcher in his investigations in many fields.

Writer Should Know History of the Magazine. In order better to understand the magazine of today, one should read the histories listed in the "Free-Lance Writer's Library." To consider its history briefly, the magazine grew out of the newspaper. The little *Courants,* which started in 1620, were in a sense magazines, and the earliest magazines were in a sense newspapers. The first magazine which authorities agree to call a magazine was started in 1665, in France, by Dennis De Sallo, who called his publication *Mercure de France.* It contained reviews, scientific reports, and book criticisms. Three years later the Germans began a series of scientific publications, *Monats Gesprache,* and in 1681 in London, the first magazine was the *Weekly Memorials for the Ingenious.*

In America in 1741, Andrew Bradford, the first American printer, started a magazine at Philadelphia, and three days later, Benjamin Franklin's magazine appeared. Franklin claimed Bradford stole his idea. Each publication lasted about six months.

Every person finds a certain fascination about old magazines if he has prowled in his grandmother's attic or done any research in the magazine files in libraries. The fascination springs from the personal quality; the human element is never absent from the yellowed pages. Magazines have always echoed popular ideologies, presented personal interests, aroused emotional responses, and interpreted the men and women of their own days. They were a factor in molding the opinion and the way of life of those people who read them, just as the current ones influence readers today. According to an outstanding magazine historian, Dr. F. L. Mott, writing in his *A History of American Magazines* (three volumes), Noah Webster in his *American Magazine,* in 1788, wrote that "the expectation of failure is connected with the very name of the magazine." Looking back into history of the periodical the researcher finds Webster's statement was accurate, owing to: (1) indifference of the readers, the majority of whom were not educated, and of the writers, who could not live from writing alone because of the low pay; (2) lack of means of distribution of the magazines; (3) lack of ability to collect for subscriptions; and (4) lack of printing equipment.

People of that time had not formed reading habits. They were too busy making a living to think about making a civilization. Between 1741 and 1794, Dr. Mott writes, there were seven magazines at one time with an average circulation of 700.

One better understands the difficulty of distribution, the historian explains, when he realizes that it took from eight to ten days to go to New York from Boston; travel westward was even more difficult and took longer. In 1789 there were 75 post offices and only a thousand miles of post roads. Because of Queen Anne's act of 1710, magazines and newspapers were not regularly admitted to the mails, and this fact explains why many postmasters of that period became publishers. The Postal Act of 1792 still did not permit magazines to be carried by the post riders. But the Postal Act of 1794 admitted magazines to the mails. Almost immediately many new magazines sprang up—and have been springing up ever since.

That interesting period of magazine history since 1794, which to the journalist reads like an adventure tale, must be summarized here. Magazines of those decades were concerned with the problems of: (1) free education; (2) education for girls and young women; (3) dress reform, which was led by Mrs. Bloomer; (4) slavery disputes; (5) the panic of 1857; (6) the development of class periodicals of all types; (7) the Civil War; (8) post-Civil War problems; (9) the building of the West; (10) the reconstruction of the South; (11) government corruption; (12) the new growth and new development of almost everything toward the end of the nineteenth century, and changing of attitudes and public opinion; (13) the growing importance of circulation, distribution, and advertising; (14) reform and new laws as a result of the muck-raking articles of the eighties and nineties; (15) the growing importance of circulation and distribution, owing to the development of the newsstand; (16) World War I; (17) the development of advertising as an important part of the magazine; (18) the magic-like improvement in mechanical production; (19) the naughty twenties and the terrible thirties; (20) World War II; (21) the atomic era; and (22) the post-atomic era.

In a little more than 200 years, American periodical history brings one to the magazines he is reading today.

If the journalism student will read the history of magazines, he will find many interesting facts: the growth of mere colonial pamphlets to books numbering 100 to 200 pages; an occasional book advertisement to pages and pages of interesting advertising; circulations of a few hundred expanding into millions; distribution of magazines by haphazard methods to a great business; printing done in small shops to plants covering hundreds of acres, such as the Fawcetts at Louisville or the Mt. Morris Publishers at Mt. Morris, Illinois. The reader of magazine history realizes what postal laws, education, transportation, advertising, distribution, and mechanical inventions have made possible for magazine subscribers today.

The Magazine in the Atomic Age. There are all manner of magazines on the newsstands and in the mail. They range from the "slicks" and the "digests" to the news weeklies; from the organs of opinion to the confession magazines; from the "pulps" to the comics. They have all kinds of aims and purposes in order to attract readers.

The types of periodicals are endless. The tables in the Appendix show that there are 21,680 publications with 4,648,900 issues annually. This total includes the magazine sections of newspapers, such as the *American Weekly, This Week,* the *Parades,* and many other Sunday newspaper magazine sections. One market book, listed in the Appendix, lists 2,800 markets, and it makes no pretense of listing all of the markets in the United States.

As one browses at the newsstand or in the periodical room at the library, he reaches the conclusion that there is a magazine published for every person with every possible interest.

Modern magazines must be interesting in order to hold their subscribers and newsstand buyers and to find new ones, for the magazine of today must be able to pay its bills. If it cannot do so, it does not have subscribers, nor can it get the big-figure advertising. Many of the magazines provide news, selective news; and they also provide interpretation and discussion of the issues before the public. As pointed out in previous chapters, modern readers desire facts.

Editors Cannot Please Readers All of the Time. Critics of the present-day magazine, who do not bother to investigate, say magazines are dominated by the advertiser. But it is the magazine which accepts or rejects advertising. National advertising agencies select the space for their clients who have things to sell by means of the magazine advertising page. Advertising is the support of the majority of magazines and enables the subscribers to buy them for a few cents instead of the dollars they cost to produce. Income from advertising makes it possible for editors to pay well for the manuscripts which they buy and to pay good salaries to the staffs which assist them.

Editors can never please their readers all of the time. One editor wrote in his class magazine that from time to time the staff were accused of being communists, fascists, reactionaries, pacifists, anti-British, anti-Russian, anti-labor, anti-business, anti-farmer; while at other times they are said to be the tools of those very groups. The successful editor strives to have variety in the magazine and to make it interesting to all of the readers some of the time. Subscribers, at best, are fickle, and so it behooves editors to make every effort to retain those they have and constantly to acquire more by careful selection of the articles they print.

Class Magazines Have a Great Influence Indirectly. Such magazines as *Harper's* and the *Atlantic,* with their small but select circulations, seem insignificant by comparison with the big circulations of general periodicals. But the quality and first-class magazines, like the religious, business, and trade publications, are doubtless a great influence in the molding of public opinion. They are read by teachers, preachers, lecturers, commentators, and speakers on radio and television, and through them the ideas and contents are relayed on to others. It would be impossible to estimate the influence of these groups in molding opinion. Indirectly, they probably reach a greater audience than all the mass magazines put together.

It is interesting to note that the periodical reading room of the New York Public Library—with its 40,000 or more periodicals, one of the greatest collections in existence—has more than 1,000 calls for magazines each day. Many magazines have to be duplicated in a few weeks because they become worn out from use.

Who reads these magazines? Businessmen and women read them to seek the information contained in the trade, technical, business papers, and house organs. Advertising men and women and research workers pore over the business forecasts, news of new products, new methods, and new processes. They read every word carefully. These periodicals, like the quality, class, and religious publications, also exert a tremendous influence on the public, directly and indirectly.

Journalists, reporters, interpretative writers, lecturers and authors also are faithful students of many of these papers. They in turn influence their readers and their audiences. There are 4,749 business and trade publications and 6,000 house organs; they are a significant factor in molding public opinion, even though the average magazine reader is not aware of the existence of these periodicals.

The library and its branches in the average small city of from

75,000 to 100,000 population has a total of from 5,000 to 10,000 or more periodicals which are in use in the periodical reading room every day. Colleges and universities have periodical collections of from 500 to 2,000 separate titles. Some of these also may be duplicated in the various university department libraries.

Readers Choose Magazines for Various Reasons. The factors that influence the purchaser's selection of magazines are interesting. They may include the name of the magazine, the cover, the size, the quality of the paper, use of color, size of type, advertising, frequency of publication, fiction, poetry, fact articles, pictures, drawings, the policy of the publication, the names of contributors, or previous familiarity with the publication over a period of years.

Foreigners cannot comprehend the American's delight in reading advertising in his periodicals and of course the Americans do not enjoy the foreigner's magazines, with their dull and uninteresting advertising, or none at all. Magazines not only accept advertising but they advertise, particularly when a new periodical is launched or when circulation is to be increased, as discussed later in this chapter.

Statistics Provide Basis for Comparison of Development. In the magazine industry, figures become out of date while one is writing them down. To give the magazine student an idea of the hugeness of the magazine business, however, this decade of banner growth and production shows that the magazine business is a gigantic one. Even though the figures on this and the following pages will be out of date before they can be set in type, they will provide a basis of comparison for current statistics on salaries, reader-interest surveys, advertising, circulation, promotion, production, and current and future trends.

Modern Magazines Pay Staffs and Contributors Generously. Salaries of editors vary much more in this decade than in previous periods. The editor of a small-circulation magazine (a baby magazine) receives more than $25,000 a year, according to a writer's magazine. In the post-Civil War period, *Harper's* paid Mr. Lowell the then unheard of salary of $2,500. Editors of the big magazines receive salaries from $10,000 to $50,000 and up. One of the highest paid receives $100,000.

Contributors are paid much better than those early ones who wrote for the honor or at most for $6 a page. The "Diary" of Capt. Harry C. Butcher, General Eisenhower's aide, which ran in the *Saturday Evening Post* brought its author $175,000. Even students in classses in magazine writing—beginners—receive anywhere from $25 to $200 or more for their first articles, while in some of the earlier periods "big-name" writers were paid only $25 to $50. A few of the student beginners have received $550 for an article—but that is unusual for a tyro, of course.

Rates for articles are by the word, as previously explained in Part I, and range from one-half cent to twenty-five cents or more per word.

Reader-Interest Surveys Are Interesting. Many types of reader-interest surveys have been devised by magazine publishers and advertising agencies. Publishers say they serve as a guide, but must not be taken too literally. They are revealing even though they are not always accurate, because of the frailty of some human beings who pretend to read more than they actually do. Because of time and expense, the majority of the surveys must be local or sectional, so that they do not give a true estimate nationally.

A recent survey of a midwest county indicated that 20 per cent of the county's adult population read one or more books a month; 44 per cent read one or more magazines a month; 45 per cent saw a motion picture or more once a month; 81 per cent read one or more dailies; and 87 per cent listened to the radio or watched television one-half hour or more daily. But an editor realizes that the reliability of those figures depends upon the intellectual interests of the people living in that county. A county which contained a large city would have a different percentage from a county the majority of whose population were laborers with a limited education.

The McFadden survey revealed that magazines are found in all homes with incomes of $5,000 per year. Exactly 22 per cent of the families with incomes between $1,000 and $2,000 per year do not have magazines, and 53 per cent with incomes below $1,000 do not have magazines. Women were found to read magazines and books more than men, because they have more leisure. Rural people read more magazines and listen to the radio more than urban dwellers, who read more newspapers and attend more movies.

The majority of reader-interest surveys conclude that people with some education prefer the printed page to the radio or television. Those with a slightly better than average education prefer newspapers and magazines, and those with a considerably better than average education prefer books and magazines.

In applying the results of reader-interest surveys, the magazine editor and writer take into consideration the factors of age, sex, education, financial prosperity, and status as home-owners, renters, employees, or employers. Even though such surveys are not absolutely dependable, they do serve as a guide to editors and writers. As pointed out in Chapter 19, the more editors and writers know about the subscribers, the better able they will be to slant their articles to interest the readers.

Circulation Studies Aid Editor and Writer. As pointed out in Chapter 19, circulation is the key to the identity of the reader. In the magazine banner decade, total magazine circulations were between four and five billion copies annually. Another study shows that a magazine is sold every second of every hour, with single-copy sales, for the first time in circulation history, running slightly ahead of subscriptions. The average annual expenditure for magazines is $10.29 per family, an advertising bureau has reported.

The *Ladies' Home Journal* sold 5,076,214 copies of its March, 1954 (latest figure available) issue. Its advertising rate was $14,600 a page and its second cover page rate in four colors was $20,000 a page at that time. The student realizes that the magazine business is a huge one.

It is impossible to keep up with circulation figures, because of the constant changes. The magazine published at Des Moines, *Better Homes and Gardens,* announced a circulation of over four million, and it is just a little magazine by comparison with others. *Farm Journal* upped its already big circulation when in 1955 it purchased *Better Farming,* which for many years had been *The Country Gentleman. Farm Journal* now has the largest agricultural circulation.

In addition to the big circulations in the United States, American magazines are achieving a substantial circulation abroad. World War II gave an impetus to magazine publishers to seek world circulation. The periodicals designed for American readers are translated into the language of the country in which they are to be distributed. *Reader's Digest* is printed in 17 foreign editions including its American one. The latter is also published both in Braille and on Talking Records. The *Digest* did not accept advertising until 1955. Its page rate at that time was $26,500.00 and its four-color page rate was $31,000. Its total circulation in all its editions is more than 10 million copies.

Syndicated newspaper magazine sections are one of the expanded developments in the magazine world. Except for local features, because of the syndicated magazine sections, newspapers do not buy as many free-lance articles as they once did. But syndicated newspaper magazine sections buy articles if they have a national appeal. *This Week,* produced by the New York *Herald Tribune,* is one of the older and larger syndicated supplements. It goes to 35 Sunday newspapers and had a circulation of 11,142,964 in November, 1955. At that time it had the largest circulation in the world. The *American Weekly,* a Hearst publication, had a city circulation of more than 9,705,000. *Family Weekly,* a non-metropolitan supplement, with its 93 member papers, had 2,217,093 circulation in the same year. Other sections are *Parade* and *Pictorial Review.* Another recent development is that of newspapers producing their own feature sections and in turn syndicating them to smaller newspapers. The five-day week, television, and the ease of obtaining the supplement with the Sunday paper were responsible for this development. The circulations of three big weekly magazines are: *Life,* 5,524,954; *Saturday Evening Post,* 5,098,186; and *Collier's,* 3,800,116.

As periodicals increased their subscriptions, a new type of magazine was distributed for a few cents through national chain grocery stores. *Women's Day* with a circulation of four million and *Family Circle* with about four and a half million are typical of this new type of women's service magazine. Grocery advertising makes them possible at that price.

Increased subscription rates due to increased production costs and the competition of television have not changed total circulation figures because magazine subscriptions continue to increase. Editors and writers are constant students of the directories listing circulations, for they are a key as to who are the readers.

Magazine Sales Are Second Largest in Retail Distribution. Where the colonial magazine did well to sell two or three hundred copies, the modern magazine now sells millions. The sale of periodicals is the second largest retail distribution field in the United States. *Magazine Industry News Letter* announced in 1955 that the two distributing agencies, American News and Union News had merged, representing an investment of about eight million dollars. About 70 per cent of periodicals at that time were distributed by more than 800 independent wholesalers plus 93,000 magazine retailers in drugstores, cigar and tobacco stands, confectionery shops, outdoor magazine stands, grocery stores, delicatessens, inside stands, hotels, book stores, office buildings, department stores, bus, rail and plane terminals, institutions, colleges, and public markets. In a typical small mid-western city of 85,000 adult population, one news company alone distributes to that city and its surrounding territory more than 42,000 magazines a week, or 2,250,000 copies a year. The magazines continue to have huge newsstand sales.

The Fawcett Distributors—the largest independent in the U. S. A.—distribute more than 225 million magazines annually. The so-called comics jumped from 25 million in 1941 to 40 million in ten years—there are now more than 200 such publications which children buy, according to the latest reports available.

Distribution by airplane resulted in a tripled circulation for *Time* magazine, which was the first to publish an air-express edition. A number of magazines now own and use planes for distribution, as well as for staff transportation.

Beautiful Periodicals Are Made Possible by Advertising. It is the income from advertising which enables publishers to give their subscribers beautiful periodicals which may be purchased from 10 cents to $1 a copy, and higher. The history and development of periodical advertising is a romantic tale as told in the books listed in the "Free-Lance Writer's Library" in the Appendix.

But a glance at the advertising rates listed in Standard Rate and Data soon convinces the student of the magazine that the advertising phase of magazine-making is a gigantic one. Advertising in magazines dominates national advertising budgets. Magazine advertising expenditures total 650 million dollars in trade, business, and farm papers.

Advertising rates vary according to page position. The back cover demands a higher rate than other pages. If the writer does not have access to directories listing advertising rates, he will gain some idea of advertising income by noting the following rates, which were selected at random:

Magazine	For One Page	For Back-Cover Page
Saturday Evening Post	$16,800.00	$25,045.00
Ladies' Home Journal	14,600.00	20,000.00
Life	20,350.00	30,600.00
Mademoiselle	2,700.00	4,100.00
Popular Mechanics	2,330.00	2,900.00
Vogue	3,400.00	4,800.00
American	7,840.00	11,415.00
Sports Afield	2,800.00	4,450.00
Fortune	3,495.00	5,245.00
Fountain Service & Fast Food .	650.00	950.00

A writer will see readily enough from the above table that advertising has made magazine production one of the big businesses of America, employing thousands of people. Noah Webster in 1788 did not foresee the success the modern magazine would attain when he said the name connoted failure.

Magazine Promotion Has Developed Rapidly. The colonial magazine grew by word-of-mouth publicity, but the modern periodical includes in its budget of operation a large sum for self-advertising or for promotion of its own circulation. The publication with a large circulation is in greater demand by advertising agencies which place their clients' advertising copy.

Promotion is designed, not only to increase circulation, but also to sell more advertising space. The *Saturday Evening Post* has spent as much as $2,000,000, and promotion on the other Curtis publications brought the Curtis total to above $3,000,000. For the same year, *Reader's Digest* spent more than $1,200,000 on promotion, and *Esquire* and *Coronet* spent more than $2,000,-000. Large staffs are employed in magazine promotion departments as well as in editorial departments.

Many magazines offer services of various types to their readers which are important as promotion and circulation builders. These services aid too in obtaining advertising and in molding public opinion. Prizes, awards, and booklets of instructions on various subjects are included in services.

Production of Magazines Has Become Big Industry in Itself. Readers give little thought to the production of the publication they are reading. But it interests writers to know that one house— Fawcett, at Louisville—publishes 6 men and women's magazines. Magazines with their large subscriptions could pay their way without advertising. Fawcett maintains a hotel for housing visiting employees from branch offices. They have more than 1,550 persons on their payroll, and they spend a million a year on advertising and promotion of various publications.

The little town of Mt. Morris, Illinois, is spoken of as the capital of magazine production. Its acres of printing presses pour out more than 150 fraternal, religious, and general magazines every month. Mail comes in by the ton and goes out by the train-load, carrying a nation-wide service to millions. The two Meredith publications at Des Moines, Iowa, employ more than 1,500 persons. The *Scholastic Journals* require about 150 full-time employees, who put out 600,000 copies a week. The Curtis Publishing Company publishes the *Saturday Evening Post*, the *Ladies' Home Journal, Jack and Jill* (juvenile), *Holiday*, and *Bride-to-Be*. The Fairchild Publishing Company publishes the business periodicals *Women's Wear, Daily News Record, Retailing, Home Furnishings, Men's Wear, Foot Wear,* and the Fairchild *Blue Book of Directories.*

This is to mention only a few of the 65 group-magazine publishers—those getting out hundreds of magazines—but it is enough to convince anyone that magazine publishing has gone a long way since the colonial postmaster set up a little printing press in a corner and issued a magazine in his spare time. The advertising and promotion alone necessary to launch a new magazine successfully would be beyond those early editors' comprehension— let alone the spending of two million in one year on promotion by such well-established publications as *Coronet* and *Esquire.*

Writers Study Current Economic Trends. Economic developments all over the world are closely interwoven with magazine production factors. The trend since 1939 has been for higher pay, shorter hours, and less production, factors which resulted in a 70 per cent increase in production costs. To offset this increase, many periodicals were forced to raise their subscription and advertising rates.

New inventions have resulted in a growing increase of the use of color, quick-drying inks, successful four-color web perfecting (two-side) printing presses which operate at greatly increased speeds, and high-speed binding equipment. These mechanical developments have made it possible for publishers to produce, not only interesting, but beautiful periodicals for the modern subscriber.

The microfilming of subscription orders and the new mailer

which addresses 8,000 wrappers an hour save time, space, and money for the production department of magazines. And these are only two of the many inventions which provide better services for the readers.

Organizations of Publishers and Writers Help One Another. The National Publishers Association was organized many years ago. It has annual conferences for the discussion of mutual problems. Its membership represents more than 400 periodicals whose combined circulation exceeds more than 100,000,000 copies per issue.

Some of the other organizations include the Association of Comic Magazine Publishers, with 35 periodicals represented, and the United States Business Papers, with more than 2,000 publisher members. There are many other specialized group organizations, but they are too numerous to list.

Writers have not been as successful in organizing as have the publishers. From time to time attempts have been made to organize national associations, but difficulties frequently arose to split the groups. There are specialized groups and state authors' and writers' leagues whose members co-operate and help one another. Writers' institutes and conferences are sponsored by some of the writers' groups; others are sponsored by colleges and universities; and still others by private groups.

Magazines of Tomorrow. The publishers of periodicals realize that their publications will have social, economic, and political responsibility to the readers of tomorrow. One person's guess is as good as another's as to the future of the magazine. With global travel a matter of hours, with the great growth of adult education, the changing of the American way of life, the trend for the family to "go back to the home" due to the attraction of television, the magazines of tomorrow probably will widen their appeals to include the family rather than one sex or the other.

Magazines will widen their scope to include world as well as the nation's market. New approaches will be developed to appeal to readers in other lands. Through reader-interest surveys editors realize that the women of tomorrow want articles that have practical application to themselves, their families, and their neighborhoods. The *McCall* reader-interest study resulted in using more articles on social and economic questions to appeal to older and more prosperous men as well as women. The modern publishers of women's periodicals recognize that they have been underestimating the minds of intelligent and well-adjusted women in the past.

Articles probably will continue to be written more informally, with understanding, inspiration, warmth, and emotion. If current circulation figures are an indication, television has not decreased subscriptions even though it has lessened reading time. Some surveys show that after two years, television owners resume reading though they probably will never read as much as before they had television.

An even greater interest in publications devoted to science is probable. European countries have shown tremendous interest in the American magazines published by the government. These were made possible because many American magazines released their copyright material to the government-published periodicals, which were designed to serve as textbooks in continuing the peace.

Future Magazine Trends Are Analyzed by Writers and Editors. Each month brings many announcements of new periodicals to be published. New magazines are constantly coming out and others are ceasing publication because they do not find readers, so it is useless to discuss new periodicals here. But the writer may discover the possible future trends from an analysis of those magazines he obtains at the newsstands or examines in the library periodical reading room.

The successful writer watches publishers' and writers' periodicals for announcements of the new magazines to appear. He, or she, also analyzes current social, political, and economic conditions to foresee tomorrow's magazine needs, just as during the late '40's keen writers sensed there would be a need for articles on housing and solutions for the teen-age problems which had arisen at an astounding rate. Anticipating the needs of the times, all sorts of magazines began expanding to use housing and juvenile-delinquency articles. And so it will be in the future; magazine writers and editors will anticipate the readers' needs.

New reader groups probably will appear, as did the teen-age public a decade ago. One of the teen-age periodicals has almost a million subscribers, and there are several other successful ones. The Negro magazines, written for and by members of the race, probably will increase in number. Theirs was a long and arduous fight to gain success in the magazine world, but they have emerged victorious.

In view of readers' preference for fact articles, rather than fiction, the feature writer is assured of a bright future. Subscribers like objective writing which enables them to do their own thinking. Only time and conditions can foretell new problems and their solutions of circulation, advertising, promotion, and production. Many of today's magazines will be gone tomorrow, new ones will appear, but others, which have withstood inflations, depressions, and wars for one or two centuries, doubtless will be succeeding even stronger than before.

Writers and Editors Are Constant Students of the Magazine.
The magazine worker, be he, or she, a free-lance writer, a staff member, an editor, or a publisher, must continually study periodicals to know their problems, their trends, and their changing appeals. He must be alert to know why one magazine fails while another prospers if he is to appeal to and hold the reader's interest.

The hobby of knowing magazines is even more important to a writer than that of photography. The latter, however, is profitable too.

A career in magazine work is a challenge, because the periodical is a growing power as a social, economic, and political force in the nation and the world. The responsibilities of magazine writers and staff workers are: (1) to write the truth with precise accuracy; (2) to select subjects wisely; (3) to choose writers to interpret significant facts carefully; (4) to edit with honesty; and (5) courageously to lead and guide the readers. If a writer has the ability, training, and desire to succeed, his future in the magazine world will be what he makes it. The opportunity is there.

Magazines will continue to enrich the literature of the day, to influence public opinion, and to sow the seeds from which great movements will grow. The periodical, once a luxury, has become a necessity in the American way of life. It exerts a tremendous influence on the opinion of the public in spite of the competition of other communication media. At the same time it is a gigantic industry in the many divisions of which thousands find satisfying, happy, and profitable careers.

Exercises

1. List three things that interested you most in the *History of American Magazines,* by Dr. F. L. Mott.

2. Define public opinion and show how magazines influence it.

3. Can you recall any events of the past year that will influence magazines in some way?

4. How do the economics of today affect circulation and advertising?

5. How many pages did you find in five magazines which you examined in the library or at the newsstand?

6. How many of the pages, as suggested in the above question, were devoted to advertising?

7. How many pages were devoted to fact articles? To fiction?

8. Did you note any promotion services offered to the reader in any of the five periodicals? What?

9. What magazine promotion have you noticed recently and where did you see it?

10. What is the total number of periodicals listed on the cover of a recent writers' market book?

11. What did you read about advertising and circulation in the most recent issues of the writers' magazines?

12. How many periodicals are there in your college or university library or in your city library?

13. What are your three favorite magazines?

14. Why did you choose the magazines you did as your favorite ones?

15. What new reader-interest surveys have you read about in the writers' publications? What did you learn from them?

16. Cite the circulation of five magazines of your choice which you found listed in Standard Rate and Data or Ayer & Son's *Directory.*

17. What are the distributing agencies for magazines in your city?

18. How many does each one distribute a month?

19. Check the advertising rates as listed in Standard Rate and Data for the five magazines you listed for Exercise 16.

20. What news have you read of magazine publishers' or writers' associations?

21. List the names of all the new magazines you have noted in the last few months.

22. What new magazines were announced in the most recent writers' periodicals, but which are not yet off the presses?

23. With what political, social, or economic problems were five magazines of your choice concerned this month?

24. List the points that you would include in a code of ethics for a magazine writer or staff member.

25. Enumerate the benefits you have had from your hobby, "knowing magazines."

26. What phase of magazine work do you now think you would be most interested in?

27. Give the reason for your answer in Exercise 26.

Report No. 8, due eighth week. Final outline for Magazine Article No. 1 based on Chapters 10, 20, and 21, or 23, depending on subject matter of article.

Report No. 9, due ninth week. Magazine Article No. 1 prepared as suggested in Chapters 11-15 incl. and 20, and 21, or 23.

Report No. 10, due tenth week. Additional background report for Magazine Article No. 2 to include any additional notes, interviews, or ideas.

Report No. 11, due eleventh week. Outlines for Magazine Article No. 2 based on Chapters 10 and 20.

Report No. 12, due twelfth week. Magazine Article No. 2 prepared as suggested in Chapters 11-15, 20 and 21 or 23, depending on subject matter of article.

Report No. 13, due thirteenth week. Additional background report for Magazine Article No. 3 to include any additional notes, interviews, or ideas.

Report No. 14, due fourteenth week. Outlines for Magazine Article No. 3 based on Chapters 10, 20, and 21 or 23, depending on subject matter.

Report No. 15, due fifteenth week. Magazine Article No. 3 prepared as suggested in Chapters 11-15, 20, and 21 or 23, depending on subject matter.

Report No. 16, due sixteenth week. Project Book, which will consist of all papers returned by instructor, carbon copies of feature articles, manuscript records, and any other material which the instructor may assign.

(Papers are to be placed in some form of a "binder" or loose-leaf notebook as suggested by the instructor.)

APPENDIX

APPENDIX

The Free-Lance Writer's Library

References and Guides for the Journalist

■.■

Almanacs and Yearbooks

American Labor Year Book. New York: The Rand School of Social Science, published annually.

Ayer, N. W. & Son, *Directory of Newspapers and Periodicals.* Philadelphia: N. W. Ayer & Son, published annually.

Editor and Publisher, International Year Book Number. New York: Editor and Publisher Company, published annually.

Irvine, E. Eastman, Editor, *The World Almanac and Book of Facts.* New York: *World-Telegram,* published annually.

McSpadden, J. Walker, Editor, *American Statesman's Year Book.* New York: McBride, Nast, and Company, published annually.

Standard Rate and Data Service. Chicago: B. & B. Service Corporation, published monthly.

The London Times Index. London: Times Publishing Company, published annually.

The New York Times Index. New York: The New York *Times,* published annually.

The Official Index to the Times. London: Times Publishing Company, published monthly.

The United States Agricultural Department Year Book. Washington 25, D. C.: U. S. Government Printing Office, published annually.

Whitaker, Joseph, *Whitaker's Almanac.* London: 13 Bedford Square, published annually.

Encyclopedias

Bridgewater, William, and Elizabeth Sherwood, Editors, *Columbia Encyclopaedia.* New York: Columbia University Press, second edition, 1950.

Hooper, Franklin H., Editor, *The Encyclopaedia Britannica.* London: The Encyclopaedia Britannica Company, Ltd., 1949.

McDannald, A. H., Editor revised edition, *The Encyclopedia Americana.* New York: American Corporation, 1949.

The Catholic Encyclopedia. New York: Robert Appleton Company, second supplement, 1950.

The Lincoln Library of Essential Information. Buffalo, N. Y.: The Frontier Press, sixteenth edition, 1946.

Books on Feature Writing and Magazines

Archer, Jules, *I Sell What I Write.* New York: Fell Publishing Company, 1950.

Bird, George L., *Article Writing and Marketing.* New York: Rinehart & Company, Inc., 1948.

Brennecke, Ernest, and Donald L. Clark, *Magazine Article Writing.* New York: The Macmillan Company, revised edition, 1942.

Browne, Benjamin P., Editor, *Christian Journalism for Today.* Philadelphia: Judson Press, 1952.

Chase, Edna Woolman, and Ilka Chase, *Always in Vogue.* New York: Doubleday & Co., 1954.

Flesch, Rudolph, *How to Make Sense.* New York: Harper & Brothers, 1954.

Gundell, Glenn, *Writing from Idea to Printed Page.* New York: Doubleday & Co., 1949.

Howard, Clive, Editor for Society of Magazine Writing, *A Guide to Successful Magazine Writing.* New York: Charles Scribner's Sons, 1954.

Lederer, W. J., *Spare-Time Article Writing for Money.* New York: W. W. Norton and Company, Inc., 1954.

Meredith, Scott, *Writing to Sell.* New York: Harper & Brothers, 1950.

Mott, Frank L., *A History of American Magazines* 1741-1850. New York: D. Appleton-Century Company, 1930.

Mott, Frank L., *A History of American Magazines* 1850-1865 Cambridge, Mass.: Harvard University Press, 1938.

Mott, Frank L., *A History of American Magazines* 1865-1885. Cambridge, Mass.: Harvard University Press, 1938.

Patterson, Helen M., *Advertising "Tie-Up" with Editorial Matter in Twenty-One Magazines.* Unpublished manuscript.

Peterson, Theodore B., *Writing Non Fiction for Magazines.* St. Louis, Mo.: Educational Publishers, 1949.

Reddick, Dewitt C., *Modern Feature Writing.* New York: Harper & Brothers, 1949.

Steigleman, Walter A., *Writing the Feature Article.* New York: The Macmillan Company, 1950.

Tebbel, John W., *George Horace Lorimer and The S.E.P.* New York: Doubleday & Co., 1948.

Wolseley, Roland, *The Magazine World.* New York: Prentice-Hall, Inc., 1951.

Wolseley, Roland, *Careers in Religious Journalism.* New York: Association Press, 1955.

Wood, James Playsted, *Magazines in the United States.* New York: The Ronald Press Co., 1949.

Books on Style of Writing

Burack, A. S., *The Writer's Handbook.* Boston: The Writer, Inc., 1954.

Flesch, Rudolph, and A. H. Lass, *The Way to Write.* New York: McGraw-Hill Book Company, revised edition, 1955.

Graves, Robert, and Olan Hodge, *The Reader Over Your Shoulder.* New York: The Macmillan Company, 1944.

Gunning, Robert, *The Technique of Clear Writing.* New York: McGraw-Hill Book Company, 1952.

Hyde, Grant M., *Handbook for Newspaper Workers.* New York: D. Appleton-Century Company, third edition, 1939.

Leggett, Glen, C. David Mead, and William Charvat, *Handbook for Writers.* New York: Prentice-Hall, Inc., 1954.

Mencken, H. L., *The American Language,* Supplement I-II. New York: Alfred A. Knopf, Inc., 1948.

Smith, S. Stephenson, *The Command of Words.* New York: Thomas Y. Crowell Co., second edition, 1949.

Turabian, Kate L., *A Manual for Writers of Term Papers, Theses, and Dissertations.* Chicago: University of Chicago Press, 1955.

Whyte, William H. J., *Is Anybody Listening?* New York: Simon and Schuster, 1952.

Books on Psychology of Writing

Bingham, Walter V. D., and Bruce V. Moore, *How to Interview.* New York: Harper & Brothers, 1941.

Brembeck, Winston Lamont, and William Smiley Howell, *Persuasion.* New York: Prentice-Hall, Inc., 1952.

Burnett, Verne, *You and Your Public.* New York: Harper & Brothers, 1947.

Frederick, J. George, *The Psychology of Writing Success.* New York: The Business Bourse, 1935.

Grace, William J., and J. C., *The Art of Communicating Ideas.* New York: Devin-Adair, 1953.

Harral, Stewart, *Keys to Successful Interviewing.* Norman, Okla.: University of Oklahoma Press, 1954.

Hovland, Carl I., Irving L. Janis, and Harold H. Kelley, *Communication and Persuasion.* New Haven, Conn.: Yale University Press, 1953.

Hyman, Herbert and others, *Interviewing in Social Research.* Chicago: University of Chicago Press, 1954.

Klare, George R., and Byron Buck, *Know Your Reader.* New York: Hermitage House, 1954.

MacIver, R. M., *New Horizons in Creative Thinking.* New York: Harper & Brothers, 1954.

Nixon, H. K., *Psychology for the Writer.* New York: Harper & Brothers, 1928.

Schramm, Wilbur, Editor, *The Process and Effects of Mass Communication.* Urbana, Ill.: University of Illinois Press, 1954.

White, Wendell, *The Psychology of Dealing with People.* New York: The Macmillan Company, 1937.

Vocabulary Aids

Adams, Ramon F., *Western Words.* Norman, Okla.: University of Oklahoma Press, 1944.

Berry, Lester, and Melvin Van den Bark, *The American Thesaurus of Slang.* New York: Thomas Y. Crowell Co., 1953.

Birkett, Sir Thomas, *The Magic of Words.* London: Oxford University Press, 1953.

Brin, Joseph, *Applied Semantics.* Boston: Bruce-Humphries, 1951.

Campbell, Walter S. (Stanley, Vestal). *Writing: Advice and Devices.* Garden City, N.Y.: Doubleday & Co., first edition, 1950.

Chase, Stuart, *Power of Words.* New York: Harcourt, Brace and Company, 1954.

Colcord, Joanna Carver, *Sea Language Comes Ashore.* New York: Cornell Maritime Press, 1945.

Devlin, J., *Dictionary of Synonyms and Antonyms and 5,000 Words Most Often Mispronounced.* New York: World Publishing Company, 1951.

Funk, Charles E., Editor, *New College Standard Dictionary.* New York: Funk & Wagnalls, 1950.

Funk, Isaac K., Editor, *New Standard Dictionary of the English Language.* New York: Funk & Wagnalls Company, 1952.

Gowers, Sir Ernest, *Plain Words: Their A.B.C.* New York: Alfred A. Knopf, Inc., 1954.

Hayakawa, S. I., *Language, Meaning and Maturity.* New York: McGraw-Hill Book Company, 1954.

Mawson, C. O. Sylvester, Editor, *Roget's International Thesaurus of English Words and Phrases.* New York: Thomas Y. Crowell Company, 1947.

Murray, Sir James A. H., *New English Dictionary.* Oxford: The Clarendon Press, 1933. Publishes supplements but not at stated intervals.

Neilson, William A., Editor, *Webster's New International Dictionary of the English Language.* Springfield, Mass.: G. & C. Merriam Company, second edition, 1947.

Onions, C. T., Editor, *The Shorter Oxford English Dictionary.* Oxford: Clarendon Press, 1933.

Opdycke, John B., *Mark My Words* (A Guide to Modern Usage and Expression). New York: Harper & Brothers, 1949.

Opdycke, John B., *Lexicon of Word Selection.* New York: Funk & Wagnalls, 1950.

Partridge, Eric, *Concise Usage and Abusage.* London: Hamish Hamilton, 1954.

Partridge, Eric, *Slang, Today and Yesterday.* New York: The Macmillan Company, third edition, 1950.

Partridge, Eric, *You Have a Point There.* London: Hamish Hamilton, 1953.

Webster's Dictionary of Synonyms. Springfield, Mass.: G. & C. Merriam Company, 1942.

Webster's New Collegiate Dictionary. Springfield, Mass.: G. & C. Merriam Company, second edition, 1953.

Books on Photography and Illustrations

Chamberlain, Katherine, *An Introduction to the Science of Photography.* New York: The Macmillan Company, 1953.

Deschin, Jacob, *Say It with Your Camera.* New York: Whittlesey House, 1950.

Feininger, Andreas, *The Creative Photographer.* Englewood Cliffs, N.J.: Prentice-Hall, Inc., 1955.

Feininger, Andreas, *Successful Color Photography.* Englewood Cliffs, N.J.: Prentice-Hall, Inc., 1955.

Giusti, George, *Drawing Figures.* New York and London: The Studio Publications, Inc., 1944.

Guptill, Arthur L., *Freehand Drawing Self-Taught*. New York: Harper & Brothers, 1933.

Hall, Ray Ovid, *Handbook of Tabular Presentation* (how to design and edit statistical tables). New York: The Ronald Press Company, 1943.

Hanson, Eugene M., *How to Make Money in Photography*. Englewood Cliffs, N.J.: Prentice-Hall, Inc., 1955.

Hicks, Wilson, *Words and Pictures*. New York: Harper & Brothers, 1952.

Keppler, Victor, *The Eighth Art: Color Photography*. New York: William Morrow and Co., 1950.

Mees, Charles E. Kenneth, *Photography*. New York: The Macmillan Company, second edition, revised 1951.

Mich, Daniel Danforth, *The Technique of the Picture Story*. New York and London: McGraw-Hill Book Company, Inc., 1945.

Morgan, Willard D., and Henry M. Lester, *Graphic Graflex Photography*. New York: Morgan and Lester, tenth edition, 1954.

Schmid, Calvin F., *Handbook of Graphic Presentation*. New York: The Ronald Press Company, 1954.

Spear, Mary Eleanor, *Charting Statistics*. New York: McGraw-Hill Book Company, Inc., 1952.

Walley, C. W., *Colouring, Tinting and Toning Photographs*. New York: Fountain Press, third edition, 1950.

The Author and the Law

Dean, Joseph, *Hatred, Ridicule or Contempt*. New York: The Macmillan Company, 1954.

Kupferman, Theodore R., Editor, *Copyright (1953) Problems Analyzed*. New York: Commerce Clearing House, 1953.

Nicholson, Margaret, *A Manual of Copyright Practice for Writers, Publishers, and Agents*. New York: Oxford University Press, 1945.

Swindler, William F., *Problems of Law in Journalism*. New York: The Macmillan Company, 1955.

Thayer, Frank, *Legal Control of the Press*. Brooklyn, N. Y.: The Foundation Press, Inc., third edition, 1956.

Wittenberg, Philip, *The Protection and Marketing of Literary Property*. New York: Julian Messner, Inc., 1937.

Books on Scientific Writing

Bates, Marston, *The Nature of Natural History*. New York: Charles Scribner's Sons, 1950.

Burch, George E., *Of Publishing Scientific Papers*. New York: Grune & Stratton, 1954.

Conant, James B., *Modern Science and Modern Man.* New York: Columbia University Press, 1952.

Davis, Ira C., John Burnett, and Wayne E. Gross, *Science, A Story of Discovery and Progress.* New York: Henry Holt & Co., rev. ed., 1952.

DeVries, Louis, *French-English Science Dictionary.* New York: McGraw-Hill Book Company, Inc., 1940.

Emberger, Meta R., and Marian Ross Hall, *Scientific Writing.* New York: Harcourt, Brace and Co., 1955.

Hogbien, Lancelot T., *Science for the Citizen.* New York: W. W. Norton and Company, 1951.

Holmstrom, John E., *Report on Interlingual Scientific and Technical Dictionaries.* Paris: UNESCO, 1951.

Houston, W. V. and others, *The Scientists Look at Our World.* Philadelphia: University of Pennsylvania Press, 1952.

Kaempffert, Waldemar B., *Explorations in Science.* New York: Viking Press, 1953.

Mott, Frank L., and Ralph D. Casey, *Interpretations of Journalism.* (Chap. XXVII, "Dont's for Writers of Science Stories," by Edwin E. Slosson.) New York: F. S. Crofts and Company, 1937.

Oppenheimer, J. Robert, *Science and the Common Understanding.* New York: Simon and Schuster, 1954.

Ratcliff, J. D., *Science Yearbook.* Garden City, N.Y.: Doubleday and Co., published annually.

Standen, Anthony, *Science is a Sacred Cow.* New York: Dutton Press, first edition, 1950.

Stauffer, Robert C., Editor, *Science and Civilization.* Madison, Wis.: University of Wisconsin Press, 1949.

Taylor, Frank, *The World of Science.* New York: W. W. Norton and Co., second edition, 1950.

United Nations Educational, Scientific and Cultural Organization *Bibliography* of Interlingual Scientific and Technical Dictionaries. Paris: UNESCO, third edition, 1953.

Wistar, Richard, *Man and His Physical Universe.* New York: John Wiley & Sons, Inc., 1953.

Books on Technical Writing

Beckman, Frederick W., and Harry R. O'Brien, *Technical Journalism.* Ames, Ia.: The Iowa State College Press, second ed., rev., 1942.

Crouch, William G. W., and R. L. Zeller, *A Guide to Technical Writing.* New York: The Ronald Press Co., 1948.

Fox, Rodney, *Agricultural and Technical Journalism.* New York: Prentice-Hall, Inc., 1952.

Mills, Gordon H., and John A. Walter, *Technical Writing*. New York: Rinehart and Company, 1954.

Nelson, J. R., *Writing the Technical Report*. New York: McGraw-Hill Book Company, Inc., third edition, 1952.

Sherman, Theodore A., *Modern Technical Writing*. New York: Prentice-Hall, Inc., 1955.

Ulman, Joseph N., *Technical Reporting*. New York: Henry Holt & Company, 1952.

You Can Write and Edit Effective Agricultural Publications. East Lansing, Mich.: Michigan State College, 1954.

Books on Business, Trade, Company, and Association Publications

Beach, Walter, *Industrial Editors*, International Council of Industrial Editors. Houston, Tex.: P.O. Box 2180, published weekly.

Bentley, Garth, *Editing the Company Publication*. New York: Harper & Brothers, 1953.

Biklen, P. F., and R. D. Bretti, *The Successful Employee Publications*. New York: McGraw-Hill Book Company, Inc., 1946.

Champion Paper Company, *Starting a House Magazine*. Hamilton, O.: H. H. Wilson Company.

Comprehensive Magazine Directory. Indianapolis, Ind.: Commercial Engraving Co., 34 North Ritter Ave., fifth edition, 1955.

Elfenbein, Julien, *Business Journalism, Its Function and Future*. New York: Harper & Brothers, 1945.

Elfenbein, Julien, *Businesspaper Publishing Practice*. New York: Harper & Brothers, 1952.

Karch, R. Randolph, *How to Plan and Buy Printing*. New York: Prentice-Hall, Inc., 1950.

Pratt, Kenneth C., *House Magazine Layout*. Hamilton, O.: Champion Paper and Fibre Company.

Schwartz, Robert J., Editor, *The Dictionary of Business and Industry*. New York: B. C. Forbes and Sons Publishing Company, 1954.

Wimer, Arthur, *Writing for the Business Press*. Dubuque, Ia.: Wm. C. Brown Company, 1950.

House Magazine Directory. New York: Gebbie Press, 19 East 48th St., New York City 17, published even numbered years.

Reference and Source Books

Aldrich, Ella V., *Using Books and Libraries*. New York: Prentice-Hall, Inc., 1946.

Bartlett, John, *Familiar Quotations*. Boston: Little, Brown, and Company, twelfth edition by Morley, Christopher, and Louella D. Everett, 1948.

Bates, Mary E., Editor, *Annual Magazine Subject-Index*. Boston: The F. W. Faxon Company, published annually.

The Bible.

Block, Maxine, Editor, *Current Biography*. New York: H. W. Wilson Company, published annually.

Catalog of U.S. Documents. Washington 25, D.C.: U.S. Government Printing Office, published monthly.

Dougan, Alice M., Joel Bertha, and Jeannette Moore-Smith, Editors, *Readers' Guide to Periodical Literature*. New York: H. W. Wilson Company, published annually.

Hilbish, Florence May Anna, *The Research Paper*. New York: Bookman Associates, first edition, 1952.

Hook, Lucy, and Mary Virginia Gaver, *The Research Paper*. New York: Prentice-Hall, Inc., second edition, 1952.

McGlaufflin, Alice C., Editor, *Who's Who in American Art*. Washington, D.C.: The American Federation of Arts, published annually.

Mencken, H. L., Editor, *A New Dictionary of Quotations*. New York: Alfred A. Knopf, Inc., 1952.

Monthly Catalog of Subject Lists. Washington 25, D.C.: Superintendent of Documents.

Monthly Catalog of United States Public Documents. Washington 25, D.C.: Superintendent of Documents, published monthly.

Muench, Alice F., and Bea Joseph, Editors, *International Index to Periodicals*. New York: H. W. Wilson Company, published annually.

Nafziger, Ralph O., and Marcus M. Wilkerson, Editors, *An Introduction to Journalism Research*. Baton Rouge, La.: Louisiana State University Press, 1949.

Smith, Esther Anne, Editor, *International Index to Periodical Literature*. New York: H. W. Wilson Company, published quarterly.

Smyth, Alice Mary, Editor, *The Oxford Dictionary of Quotations*. New York: Oxford University Press, 1941.

Social Register. New York and Boston: Social Register Association, published annually.

Statistical Abstract of the United States. Washington 25, D.C.: U.S. Government Printing Office, published annually.

Stevenson, Burton Egbert, *Home Book of Quotations*. New York: The Macmillan Company, 1948.

Thompson, Nina R., and Regina G. Grookman, Editors, *Cumulative Book Index*. New York: H. W. Wilson Company, 1956.

Thorpe, Willard L., Editor, *Dun's Review*. New York: Dun & Bradstreet, Inc., published monthly.

Ulrich, C. F., Editor, *Periodicals Directory*. New York: R. R. Bowker Company, published alternate even years.

White, David Manning, and Seymour Levine, *Elementary Statistics for Journalists*. New York: The Macmillan Company, 1954.

Winchell, Constance M., and O. A. Johnson, *Guide to Reference Books,* by Isadore G. Mudge, 7th ed. (Suppl. even years, 1951.)

Who's Important in Medicine. New York: The Ronald Press Co., 1945.

Who's Who. New York: The Macmillan Company, published annually.

Who's Who in America. Chicago: A. N. Marquis Company, published biennially.

Who's Who in the Middlewest. Chicago: A. N. Marquis Company, published irregularly.

Who Was Who. Chicago: A. N. Marquis Company, 1950.

World Who's Who. New York: The American Universities Medical Research Publications, Inc., 1947.

Aids for Writers

A Manual of Style, 11th revised edition. Chicago: University of Chicago Press, 1955.

Brentano's Publishers' Magazine Service, 586 Fifth Ave., New York 19, N.Y.

Copy Fitting Tables. Brooklyn, N.Y.: Mergenthaler Linotype Company.

Current List of Trade Magazines. Indianapolis, Indiana: Commercial Engraving Publishing Company, 34 North Ritter Ave., issued annually.

Federal Government Manual of Style, Washington, D.C.: U.S. Government Printing Office, revised frequently.

Howard, Clive, Editor, *Successful Magazine Writing*. New York: Charles Scribner's Sons, 1954.

Paper Manufacturer—Champion Paper and Fibre Co., Hamilton, Ohio.

Paper Manufacturer—Kable Brothers, Mt. Morris, Ill.

Paper Manufacturer—S. D. Warren Company, 89 Broad St., Boston, Mass

Schulte's Book Store, Inc., 80 Fourth Ave., New York City.

Taylor Publishing Company, 1608 Oakridge Dr., Dayton, Ohio: *Character Counter*. (Device to estimate typed copy.)

Union Library Association, 121 East 24th St., New York City 10.

Wilson, H. W., Periodical Dept., 950 University Ave., New York City. (Magazine Service.)

Word Division. Washington 25, D.C.: Government Printing Office.

Aids for Scientific Writers

How Does Your Writing Read? Washington 25, D.C.: U.S. Government Printing Office.

Prefixes & Suffixes. Washington, D.C.: Reference Service, U.S. Civil Service Commission.

Stewart, Jeffrey R., *Stewart's Scientific Dictionary.* Alexandria, Virginia: Stewart Research Laboratory, 1953.

Swartz, Harry, M.D., *Intelligent Laymen's Medical Dictionary.* New York: Frederick Ungar Publishing Company, 1955.

The Scientific American Reader. New York: Simon and Schuster, 1953.

"Transactions" (A Bulletin), American Association of Cereal Chemists, W. F. Geddes, Chief Editor, January, 1945.

Scientific and Technical Periodicals

American Journal of the Medical Sciences. Philadelphia, Pa., published monthly.

Atomic Energy Newsletter, Atomic Energy News, Inc., New York, published fortnightly.

Iournal of Biological Chemistry. American Society of Biological Chemists, Inc., Williams and Wilkins Company, Baltimore, Md., published monthly.

Journal of the American Chemical Society, Washington, D.C., fortnightly.

Journal of the American Medical Association. Chicago, published monthly.

Journal of Nutrition, American Institute of Nutrition. Wistar Institute of Anatomy and Biology, Philadelphia, Pa., published monthly.

Nucleonics, McGraw-Hill Book Company, Inc., New York, published monthly.

Proceedings of the American Institute of Electrical Engineers, published annually, in 2 parts.

Psychological Abstracts. The American Psychological Association, Inc., Lancaster, Pa., published monthly.

Review of Biochemistry. Annual Reviews, Inc., Stanford, Calif., published annually.

Review of Nuclear Science. Annual Reviews, Inc., Stanford, Calif., published annually.

Science. 1515 Mass. Ave., N.W., Washington 5, D.C., published weekly.

Science Illustrated. 330 West 42nd St., New York 18, N.Y., published monthly.

Science Service. 1719 N St., N.W., Washington 6, D.C., published weekly.

Scientific American. 24 West 40th St., New York 18, N.Y., published monthly.

Guides to Selling Articles

Hanrahan, J. K., *The Literary Market Place.* New York: R. R. Bowker Company, 1955.

Herbert, Agnes, Editor, *Writer's and Artist's Year Book.* New York: The Macmillan Company, 1954.

MacCampbell, Donald, *Marketing Your Literary Material.* New York: McBride Publishers, 1954.

Mathieu, Aron M., and Ruth A. Jones, Editors, *The Writer's Market.* 22 East 12th St., Cincinnati, Ohio, published annually.

The Catholic Writer Year Book. Pence, Wisconsin: The Marolla Press, published annually.

Writers' Publications

Abbott, Richard K., Editor, *Writer's Digest,* 22 East 12th St., Cincinnati 10, Ohio, published monthly.

Brown, Morgan, Editor, *Tide,* Tide Publishing Company, Inc., 232 Madison Ave., New York 16, N.Y., published weekly.

Brown, Robert U., Editor, *Editor and Publisher,* 1700 Times Tower, 1475 Broadway, New York 18, N.Y., published weekly.

Bursack, A. S., Editor, *The Writer,* 8 Arlington St., Boston 16, Mass., published monthly.

Crawford, Nelson A., Editor, *Author and Journalist,* 1313 National Bank of Topeka Bldg., Topeka, Kan., published monthly.

Dewberry, Frances, Editor, *The Matrix,* Box 7619, University Station, Austin 12, Texas, published bimonthly.

James, Mertice M., and Dorothy Brown, Editors, *The Book Review Digest.* New York: H. W. Wilson Company, published monthly.

Kesler, Carl R., Editor, *The Quill,* 35 East Wacker Drive, Chicago 1, Ill., published monthly.

Nixon, Raymond B., *Journalism Quarterly,* University of Minnesota, Minneapolis 14, Minn., published quarterly.

Peterson, Eldridge, Editor, *Printer's Ink,* 205 East 42nd St., New York 17, N.Y., published weekly.

Quinlan, Roy, Editor, *Magazine Industry,* 40 East 49th St., New York 17, N.Y., published weekly.

The Catholic Writer. Pence, Wisconsin: The Marolla Press, published quarterly.

Periodicals

Local Newspaper.

Nation's Business. Alden H. Sypher, Editor, U.S. Chamber of Commerce Bldg., Washington, D.C.

Nearest Metropolitan Newspaper.

Newsweek. Chet Shaw, Editorial Director, Broadway and 42nd Street, New York 36, N.Y.

New York Times. Arthur Hays Sulzberger, President, Board of Directors, Times Building, 229 W. 43rd St., New York 18, N.Y.

The Reporter. Max Ascoli, Editor, 136 East 57th St., New York 22, N.Y., published fortnightly.

The United States News & World Report. David Lawrence, Editor, 24th and N Streets, N.W., Washington 7, D.C.

Time. Henry R. Luce, Director, 9 Rockefeller Plaza, New York 20, N.Y.

Picture Syndicates

Acme Newspictures, Division of NEA Service, Inc., 461 Eighth Ave., New York 1, N.Y.

Central Feature News, Times Bldg., Times Square, New York 18, N.Y.

Columbia News Photos, 36 West 44th St., New York 36, N.Y.

Free Lance Photographers Guild, Inc., 219 E. 44th St., New York 17, N.Y.

Globe Photos, Inc., 152 W. 54th St., New York 19, N.Y.

International News Photos, 235 E. 45th St., New York 17, N.Y.

Keystone Pictures, Inc., 219 E. 44th St., New York 17, N.Y.

King Features Syndicate, 235 E. 45th St., New York 17, N.Y.

Livingston News and Photo Service, 137 Sutherland Rd., Boston 46, Mass.

Los Angeles Times News Bureau, 202 W. 1st St., Los Angeles, Calif.

Medical News Service, 1407 L St., N.W., Washington 5, D.C.

Religious News Service, 381 Fourth Ave., New York 16, N.Y.

United Feature Syndicate, 220 E. 42nd St., New York 17, N.Y.

United Press Pictures, 461 Eighth Ave., New York 1, N.Y.

Opportunities to Sell
Feature Articles

███

To show the beginner in free-lance writing the scope and the opportunities to sell his feature articles, the following tables are presented. They were compiled by making a study of the number of periodicals listed in the *Directories* of Standard Rate and Data Service for 1955, and the number of feature sections listed in the latest N. W. Ayer and Son's *Directory of Newspapers and Periodicals*[1] for the year 1955. In order to keep the figures on a uniform basis, the following tables were also computed from the latter directory. In reality the figures for opportunities to sell are much larger, because the tables were calculated on the basis of one feature article to each publication although each publication uses from one to twenty or more feature articles in each issue.

OPPORTUNITIES TO SELL TO MAGAZINES

Type of Publication	Number of Magazines	Total Annual Issues
Agricultural and Farm Papers	1,068	12,816
Education and Social	73	876
Entertainment	129	1,548
Fraternal Publications	146	1,752
Home and Garden	32	384
Magazines of General Circulation	633	24,972
Newspaper Magazine Sections	487	25,324
Newspapers of all Types	12,398	4,525,270
Religious Publications	683	8,196
Sports	142	1,704
Trade, Technical, and Class Publications	4,749	56,988
Women's Publications	41	492
Young People and Children	37	444
Totals	20,618	4,643,390

Check Sheet for Preparation of Manuscripts

Before writing manuscript, read directions in Chapter 14. In addition to requirements in Chapter 14, the following are required by your instructor:

1. Make a carbon copy of everything you write for print; one copy for the editor on good grade of typewriting paper, the other for your own files. Hand in both copies to your instructor in large manila envelope. Do not fold.

2. For classroom purposes, make a third "cover sheet" for instructor. On this add at least 3 possible markets where you plan to send your manuscript. Add them to your file cover sheet, also.

3. Be sure that your note to the editor contains "salesmanship" points that will convince him he should at least read your manuscript.

4. Pictures, drawings, etc., should have "cut line" (or title) typed on a piece of paper and cemented or attached with "Scotch tape" on lower edge of photograph or drawing. (See Chap. 15.) On the back, paste a piece of paper (or use "Scotch tape") upon which you have typed the caption of the article, your name, street address, city and state. Do not write on back of any photograph or drawing for it may ruin it for reproduction.

5. Before you write in the amount of postage on your cover sheet, be sure you have included all material to be mailed: one copy of the manuscript, pictures, drawings, return manila envelope, cardboard packing, and return post card, and that you have weighed it on a postal scale at a postal station or on one in the Journalism office. Attach stamps to return envelope for return of your manuscript with a clip; do not stick stamps on return envelope, but do paste stamps on the outer envelope before you hand it in to your instructor.

6. Purchase large manila envelopes of two sizes, but be sure that both are large enough to contain all manuscript material without folding or breaking any pictures. Or, if you cannot get two sizes, you will have to fold the envelope that you enclose to the editor for the return of the manuscript. Be sure to put your correct address on the envelope for the return of the manuscript. Be sure to put your address in upper left-hand corner of envelope that you send to the editor so, in case publication no longer exists, it will be returned.

7. Attach to the editor's manuscript a post card addressed to yourself.

[1] N. W. Ayer and Son, *Directory of Newspapers and Periodicals.* Philadelphia, 1955.

Evers, Betty
Writing and Selling Feature Articles
Miss Patterson—Sec. A, 10 TTF
Nov. 21, 1957

SAMPLE
PUBLICATION ANALYSIS
WOMEN'S—MEN'S MAGAZINES,
page ——

Time spent:
Research ...... 1½ hrs.
Typing ...... 1 hr.
Total ...... 2½ hrs.

	Woman's Home Companion Sept., Oct., Nov., 1957	Ladies' Home Journal Sept., Oct., Nov., 1957	True Sept., Oct., Nov., 1957	Argosy Sept., Oct., 1957
I. Identification: Publisher, Ed., Where, Price	Crowell-Collier Pub. Co., Paul C. Smith, 250 Park Ave., NYC, 35 cents.	Curtis Pub. Co., Independence Square, Philadelphia 5, Pa., 35 cents.	Douglas S. Kennedy, 67 West 44th St., New York 36, N.Y., 25 cents.	Alden H. Norton, 205 East 42nd St., NYC 17, 25 cents.
II. Make up: 1. Like 2. Dislike	1. Red explanation lines at top of articles, large clear type, interest-arousing arrangement of pictures 2. Too much adv. mixed in between articles	1. Much color, different style for each art., adv. in side columns 2. Broad type, hard on eyes, too much script in titles —loses its effectiveness	1. Large clear masculine type, short boxed articles, good color 2. Pictures unbalanced on pages	1. Good make up, good quality paper, clear pix. Like tone
III. Advertising: 1. Different appeal 2. Type reader 3. One tip	1. Middle-class to the housewife 2. Average American housewife or young career girl 3. Twins — fraternal and identical, twin studies of statistics	1. Mainly middle-class older women 2. Housewife with children or older career woman 3. New music store on State St., unique in Madison	1. Masculine appeal only 2. Business men, young & middle age, sportsmen, politicians 3. Early picturesque weather vanes	1. Masculine appeal

512

IV. General Policy: 1. What change 2. Give reason 3. What type art. could you submit	1. Move adv. back further, take adv. from between the story columns 2. Breaks continuity of articles 3. Int. or pers. exp. on children, household, current topics	1. Use colored ads. 2. Too many such ads, lack of color makes ads less effective 3. Int. or pers. exp. on clothing, training children, jobs, furs, gifts	1. Very little except to rearrange page balance 2. Pages appear lop-sided 3. Pers. exp. on success current topics in news, travel, sports	1. Use smooth paper, get adv., colored pix, more articles 2. Lift to a higher class appeal with such changes 3. Int. & pers. exp. on sports & current events
V. Feature Articles: 1. Type & appeal 2. Analyze one; 5 suggestions for improving yours	1. Int. pers. exp., narra.; appeal to alert housewife who wants to keep up with the world 2. "American Ting-Hao Boys" Lively, smooth, begin, quotes, narr. vary style	1. Pers. exp, intv.; appeal to housewife and career woman 2. "No Boy Problem in My House," short, 700 words, concise, personal appeal. Short sentences, begin with question	1. Pers. exp., appeal to young men, & intv. of well-known people 2. "Hardware's Bob Hope" Success story, light but well-written. Use humor, short P, be frank, use *good* English	1. Intv., pers. exp. appeal to middle-class man 2. "Amusing Experience," brief, easy, amusing. Clear lang, variety, narr. plain vocab. definite
VI. Tips: Authority, Source, and 3 markets	Selecting a wardrobe for college girl (from art. on becoming clothing) See Manchester's Sport Shop. Mademoiselle, Seventeen, Glamour	Madison's Youth Problem (from article on the boy above); intv. Prof. Becker, Marie Brown (social case worker), Mgr. of The Loft. Parents, Today's Woman, C. S. Monitor	Men's Toiletries in a Woman's Perfume Shop (from toiletries art). Intv. Mrs. Hansen at Perfume Shop. Glamour, True, American	Early River Boats in Wisconsin (from poem "Old Man River"). Intv. E. P. Alexander and do library research. C. S. Monitor, American, N. Y. Times Magazine, Mil. Jour.

Fig. 14. Sample Chart for Publication Analyses, Chapters 1-16.

(If one prefers, he may place publications in left column and place the present left column at top of chart.)

On the other side of the card write the city and state in which the publication is located and the following statement; e.g.:

> Philadelphia, Pa.
>
> ————, 19—

Your name
Your street address
City, zone, state

Dear Mr. ————:

This is to acknowledge receipt of your manuscript, (include caption)

———————————————, which came in today's mail.

(Signed)—————————————————

Editor, (Name of Publication)

8. On *outer* envelope write lightly in pencil the day, date, and hour of your discussion group, to aid your instructor in sorting articles. After it is returned to you in discussion group you can erase this notation before mailing.

9. When you get your article back from your instructor, make all suggested changes, retyping article if necessary, making it correct in every detail, and mail out as quickly as possible, or not later than three days after you get it back from the instructor.

10. Report to your instructor when you sell an article and show him your letter of acceptance or check.

Index